THE MANUAL FOR SUCCESSFUL HUNTERS

WHY 10% OF THE HUNTERS TAKE 90% OF THE GAME

TONY RUSS

Cover Photo: Alberta whitetail deer, by Chris McKinnon, McKinnon & Co. Outfitters, P.O. Box 3237, Fort Saskatchewan, Alberta, Canada, T8L 2T2, 780-331-2440 or 780-992-0901.

Editor: Diane O'Loughlin
Illustrator: Tony Russ

First Edition, May 1999; Second Printing, March 2002
Produced in Alaska
Printed in the United States of America

Northern Publishing
P.O. Box 871803
Wasilla, Alaska 99687-1803
E-mail: tony@tubooks.com
Web Site: tubooks.com

TABLE OF CONTENTS

SECTION IV. HUNTING GEAR & FOOD

SECTION V. FIREARMS & OPTICS

SECTION VI. ANIMALS & THEIR SENSES

SECTION VII. THE HUNT

TABLES, CHARTS AND ILLUSTRATIONS

ACKNOWLEDGMENTS

This book is an accumulation of hunting information from many sources and its success is a direct result of the quality and quantity of those sources. I would like to thank everyone individually, but if I could remember all their names—which I cannot—the list would be endless. I will have to settle for thanking them in groups, trusting that each individual knows who he or she is.

The first group I must thank is the writers who supplied the vast amount of written information I used for this book. They gathered information on specific topics that I was able to compile into a comprehensive book covering the wide range of hunting situations across North America.

I must thank all the hunters I've guided from around the world who related their hunting experiences and explained their tactics which I learned so much from. I also must thank all the guides I've worked with whose professional knowledge was extremely valuable. Then there are all my hunting partners over the years who all helped me become the hunter I am today. Thanks to all these hunters; everyone has made a difference in what I know about hunting and how much I have passed along in this book.

Thanks to those who donated many of the photos for this book. Photos are crucial to a book of this type as they help me explain what I cannot always convey in words. Thanks to Dave Widby for taking the time to help me find useful photos in his large collection, and thanks to George P. Mann for donating numerous photos. Thanks also to Chimo's sporting goods in Wasilla for their assistance with some necessary photos.

Thanks to my editor, Diane O'Loughlin who was able to do the work in a timely manner while juggling the many other responsibilities in her life. And, once again, thanks to Joan L. Baxter, my high school English teacher who taught me and still inspires me.

I also want to thank all the hunters I've met and talked to over the years who passed along their hunting experiences and lessons–which I've learned from. They have all helped complete this book.

My thanks to everyone I've listed and anyone I've omitted. This book could not have been written without you.

INTRODUCTION

Part of my research for this book was gathering information from dozens of books and hundreds of magazines over the past few years. I also questioned dozens of experienced hunters about their hunting skills. I filtered, sorted and then organized this information together with my hunting knowledge gained from thirty years' experience of big game hunting in North America. The result is this book covering the skills and knowledge necessary to successfully hunt big game animals in North America.

People hunt for numerous reasons. Obtaining food tops the list for many—and justifiably so. Gathering food is one of the basic driving forces in humans which is necessary to our welfare. Of course, nowadays most people gather food indirectly by earning a paycheck which is later used to purchase/gather food. Recreation, camaraderie, adventure, excitement, the challenge, and enjoying nature are other reasons hunters participate. For most of us, it is a mixture of several of these reasons. The total experience of getting up early, getting away from the constraints of everyday life, being with good friends and feeling truly alive are all part of the hunting experience which keep us involved in this activity year after year.

The key word in the title of this book is success. To some extent, hunting success always implies that a game animal has been taken, and this book title is no different. However, hunting success also implies some or all of the other reasons we hunt. A successful hunter must also play by the rules (laws) and adhere to high ethical standards. This includes: knowing and obeying all laws, respecting landowners' land and property, respecting other hunters' rights, respecting wildlife, putting hunting safety above killing animals, reporting violations and becoming educated hunters. For the sake of compatibility, this definition of hunting success has been influenced by the current attitudes of the public toward hunting.

The skills and information in this book are intended for a comprehensive preparation of a big game hunter—from physical conditioning to philosophy. Few hunters want or need everything this book has to offer, yet everything here is of use for big game hunting in North America. Hunters will no doubt pick and choose which sections they will only skim through and which sections to study in detail. For myself, I have found that every hunting skill included here has been of use to me at sometime in my hunting career. And, since I don't know what demands future hunts may place on me, I never pass up an opportunity to learn hunting skills even if I see no current need for them.

In my opinion, whitetail hunters have the most developed hunting strategies of all hunters. This is logical since there is more effort spent on hunting whitetail deer than any other species. Much of this book is based on what has been learned by hunters who pursue whitetail deer, so it is directly useful to the 90% of North American hunters who prefer to hunt this species. However, I have found that every skill and technique used by whitetail hunters can be applied in some way to hunting other North American species. Using these highly developed whitetail techniques gives hunters a big advantage when pursuing other species which have not dealt with hunters using these methods. A hunter who applies whitetail tactics in a discriminating way when hunting other species is often way ahead of the game.

Perhaps more than anything else, hunting success comes from a positive attitude. Hunters who expect to see game will have more opportunities because they are alert and focused. As any experienced hunter can attest to, it only takes a few seconds to change the outcome of a hunt. Being in the right place at the right time is necessary, but the hunter must be alert to take advantage of any situation. Hunters with positive attitudes do everything as if it counts, and this often makes all the difference.

While compiling the information for this book, I have learned a considerable amount of hunting lore. I also know that when I go back and study it in the completed form I will be able to make many connections and come to numerous conclusions which will improve my own hunting success. As I stated at the beginning, this book is an accumulation of the hunting knowledge of many people, not just my own. I think an accumulation of information like this book can be greater than just the sum of its parts. With that in mind, I hope you find this a useful source of information which will lead you to greater hunting success. Good hunting.

Tony Russ — February, 1999

The author with his 1997 Dall sheep. This ram was awarded the Archery Gold Medal at FNAWS for 1997.

PART I.
THE BASIS OF SUCCESS IS EDUCATION

Chapter 1

BECOMING AN EDUCATED HUNTER

Regardless of how much we know about hunting or how good our skills are, we can always learn more. In fact, the desire to keep learning is one of the key elements in becoming a better hunter. Hunters who are consistently successful usually know more about some aspect of hunting than less-successful hunters. Perhaps they know more about the animals they hunt; or maybe they are highly skilled with their gear and weapons; or they have an intimate knowledge of the land they hunt. Superior knowledge or skills improve their success.

In addition to directly affecting our hunting success, there are other good reasons we should become educated hunters. As the world becomes a more urban society, people are more removed from the realities of life—and death. This has resulted in a decline in hunting's acceptance by the general public. Improving the image of hunters is one way to fight this decline. And education is one way to improve our image as hunters.

We have to promote an image as responsible, educated hunters if we want to maintain our current hunting opportunities, let alone gain more seasons and areas to hunt. The way to do this is by first educating ourselves thoroughly about hunting and the responsibilities that go with it. Then, as we recruit more hunters, we will need to educate them as well. Kids especially need experienced instructors to help them become responsible members of the hunting fraternity.

Hunter Education

Early in this century hunters realized the need for hunter education to improve safety, hunter ethics, and our public image. In the 1920s a Hunter's Code of Ethics was written and promoted for these reasons. Formal hunter education, focusing mainly on safety, began in New York state in the late 1940s. Other states gradually joined in. Then in 1972 the National Rifle Association (NRA) joined with the state hunter education volunteers and organized the current nationwide Hunter Education program. From 1972 through 1996 over 20 million hunters have been certified through formal training. This program teaches safety, wildlife management philosophy, hunting techniques, and hunter/landowner relationships. There is now some kind of hunter education available in all 50 states. Forty-seven states and seven provinces in Canada currently have mandatory certification requirements. These programs are run by state fish and wildlife agencies with volunteer instructors.

The primary source of hunter education material and standards is the International Hunter Education Association. The IHEA consists of state and provincial Hunter Education administrators, tens of thousands of volunteer instructors, and representatives from conservation organizations and the shooting sports industry. The IHEA is an affiliate of the International Association of Fish and Wildlife Agencies. Together they provide leadership in hunter education. Their common goal is hunters that are safe, responsible, knowledgeable and involved. Hunter education cards from any member of IHEA meet hunter education requirements in other member states and provinces.

The International Bowhunter Education Program (IBEP) is a hunter education program designed specifically for bowhunters and supported by the National Bowhunter Education Foundation. This program covers much of the same material as the IHEA program with the exception of the weapons segment. Participants in the IBEP program are required to show proficiency in knowledge and use of bows and arrows as weapons. This program also includes more instruction on blood-trailing and game recovery. Hunters with an IBEP certification card meet hunter education requirements in most states and provinces. However, basic hunter education certification does not meet most bowhunter education requirements.

There is a recently developed program called "Becoming an Outdoors-Woman" which was designed to educate primarily women, although it is not closed to men. Many women who would otherwise not venture into the outdoors to try hunting get a chance to do so thanks to this wonderful program. Because our population has a growing number of single-parent families run by women, this is also a great way to pass on information to kids who might never be exposed to outdoor activities—including hunting. If the heads of these households (women) don't teach their kids to hunt, most of these kids will never start. Programs like these are great. Without them, the numbers of people who hunt will certainly decline and we will have less hunting opportunities in the future.

The NRA also owns and operates a hunter education facility for youth called the Wittington Center. Located in New Mexico, this facility is set up to handle teenagers during intensive two-week courses. The participants live on the grounds while taking muzzleloading, pistol, shotgun, and rifle training sessions. They also take camping and survival classes. Safety is emphasized above all else.

Tyler George relies on his father Stan, for his hunting education.

After a hunter has a good basic understanding of what it takes to be a successful hunter there are many ways to continue learning. State fish and wildlife agencies are always a good source of information. They know about game habits, population statistics, and hunter success. They keep yearly harvest records and perform game biology reasearch to develop better management principles. In some states, like my state of Alaska, the Department of Fish and Game even puts on educational seminars designed to improve hunter success. Sports shows are likely places to learn about the latest hunting tactics or find the newest hunting gear. Reading is another great way to learn, although facts show that the average hunter does not read books about hunting. Hunters who <u>do</u> keep up with the latest hunting information are more likely to be successful hunters.

Past Successes and Future Prospects for Hunting

Even the most successful hunters need the opportunity to hunt. Unfortunately, there are some real threats to our hunting opportunities.

Statistics show that hunters comprise only about 10-12% of the U.S. population, and anti-hunters comprise about the same percentage. The other 75-80% are neither dead-set for, or against, hunting. These non-hunters are the people we, as hunters, need to support us. According to *Beyond Fair Chase* by Jim Posewitz (pp. 111-112), "What critics of hunting find objectionable are: unethical hunting behavior, killing only for trophy, and killing for fun. Aspects of hunting that are seen as positive are: hunting for food, hunting to manage wildlife populations, hunting as a way of appreciating nature through participation, and the conservation achievements of hunters." To know and understand what is objectionable to non-hunters is the first requirement of getting them on our side. And hunter education is the first step toward presenting a good public image to these non-hunters who make up the majority of the U. S. population—the majority who will decide the future of hunting.

As individuals we should also know some of the history and realities of hunting to fairly represent ourselves to those who question our choice to hunt. First, all hunters should know that regulated hunting has never caused a species of game to be put on the endangered species list (and never will under current management practices). The main factors affecting the future of wildlife are human population growth, human poverty, land development, and social pressures. The first three have a negative impact on wildlife; the last one can be positive if we decide to be good stewards of our wildlife and their habitat. One example of our good stewardship is the way hunters have helped to create National Parks, Refuges and Preserves.

As hunters, we should be familiar with the commendable history of hunting in the U.S. In the early 1900s, game was rapidly dwindling and some people felt all large wildlife species would soon be gone from North America. But in stepped the American hunter/conservationist. Hunters helped pass game laws restricting their activity, but necessary to protect the remaining herds. The Federal Aid in Wildlife Restoration Act, commonly called the Pittman-Robertson Act because it was sponsored by Senator Key Pittman and Representative A. Willis Robertson, was passed in 1937. It provides for an excise tax on firearms, ammunition, and archery gear. This P-R money collected each year is used by the states to acquire wildlife habitat, perform wildlife management and research, and operate hunter education programs. P-R money and hunting license money together provide the majority (over 75%) of state fish and wildlife agencies' budgets. All wildlife species, both game and non-game animals, are managed and provided for with P-R money for the benefit of hunter and non-hunter alike. Since the early 1900s, with the help of sportsmen's dollars, our wildlife has made an incredible comeback. Some examples of the growth of game populations in this century are: whitetail deer—once as low as 300,000/ now up to 20,000,000; Rocky Mountain elk—once as low as 41,000/now up to 1,000,000; pronghorn antelope—once as low as 12,000/now up to 1,000,000. These numbers show how positive an effect hunters have had on wildlife populations in America; we should be proud of it.

Rocky Mountain elk are one of several animals which have made tremendous comebacks with the help of hunters. George P. Mann with a very good bull elk.

There are two other Federal laws that were supported by hunters to protect wildlife. The first is the Lacey Act which prohibits interstate shipment of illegally killed wildlife. The second requires a Cites Permit to export certain endangered species and is enforced worldwide. An educated hunter should be aware of both of these laws and their importance to protection of our wildlife.

Education is the cornerstone of continued success for hunters and wildlife. State fish and wildlife agencies, hunter education programs, sports shows, and hunting publications are a few of the many ways to learn more about hunting and increase your chances of success. By improving the public image of hunters, educated hunters improve the outlook of hunting. The continued success of wildlife in our country depends on the faithful stewardship by a strong hunting community.

Mary Anderson with one of her Dall sheep. Hunters only harvest two or three percent of Alaska's Dall sheep population yearly and the hunter success rates have remained constant for the past two decades. Effective wildlife management is good for both animals and hunters.

Chapter 2
WILDLIFE MANAGEMENT

Hunter success rates are directly related to changes in wildlife populations. Healthy wildlife populations are the direct result of effective wildlife management. Therefore, as hunters, we should support effective wildlife management. It is good for us and wildlife.

Basic Concepts of Management

The science of wildlife management has some unique concepts and terms unfamiliar to most hunters. Understanding these concepts and terms can help us appreciate the animals we hunt, communicate with wildlife managers, understand reasons for seasons and bag limits, and explain to non-hunters how regulated hunting helps—not hurts—wildlife populations.

Animal *Habitat* is one of these basic terms. Habitat is where wildlife lives; it is their home. Good wildlife habitat has food, water, shelter, and open space—all arranged in a convenient manner. Abundant habitat is necessary for healthy wildlife populations. Habitat management is the first priority of wildlife managers. Since so much of our land is in private hands and out of direct control of public wildlife managers, private landowners also play a significant role in habitat management.

The *food chain* is another basic concept of wildlife management. Basically it is the movement of nutrients from lower life forms to higher life forms and back again. The food chain is also called the *food pyramid* because the shape of a pyramid illustrates how a large number of organisms is needed at the bottom of a food pyramid to support a much smaller number of higher life forms at the top of the pyramid. Figure 2.1 shows a very simplified food pyramid. The base of the pyramid represents a large quantity of grass, the middle section—a small number of deer, and the top—a few cougars. A small number of deer need a large amount of grass to survive

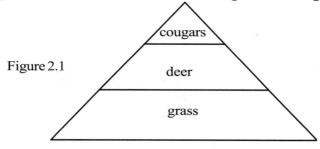

Figure 2.1

and flourish. And a very few cougars live off the small number of deer. The cougars in this example are predators. Predators are virtually always at the top of the food chain, which is why there are always less of them than prey. Prey animals often outnumber predators by 100:1 or more.

Carrying capacity is a term describing the number of animals an area of habitat can support. The quantity and quality of habitat in an area determines the carrying capacity. If a population of animals exceeds the carrying capacity, the habitat may be damaged—possibly severely. Good examples of this concept are caribou herds which depend on very slow-growing lichens for their winter food supply. Some of these lichens may take fifty years to grow one inch tall in the harsh Arctic environment. If a caribou herd grows too large and overgrazes an area, it may take decades for the lichens to grow back to a point where the habitat would have the same carrying capacity as before the overgrazing occurred.

Animal populations above carrying capacity of their habitat tend to be self-limiting to some degree. As a population grows, there is less food per animal and thus, more chance some will starve during long, severe winters or during times of drought. There is also more chance the increased population will attract and feed a growing population of predators. Disease also tends to travel faster through a dense population than a sparse one. On the other hand, a population well below the carrying capacity of an area usually grows quickly. A sparse population tends to have plenty of food per individual, it attracts fewer predator populations, and diseases tend to be localized and not become epidemic. Animal populations are affected by a multitude of diverse factors which people spend their entire lives studying and trying to understand, but this simple explanation gives a general idea of the basic interactions of populations, carrying capacity, and habitat.

One significant change which has occurred in most food chains in our country is the removal of most large predators by man. As man populated the U.S. we displaced or killed off most predators. Since predators also perceived us or our domesticated animals as prey, they were often killed in defense of life or property. Prey species, on the other hand, can live in close proximity with man and survive just fine. Whitetail deer are the classic example of large animals which can literally live in man's back yard—sometimes without being noticed. Large predators require a dense prey population and lots of open space. As population and development expanded in our country during the twentieth century, both of these factors were limited. Small pockets of large prey species survived all over the U.S., but only a few large areas were left undeveloped to sustain healthy populations of large predators like grizzly bears and wolves. When our large prey species made spectacular comebacks in the middle of this century, the predators didn't—mostly because of the presence of man and extensive land development; there were not enough of the open spaces large predators require for good habitat.

Wolves particularly need large areas with little interference by man. They avoid man and seldom live near civilization; they just move away. My forty-odd years' experience here in Alaska (where there are about 10,000 or so wolves) is a good example of wolves' avoidance of man. Although I have always been an outdoorsman—hunting, fishing, boating, camping, skiing, flying, and now a professional hunting guide—spending as much as 150 days per year in remote areas and regularly seeing wolf tracks, I have sighted less than twenty wild wolves in my entire life. They just don't like us humans and stay away from us as much as possible. The point is—in most areas (Alaska is an exception) there are now very few large predators in relation to the large numbers of prey species; in some places there are none. Basically,the top predators have been removed by man and we now fill that niche in our environment. Without man—the hunter—performing as a top predator, our large game populations would soon exceed carrying capacity in most areas of the U.S.

These elk will have to compete for a limited winter food supply.

Effective Management

Wildlife managers are continually doing research and population surveys on our game animals to determine the best management practices and goals. Research results help biologists understand animal habits and their habitat requirements. Surveys indicate direction and magnitude of population changes and overall herd size. Managers also rely heavily on harvest data from hunter reports to keep track of herd size.

Effective wildlife managers use all available information to balance animal numbers with available habitat. When nature is left alone there are typically huge swings in populations. Figure 2.2 shows a graph of a typical animal population that is left unmanaged. Populations grow until well above carrying capacity in an area and then crash; the huge die-off of animals is usually caused by starvation and/or disease. These cycles of rapid growth–then population crashes, are followed by long periods of low population as the animals and their environment recover. During these population cycles the number of animals can change a hundredfold. Changes of this magnitude can cause severe habitat damage which might prevent a population comeback for fifty years or more; and that is assuming animals are in an unaltered habitat. If you also consider the changes we have made to the habitat and the predator-prey balance, the situation is much worse. Whitetail deer are an example of an animal that can easily become overpopulated in an area. Such overpopulation causes crop damage, habitat damage, and highway safety problems—currently up to 500,000 deer die per year in automobile collisions; eventually this overpopulation leads to mass starvation or die-offs due to disease.

Figure 2.2

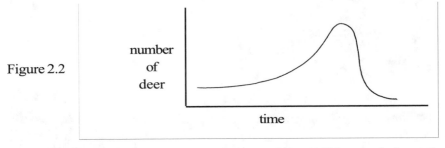

number of deer

time

Wildlife managers try to maintain stable wildlife populations. A more consistent level in an animal population provides many more healthy animals in the long run for increased hunting and viewing opportunities. This also protects habitat and reduces the chance of losing entire populations which would reduce the diversity of the gene pool. A diverse gene pool allows more possible adaptations within a population, which helps the population change to keep up with environmental pressures. This is the reasoning behind the spotted owl controversy in the Northwest and attempts to keep the Florida Key deer herd from becoming extinct. Biological diversiy is a good thing. We are always learning from animal studies and improving our lives from this. The more animal diversity, the more we can benefit from them and the more we can learn to better protect animals and the environment.

Wildlife conservation involves protection of habitat and wise use of our wildlife resources. The most useful tool to manage wildlife is regulated hunting. Managers manipulate seasons, bag limits, legal animals, and hunting methods to control wildlife populations. They balance goals of hunter success, quality hunting opportunities, wildlife viewing opportunities, non-hunting outdoor recreation opportunities, public safety, habitat protection, preservation of genetic diversity, etc., to provide as much possible benefit to man. Without hunting as a tool and in the absence of other predators, managers can do little to help populations of large species of wildlife. Predator/prey relationships among smaller game and non-game species have been less-affected by man and don't need as much management as larger game species. Still, wildlife managers have to keep a close watch on an entire *ecosystem* (animal and plant populations which interact plus the space they live in) to keep a balance between habitat, prey, predators, and man.

Wildlife preservation means protection of habitat and no use of wildlife resources. This is the situation in some of our National Parks where no hunting is allowed. Although this approach has its merits, without large predator species there are often population boom/bust cycles in these situations with a resulting destruction of habitat. The overpopulation of Yellowstone Park by bison and elk is a good example.

Wildlife law enforcement is good for hunters, non-hunters, and wildlife. Wildlife belongs to everyone and should only be hunted in accordance with wildlife regulations. People who disregard the regulations—poachers—are stealing our wildlife. They are not hunters, they are thieves. They are simply criminals in our society and should be regarded as such. They give hunters a bad name and adversely affect wildlife. Since wildlife managers don't get harvest reports from poachers they can't accurately determine populations and can't manage our wildlife as well. Poor management hurts hunters, viewers, and wildlife populations. Poachers should be turned in by hunters and non-hunters alike.

Wildlife management and research is also funded by conservation organizations—whose members are mostly hunters. Organizations such as the Rocky Mountain Elk Foundation, the Foundation for North American Wild Sheep, Ducks Unlimited, the Ruffed Grouse Society, etc., raise money to donate to research projects, animal transplants to replace lost populations, and habitat acquisition and enhancement projects. Millions of dollars are donated by these sportsmen's groups each year to help wildlife. This is another way hunters are paying the bill for protection and enhancement of wildlife in America.

A basic understanding of wildlife management principles is beneficial to hunters. It helps us appreciate and support management goals and game regulations. It can make us more successful and responsible hunters. We can also pass this understanding on to other hunters, non-hunters, and landowners. Any time we improve the public's understanding of the relationship between hunting and wildlife, we will increase our hunting opportunities. In the long run, this benefits hunters, non-hunters, and wildlife.

Wildlife managers work to increase opportunities for hunters and non-hunters alike. This trophy Alaskan moose presents a fabulous viewing opportunity for everyone in this neighborhood–especially the hunter whose trees the moose is eating.

Chapter 3
HUNTER ETHICS

Ethics are basically what is considered right and wrong by a society. These moral codes vary depending on the culture and customs of each society. They are not always written down, but they are usually understood by all adult members of a society. Ethics are as important in hunting as in any other activity in our lives, maybe even more so because of how closely hunter behavior is scrutinized and questioned.

Some of the basics of ethical hunting in our culture are:

•Shoot only when you are confident you can kill cleanly; this one rule alone prevents most of the unethical hunting behavior.

•Obey all safety rules, hunting regulations, public laws, and property laws; be a good citizen.

•Be responsible and know all of the applicable laws, rules, and regulations; wherever you may be hunting.

•Know and respect the animals you hunt; the American Indian had a thorough knowledge of and a deep respect for animals they hunted and needed to live. We should do no less.

•The first hunter arriving in an area or spotting an animal deserves the first try at the animal; back off and give the hunter some space.

•An animal belongs to the hunter who made the (first) fatal shot; help bring the hunter and his/her game together if you have the opportunity.

•When hunting on private land, treat it as if it were your own; always ask for permission and any limitations.

For an in-depth discussion of hunter ethics and tradition see *Beyond Fair Chase* by Jim Posewitz, published in 1994 by Falcon Press Publishing Co., Inc., Helena, Montana.

Most hunters are the children of hunters. Our hunter ethics have been handed down from others. However, due to the evolving role hunters and hunting plays in our modern world, these ethics are changing. We still fill a niche in the world, that of the hunter, but this niche is changing.

We must first realize that we don't hunt to kill, we kill to hunt. Killing is not an enjoyable action for hunters; it is not easy to kill an animal and watch it die and we do not take it lightly. People who do enjoy killing are mostly in prison—we hope. The killing is not the real purpose of the hunt. We do hunt with that end in mind, but we only kill to possess the meat, hides, and horns of the animals we hunt. It is part of the hunt, but certainly not the reason we hunt. Hunting is what our ancestors did for thousands of years. We evolved as hunters; it is still part of who we are.

As residents of North America, we have the best hunting opportunities of anyone in the world. This is both due to our government-mandated personal rights and freedoms and the sportsmen's dollars that pay for management and conservation. We also have great opportunities to get out into the woods at other times than hunting season to enjoy wildlife and learn more about it. Seeing wildlife at another time of year will give you new understanding, insights, respect and appreciation of our wildlife. This, in turn, can help you clearly recognize and appreciate your ethics.

Recognizing and following personal hunting ethics is essential to becoming a successful hunter. To be truly successful, hunters must be satisfied with their actions. To be satisfied with their actions, hunters must follow their ethics. Therefore, truly successful hunters follow their ethics. Bagging game must be of secondary concern to ethical hunters.

It helps to remember that even the ultimate American predator, the cougar, does not make a kill every time it hunts. Taking an animal is not the only measure of a successful hunt. Nor is taking the largest animal essential to success. A meaningful trophy is any animal you are proud of because of the manner in which you took it. A successful hunt is one in which you followed your ethics, regardless of the amount of game you bagged. Long after the hunt is over, memories are the real trophies, and ethical hunting produces good memories.

Hunter ethics are passed on by veteran hunters to beginners. Todd Fisher with his son Greg, in pursuit of caribou in Alaska.

PART II. – THE HUNTER

Chapter 4

PHYSICAL CONDITIONING

Physical conditioning can play a significant role in the success of a hunter. There are some instances when only mild physical exertion is required to complete a successful hunt, but these are exceptions. Most big game hunts range from moderately physical to extremely physical. Backpack hunting for Dall sheep or Rocky Mountain elk can be a supreme test of anyone's strength and endurance. Even tree stand hunters will benefit from good strength, flexibility, agility, and stamina.

The animals we hunt are always in good physical condition. It follows that hunters who are better able to keep up with game have a better chance of succeeding. As hunters we are acting as the predators in nature's scheme. Nature's predators are in great physical condition; the most successful hunters have learned from this. When was the last time you saw an overweight cougar or an out-of-shape grizzly bear?

Conditioning Strategy

The amount of effort a hunter puts into physical conditioning depends on many things. The age of the hunter, the time spent afield each year, physical conditioning from an occupation or other activities, the type of hunting, and determination to get game are some of the factors. At some time almost every hunter feels the need for improving his or her physical conditioning. Maybe it is the hunt of a lifetime the hunter has spent years saving for; or maybe it is just to recuperate after a serious injury. Regardless, the first step is the same—get a medical okay before embarking on a training program. Even people in their twenties should get a basic physical. A few years back we lost a 29-year-old guide here in Alaska to a heart attack—while he was in the field. He was predisposed to heart problems and didn't know it. A simple physical can identify some obvious problems, and if you are over 40 you should probably get a comprehensive physical if you haven't had one recently; it could be a real life saver.

Physical conditioning takes many forms. Hunters should design an exercise program that takes into account their current health, time constraints, and ambitions. The more accurately you analyze your situation, the more effectively you can prepare yourself.

Personally, I like to use a cross-training approach to physical

conditioning. I have divided my program into four parts:
-cardiorespiratory conditioning
-strength training
-flexibility and agility training
-stamina

Hunters should evaluate themselves in respect to these four parameters. Train your weaknesses. Realize the limitations a weak back or poor wind will put on you. Some weaknesses can be realistically improved, others cannot. Make an accurate analysis and then design a program that most efficiently improves your situation.

I remember one guided sheep hunt I went on (with me as the guide) that vividly illustrates the need for a cross-training approach to get into top "sheep shape." The hunter I was guiding was a marathon runner and in excellent shape—for running. He did not have any excess body fat and his cardiorespiratory (c/r) conditioning was great. On the trip in he carried 25 lbs. and I carried 45 lbs. I needed to stop and catch my breath more often than he did. This was my first hunt of the season and my cardiorespiratory system wasn't in great shape—yet. But on the way out, when I packed 95 lbs. to his 55 lbs., he was dragging long before we made the airstrip. His final words as he set down his pack were "If Bill [the pilot] doesn't come in, my bones will be here forever, because I'm not carrying that pack one more step." A sheep (or elk) hunter needs physical fitness in all four of the areas I have listed. Any shortcomings in a hunter's physical conditioning will show up during something as strenuous as sheep hunting. However, if you mainly hunt whitetails in farm country, you may not have to carry a heavy pack over rough terrain. Maybe aerobic training to control your weight, retain your flexibility, and maintain your overall health is all you feel the need to do.

Cardiorespiratory Conditioning

Climbing steep slopes at high altitudes with a heavy pack to hunt sheep or elk, fast-walking over uneven tundra or up a mountain to intercept a grizzly bear or caribou, or moving quickly down a dry wash to catch moving antelope all require good cardiorespiratory fitness. Aerobic exercise improves your c/r fitness and can be any activity that makes you breathe hard for a long time. Running, biking, swimming, racquetball, jumping rope, hockey, basketball, soccer, and of course mountain climbing are some of the ways to improve your c/r fitness. For indoor training I like the stationary bike, skiing machine, and the stepper/climbers that have become so popular lately. The stepping machines can duplicate the mountain climbing motion very well. Hunters wishing to get the most out of their conditioning program should use exercises that most closely approximate the motion they will be using on the hunt. This helps build the specific muscles they will use as well as their c/r fitness. This means the stepper/climbers are great for hunters who will be climbing steep slopes, and although swimming does build c/r fitness and flexibility, it does very little to build walking or climbing muscles.

The author (right) and Mike Traub are both seasoned sheep hunters. They know climbing steep slopes with a pack requires strength, stamina and cardiorespiratory fitness.

Of course, there are other factors to consider. All hunters don't have access to a variety of training options. Jumping rope is a great option to build muscle and burn calories fast for those with little space, time, and money; and it is easy on joints—something older hunters have to consider. Over the past 42 years, I have found that varying my exercise program reduces the risk of joint problems for me. There are also some exercises which bother my knees, so I avoid them as I get older. Personal preference also affects what exercise option you choose. It is better to pick an exercise you like and will stay with, rather than one you hate and will avoid doing. Choosing something the family can do together (like swimming or biking) may also help hunters keep up a regular exercise program. Regularity in your exercise program plays a big part in its effectiveness.

The accepted pattern for aerobic training is to work out at least three times per week for at least 20 minutes each time at your target heart rate. Your maximum heart rate is determined by subtracting your age from 220. Your target heart rate is either 70% or 80% of your maximum heart rate, depending on which expert you agree with. A 40-year-old would have an 80% target rate of 144 beats per minute [(220-40) x .80]. There are personal heart rate monitors available now for constant monitoring or you can do it the old fashion way by checking your pulse occasionally. Whether you like to run, swim, or use apparatus like I do, you can use these guidelines to begin. Of course, if you want to get into better than just passable shape, and your doctor has given you the okay, you will need to do more than this basic aerobic training. Your goals and the hunt you have planned will determine your training program.

Strength

Brute strength can be very useful to a hunter. Whether you're pulling yourself up a steep mountainside through thick alders with a loaded pack, hoisting that last load of moose or elk onto your back, or drawing your bow as slowly as possible to avoid spooking a bear, strength is a handy commodity. Strength helps you overcome difficult physical obstacles during a hunt, but it also allows you to continue at a sub-maximum level for a much longer time. It is much easier to carry a 60 lb. pack all day after regularly training with a 120 lb. pack. Most of our strength lies in the large muscles of our legs, hips, and lower back. These are the muscles which should be trained to increase overall body strength.

Leg, hip, and back muscles can be trained for strength most effectively with weights. Leg presses, squats, leg extensions, lunges, and calf raises are standard exercises for legs and hips. Good back exercises include deadlifts and good mornings. There are numerous modifications of these basic exercises that can be found in any weight-training guide or by asking any competent weight-room attendant. In general, I use low to moderate repetitions (4-10) when I am training for strength. If you are not familiar with weight training, you should first consult a good trainer. Weight training can dramatically increase your overall body strength if it is done properly.

Another good way to train your legs is to climb stairs. Long staircases are available to almost everyone and they are free to use. Make climbing stairs a lunchtime activity if you work near or in a tall office building. You can even make this closer to the real thing by carrying a pack. This may draw strange looks from others, but occasionally you will get a knowing smile from a fellow hunter who has been there and understands. A few years ago I realized how much just a little stair climbing can affect leg strength. After remodeling my single-level home into a two-story home, my legs showed a noticeable improvement. And this was from climbing only one flight of stairs several times a day.

By far the best way to get into backpacking shape is by packin'. That is just what it sounds like—walking or climbing with a loaded pack. Get your pack and some sandbags (or any weight) and you are set. I've trained in this manner for about 20 years. Each spring I start out with a light pack and work up to a heavy one by fall. I like to get out early in the morning and walk for about an hour. I wear my hunting boots to accustom myself to their feel and work out any trouble spots. I used to go packin' three to four days a week during the summer months. In three or four months' time, I was ready. Lately I have discovered that I only need two to three weeks to work up to a heavy (120 lb.) load. Coincidentally, I have noticed some aches and pains associated with overuse of some of my joints, so I cut back on my training. I guess moderation is the key—particularly as we get older.

Hunters should also train their upper bodies for strength if they want to get into their best hunting shape. Arm strength is handy when the only way up a steep face is hand over hand through the alders. I remember the first bowhunt I went on when I ran into a vertical rock face. Luckily, I was able to use the overhanging alders like ropes and pull myself up and over the bare rock. There are a variety of situations like this when arm and hand strength can come in handy while you are hunting. The weight room can also be useful for upper body training, although not as important as with the lower body. Calisthenics and home gyms/apparatus can also provide all the upper body training you need. Good exercises for the upper body are plentiful whether you train with weights or just do calisthenics. Regardless of the exercises you choose, remember to select with your situation in mind.

Upper body strength can be increased with heavy weight work on exercises like the bench press.

One more benefit of weight training as you get older is protection of joints. Keeping, or getting, muscle mass around joints cushions them from some of the stress placed on them. We older weight trainers have to realize that we do have to be more careful when handling heavy weights so as not to injure ourselves, but we can still work out. Even though we all tend to lose some muscle mass as we get older, a proper weight training program can significantly slow down the process and help keep us hunting into our sixties, seventies, or even longer.

Louis Cole, in his early 80's, with his first bow-killed deer.

Flexibility and Agility

Along with strength training, hunters should include stretching exercises. Weight lifting has a tendency to tighten muscles, but even without weight training our muscles shorten with use and age. You may not feel the need to improve your flexibility, but you need to stretch just to maintain the range of motion you do have. There are times when hunters have to lie motionless in cramped positions for long periods, travel in a hunched-over position to stay out of sight of game, or simply straddle logs while hiking; flexibility helps in all these and many other situations. Stretching also helps prepare you for exercise and loosens you up after exercise. Whether you are going on one of your training runs or waking up in your tent on a frosty morning with stiff, sore muscles—stretching can help. Loosening up by stretching allows you to work out harder and it can prepare you for a difficult stalk. When your muscles are still warm from a hard training workout or a day in the field, stretching will loosen muscles before they begin to tighten. This will help relax your muscles and let you sleep better and recover quicker.

Flexibility also helps heal old injuries and prevent new ones. There is nothing worse than pulling a muscle or straining a ligament during a physically demanding hunt and having to turn back. It pays to get into the habit of stretching every day to maintain your flexibility. The old adage "use it or lose it" is very appropriate when talking about flexibility and range of motion. If you always warm up before any strenuous exercise, it will save you numerous minor injuries over the years and extend the length of your hunting career.

The most important stretches for hunters work the legs, hips, and lower back. These are the muscles most often used when hiking and carrying a pack. A more thorough stretching regime also includes arms, shoulders, chest, and neck. One of the best times to do your daily stretching is just after showering when your muscles are warm and loose. You will be able to stretch your muscles farther and benefit more. When stretching, the minimum time to hold a stretch is six seconds. Fifteen seconds is better. If you really want to see an improvement during just one session, hold each stretch for a count of 60. Breathe deeply and let the muscles, tendons, and ligaments loosen as you breathe. Don't push beyond a slight pull; forcing soft tissues to your pain threshold will most likely cause injury sooner or later. (I currently have a five-year-old shoulder injury from an overzealous stretch.) Holding to the count of 60 will let your body's immediate reaction to protect itself from overstretching pass and you should see a loosening the first time you try this (unless you are already as flexible as an Olympic gymnast). Remember to *breathe deeply*, it is a vital part of any stretching you do.

Flexibility also helps improve agility. Agility is obviously important to a sheep hunter scrambling over loose rocks with a heavy pack, but it also affects balance which is so very important when trying to minimize noise while still-hunting through the woods or creeping toward a stand before first light. Agility is difficult to work on specifically. Lunges are probably the best exercise to improve agility, while also improving leg strength. Agility will also improve as a result of all the other training you do. Having excess strength will certainly help your balance as you walk over rough terrain with a loaded pack, and c/r fitness helps you maintain control during quick stalks over rough ground where noise has to be kept to a minimum.

The best agility training (for backpacking) I can suggest is to actually go walking with a loaded pack on uneven ground. Your center of gravity changes as you carry heavier loads so experiment until you feel comfortable and stable. If you incorporate agility training into your packin' trips, you can improve agility as well as fitness.

Stamina

Stamina is the last parameter of conditioning you should work on while training. Stamina is the sum total of all the conditioning you have done. Stamina is both physical and mental endurance. It is the ability to keep going for prolonged periods of time, which depends on the muscles' ability to absorb oxygen and keep working. Training for stamina involves pushing yourself beyond the length or intensity of the last workout. After you have been on an exercise program for several weeks and are in fairly good condition, work on stamina. Interval training during workouts will increase your stamina. Thirty-second bursts of training at 90% of your maximum during aerobic exercise is a good way to add interval training to your workouts.

Stepping machines, skiing machines, bicycles and treadmills can all provide good aerobic workouts to improve stamina.

Another way of increasing stamina is to force yourself to keep going after you are tired. For me, this means having a longer and tougher workout, or two in one day. Maybe I will combine an aerobic workout in the morning with a weight training workout in the evening. Or, I will go on a three-hour packin' trip which includes some steep hills. Pushing yourself beyond your normal workout will help build stamina of body and mind. During my years as a guide I have seen many clients who lacked mental endurance, even though they were physically able to continue. A typical comment from clients as we've arrived at a remote airstrip at the end of a hunt has been, "I couldn't have made it one step farther." Of course, they could have gone a lot farther. Their bodies had much more endurance than their minds.

Perhaps the most useful way to build stamina is by taking scouting trips or training outings over rough terrain or long distances. Actually going into the area where your hunt will be is a great way to increase stamina as well as look over the country. If you can't get to your hunt area in the off-season and there are no steep mountains nearby, then just take a couple days and go hiking with a heavy pack. Find steep hills or at least long hills to climb. This will prepare you for the rigors of the hunt. The harder you push yourself in training, the more likely you are to be physically and mentally prepared for the hunt.

Stamina is somewhat exercise-specific. This means if you want to be a tireless mountain climber, you should practice climbing mountains. Running will help your c/r fitness, but it mainly builds running muscles and mental stamina for running. The closer your training comes to the real thing, the better off you will be. This reflects both the mental and physical endurance needed for stamina. A perfect example of this is something I have noticed for years. I often see old guides with pot-bellies and bean-pole legs. I'm sure many of them were impressive physical specimens in their younger days, but not now in their later years. Yet, many of these guides have physical and mental stamina far beyond what most people would guess from their appearance alone. They can out-climb and out-pack almost any client—regardless of how physically fit the client appears to be. The mental and physical training over dozens of years of climbing mountains gives these old, pot-bellied guides more stamina than most flat-landers can even imagine. This never ceases to amaze me. Now, after twenty years of walking the mountains myself, I am benefiting from this same phenomenon.

Pain, Injuries, & Therapy

It is useful to understand current theories on muscle pain, how it is caused, what it means, and when to stop exercising. Even if you are not engaged in an exercise program you can benefit from being able to distinguish between types of pain. The old theory of the classic high school coach who believed muscle soreness was good is history. New theories about pain and injury can help hunters avoid unnecessary muscle soreness and injury, so they can continue hunting at 100%.

Muscle soreness after exercise means you have broken down muscle tissue. This is common after a dramatic increase or change in physical activity. More exercise will just break down more muscle tissue—not heal it as my old high school coach believed. Exercising really sore muscles will only impair your training program. What your muscles really need is rest. Current weight training programs reflect this new understanding. Just twenty years ago the common practice was to exercise a muscle every two days with weights. Now it is common to rest a muscle for three to seven days after an intense weight training workout. These longer rest periods let the muscles recuperate, let soreness disappear, and reduce the chance of injuries. The best way to encourage sore muscles to heal is to promote a good blood flow to the general area by engaging in an exercise that doesn't target a sore muscle specifically, but still requires flexing it. Exercises like walking, cycling, swimming, and stretching can help sore muscles heal without putting severe demands on them.

Since we all exercise in some way, a good skill to learn is how to distinguish between good pain and bad pain. Only a few types of pain while exercising are good; most pain is not. It is okay to perform an exercise to complete failure and even "feel the burn" of really tired muscles. Aerobic workouts when our bodies are calling for oxygen is also an okay type of pain. But there is a very fine line between this and harmful pain. Most pain while exercising is your body's way of telling you to stop. Whenever soft tissue (muscles, tendons, ligaments) are hurting from the first repetition of an exercise, it is time to stop and reconsider. Your body is telling you it needs rest and time to recuperate. Change your exercise program until the pain is gone.

To avoid severe muscle (or any soft tissue) soreness, always begin an exercise program slowly to let your body adapt. By doing this you can avoid interruptions in your program and, more importantly, avoid injuries. This is particularly important as we get older and our bodies don't recover or heal as fast. At 42 years old, I often take an extra day off from my daily weight training routine if I feel a little stiff and not quite ready for a tough workout. On these days I just stretch and do light isometrics. My normal routine allows me to rest each muscle 3-5 days between workouts. It seems to have paid off as my old injuries have been healing and I haven't had any new ones.

No matter how careful we are, we all sustain some injuries during our lives. The most common ones from exercising are tendinitis, strains, sprains, bursitis, and stress fractures. If you have a sudden pain during exercising, a sharp, isolated pain following exercise, a recurring soreness anywhere after exercise, swelling, or bruising, you have probably injured yourself and should check with a qualified medical person who can tell you the best treatment. However, if you are on a hunting trip or away from medical services, you should be familiar with some basic treatments.

The first thing to always remember is—the worst time to assess an injury is *during* exercise. While we are exercising, our bodies manufacture endorphins which are natural painkillers—strong enough to cover the pain of even a stress fracture. The best time to assess an injury is eight to twelve hours after the injury, after the endorphin high has worn off.

The standard treatment for muscle or other soft tissue injury is the RICE treatment. RICE stands for REST, ICE, COMPRESSION, & ELEVATION. Rest to let the body recuperate; ice the area, use compression, and elevate the body part above the level of the heart–all to reduce swelling. As you can see, swelling is a major concern. The more fluid accumulating in an injured area, the more chance of further injury. The pressure from the accumulated fluids can rupture more cells and cause further injury and swelling. The pressure also stresses injured tissues and prevents a healing blood flow to the area. Aspirin and other anti-inflammatory medications also help after mild injuries. I carry them whenever I go hunting and use them before any exercise (like mountain climbing) that might cause my knees to become inflamed. Some medical doctors recommend taking anti-inflammatories for up to two weeks before a difficult mountain-climbing trip (or hunt) to help prevent excessive swelling of joints (knees, hips, ankles) and possible overuse injuries.

Injury prevention and rehabilitation are necessary for hunting longevity. G.Fred Asbell was in his fifties when he took this ram.

Stretching is one of the best ways I have found to prevent, locate, and rehabilitate minor muscle injuries. More flexible muscles, tendons, and ligaments can take extra pulling and stretching without complaining. Frequent stretching will help locate minor muscle pulls or tears and treat them before they become major problems. Stretching is also a great way to *slowly* work a muscle back into usable condition and recover any lost range of motion. Daily stretching will also help us relax and reduce stress for overall health benefits.

If your doctor or you cannot find effective ways to heal old injuries, I would suggest trying a physical therapist. I have had limited success consulting a sports doctor for my injuries. However, a physical therapist is specifically trained for rehabilitation of physical injuries. When I was 37, a physical therapist was able to completely heal a 20-year-old muscle injury in my back in one session. I had felt mild soreness in the muscle dozens of times a year. Since seeing the therapist, I have not noticed it once in the past five years. It is worth going to this type of specialist to regain your previous physical abilitites.

You Are What You Eat

Diet accounts for 80% of the results of physical training. This is a statement I have read many times and didn't fully understand until I drastically changed my own diet. After I changed to a very good diet, my conditioning program was much more effective. (Remember, diet doesn't necessarily mean a *reducing* diet, but rather, just the sum total of what you eat.) All the information we read and hear about eating whole grains, fruits, and vegetables–while cutting down on fats is amazingly good advice. If you have doubts about how significant diet can be, I suggest you try a strict low-fat, high-protein diet with lots of fruits, vegetables, and complex carbohydrates. In just a few weeks you will be amazed at the effect a good diet has on your body. For a more detailed explanation of nutrition for the hunter, see chapter five.

If you are going to spend significant amounts of time on a physical conditioning program, why not also eat sensibly to get the greatest benefit. If you need to shed a few pounds, this is the best method for that, too. Ideally, you should not look at this as a "diet" to endure for a short time and then plan on returning to old eating habits. Eating *well* should be a habit. Eating in this manner doesn't mean going hungry. I have a hard time not losing weight if I am eating right—even though I eat whenever I get hungry. I have to force myself to eat more just to maintain my weight—*if I am eating properly*. On the other hand, when I am not eating properly, the pounds always seem to gather on me. It is not the quantity of food we eat that puts on the extra pounds. It is those sugary and fatty foods that have so many concentrated calories that do it, as well as the timing. Eating a good breakfast is good for our health and helps keep our weight down. Fasting all morning is hard on our hearts and then eating two heavy meals and snacking late at night usually puts on extra pounds of fat. Late-night eating tends to turn to fat overnight because of the way our metabolism works—and because these foods are usually fat-laden and, therefore, easy for our bodies to store as fat.

Actually, I have found it is better to carry a couple extra pounds of bodyweight when I go on a very physical hunt like a sheep hunt. In this way, I am carrying extra energy in a very convenient form that will help me through demanding hunting days when I don't get as much good food as I should. It is easier to carry this available energy on my body rather than in my pack. These extra pounds are typically gone before the end of the hunt. But I am talking about two or three pounds—not twenty or thirty. It is not a good idea to try to lose a *significant* amount of body fat on a hunt. Demanding hunting days require good nutrition and plenty of calories so you can perform at your best. Don't fall short on a once-in-a-lifetime hunt because you lacked energy for that last climb to get in position for the shot. It is also just plain risky to intentionally skip meals in remote areas where you never know when a survival situation may present itself.

There is one more aspect of conditioning hunters should consider when determining how much, if any, physical training they need. This last aspect is mental toughness. Stamina is a result of physical conditioning; mental toughness is a result of *all* the preparations you go through before a hunt. If you take the time to design a suitable physical conditioning program and stick to it, you will have confidence in your physical abilities. That confidence will improve your mental toughness and might make the difference between success and coming up just short of a satisfying, successful hunt.

Stamina is vital to success on many hunts—like blacktail hunting on Kodiak Island. Dave Widby with a nice buck.

While you are getting into hunting shape is a perfect time to test gear. Nothing is worse than having new boots and getting blisters after five miles of a 35-mile trip (as I have done—luckily it was just a scouting trip). Current footwear is supposedly broken in from the factory, but I still like to get new leather boots soaking wet and then walk them dry. And the

Cougar hunts can involve many miles of hiking after a pack of hounds so it is best to break in boots before the hunt and be in good walking shape. This is George E. Mann with his tom cougar.

new pack designs are great—if you know how to use them. Training walks will provide the opportunity to learn how to adjust them so you can be ready on opening day. Don't handicap yourself because you don't know how to "operate" new equipment.

When testing new boots and packs, try carrying your gun or bow as well (if you have a suitable route for toting a weapon). Toting a heavy gun while packing heavy loads can be tiring. Training walks help determine whether or not to carry your chosen weapon over the distances required while hunting. I once guided a 140-pound sheep hunter who had absolutely the heaviest gun I have ever felt. I still don't know how he was able to carry that piece of artillery. He will think twice before choosing that gun for his next sheep hunt. Testing equipment beforehand can make a world of difference on a physically demanding hunt.

Depending on the hunt you are planning, there may also be some specific training you need to improve your odds of success. For instance, the mountains Dall sheep inhabit are steep and dangerous. Sheep hunters often climb fifty- or sixty-degree slopes which require use of their hands as well as feet. This can be *frightening* for someone who is afraid of heights. If you are about to go on such a hunt, you don't have any climbing experience and you doubt your ability to climb steep, rocky faces, I advise you to do some mountain climbing. Maybe you can go to one of those rock-climbing gyms to just get used to the feeling of being in steep, rocky places. It is great exercise for your body and will also help prepare you mentally for the hunt.

Even if you are just going on a hunt where you will be in a tree stand and have no prior experience, a little practice can help. Borrow a tree stand, set it up in your back yard, and practice climbing the steps and getting into the stand. Then go through the motions of hunting from it— sitting still, moving your weapon, and shooting from it. Find out beforehand how to do everything the hunt might require. Everything you do to prepare yourself physically and mentally for your hunt will pay off.

The Real World

There are only a few hunters who have the time and ambition to follow all the suggestions I have made about physical and mental conditioning. The only big game animal many hunters ever pursue is whitetail deer and conditioning is not so much of a factor for them. Much of whitetail country is relatively flat and hunting is not so strenuous as it is in the Rockies, Canada, or Alaska. However, even the most hesitant, flat-land whitetail hunters might want to consider a little pre-hunt conditioning of a milder nature.

Several weeks before hunting season starts you can just start walking instead of riding. Whenever there is an opportunity for a short walk instead of riding in a vehicle, take the walk. Don't ride an elevator if you can walk stairs. Studies have been done on the aerobic health of people who live in two-story homes versus people in single-story homes. The people who walk stairs in their home always show a noticeable advantage in their aerobic capacity. As I mentioned in the c/r section, my personal experience has confirmed this. My executive friend/hunting buddy who has a limited amount of time to exercise also finds stairs a simple, but effective way to improve conditioning. He only uses the stairs to his fourteenth-floor office in the afternoon—so he doesn't sweat up his business clothes early in the day. If you're bound to a desk all day or spend time commuting you can also get a little productive exercise. Just flexing your muscles frequently while sitting can improve muscle tone. I often do sets of 100 reps of isometrics while riding in vehicles to do something constructive with the time. It is real exercise—you can easily work up a sweat doing this. All the little things you can do to improve your physical conditioning will prepare you to step into your role as predator.

I have not covered all the possible forms of exercise you could use to achieve a high level of physical and mental conditioning in order to become a better hunter, but I have given you some examples and a basic framework to work around. I am really into Dall sheep hunting here in Alaska. I try to stay in good shape all year. I go to great lengths to tailor my physical conditioning program to improve my sheep hunting success. As your own personal trainer, you should first analyze your strengths and weaknesses, decide on your goals, then design a conditioning program that suits you. It is a good idea to exercise regularly just to maintain our general health. Maintaining or improving our fitness to hunt successfully just gives us a good excuse to exercise year-round. Whatever you decide, remember that your physical and mental condition will affect your success as a hunter; so *any* improvement will increase your chances of success.

Tony Russ on a summer training hike in the Chugach mountains near his home in Alaska.

Chapter 5
NUTRITION FOR THE HUNTER

Hunters who have a basic understanding of nutrition are better able to provide the proper fuel for their bodies. When our bodies are properly fueled we can hunt longer and more effectively. We won't suddenly run out of gas just before a difficult stalk or lack the necessary alertness while on a stand. Good nutrition and eating habits not only provide plenty of energy for the hunt, they also affect our long-term health and physical abilities—both of which can significantly affect our long-term hunting success.

Nutrient Types

Food calories come from three basic types of nutrients—proteins, carbohydrates, and fats. A healthy diet contains some of each of these three nutrients. A knowledge of how our bodies respond to each nutrient, which foods supply these nutrients, and the role vitamins and minerals play in nutrition will help hunters "balance" their diets both in the field and at home.

Protein is the most critical nutrient in our diets, as well as the most expensive. Proteins are mainly used to build and repair soft tissues (muscles included), but some proteins are used to simply maintain our metabolism. Proteins are made of smaller units called amino acids. There are twenty different amino acids—of which eight to eleven (depending on which expert you believe) are essential. *Essential* amino acids cannot be made by the body in sufficient quantities; we must get them from the foods we eat. *Nonessential* amino acids can be made by our bodies from other nutrients (carbohydrates or fats) we've eaten. Proteins which are called *complete* proteins have all the essential amino acids. Complete proteins can be used (as is) to build the proteins our bodies need—we don't have to supply any other amino acids to use <u>all</u> of a complete protein. An *incomplete* protein, on the other hand, may not be entirely usable by our bodies as protein. It may be partially wasted, unless we supply the additional amino acids it is lacking by eating other foods at the same time that have these amino acids. Thus, not all proteins are created equal. Corn, wheat, rice, potatoes, beans and nuts are some foods with incomplete proteins. With a thorough knowledge of protein composition a person can combine these foods in the right proportions in a meal to get complete proteins. For most of us it is easier to rely on foods with complete proteins for our protein requirements. Of course foods with incomplete proteins should still be used to supply calories, vitamins, minerals and variety to the diet. In order of quality: egg whites, fish, milk, game meat, lean beef, and poultry contain high quantities of complete proteins.

Roy Wallis cooking sheep ribs from his 1998 ram. This is one of the most satisfying ways for a hunter to get high-quality protein.

Carbohydrates are the most commonly used nutrient to supply energy for our muscles. They are inexpensive and they also contain vitamins, minerals, and fiber necessary for optimal health. After digestion, energy from carbohydrates (or other nutrients we ingest and eventually use for energy) is stored in the liver and muscles as glycogen, then turned to glucose when needed to fuel the body. Carbohydrates come in two forms—starches and sugars. Starches are called complex carbohydrates. Sugars are simple carbohydrates. Ingesting a large amount of a sugar—particularly without other nutrients—produces a sudden energy surge and then a sudden drop in energy. Starches supply the body with a longer-lasting, more even flow of energy. Overconsumption of sugars can also lead to diabetes in older people. Fruit and sweeteners (table sugar, honey, molasses) are the most common sources of sugar. Common sources of starches are potatoes, pasta, rice, beans, and bread.

Fat is the nutrient that Americans overeat the most.

Overconsumption of fat, along with obesity, are the reasons heart disease is still the number one killer of men and women in America. Fat is not all bad, however. Some essential vitamins come associated with fats and oils as part of a healthy diet. Fat is also an essential nutrient necessary for good health, and it is very useful as a concentrated source of energy. One gram of fat has nine calories, compared to four calories in one gram of carbohydrate or one gram of protein. That is why animals put on *fat* for the winter. It is the most concentrated way to store energy to use until spring. It is also why people who have enormous calorie requirements—distance runners, mountain climbers, heavy laborers—eat diets higher in fat than most people. Fats come in both liquid and solid form. Unsaturated fats like corn oil, olive oil, or peanut oil are usually liquid at room temperature. Saturated fats (the ones usually linked to heart disease) like butter, cheese, lard and suet (animal fats) are usually solid at room temperature.

A Balanced Diet

Balancing our diets to include the right proportions of these three nutrients is not always easy, but greatly affects our current and long-term health. Eating too much sugar and skipping meals can cause sudden peaks and troughs in our energy level and cause us to lack staying power for long, strenuous days of hunting. The results of a poor diet over many years may be obesity, heart disease, poor circulation, or other infirmities which limit our hunting abilities. Just a little attention to their diets is all that is necessary for most healthy hunters to enjoy continued good health.

The Daily Value (previously called Recommended Daily Dietary Allowance—RDA) is the amount of a nutrient that a healthy person needs to maintain good health. These amounts include protein, calories, minerals, and vitamins. The Daily Values (DVs) are different for men, women, and children and are also based on age and weight. Various DV tables are available from different sources and their numbers differ slightly, depending on their source. The United States' DV table is made by the Food and Drug Administration; the National Academy of Sciences also produces a DV table ; food manufacturers will sometimes use a scientific study to base their own Daily Value on; etc. However, Daily Values are consistent enough between different tables to be useful for diet management.

The most disagreement about Daily Values surrounds vitamins and minerals. Most people are aware of the fabulous claims some advocates make about mega-doses of vitamin C or E. There are even some that claim we need over 100 trace minerals to maintain good health. Books have been written on each one of these claims alone so this basic explanation of nutrition won't dwell on these claims. Let it suffice to say that there is some controversy about vitamin and mineral Daily Values and plenty of literature exists if you want to read about these in depth.

The DV for protein for a 30 year old, 160 lb man, doing moderate activity is about 60 grams. A 30 year old, 120 lb female, doing moderate activity needs about 50 grams of protein. (The actual DV formula is 0.37 x bodyweight = no. of grams of protein) You can adjust the protein DV up or down proportionally for your weight. Many sports trainers and most bodybuilders claim this requirement jumps tremendously for those involved in strenuous exercise—like distance running, heavy weight training, or hunting in the mountains all day. It doubles or triples according to some. This would mean if you are on a very physical hunt (like a Dall sheep hunt when you climb mountains with a pack for 8-14 hours a day) a 160 lb man might need 120 grams of protein (100 grams of protein for a 120 lb female in the same situation) or more to maintain and rebuild body tissues. A person on a strenuous weight training program would have the same elevated protein requirements. I do not claim to be an expert, but I have been involved in heavy weight training for over twenty-five years and also been on many, many sheep hunts and I tend to agree with the high-protein advocates. I have tried it both ways and more protein sure seems to help; I am able to build more muscle while training and I don't lose as much on week-long sheep hunts. It also seems to be logical—since your calorie requirements on a grueling hunt doubles or triples, your protein requirement should also increase significantly. However, there are still some experts who insist exercise doesn't increase the DV for protein and large quantities of protein might even be harmful to our livers.

A balanced diet is necessary for hunters to keep going all day long. Here, Kris Widby takes a break after many hours of beating the brush in search of Sitka blacktail deer.

The DV of calories for a 30 year old, 160 lb man, doing moderate activity is about 2,800. The DV for a 30 year old, 120 lb woman, doing moderate activity is about 2,000 calories. The calorie DVs are slightly higher for younger people and slightly lower for older people of the same weight. The way we "balance" our intake of nutrients (proteins, carbohydrates, and fats) to get these calories greatly affects our health.

Carbohydrates should make up the bulk of most diets (diet here means the food a person eats, not a *reducing* diet), both in size and calorie content. Carbohydrates are inexpensive, of great variety, bulky so they make us feel "full," and accompany many essential vitamins and minerals. A commonly recommended proportion of calories from proteins/ carbohydrates/fats for healthy people is often 10/60/30. That is, 10% of your calories should come from proteins, 60% should come from carbohydrates, and 30% should come from fats.

If you follow this 10/60/30 recommendation, you would be getting only the minimum amount of protein for a moderately active person. However, if you are on any exercise routine or have a physically demanding occupation, this should be increased; 20% is a better amount for proteins, and I often get 30% when I am in heavy training.

The other critical part of this calorie ratio is fat (fats and oils are both in this group). Fats are moderately costly and found in many foods. Americans have averaged over 40% of the calories in their diets from fats in the 1980s and 1990s. This is part of the reason Americans are overweight (one in three of us are obese) and have a high rate of heart disease. Experts began recommending 30% in the mid-1980s as a stepping-stone approach to eventually getting the number down to 25% or even 20%. The theory was 30% was a reachable goal since Americans averaged over 40%; then 20% could be recommended after we reached 30%. An ultimate, reasonable goal for fat calories in your diet is 20-25%. A better calorie ratio is then 20/60/20, or 30/45/25 if you are into heavy endurance training or bulking up with weight training.

To find the protein/carbohydrate/fat calorie ratio of one food, an entire meal, or a daily diet, use the following formulas:
-protein grams x 4 = protein calories, *then take*
    protein calories ÷ total calories x 100 = percent protein calories
-carbohydrate grams x 4 = carbohydrate calories, *then take*
    carbohydrate calories ÷ total calories x 100 = percent carbohydrate calories
-fat grams x 9 = fat calories, *then take*
    fat calories ÷ total calories x 100 = percent fat calories
Food example: Skippy Reduced Fat peanut butter; two tablespoons have 190 calories total with **12** grams of fat, **7** grams of protein, and **15** grams of carbohydrates; *so*

7 x 4 = 28 (protein calories), *then* 28 ÷ 190 x 100 = **15%** of the calories come from protein, *then*

15 x 4 = 60 (carbohydrate calories), *then* 60 ÷ 190 x 100 = **31%** of the calories come from carbohydrates, *then*

12 x 9 = 108 (fat calories), *then* 108 ÷ 190 x 100 = **56%** of the calories come from fat; *so*

the calorie ratio of Skippy's is **15/31/56**

(Labels only list whole grams—not fractions so the totals do not always equal exactly **100%**.)

Meal example: Skippy Reduced Fat peanut butter (two tbsp. = 190 calories total with protein/carbohydrate/fat ratio of 15/31/56) sandwich with reduced sugar fruit spread (two tbsp. = 88 calories total with ratio of 0/100/0) on whole wheat bread (two slices = 160 calories total with ratio of 20/61/19), an 8 oz. glass of 1% milk (8 oz.= 100 calories with ratio of 32/57/11), a medium-size apple (apple = 70 calories total with ratio of 0/100/0). Total calories for the meal is 608. Combined ratio of protein/carbohydrate/fat for the meal is 15/60/25 which is a fairly good ratio for one meal.

Daily diet example: Depending on how many calories you want to get for the day, add two, three, or more meals to the peanut butter sandwich meal analyzed above plus snacks to get the daily calorie goal while keeping the ratio for the whole day in the right proportions. If one meal comes out heavy on fat, compensate with a low-fat meal. Every food or meal you eat will not have precisely the correct ratio of protein/carbohydrate/fat, but the idea is to "balance" the diet over a day's time; sometimes even over a week if necessary. However, the optimal diet will have the target ratio met at *each meal*. Fat and carbohydrate both contribute mainly to our energy stores, so you balance these out over a day's time with each other to some extent. However, dietary protein cannot be kept in our system intact for more than a few hours. And the average person can only use about 30 grams of protein at one meal. Protein is either used to build and repair our bodies within a few hours or it is broken down into smaller components and used for energy. So we need a constant supply of protein (ideally every 3-4 hours) for optimal health and optimal results from heavy exercise. If our diet is protein-deficient for one day or even one meal, it has a negative effect on our performance and health. That is why protein is the most valuable nutrient.

Eating Habits

The typical eating habits of Americans are not conducive to healthy diets. For the most part we get enough protein in our diets because of the large quantities of high-quality protein foods we eat—like red meat, fish, poultry, and dairy foods—and because most Americans lead a sedentary lifestyle requiring only a minimum amount of protein. The problem is that many of these high-protein foods also have a high percentage of fat. Instead of eating only 3-5 oz of meat or fish (which supplies the maximum supply of protein an average person can use at once—30 grams), we often eat 10 oz, 12 oz, or more. The excess protein is not entirely wasted because it can be used for energy or stored as glycogen for future use. (However, if not used within 48 hours, it will be stored as fat.) But the amount of fat accompanying these large pieces of protein-rich foods is: 1) rich in calories—remember that one gram of fat has 9 calories versus only 4 calories for the same gram-size chunk of protein; 2) eaten with a lot of other calories to produce a huge caloric intake which is seldom used before the next meal; 3) already in fat form so it can easily be stored by the body as (of course) fat.

There are three obvious solutions to this problem eating habit. First, eat less meat, fish, or poultry at one sitting. Second, eat cuts of meat with less fat and trim visible fat. Most game meat has similar quantities of high-quality protein as beef, but much less fat within the meat. Venison, for example, has one-third the marbling fat (fat you don't see in the meat) of beef. Trim visible fat from red meat and don't eat the skin or fatty tissue next to the skin on fish or poultry. Third, be sure to eliminate fat and as many calories from all other parts of the meal if you do eat a large portion of meat, fish, or poultry accompanied by a a lot of fat.

Fruit is a healthy snack containing essential vitamins and minerals.

There are other reasons why limiting the amount of fat in our diets can improve our health. If you are overweight, reducing calorie-rich fats is the easiest way to quickly reduce total caloric intake. Then, you can replace a few of those calories with bulky, but much less calorie-rich foods like fruits and vegetables which will make you feel fuller and leave you more satisfied. Also, eating more fruits and vegetables will increase your vitamin and mineral intake and help you meet or exceed those DVs. The amounts and types of vitamins and minerals we need for good health is so controversial that getting more of these nutrients is always a good idea.

There are a few pitfalls to avoid when reducing fats in your diet to reduce calorie intake. People often make up for eating lower-fat foods by increasing the amount they eat. Some of the fat-free foods often have plenty of sugar in them to make up for lost taste, so you can't eat these foods with abandon—they may still have lots of calories. A calorie is a calorie no matter what type of nutrient it comes from. Furthermore, America's obesity problems has *two* causes. In addition to eating too much, we don't get enough exercise. Americans currently eat 10% fewer calories than they did 100 years ago, but they are more obese now. Reducing calorie intake is the answer to one part of the problem, the other is getting more exercise. We have machines to carry us, mow the lawn, move the snow, blow the leaves, open our doors and windows, open cans, and even brush our teeth. The more we use these machines the more we will need to: A) reduce our calorie intake or B) get regular exercise doing something else.

An Eating Strategy for Hunters

The last part of this short course on nutrition for the hunter is a daily eating strategy to control your weight, maintain a consistent energy flow throughout the day, and sustain your health. After rising in the morning, your blood sugar is low after fasting all night. While you slept, your body has used stored glycogen to recover from yesterday and maintain necessary functions. You should replenish these glycogen stores soon after rising by eating at least 500 calories by mid-morning. If you don't, your body will take glycogen from muscle stores—your muscles will then function at less than 100% until these glycogen stores are replaced when you do eat. Also, when the deficit becomes great enough your body will actually break down your muscle protein to use as energy, so you will lose muscle size. This is counterproductive to good health and weight control since muscle tissue uses more energy than other tissue types, thus the more muscle mass you have the more energy you expend during any physical activity.

Furthermore, a good breakfast should contain a good quantity of carbohydrates because these are most easily digested by the body to quickly replenish glycogen stores. Fats and proteins are much harder for the body to digest to use as energy—eat these in moderation in the morning. One more reason to eat a good breakfast is the body's survival reaction to lack of food in the morning. The body will overreact and by evening—even if you have eaten a good lunch—your hunger will be insatiable and you will tend to overeat to compensate. Plus, evening meals—and breakfast skippers

*One way to reduce fat in our diets is to eat more wild game like this
bison Tony Russ took in 1992. Bison meat is excellent eating.*

often eat two—are usually much larger *and* more fat-laden. This is a
cycle that is hard to break because evening overeating eliminates hunger
in the morning. Breaking the habit takes a few days of sensible eating at
dinner until the morning hunger returns.

Once a good breakfast is eaten with plenty of carbohydrates, some
fats and ample protein, follow it with a (balanced) lunch with enough protein,
carbohydrates, and fats to provide energy until the next meal. It is actually
easier to maintain a balanced diet, get ample protein, and sustain energy
levels if four or more (smaller) meals are eaten, rather than the standard
three. The basic strategy about daily eating is to eat an increasing amount
of protein and decreasing amounts of carbohydrates and fats as the day
progresses. Eating a surplus of fat or carbohydrate in the evening tends to
lead to excess glycogen in the system at bedtime which may be stored as
fat—depending on the situation. These should be eaten early to provide
energy for the day, then plenty of protein should be available in the evening
meal to repair and rebuild tissue after a hard day.

There is one more useful nutritional strategy concerning eating
habits and exercise. Not only does diet account for 80% of the results of a
physical training program, the timing of the follow-up meal is also important.
To get the most from workouts, eat at least several hundred calories of
carbohydrates and 10-20 grams of protein within one hour of finishing
your exercise, as well as plenty of cool drinks to rehydrate your body.
After exercising, your glycogen stores are depleted and need to be

*Hunting for mountain animals is usually an exhausting undertaking
and depletes a hunter's glycogen stores after the first day or two.
To prepare for such a hunt, hunters should make sure they get good
nutrition and sufficient rest for the week preceding the hunt, and
then, adequate nutrition during the hunt. This goat was taken by
Tony Russ in 1995 in the Kenai Mountains of Alaska.*

replenished immediately. Otherwise, your body will take more glycogen
stores from the muscles—or even use muscle protein—for energy. Also,
to begin rebuilding muscle as soon as possible you should get some protein
into your system. For the best results from any training program, feed
your muscles immediately after a workout.

Even a basic understanding of nutrition can help hunters
eat properly to maintain energy levels and good health. There is no need to
always count calories, constantly read labels for DVs, or follow a strict
diet. Just learning the basics about nutritional contents of common foods,
then remembering and following some general guidelines about healthy
eating habits most of the time is all it takes. Hunters who do pay atttention
to their nutritional requirements improve their chances of success.

Chapter 6
WATER & THE HUNTER

Water is *vital* to a hunter. Our bodies are 60% water; our muscles are 70% water. The average person loses ten cups of water per day; an active hunter can lose two or three times that amount. If we are dehydrated by only three percent, our muscles lose ten percent of their contractile strength; and our concentration, coordination, reaction time, and stamina are all impaired. A three percent dehydration also makes us more susceptible to hypothermia or heat stroke. Although most healthy people can last several weeks without food, three days without water can cause death. Because water has such a significant impact on our performance, *successful hunters always make water a primary concern while in the field.*

A Hunter's Water Needs

A moderately active hunter will lose at least ten cups of water each day. Of this ten cups, three and one-half cups will be replaced from the food he or she eats—but this may be much less if the hunter is on a backpack hunt where drier, lighter-weight food is standard fare. Another half-cup of water is normally generated as a by-product of daily metabolism. The other six cups or more the hunter needs has to be replaced by drinking fluids; thus the recommendation for healthy people is to drink six to eight cups of water per day to avoid dehydration. An active hunter requires more than this minimum to perform at maximum capacity. Just one hour of strenuous hiking can require a hunter to drink an extra four cups of water to remain fully hydrated.

The body's thirst mechanism cannot keep up with its need for water. Thirst actually signals that our body is already slightly dehydrated. If we drink only in response to thirst, we only replace about half of what our bodies need to perform at 100% capacity. To compensate, we should drink fluids at the slightest indication of thirst and continue drinking a little more. By doing this, we can keep our bodies fully hydrated and perform at our maximum physical capacity.

Prolonged, strenuous physical exercise common to backpack hunting puts enormous demands on our bodies. This creates a need for large quantities of water to remove toxins from our bodies created as a result of this exertion, as well as to break down fats our bodies are using for energy. Re-hydration is most effective with cool (rather than warm) drinks within the first hour after exercise. Sports drinks (like Gatorade) also replace some of the electrolytes we lose and are absorbed faster than just plain water. Whether on an actual hunt or just training, these sports drinks re-hydrate us better and will slightly enhance our performance. It is also a good way to simultaneously put carbohydrates into our systems.

A wise precaution to take on a backpack hunt is to have a water-carrying capacity of at least two quarts per hunter. If you know there is water available along your route, you can just carry the portion of these two quarts you will need until you reach the next water source. However, when uncertain about the next water source or traveling in unfamiliar country, it is always wise to carry extra water. I have run out of water only once, and I will never do it again. My partner and I were packing a sheep back up a mountain to camp after a long day of hunting. After just two hours of climbing without water, our mouths were so dry we couldn't swallow food to get more energy to continue. We were exhausted and had to bivouac on the mountainside overnight with no gear except our clothes. By morning we were mildly hypothermic; luckily for us it was early in the sheep season and not too cold.

When hunting in the mountains you can often look ahead and plan your route to pass by water and replenish your supply. This may save carrying extra water or having to backtrack if you run out. Thinking ahead about water supplies is a mark of an experienced—and probably more successful—hunter.

Water Quality

The quality of your water supply is also very important. Unfortunately, there are basically no natural bodies of water that are not suspect as far as safety goes. Harmful concentrations of bacteria, viruses, or protozoans abound in 80-90% of the world's natural bodies of water. Even mountaintop springs in Alaska may make you ill.

One common protozoan hunters should be familiar with is called Giardia lamblia. It causes Giardiasis—popularly called "beaver fever" because of the typical mammalian carrier. It is commonly found downstream of beavers, but it also can be found upstream of any possible beaver habitat because it can be carried by other mammals as well. It is frequently contracted by hunters in Alaska and other remote hunting lands where the water seems so (deceivingly) pristine. The diarrhea, loss of appetite, cramps, and nausea often don't appear for seven to ten days—which can be a blessing if the hunter has left the field and is back home closer to medical services. Even if the symptoms stop after a few days, the disease needs to be treated to prevent reoccurrences typical of this illness.

There are several ways for hunters to treat water to make it safe for drinking, but the most reliable is by boiling. Boiling for even one minute kills protozoans (preventing Giardiasis), viruses (hepatitis and polio viruses included), and bacteria. It is the one surefire method hunters can use to kill organisms if in doubt about the potability of any water source.

This hunter is getting a cold drink in a wilderness area of Alaska. Precautions should always be taken whenever using unproven water sources.

Another method of treating water is adding iodine. Iodine comes in tablet, crystal, or liquid form. Iodine is difficult to use because extreme care has to be taken to ensure every drop of water gets treated; it also gives the water a distinctive taste unpleasant to some people. Iodine does not kill the protozoan cryptosporidium which is becoming more common in our water supplies.

There are also a wide array of compact filtering and/or purification systems designed for campers and hunters requiring potable water in the field. They are available as just filtering devices, purifiers, or as systems that do both. There are many varieties and sizes which can meet the needs of any size group, from a single hunter to a large camp with dozens of hunters. The better filtering devices are supposed to remove all bacteria and protozoans, but may not get all the viruses. The purifiers are better at removing the viruses, but don't always remove very small protozoans (like Giardia). A system which combines a filter with a purifier is thus, more reliable than either one alone. One advantage filtering systems and purifiers have over boiling is the ability to remove harmful, inorganic particulates— like heavy metals, chemicals, and other pollutants found in many urban areas. However, claims made about any water filter or purifier should be examined closely, as they are not always justifiable. Careful research should be done before buying to ensure a particular device will meet a hunter's needs.

Since most of my hunting is done in Alaska and I don't have to worry too much about inorganic particulates, I usually rely on the boiling method to produce potable water. Of course, the other way to have enough safe drinking water is to always bring it with you. This is impractical when backpacking, but okay when you have transportation to your campsite.

Regardless of how you get potable water when in the field, be sure and get enough of it. An ample water supply is vital to good health, maximum performance, and a successful hunt. Successful hunters plan ahead to bring plenty of water, ensure there will be plenty of (safe) water available, or bring the means of producing enough water from available supplies.

A hunter's need for water cannot be matched by the body's thirst mechanism, so drink more than you think you need.

PART III. – VITAL SKILLS

Chapter 7

FIRST AID

Many items of hunting gear (guns, knives, axes, saws, etc.) can cause severe injuries. Hunters also put themselves in dangerous situations: they climb treestands, ride horses, scale mountains and generally push themselves to their physical limits. They frequent backcountry and wilderness locations hours or days away from medical assistance. First aid skills are therefore, a practical and logical part of every hunter's repetoire.

First aid is the physical and emotional help given immediately to a victim of an injury or sudden illness. First aid classes are available from community schools, hospitals, clinics, nurses, private businesses, etc. for a nominal fee. Basic first aid and CPR training classes are usually less than eight hours each. These skills are useful for everyone—not just hunters—because any one of us may be the first person available to administer first aid in an emergency situation.

The following procedures should be carried out by trained medical personnel whenever available. Being able to recognize the urgency of a situation can sometimes mean the difference between life and death or permanent disability and full recovery. Other medical situations may not be urgent with plenty of time to wait for trained medical personnel; the best course of action may be to keep the victim warm, comfortable, and immobile until professional help can arrive. Basic first aid and CPR (cardiopulminary resucitation) training can go a long way toward helping a hunter properly evaluate and determine the proper course of action in many cases.

(Note: When ABCs are indicated in the following descriptions, this stands for Airway, Breathing, and Circulation. The first thing to do in a potentially serious medical situation is to clear and maintain the airway, check and restore breathing, and check and restore circulation—the three things taught in a CPR class.)

Bleeding – Minor – Apply direct pressure with clean (sterile if possible) dressing, wash, clean with soap, apply ointment, tape closed. Major – Apply direct pressure with clean (sterile) dressing, elevate injury above heart, cover and/or tape edges together. Severe – Apply direct pressure with clean (sterile) dressing, elevate injury above heart. If bleeding stops, apply pressure bandage and tape. Use a tourniquet as a last resort because this will often result in loss of limb. Tourniquet = any tight band which constricts blood flow and is applied closer to heart than the injury; can be made of belt, towel, or cloth band; loosen every 30 minutes for one minute, then reapply. If embedded object caused bleeding—like a broadhead or knife—leave it in unless it is very loose. Do not wiggle or remove; it will help stop bleeding if it is tight in wound. Cut off the protruding shaft (arrow) to shorten it, then stabilize it.

Broken Bones, Sprains – These are not easy to tell apart. Open fractures are obvious because bone protrudes through skin; pain, numbness and swelling occur. Treat open wound before splinting; check ABCs. Closed fractures: signs are pain, swelling, bluish color, and numbness. Splint area; use available padding and splint material to support joint on both sides of fracture. Elevate, use indirect ice pack (not on skin). Sprains: these are injuries to ligaments which cause pain, tenderness, swelling, and bluish color hours later. Splint limb and elevate above heart. Ice for 20 minutes hourly up to 72 hours.

Burns – Minor – Indicated by pain, reddened skin, and possibly blisters. Apply cool, running water immediately, dry, apply burn ointment if skin is unbroken, and cover with (sterile) bandage. Major – Indicated by white, charred skin. Use ABCs first if needed; wrap with clean, dry cloth; treat for shock (see **Shock** instructions).

Diarrhea – Usually from food poisoning or infection in intestinal tract. Frequent watery or even bloody stools, can be accompanied by nausea, vomiting and abdominal cramping. Severe dehydration can occur. Rest and plenty of fluids (Gatorade is good) and anti-diarrhetic like Immodium A-D if watery—not bloody—stools.

Frostbite – Discolored skin—white or gray, numbness. Immerse in warm water until area is soft or put area in armpits; do not rub or squeeze; do not use hot heat source. Do not thaw until danger of re-freezing is gone.

Heart Attack – Signs are chest discomfort like tightness or squeezing, mainly in center of chest; may spread to either shoulder, arm, neck or lower jaw. Usually lasts at least two minutes and may come and go. Accompanied by sweating, nausea, and shortness of breath. Use ABCs if unconscious. Have patient sit or lie down and rest.

Heat or Sun Stroke – Indicated by hot, dry skin–usually with no sweating, rapid breathing, dizziness, nausea, confusion, seizures, and/or unconsciousness. Get patient in shade, cool rapidly with water, ice, cold metal or rock–whatever you can find; give cool drinks if conscious.

Hypothermia – Variable signs – loss of judgement, loss of visual acuity, shivering, slurred speech, poor coordination, hallucinations, warm flashes, decreased limb function, and/or higher blood pressure and pulse at first followed by depressed blood pressure and pulse. Mild Hypothermia treatment – Place victim in warm environment, exercise to warm, give food and warm liquids, apply heat packs, give warm bath or shower if alert, or get skin-to-skin contact with a warm body in a sleeping bag. <u>Severe Hypothermia treatment</u> – Treat as for mild hypothermia if pulse and breathing are present, but do not give warm bath or shower. Do not give anything by mouth, and do not exercise victim. If pulse and breathing are absent for 45 seconds, start CPR.

Backcountry hunters should know basic first aid, including the symptoms of hypothermia and how to treat them.

Insect Bites – <u>Ticks</u> – Early removal can prevent transmission of disease or poisons which may be fatal. Coat tick with grease or petroleum jelly, use blunt tweezers to remove tick–do not squeeze body of tick which may force toxins into victim, clean area, use antiseptic and cover. <u>Bee Stings</u> – Allergic reactions are facial swelling, difficulty breathing, or signs of shock. Allergic persons should have bee sting kit. They need epinephrine as soon as possible. Non-allergic victims just suffer minor pain. Remove stinger with outward scraping motion using fingernail or knife; do not squeeze stinger or attached sac because this may drive venom into victim. Clean area; use ice or cool water to soothe; baking soda paste may ease pain.
Neck & Head Injuries – <u>Neck Fracture</u> indicated by stiff or painful neck, inability to move limbs or any body parts, or tingling sensation. Treatment is to immobilize head and neck with padding and splint and, *moving victim very carefully*, slide victim onto body-size board and tie to board. <u>Head Injury</u> – Indicated by scalp wound, skull fracture, blood from nose–mouth–ears, unconsciousness, headache, vomiting, convulsions, or different-sized pupils. Treatment is ABCs first, then immobilize head and

neck, keep warm, treat gently, victim should lie down; treat for shock.

Poisoning – <u>External</u> – Acids, bases, solvents or poison ivy, sumac, or oak; flush with water at least 15–20 minutes. <u>Internal</u> – Do not cause vomiting unless sure it was not caustic. Treatment is ABCs, then CPR.

Shock – This is a secondary condition resulting from trauma or injury and is life-threatening. Symptoms are anxiety, thirst, sweating, paleness, rapid or weak pulse, dizziness, or unconsciousness. It often results in death if not treated immediately. Treatment is ABCs, then CPR; handle victim gently, have victim lie down, keep warm, elevate feet 15 inches unless neck injury or other broken bones and reassure patient. If unconscious and no neck or head injury or broken bones, place victim face down with head to one side.

Snakebite – Indicated by swelling, blistering, bruising, numbness and tingling, dizziness, nausea, vomiting, and shortness of breath. Immobilize affected area if possible, keep victim inactive, keep affected area below heart, and use vacuum pump if available.

Stroke – Caused by lack of blood circulation to brain; indicated by loss of or trouble with speech, dizziness or loss of consciousness; weakness or numbness in arm, leg, or one side of face; or trouble with vision in one eye. Treatment is ABCs.

In addition to giving hunters the *ability* to administer life-saving first aid should the situation arise, a *knowledge* of first aid builds confidence in their self-sufficiency as hunters and wilderness travelers. Hunters with this type of confidence are more willing to travel deeper into uninhabited areas where safety is an important concern. Since remote areas often present better hunting opportunities, these hunters are more often successful than others who stay closer to civilization.

Tony Russ with a barren ground caribou in 1983.

Chapter 8
SURVIVAL

Anyone who hunts regularly will likely encounter a few survival situations in their lifetime—whether they recognize them or not. Just the fact that hunters seek out remote and/or uninhabited areas to enjoy their pastime puts them at risk. Most hunters have been caught out after dark in unfamiliar country at least once, and for many it is a regular occurrence. Many hunters have also found themselves wet, cold and several miles from shelter at times. Situations like these may precipitate a long, cold night without adequate shelter—at the least—and just a minor injury in these circumstances greatly increases the danger to the hunter. Proper preparation is a significant factor in determining the outcome in these and other potentially life-threatening situations. Hunters who have adequate skills and knowledge can make it through these unexpected bivouacs with only slight discomfort; less-skilled hunters may not return from these situations.

Preparation and Confidence

A significant part of preparation is to have a good background in first aid—as discussed in Chapter Seven. Having actual practice in first aid procedures will help an injured hunter stay calm and rational. In a situation with a serious injury—like a severe bleeding wound—a hunter's reaction in the first few minutes can be crucial to the outcome.

Even when there is no injury involved, hunters regularly make choices that affect their health or even survival. When a hunter realizes he is many miles from camp or a vehicle with little daylight remaining, the decision whether to continue walking or stay overnight can determine whether or not he survives. The hunter's knowledge of the area, his physical condition, clothing, gear, the type of terrain, the weather, and if he followed the basic rule of telling someone where he was going all affect this decision. The more experienced and knowledgeable a hunter is, the more prudent these decisions will be.

Staying Warm and Dry

One of the most common threats to a hunter's well-being is hypothermia. Knowing how to avoid this gradual drop in body temperature which eventually leads to death is the single most important survival skill a hunter can possess. Knowing the first aid which should be given to a hypothermia victim (presented in Chapter Seven–"First Aid") also helps to understand how to avoid the situation.

Hypothermia occurs most often in cool, wet conditions—to avoid hypothermia, stay warm and dry as much as possible. Temperatures which most often cause hypothermia are around 40 to 50 degrees. Because many people don't recognize the threat of hypothermia at these cool temperatures they don't dress and act accordingly—whereas at below-freezing temperatures most people do recognize the danger, so their appropriate dress and actions prevent hypothermia.

Other factors greatly increasing the chances of hypothermia are exhaustion and dehydration—conditions which hunters commonly experience in the field. Alcohol consumption also predisposes a person to hypothermia, as does any other factor that prevents body heat generation from keeping pace with heat loss. Because this condition is not traumatic, but often a cumulative result of many hours of slow heat loss (usually from exposure in an outdoor situation), it can sneak up on the most experienced outdoors enthusiasts; which is another reason it is such a threat to all hunters and one which has to be guarded against continually.

One of the best ways to guard against hypothermia is by choosing the right clothing. If the temperature is expected to drop below 60 degrees Fahrenheit during a hunt, hunters should consider hypothermia a real threat and plan accordingly. Wet cotton clothing is actually worse than dry skin for insulating value. Cotton should only be worn when temperatures will not drop below 60 degrees, the distance to shelter will always be short, reliable transportation is available, or hunting companions will always be nearby. Even then, I am very leery of cotton because of the ever-present possibility of injury, which—combined with wet weather— could still lead to hypothermia in the most unlikely hunting situations.

It is much safer to wear wool or synthetic clothing during any outdoor recreation. Wool retains 60% of its insulating properties when wet, and most synthetics do better than that. For adamant cotton enthusiasts, light cotton garments can be worn under wool or synthetics for comfort, then removed if sweat accumulation makes them useless—which is common in cool weather hunting. The new synthetics (like Thermax and Coolmax) are almost as soft as cotton and a lot more comfortable after just the slightest sweat buildup from activity. Personally, I do not wear any cotton in the field. Hunters often go afield with only the clothing on their back, so they should make it a policy to dress in clothing that is the most efficient at keeping them warm—and alive—under any possible circumstances. Chapter Twelve has a detailed discussion on clothing for the hunter.

The one disadvantage to wearing synthetics may be for those

Hunters can face a survival situation at any time. Here, Bob Ameen rejoices after an unexpected, early snowfall finally stopped after six feet fell in 24 hours in the Chugach Mts. of Alaska.

hunters who often fly in small aircraft, because synthetic clothing does burn readily. In the case of an aircraft accident and ensuing fire, it would be better to be wearing wool clothing.

Since staying dry is such a high priority, hunters also need to have an established procedure for water crossings to avoid mishaps. Always unbuckle your pack and unsling your rifle or bow when crossing moving water. (While crossing in a boat, these items should be off your back.) Both packs and guns should be dropped if you slip while crossing fast-moving water where your life might be at stake. Before crossing, you should determine how dangerous the water is and make a plan if you do slip. If there is a danger of being swept downstream, tie your gun and pack together with a short length of rope and plan on releasing them if necessary. After you are safely across, they will be much easier to retrieve with a rope between them to snag on rocks or logs. If the stream is narrow but fast, you can also tie them together with a rope that goes loosely around a log on the beginning side. When you complete your crossing, just untie one end and pull the free end—attached to your gear—around the log and back to you. Both your pack and gun are important items in your survival on a backcountry hunt, but when crossing fast-moving water, your immediate safety is the first priority—plan ahead so you react quickly.

Hunters should also have a policy about crossing ice. Follow the water-crossing precautions about unbuckling your pack and gun as well as releasing them—think ahead so you are not caught unaware. It is always best to go around ice whenever possible, but if you must cross, carry a stout pole at least ten feet long. A strong pole will likely support you and often allow you to get out of a hole and back onto solid ice by yourself.

In addition to water crossings, there are other reasons you might get separated from your pack, gear and gun. Anytime you are traveling in remote areas by plane, boat, horse, or even land vehicle, always remember that accidents do occur. Plan for your survival; you might have to depend on what is on your person. Therefore, another good policy is to always carry survival items on your body. Matches (waterproof or in a waterproof carrier), a knife, map, and a compass—in order of importance—are good items to habitually carry on you when involved in any phase of a hunting trip. These items will get you out of most unexpected situations in good health. For better insurance if staying out overnight is a real possibility–a pocket-size space blanket, a few firestarters, disposable hand or bodywarmers, and some trail food can also be carried in large pockets.

Heat Transfer

Understanding the physics of heat transfer can also help hunters avoid hypothermia and just stay warmer at all times. The four ways you can lose heat from your body are convection, conduction, radiation and evaporation. *Convection* occurs when heat near your skin is removed away by air currents. Clothing protects us from this form of heat loss to the extent that it is windproof. The stronger the wind and the colder the temperatures, the thicker and less porous the clothing must be to prevent convection heat loss. Even with thick, windproof clothing we will still lose a lot of heat if our heads and faces are exposed to the wind. Exposure to wind is often a significant factor in causing hypothermia. Table 8.1 shows

Table 8.1
Perceived
Temperatures

Exposed flesh freezes quickly below these levels of temperature and wind; to avoid frostbite, make sure to cover all skin in these conditions.

thermometer readings — degrees fahrenheit

miles per hour of wind speed	30	25	20	15	10	5	0	-5	-10	-15	-20	-25	-30
0	30	25	20	15	10	5	0	-5	-10	-15	-20	-25	-30
5	27	21	16	12	7	1	-6	-11	-15	-20	-26	-31	-35
10	16	9	2	-2	-9	-15	-22	-27	-31	-38	-45	-52	-58
15	11	1	-6	-11	-18	-25	-33	-40	-45	-51	-60	-65	-70
20	3	-4	-9	-17	-24	-32	-40	-46	-52	-60	-68	-76	-81
25	0	-7	-15	-22	-29	-37	-45	-52	-58	-67	-75	-83	-89
30	-2	-11	-18	-26	-33	-41	-49	-56	-63	-70	-78	-87	-94

how much wind speed effectively reduces perceived temperatures. As you can see, the first ten miles per hour of wind effectively reduces temperature by about fifteen degrees. Convection heat loss by moving air can be a substantial drain on body heat in a survival situation. Seeking shelter from the wind is a high priority for retaining body heat.

Conduction heat loss occurs by body contact with cold items or substances. Leaning against a cold rock, sitting on a cold treestand seat, or being immersed in water are good examples of conduction. This is why sleeping on the ground without a sleeping pad is so cold. The cold ground drains our body heat. When forced to bivouac, one of the most important things to do is find dry material to put between you and the ground. Branches, grass, leaves or any dry vegetation will work. Conduction is also why we lose heat so quickly in cold water. Heat travels 30 times faster through water than air. A person has 30 minutes to 3 hours before dying of hypothermia in 40 to 60 degree water. A person in 35 to 40 degree water only has 15 to 60 minutes to live; in 32 degree water you have less than 15 minutes to survive. Hunters who commonly travel near or over water should be aware of these numbers and take proper precautions.

Radiation heat loss happens as our skin slowly gives out our body heat through the air. This is the heat you feel when you get close to a warm object without touching it. The majority of body radiation is stopped if we are wearing clothing. Radiation is not usually a significant source of heat loss.

Evaporation heat loss occurs when water evaporates, removing substantial amounts of heat as it does so. Evaporation is why being wet makes us feel so cold. The moisture on our skin or in our clothing is constantly evaporating and taking our body heat with it. This is why wearing wet cotton clothing is colder than wearing no clothing, but having dry skin. Wet cotton clothing has probably caused more hypothermia cases than just about any other factor. This method of heat loss is the reason staying dry is so critical to avoiding hypothermia and surviving in the outdoors.

The major points about heat loss to remember are: 1) Remain as dry as possible, and wear nonabsorbent clothing which retains its insulating values even when damp. 2) Stay out of the wind as much as possible, and wear windproof clothing. 3) Insulate yourself from the cold ground or cold objects to retain body heat.

Any kind of *dry* vegetation like grass or leaves also makes a good impromptu insulation for inside your outer layer of clothing. The more air you can trap around your body, the less heat you will lose by conduction, convection and radiation. The same approach works with dry vegetation for sleeping. A thick layer of spruce or pine boughs underneath you and another layer over you can often make a comfortable bivouac bed. The thicker the layers, the better. Dry moss is even better for this. Of course, since there is no tent or layer of nylon to stop the wind, the more protected this bed is from the wind, the warmer it will be. Anytime you can find a dry cavity like under a large rock (but not touching it) or beneath a log for sleeping—or just waiting out cold weather—you will be much warmer. And if two people get into a small cubbyhole, your body heat will be shared as you conduct and radiate heat back and forth. Myself and a client were once caught at night next to a glacier without a tent or sleeping bags at about 40 degrees. We piled some rocks into a small semicircle next to a large rock, draped an opened garbage bag over the top, stuck our feet into a pack, and laid on his fresh sheep hide. It wasn't real comfortable, but we did get some sleep.

A fellow sheep hunter told me of his night out after a successful, but unexpectedly long, stalk. With wet clothes and no tent when darkness caught him, he crawled into a cavity in the mountainside. He stuffed moss inside his clothes and pulled more moss over him. He said the dry moss had absorbed all the moisture from his clothes by morning, and he was warm as well. A workable knowledge of heat transfer can help a hunter improvise—and survive—in many unfavorable situations.

Hunters who have never been forced to stay out overnight might try a trial run to build confidence in their survival skills. For safety, a pair of hunters should take their complete pack of gear to a remote area where cutting vegetation is allowed. Then they can set their gear aside and try to make a comfortable bivouac camp with only what they might have on their persons during a typical day hunt. Try this both with and without using fire. Hunters with this type of experience behind them will be more comfortable in the outdoors and a lot more prepared for the unexpected—both mentally and physically.

Although surviving in hot weather is an unusual circumstance for hunters to encounter, it is part of a thorough education in survival. In hot weather the hunter is trying to promote body heat loss, so the strategy is just the opposite of dealing with cool temperatures. Try to stay in breezy, shady areas during the day and make a bed of *moist* vegetation at least a foot thick—you will not absorb heat from the hot soil and the air is much cooler just a foot up. An average adult male needs two and one-half to three quarts of water per day to survive—water which may not be available on the ground's surface. A solar still can easily produce this amount if plenty of moist vegetation is available. A solar still consists of a sheet of waterproof material suspended a few inches over a pile of freshly cut vegetation. The vegetation gives off moisture which condenses on the underside of the sheeting. A small weight which has been placed on the top of the sheet creates a downward bulge—causing the moisture to drain toward the bulge, collect, and drip into a strategically placed container. This survival skill can be practiced in any backyard using a plastic bag and grass clippings.

Fire

A (survival) skill that every hunter should master is that of "fire." In a survival situation, the difference between life and death may depend on your ability to start and maintain a fire. Fire is not only an important survival skill, but it is usually considered a necessary requirement for those who would call themselves hunters.

Fire-building is one the first skills a hunter should learn. Fire not only warms you, but it keeps you company. This solitary hunter has an evening's supply of firewood close at hand.

The first considerations are the design and placement of the fire—they are interconnected. An experienced fire-builder will apply heat transfer principles when determining how to design and where to place a fire (although they may not realize this). *Convection* and *radiation* together determine the best place for a fire if its primary purpose is heat—for comfort or survival. A fire constantly draws air toward its base to continue burning. Air moving by a hunter to feed a fire can negate some of the warming effect—because of convective heat loss. By situating a fire near a large rock, earth bank, log or tree there will be a sort of windbreak on one side to back up against. Then the hunter will not feel a cool wind at his or her back while trying to warm up. This windbreak will also *radiate* the fire's heat toward the hunter's back and return some of the heat that otherwise would have been wasted. A semicircular, overhanging shape for this windbreak is ideal as it directs heat in and down toward the hunter. Sometimes a strategically placed heat reflector opposite the hunter can also radiate heat back, but this is difficult to accomplish in most conditions.

I spent one night out with a client and no camping gear after a glacial creek swelled too much so we couldn't recross to our tent. Even though I took a dunking in the creek right at dark, my synthetic clothes dried by the time we gathered firewood and started a fire—about an hour. We removed a few of the lowest branches from a large spruce tree to create a waterproof hollow and then crawled up against the trunk. We built a small fire that couldn't start overhanging branches on fire, but placed it close to provide lots of *radiant and convective* heat. Every couple hours, the cold would wake one of us just as the fire burned low and we would refuel it. It was a pretty cozy night, considering the situation; I got almost a full night's sleep.

A survival fire should always be placed in a sheltered area, but the exact location can make a huge difference in the amount of heat a hunter receives. If the fire is on a slight downhill slope from where the hunter will huddle, this will also help heat the hunter yet provide enough oxygen for the fire. It is best not to build a fire in a depression, however, because it will lack oxygen and won't burn well.

One more tactic to remember is to surround a heating fire with small boulders. After they are warm take a few to curl around while you sleep (heat *conduction* will warm you) and then trade off for warmer ones during the night as your boulders grow cold. Larger boulders will hold their heat longer, but will also take longer to heat.

If time and conditions are right, an all-night bed of coals can be designed. First, as a large fire burns down to coals, bank a six-inch ridge of soil all around it to reduce the oxygen supply to the coals. Arrange it so the coal bed will be close to—and preferably paralleling—your bed. Cover the coals with ashes just before you retire so they burn slow enough to provide heat all night. It takes some practice to design this fire to supply sufficient heat all night, but it can work if done properly.

The size of a heating fire is also important. This is determined in part by the amount of available fuel—and the risk of starting a forest fire. A small fire can provide nearly as much warmth as a huge fire because it can be placed closer to a bivouac bed, it doesn't create as much moving air to cool you, and it doesn't create as much of an updraft to remove heat. A small fire also doesn't use up fuel as fast—a consideration in any survival situation. A small to medium fire is the optimum size.

It is best to gather an entire night's fuel before dark and place it in a convenient location for feeding into the fire during the night. Long sticks or logs do not have to be cut, just fed slowly into the fire as their tips burn off.

One of the primary requisites about a heating fire is that it keeps going. The best designs for this are either a tepee shape or a crisscross

Warming fires can be used by hunters to provide light as well as heat. These three hunters are enjoying their fire while waiting to be picked up after a successful deer hunt.

pattern with lots of space for air. Air is needed to provide oxygen and to allow steam to escape without lowering the fire's temperature too much. Other fire designs are cooking fires which can be: 1) Flat, with two large logs surrounding an inner core of coals; with pots or pans supported on the two logs. 2) Flame/coal fires—with one side of coals, and one side in flames to create more coals, which are moved as needed to the cooking side.

    Fires are designed in many ways to suit different purposes, but the principles of starting any fire are the same—you need an initial heat source, fuel, and oxygen. If you supply these three items in the right quantities and arrangement, you can build a fire. It is simple to do in a dry, warm, non-breezy environment with dry fuel—like a home fireplace. The difficulty comes when cool, wet, windy weather combines with cold hands and a lack of dry fuel. Adverse conditions bring out the skill—or lack thereof—of a hunter. As with many skills, knowledge and practice are the keys to proficiency.

The first thing needed to build a fire is an initial heat source. For this requirement, wooden matches are better than paper, waterproof matches are better than regular, and having two lighters (in case one fails) is best of all. I carry both wooden matches (in a Zip-loc bag) and a couple of lighters whenever practical. There are always new fire-starting gimmicks on the market—like the magnesium firestarters which require scraping with a knife—but matches and lighters are still the most-relied on as an initial heat source.

The big ones—like this large Alberta whitetail—are very often taken late in the day and hunters end up being caught out after dark—when fires can be comforting or essential to survive until morning.

Firestarters often make fires possible in impossible situations. Plain birthday candles, leftover candle stubs, one-inch sections of paraffin-soaked, tightly-wound newspaper, or strips of plain inner tubes are examples of reliable firestarters. Any of these will provide several minutes of fire-starting flame even in wet weather. Anytime I am outdoors and carrying even a small day pack I have a few firestarters with me just in case; I believe in the Boy Scout motto "Be prepared."

The smallest size of fuel for a fire is called tinder. Jansen in *lightweight Backpacking* defines tinder as:
"1) Tinder is dry; it snaps and crackles when crushed or broken. It is eager to help you, not reluctant. Listen for the sound.
2) Tinder is small in diameter or paper thin in section; or can be cut and shaved to these sizes with a knife.

3) Tinder is usually dead wood or dead weeds.

4) Wood tinder is usually silver-gray colored. Weed tinder is silver-gray or light beige."

Good places to look for tinder are underneath foliage, against tree trunks, inside hollow logs, or wherever dead organic material is protected from the rain. Birch bark and the lower branches (often dead) of spruce, pine or hemlock trees are all excellent tinder material. Pine or spruce needles and small twigs are the next best tinder components.

Kindling is the next size of fuel needed for building a fire. It is toothpick to pencil-size material. Dry twigs, split branches or large wood shavings make good kindling.

Using split wood for kindling or larger fuel is almost always preferable. A wood fire burns when wood is heated sufficiently for flammable gases to escape and ignite. Along with these flammable gases there is always some moisture trapped within the wood which escapes as steam. The less moisture in the wood, the hotter the fire. When firewood has been split there are more pores exposed to allow the moisture, and gases, to escape quickly. This makes for much easier starts and continued burning. Most bark on firewood—particularly kindling size—also tends to trap moisture and lower a fire's temperature. With the exception of *very dry* wood, de-barking firewood will allow it to burn hotter and faster.

Site selection is next. A level area is usually best. A fire in a depressed area will lack air and not burn well, an elevated fire sends its heat even higher than usual and may get too much wind. To reduce chances of a wildfire, choose an area with mineral soil with no overhanging branches. Find a sheltered spot and, if it is a bivouac fire, select your bed with a reflector/windblock at the same time. Selecting a fire site is crucial to how comfortable you will be.

After tinder, kindling and various sizes of larger firewood have been collected by the fire site, it is time to arrange the initial fire. With your back to the wind and more windblocks to the sides if necessary, scrape down to dry soil (if necessary and possible), place a loose pile of tinder over a firestarter and loosely lean or "tepee" kindling over the tinder. One of the vital ingredients of a fire are gaps which let air feed the flame from all directions. The most common reason fire building fails is lack of oxygen. This is why loosely spaced tepee-like or crisscross arrangements are so often used to build fires.

Be sure to have slightly larger kindling nearby before you start. When everything is ready, hold the initial heat source below the tinder until a good flame appears. Sometimes this is best done by lighting a very thin, long piece of kindling and poking the burning end into the center of the pile. If there is a firestarter in the center, start it going first and let it ignite the tinder. It is a good idea to have plenty of small kindling nearby to ensure the fire catches. Blowing gently toward the base of the fire from a low position helps add oxygen and helps a stubborn fire grow. (Air generally contains about 21% oxygen; once-breathed air still has about 16% oxygen—which is still concentrated enough to fuel a fire.) Firewood should be added a little at a time in gradually increasing sizes. Large amounts or pieces of wood usually contain lots of moisture. As this moisture evaporates from the wood, heat is drawn from the fire—just as evaporation draws heat from our bodies. This cools the fire and may put it out. This is particularly true when the wood is obviously damp. In this case, more kindling and smaller diameter wood—which contains less moisture and dries out quicker—should be used until the fire is sufficiently large and hot enough to add the larger, damp pieces. To ensure the fire continues burning, always keep kindling handy to add to the center as needed. This will maintain a hot core and prevent the fire from going out.

When the wood is damp or even if it seems to be dry, preheating is a good practice. Preheat wood by standing it up around the far edge of the fire (away from you) to dry and warm it. By doing this, some of the moisture will have left before the wood is added and your fire will burn hotter. Very damp wood will visibly steam when it gets hot enough. It can be surprising just how much moisture is in apparently dry wood. This standing wood may also radiate some of the fire's heat back toward you.

The last step in successful fire building is extinguishing it. First pull all partially burnt firewood away from the center of the fire. Next, rub off any burning surfaces on rocks or into a mineral soil. Then dig through the ashes and into the surface soil to expose all coals and hot spots. Finally, douse the entire area with water whenever possible. Spend as much time as necessary to ensure your fire is **out**. This is as much a part of being a responsible hunter as making a clean kill.

Lost?

Another situation which commonly threatens hunter survival is becoming lost. Any hunter who has spent any time in unknown country has experienced at least a temporary disorientation. When this occurs the first step is to stop and evaluate the situation. A hunter can often remember landmarks that will lead back to familiar surroundings or the hunter can simply backtrack if conditions are right. Sometimes drawing a simple map on the ground will help a hunter identify his location. Remember that the sun rises in the east and sets in the west. Even on overcast days the sun's location can be ascertained by the bright glow.

The worst thing for anyone to do when disoriented is to move quickly without thinking. A hunter in this state is likely to not remember how far or which direction he has traveled, and it is easy to get into more trouble if traveling after dark. It is much wiser to immediately stop and try to remember your route up until the present point. If this doesn't produce

Dave Widby and Bill Parker returning several hours after dark on a successful deer hunt. Being prepared with headlamps helped them from becoming lost and spending a cold night on a mountain.

definite answers, the next thing to do is make a plan. If time and weather permits, a strategic travel plan to find the way back will usually work. But if the weather conditions, the hour of the day, and the possible distance to safety are unfavorable, a decision to bivouac may be best. This is the time to think "survival" above everything else.

Once a hunter establishes that he is actually lost, there is a routine to follow called the 5 "S" plan. The five S's are:

Safety - Mostly from yourself—keep your head, sit and think clearly, and make wise decisions.

Signals - Build a smoky fire by day, a bright fire at night; fire three shots.

Shelter - Find shelter for the night, with a fire if possible.

Sustenance - Preserve the food you have and only eat wild foods if they are 100% safe.

Socks - Keep your feet dry; wet feet usually cause trouble.

These five S's are an easy way to remember important things to do in any survival situation, not just when you are lost.

Another good rule to follow when you are forced to bivouac is to leave the last two hours of light to set up camp. Choosing a proper location, constructing a shelter, and gathering firewood should be done before dark. When darkness settles in it is more difficult to do any of these chores effectively or safely.

One tactic which can be used in less remote areas where there are a lot of roads crisscrossing the land is to follow a stream downhill until you cross one of the roads. In remote areas with few roads or in flat swampy country this may just lead to trouble. The hunter must stop and decide if this is an appropriate maneuver under the circumstances.

Every hunter should understand how to use and interpret the three-shot help signal. Firing three slow, spaced shots is a help signal. To avoid the shots being mistaken for hunters shooting at game, this signal should be used after dark and repeated if necessary as ammunition allows. If urgent help is needed, like when immediate medical help is necessary, the three-shot signal can be used during daylight and repeated several times to confirm the request. Hunters (or anyone within hearing distance) who hear this signal reply with *two* shots. The persons giving the three-shot help signal are to remain at their position and repeat the signal until the rescuers can find them. This is a universal signal understood everywhere, but it must be applied correctly to be effective.

The vast majority of survival situations hunters face are short term— 48 hours or less. In these cases the main obstacles are to stay warm, dry and get enough water. Accomplishing these three tasks will get hunters through almost any situation. Occasionally a hunter will be in a survival situation where obtaining food becomes a priority. The first principle of food-gathering is making sure it is safe to eat. Eating unfit food will certainly cause a bad situation to deteriorate quickly. Knowing what wild foods are edible is a good skill for any hunter to have, but it is usually area-specific. Handbooks are written on the subject and local classes are usually available to teach this skill.

It is useful to realize that we can survive for weeks in most situations without food if we have plenty of water. However, if food does become a necessity, any large wild game animals can be taken to sustain a hunter regardless of seasons or bag limits. But this is only allowed in real emergencies—not when a hunter has been hungry for a few hours and will probably get out safely within a day or two. Game officials will prosecute hunters who shoot illegal game unless it is a health or life-threatening emergency. If there is a real necessity, the best survival strategy is to spend your time and effort trying to take a large animal rather than trying to eat a few berries or catch small animals like squirrels or birds. Making one large kill will solve your food problem for weeks and likely see you through any survival predicament.

Hunters who have a good background in survival skills and strategies and who recognize their survival can depend on the choices they make in many situations are better hunters. They are more confident in their abilities and thus able to travel farther and harder when hunting circumstances demand it. Continuing to follow a fresh track, following a wounded animal into the night, or staying overnight in the field when a once-in-a-lifetime trophy is near are all possible when a hunter knows he has the ability to survive comfortably. For these hunters, an overnight bivouac becomes just a part of the hunt and not a life-threatening event.

A proud hunter with a 193-point non-typical whitetail.

Sheep hunters have to know how to survive after dark on a mountain because this scenario with a hunter descending late at night is a frequent occurrence when pursuing these mountain animals.

Chapter 9
CAMPING

Building a safe, satisfactory camp and living comfortably in a camping situation are vital skills of a successful hunter. Although most whitetail deer hunting occurs in close proximity to urban areas where camping is not necessary, much of the big game hunting in North America still involves camping. Any hunter who expects to hunt a wide variety of game should also expect to camp out a good share of the time. Hunters with good camping skills are more likely to get the necessary rest for demanding days afield. This will lead to higher success and more satisfaction in their hunting experiences.

Site Selection

The most important skill of camp building is site selection. Critical evaluation of a possible camping site is the first and most crucial step in selecting a safe, comfortable location. Hunters should know what to look for and what to avoid when setting up a hunting camp.

The basic element to look for is a dry, level, brush-free location for the tent. It is useful to mentally picture the erected tent when searching for the ideal spot. A mineral soil is better than an organic soil, both for drainage and ease of smoothing out the bumps. Look for a place that can be easily located in the dark in case you are out late. Look for a tall tree or bush that can be flagged to help identify camp to weary hunters who return late. (Campers can also hang a twilight-activated, waterproof light near camp for a locator beacon; these are available in marine supply stores and can be life-savers.) Nearby drinking water and firewood are also desireable qualities of a good campsite. If heavy snow is likely, high—but strong—overhanging trees *might* be adviseable. Remember that limbs and trees can break under a heavy snow load, so consider this possibility.

Although nearby drinking water makes for a good camp, camping too close to water is dangerous, *so don't camp too close to bodies of water whose levels may suddenly rise.* This is probably the most common mistake of inexperienced campers. Bodies of water—both running and stationary—often rise quickly. Precipitation can bring water levels up at the rate of several inches per hour. Bright sunny days in glacier country can cause water to rise even faster—sometimes at the rate of several feet per hour. Stay away from dry streambeds if there is any possibility of quickly rising water and always have a way out when you are camped near water. If you are always aware of the danger of rising water when camping, you will make good site selections. On one of my guiding trips in Southeast Alaska we were camped next to a lake with steep slopes on every side. We were camped in one of the few flat spots available. After a week of rain and rising water the entire shoreline up to the mountain slopes was underwater. We had to float our sleeping and cooking tents on 55 gallon barrels and walk between the two in our hip boots. It wasn't great camping, but with a little ingenuity, we kept our gear dry.

If there are flying insect pests, situating the camp to take advantage of the predominant breeze may be desireable, but if heavy winds are possible, the danger from the wind has to be weighed against the benefit of fewer bugs. When camping in open mountain terrain, the danger from the wind is one of the paramount concerns and counts very heavily in site selection. While hunting in the high mountains here in Alaska I once came upon a "guide" and his client who were setting up their tent on top of a completely exposed knob jutting out from a mountain slope. They claimed it gave them a good view. Had one of the regularly occurring windstorms come down that glacier valley their tent would still be airborne—even if they were in it. I convinced them to move down to a more sheltered spot, although I was tempted to let them learn the hard way (which is the way I learned).

Waking up in the middle of a rain and windstorm as your tent is blowing away is not fun and usually a soggy experience. And in some situations getting your gear wet may put your life in danger. Look for and avoid locations that may be wind funnels or any areas that look unprotected. Stunted trees or horizontally growing vegetation is always a good sign of strong winds. Moving a tent even twenty feet to benefit from a windbreak can make a significant difference.

When hunting in flat, forested country where insect pests may drop out of trees or brush as well as attack from the air, choosing an open area may be the best choice. However, if you want to erect a tarp, brush and short trees are useful to have nearby. But if you camp under trees and it rains or snows, the dripping can be annoying. If there is a possibility of lightning in the area, you should avoid getting near the tallest trees. Avoid trails and roads however tempting they may be; animals and people use these regularly and will cause unwelcome disturbances—or worse—in camp. Each site is unique. All these factors and more must be taken into consideration to choose the best site available.

Carefully plan the location of a campfire (if appropriate) and a latrine. The main purpose of the fire—whether for cooking or heating—will often determine its location. Remember that nylon tents melt or burn easily, so place the fire downwind far enough for safety. Cooking fires are

Hunting camps are seldom as chilly as this one in the frigid north of Alaska, but hunters who are able to set up a comfortable camp anywhere will have more enjoyable hunting experiences.

often only coals and not much flame. The best woods to produce good cooking coals are hardwoods. Resinous woods like spruce, fir and pine are good to get a fire going, but birch, oak, and maple will make better coals and last longer. (For a lengthy discussion on fires see Chapter Eight—"Survival.")

Rock rings around a fire are handy to set cooking pots on and to contain the fire. Green sticks with the bark left on should be used for hanging pots over a fire because they won't catch fire as quickly as dry sticks. Soaking hanging sticks in water will help extend their usefulness. Red meat can be adequately cooked over an open fire if chunks are skewered on a sharpened green stick which is then propped up at an angle over the fire. It is best to first thrust red meat into flames briefly to seal in the juices before cooking in this manner. While waiting to be picked up by a Super Cub after my dozens of Dall sheep hunting trips in Alaska, I have cooked many pounds of wild sheep meat in this manner. At times we have almost consumed a whole sheep before the pilot has been able to get us out of the mountains. This is such good fare that we sometimes hope the plane is delayed just so we can enjoy this open-fire delicacy a while longer. Any hunter who has not had wild game cooked in this manner is missing one of hunting's finest pleasures.

Baking foods can even be accomplished around a campfire if the proper arrangement of coals and reflectors is used. Aluminum foil can be used to wrap fish, game meat, or bread dough—which is placed on a bed of coals and then covered with more coals. Lightweight, collapsible outdoor ovens with built-in thermometers for better temperature control.

The latrine should be downstream from your water source, off any trails, and somewhat secluded if it is not too buggy. The size depends on the length of stay, the number of campers and any regulations in the area. A lighter can be left in a Zip-loc baggy nest to the latrine to burn any paper—if required in the area. Leave at least the top six inches empty for backfilling with soil before you leave the site. If your stay is extended, another latrine can always be dug to provide for the extra time.

This tent site, which has been used by hunters for several decades, is under a protective boulder the size of a house. This protects it from rain, wind and the eyes of game animals.

Setting up the Tent

Once the campsite has been carefully selected, the tent can be erected. The exact tent site is critical. By putting the tent on a slightly raised area you can avoid possible moisture problems. If the center of the tent is slightly higher than the edges (one inch rise every four feet of distance), any water that may get inside the tent will run away from the center. If heavy rain or snowmelt is expected, trenches can be dug around the tent directly under the outer edges of the rainfly to catch excess water. Trenches do mar the landscape so this should be done only in remote areas when absolutely necessary. The depth depends on the circumstances. Avoid placing the tent entrance in a low spot, or a puddle will form at the doorstep during wet weather. A tarp can be placed under the tent to prevent moisture from seeping through the tent floor, but make sure the tarp edges are not protruding outside the tent walls to catch water—which will then run under the tent floor and soak it.

Mountain tents should be pitched with the low end into the prevailing wind to minimize its effect. The entrance to a tent should face a campfire for convenience. Also, placing any gear or food in view of the tent entrance enables campers to watch for marauding critters. Keeping a clean camp will reduce chances of this happening, but it is always a possibility.

Overhanging limbs should be removed near the chopping block, away from the fire location, and from above the tent. This makes chopping wood much safer, reduces the chances of a wildfire, and prevents branches from making disturbing noises on the tent during windy nights. Dragging brush away from the campfire also reduces the chances of a wildfire. Marking tent guy lines with flagging tape or placing rocks next to them as markers prevents tripping and possible injuries.

To make a more comfortable bed, dry vegetation can be placed under the tent. This will also prevent moisture from entering the tent floor in wet locations. Be sure this is allowed in the area you are camping before gathering grasses (best) or evergreen (next best) boughs for under the tent. When the right vegetation is plentiful, up to a foot of bedding material can be quickly gathered and layered to make an excellent bed.

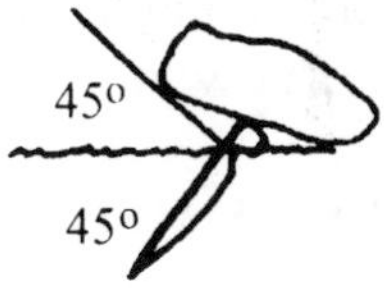

Tent stakes should be driven in at a 90 degree angle to the guy ropes they hold. Guy ropes are usually at about a 45 degree angle to the ground, so this means stakes are usually at about a 45 degree angle to the ground—45 plus 45 equals 90 degrees. It is always a good practice to place rocks on tent stakes to help anchor them, especially in loose soil or windy conditions.

Figure 9.1

If the soil is too loose to hold stakes at all, a deadman can be used. A deadman is usually a short log which is buried perpendicular to a guy rope— which is tied to its center. The depth depends on how loose the soil is, but 12-16 inches is usually sufficient. Deadman anchors are also used in snow or ice to hold tent guy ropes.

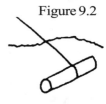

Figure 9.2

Another good practice if there is any chance of strong winds, is to place windbreaks around the tent. When mountain camping I always pile a ring of rocks around the tent to help deflect the wind. It helps me sleep better and is good insurance that the tent will be there in the evening when I return from a full day of hunting. Even twelve-inch high barriers around a tent keep a significant amount of wind from getting under the rainfly and causing problems. Logs, sod, or any material that is available can also be used to make a windbreak.

Tepees make good, albeit uncommon, hunting camps. A small campfire can be built inside a tepee because the small top hole lets the smoke escape—without letting a significant amount of precipitation in. Tepees usually must be custom made and need long, often cumbersome poles to set up. However, camping in a tepee can be a unique way to take a step back in time and feel a link to the Native hunters of North America.

Knots to Know

Setting up a comfortable camp typically requires using rope and twine, therefore knot-tying skills are quite useful for camping—and hunting in general. Although some hunters use "Granny" knots for everything, it is quite easy to learn how to make and apply a few common knots which have many more uses than a "Granny." Here are six common knots which will serve campers and hunters in almost any situation.

DOUBLE HALF-HITCH - One or two half-hitches are quick knots to use for a short duration under constant tension. One half-hitch will come loose by itself, but it can be tied and untied quickly and is useful for temporary purposes. When used in conjunction with other knots, a half-hitch or two can snug up the free end of other knots—like a bowline.

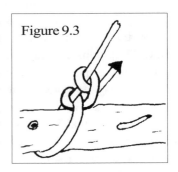
Figure 9.3

CLOVE HITCH - Also a quick knot, this is used to tie over a tight line or a solid object like a branch, log or post. It should be secured with a half-hitch. It is good for lashing bulky items to a packframe or tying a horse to a hitching post.

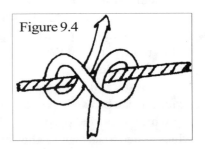
Figure 9.4

QUICK-RELEASE CLOVE HITCH - By doubling the free end of any knot as it passes through the last gap, the knot is made into a quick-release version—just pull the free end to untie quickly.

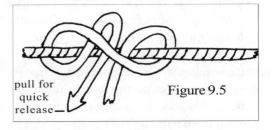
pull for quick release—
Figure 9.5

SQUARE KNOT - This is used to join two pieces of the same diameter and material, like broken shoestrings, rope, or twine.

Figure 9.6

FISHERMAN'S KNOT - This is a better way to join two pieces of rope, particularly of different sizes. Use it to add on to tent guy lines or make one long line out of several shorter ones in the field.

Figure 9.7

BOWLINE - The most secure way to tie a non-slip loop at the end of a rope. If used underwater, tie the free end snug with a half-hitch. Use to attach guy lines to tent loops, a line to a tree, a drop loop in the end of a boat line, two loops to each other, or a safety line for someone in distress.

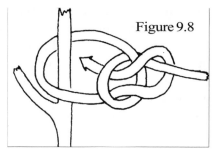

Figure 9.8

TAUT LINE - A good sliding loop which tightens under a load. Use for tent guy lines that are easily tightened, when lashing any load, or for any line that needs to be taut. To tighten, slide the knot toward the far end. Use a quick release if concerned knot may tighten too much under a load.

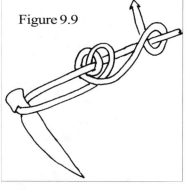

Figure 9.9

Camp pests can be a problem, especially if camp is not kept clean and food is not stored in airtight containers. To keep flies and hornets away from camp, a trap can be made by hanging meat or fish scraps over a water-filled bucket about 50 feet from camp. Insects gorge on the meat and fall into the water and drown. (This also works well around your home garden or backyard.) For a warning system of bigger pests coming into camp, line from a fishing reel can be strung all around camp at knee height. Any animal catching the line will pull on the reel's drag and alert campers to its presence.

As mentioned in Chapter Eight – "Survival," rocks warmed by a fire can be used as a heat source while camping. One of the most beneficial ways for campers to use warmed rocks is to dry footwear. Wet feet are one of the worst problems of extended hunting trips—in any kind of weather. Hunters often have no way to dry boots at night when tent camping. If small to medium-sized rocks are heated next to the fire or even by the campstove in the evening, these rocks can be placed in or around boots at bedtime. At least some of the moisture can be driven out of footwear in this manner. This method can also be used to help dry other wet gear.

The last chore a competent camper always does is dry his or her gear thoroughly after returning home. Canvas or nylon tents put away with even a little moisture will mildew and rot, and their useful life will be shortened considerably. Modern gear will last many seasons if it is dried completely without high heat and then stored in a dry, cool place. It is best to air-dry canvas, nylon, leather and most synthetics in slightly warm temperatures. High heat shortens the life of most camping gear.

Hunters with good camping skills can hunt in more locations and hunt more comfortably in adverse conditions. Having good camping skills increases the enjoyment of these hunts. Comfortable hunters sleep better and are more alert and effective. It is always interesting to hear how much cold and discomfort a hunter had to endure to be successful, but I would bet in most of those situations if the same hunter would have been a good camper he could have been warm and comfortable on the same hunt—and even more successful. There are plenty of unavoidable obstacles successful hunters have to endure, but uncomfortable camping is not one of them.

Relatively flat, smooth tent sites can be found or made even in steep terrain—and the effort is usually rewarded by a better night's sleep.

Chapter 10
PHOTOGRAPHY

"A good snapshot stops a moment from running away."
-Eudora Welty

Good photos are the best way to record our hunting adventures. Memories of past hunts are what keep them alive in our minds to enjoy for the rest of our lives. When we begin to forget the details that made a hunt memorable, photos can bring back all the excitement and companionship that made it a great experience. Even a mounted trophy cannot remind us of all the moods and feelings of a hunt the way a good array of hunt photos can.

Subjects to Photograph

Hunters who commonly take a good variety of quality photos will maximize their enjoyment of their hunting experiences. The scenery, weather patterns, companions, etc. are all part of a hunt in addition to any trophy taken. The best strategy is to take numerous photos of a variety of subjects. After the hunt is over, photos can be sifted through and just the best ones retained for a photo library of hunting memories.

The subjects you choose to photograph on a hunt vary with each experience, but the following list is a good starting point.

MODES OF TRANSPORTATION- airplanes, off-road vehicles, boats, pack animals, hiking and climbing, etc.

CAMP SHOTS- setting up camp, camp rituals, camp equipment, mealtime, campfire scenes, camp scenery, sleeping quarters, etc.

EQUIPMENT- guns, bows, packs, decoys, unusual equipment, etc.

ANIMALS IN CAMP- game animals, birds, camp pests, etc.

GUIDES - outfitters, wranglers, trackers, skinners, packers, pilots, boat captains, etc.

SCENIC SHOTS OF HUNTING AREA- from planes or boats, sunrise, sunset, weather extremes, terrain extremes, etc.

HUNTERS IN ACTION- planning strategy, scouting for game, still-hunting, in heavy brush, on stand, glassing for game, calling game, driving game, tracking, skinning, packing game, caring for meat, etc.

MOOD SHOTS- weary hunters returning late to camp, a grueling hike, misty mornings, relaxing in camp, etc.

TROPHY SHOTS- (the most important subject for hunters to learn how to photograph) the trophy by itself, the hunter with his/her trophy, the hunter and guide with the trophy, etc.

After learning *what* to photograph, hunters need to learn *how* to take good photos.

Composition

One key to taking good photos is thinking about what the final photo will look like. Think about professional photos and what makes them pleasing to the eye. You must consider positioning, viewpoint, shape, color, scale and focus. There are some guidelines for good photography, but no absolute rules. Variety and experimentation will often produce some great shots that break one or more of the guidelines of good photography.

Positioning and viewpoint are the two ingredients of composition in good photography. The guideline for positioning is called the "rule of thirds" (see Diagram 10.1). If a photo is divided into thirds with four imaginary lines (the dotted lines), the four points these lines intersect (the small circles) show the best locations to position the subject. Positioning a subject or the horizon in the center of a photo typically produces a dull picture; the exception is when the subject has strong geometric lines and is symmetrical—like a rectangular building. Hunters should apply this "rule of thirds" to most photos. Experimenting with different positions in the frame will usually indicate where the best position is for a given subject and view.

Figure 10.1

Viewpoint refers to where the photographer is located when taking the photo. One good guideline is to get close when there is one main subject—like trophy shots. Filling the frame with the subject provides emphasis to photos. When photos are taken from a distance the subject can be lost in the background, resulting in a dull photo. However, when the background is important to the composition of the photo, the photographer must back up a sufficient distance to properly frame all of the subject.

Trying all angles and distances will improve the variety and quality of your hunting photos. Lie down, stand on top of something, get real close or step back and look through the viewfinder. This kind of experimentation with viewpoint can help any photographer improve his photo composition.

Viewpoint also changes the shape and relative size of your subject(s). One very common practice is for the photographer to get very close to the animal and position the hunter several feet behind it. This makes the animal look larger than life in comparison to the smaller, distant hunter. This is a useful technique to remember when a photographer wants to emphasize any subject in the foreground, not just trophy shots.

Lighting is another critical part of taking quality hunting photos. There are several guidelines to remember. Don't take photos directly into sunlight or artificial light—unless you are backlighting or silhouetting for emphasis and you adjust the exposure setting accordingly. On overcast

Composition and subject are both important to good trophy shots.
Here is Dave Widby smiling with a nice mule deer.

days remove as much sky as possible from the photo to avoid underexposure of your subject. Use a flash or fill-flash in low light conditions. Have people remove or adjust hats to avoid shadowed faces, or use a fill-flash if you are within range of the flash. Move around the subject as you look through the viewfinder to discover where the light best shows off your subject.

Additional guidelines for top quality photos include holding the camera as *still as possible* and *gently* squeezing the shutter to get sharp pictures. Only hand-hold a camera when using a short lens at fast shutter speeds; shots at less than 1/30th of a second need to be taken from a tripod or other stable platform. Use shutter speeds of at least 1/250 when shooting from moving vehicles. Use a high aperture setting for maximum depth of field when taking scenery photos. Don't position your subject too close to the edges of the frame. This often results in part of it being cut out or so close to the edge that it distracts the viewer. Make a habit of using the center outlined area for both focusing and light meter adjustments and then adjust the framing of the subject. With autofocusing cameras the typical procedure for this is to 1) hold the shutter release halfway down while it makes the adjustments, 2) keep the release partially depressed while you frame your photo, 3) and then fully release the shutter. Remember to take unposed shots to get the real mood of the hunting experience.

Taking trophy shots is the most important photography skill for hunters to master. One key is to take *lots* of shots of the animal and the hunter with the animal. After all the time, effort and money that is spent on a hunt, it is a shame not to spend at least thirty minutes and one roll of film

*Hunting photos should include various activities and poses
to capture the different moods of the hunt. These will
enhance the memories hunters take home.*

to record the memories for future enjoyment. As a sheep and bear guide in Alaska I often spend over an hour moving an animal and posing it to get just the right shots—often using two or more rolls of film. I have never had a hunter in the field complain and have gotten many heartfelt thanks after the photos came back.

The first thing to do in anticipation of trophy photos is to place your gear out of sight. Gear strewn around in the background will distract the viewer from the main subject. Try to take trophy photos ASAP before the eyes glaze and while the animal looks its best. Also plan on taking some photos before moving the animal—often the underside of the animal will have more blood on it after lying there for even a few minutes. Always remember to remove as much blood as possible, tuck the tongue in or cut it off if necessary, and close the mouth if possible. A few paper towels can be carried in a Zip-Loc bag to wipe off excess blood, or clean vegetation can be used.

Before beginning the photo session, the immediate area should also be cleaned of blood, gore, and distracting grass and brush. There is nothing worse than getting trophy photos back two weeks after a successful hunt only to have a annoying twig or blade of grass across the trophy's face in every photo. Carefully examining the scene through the viewfinder before taking photos will identify these distractions so they can be removed.

When taking trophy or hunter-with-trophy photos, always take some close-ups to emphasize these subjects. Fill the frame with just the head and neck of the trophy and then do the same with just the hunter's face and the trophy. Even when adding scenery to a trophy shot, the animal should be close enough to display it well. If the trophy is hard to see, the scenery will become the main subject of the photo. Don't let scenery or background subjects detract from a trophy photo. By looking through the viewfinder with a critical eye, these types of distractions can be eliminated before the shutter is released. Make sure the *trophy* is the main subject of your trophy photos.

For trophy photos the hunter should also be *posed* properly. The hunter's hands should not be wrapped around the horns where they will be visible from the front, but kept behind the horns where they will not catch the viewer's eye. Have the hunter adjust any out of place clothing or clean a dirty face; and watch for anything in the background that seems to grow out of the hunter's head—like a tree.

Watch for shadows that fall on the trophy or the hunter. If necessary, move the animal to have good lighting or to find a better background. Wait for clouds, fog, rain showers, or snow squalls to move either in or out—this may provide better lighting, a dramatic background or affect the mood of the photo.

Don't forget that cameras malfunction and film processors make mistakes. For insurance against these and other hazards always use two cameras and/or two rolls of film when possible. And carry extra batteries for the camera. Give yourself every opportunity to get great photos of the hunt. As a bear guide I take brown bear hunters who spend upwards of $15,000 for a ten-day hunt. I can't imagine not taking every precaution to get good photos, since this is a once-in-a-lifetime hunt for many of these hunters. With this level of investment, a few additional dollars for an extra camera is certainly justified. Even bringing a disposable camera as an extra on special hunts is a good idea; they take pretty good pictures, too!

Hunting Cameras and Film

The camera you choose to take hunting can have a significant impact on the quantity and quality of your hunting photos. For most hunting purposes a small point-and-shoot 35mm is the best choice. A hunting camera should be light and compact enough so it will always be available and not left back at camp or at home. As the name implies, the point-and-shoot models do almost everything for the photographer. A full-size 35mm camera can do more and take better photos than the point-and-shoot models, but they are much bulkier and require more expertise.

In addition to the auto-features commonly found on most point-and-shoot 35mm models, there are a few features which the optimal hunting camera should have. A waterproof model is essential for hunting in damp climates and is good insurance in case of accidental submersions in even the driest climates. Here in Alaska I have lost three cameras to moisture buildup which eventually led to malfunctions—usually during a hunt. My current camera is waterproof to 10 feet underwater and it has lasted much longer than the previous, non-waterproof models. However, I still carry my camera in a Zip-Loc to protect it from moisture, dirt and physical abuse.

A timer is also essential on a hunting camera to take pictures of you and your trophy when you hunt alone, or pictures of you and your hunting companion(s). Other features like zoom lenses, an auto shutoff and a panoramic mode may improve your hunting photos, but they are not really essentials.

Once you buy a hunting camera, the first thing to do is *read the manual*. This not only helps you avoid real blunders, but you will know the capabilities of your camera and take the best hunting photos possible.

There are a few simple guidelines when choosing film for hunting photos. Color slides or black and white prints are best if you plan to sell them. Otherwise, most people choose color prints for personal use. Any brand film will suffice. The quality of the developing can significantly affect the quality of your photos, so if you have some one-of-a-kind photos on a roll of film, choose your developer carefully. The more expensive photo shops will usually do a much better developing job than you will get from a photo booth in your local variety store.

The film speed you should use depends on the amount of light available when the photos will be taken. 100ASA is used for daytime shooting in bright light situations. 200ASA is used for conditions with less than bright light, like overcast days. 400ASA is used for low-light levels—like at dusk. Anything outside of this 100-400ASA range is generally used only by professionals who know the specific applications. 200ASA is a good all-around film to have with you to cover most situations. I carry mostly 200ASA as my standard film and some 400ASA for lower light photos, or if I will be exposing an entire roll using a flash. Whatever film you choose, take twice what you think you will need. Film will keep until the next hunt and it is cheap in relation to the price of most hunting trips. Don't run out of film and ' let the moment run away.'

PART IV.
HUNTING GEAR
AND FOOD

Chapter 11
HUNTING KNIVES, AXES AND SAWS–AND HOW TO SHARPEN THEM

A sharp hunting knife is the second most important item for a hunter, the hunting weapon being the most important one. A hunter's skill level is often gauged by the knife he or she carries–its design and the sharpness of its edge. Some of us think the definition of a hunter should even include ". . . one who carries a keen-edged blade." At the least, a knife is a mandatory piece of gear for any successful hunter.

A sharp knife is one of the most important tools a hunter carries. Todd Fisher is shown putting an edge on his Buck knife.

Knives

Knives are far safer and more useful when they are sharp. Dull knives rip and tear rather than cut cleanly. A dull knife requires more pressure to cut, which can result in injury if the knife suddenly slips. Sharp knives save time for the hunter in the field, preventing a cold night on the mountain or an after-dark walk back to camp. A dull knife can put damaging holes in a prized trophy cape and jagged, wasteful edges on tasty game meat. Regardless of their composition, all knives get dull with use. Choosing and sharpening knives are skills at which successful hunters should excel.

When choosing a knife, hunters should consider design, construction, and function. There are two basic designs: fixed-blade and folding knives. A fixed-blade knife (a one-piece sheath knife) is generally stronger and safer than a folding knife–assuming they are both sturdily constructed. This doesn't mean that many high-quality folding knives with locking blades aren't serviceable as hunting knives, but just that they do break more often and can't be used for as rough of work as a fixed-blade sheath knife. On the other hand, a fixed-blade knife is longer and more cumbersome when carried on a belt than a folding knife. Neither design is necessarily heavier or lighter than the other, it depends on which models you compare. The folding mechanism often makes a lock-back knife as heavy or heavier than a fixed-blade knife. However, folding knives often have two blades and assorted tools which are very useful to a hunter in the field. Both designs are popular and it often boils down to personal preference, as neither type is clearly the better one.

The function of a knife is determined by the shape, length and thickness of the blade. In general, a blade with a long, curved shape from heel to tip is made for skinning. The entire curve can be used to skin an animal, versus just the tip on a very pointed blade. A very pointed blade (like a fillet knife) will get dull very quickly when skinning because only the tip is being used. All other construction features being equal, the skinner would only have to be sharpened a very few times compared to the pointed blade. However, the pointed blade is useful to start cuts on an animal and reach into tight spots. A wide skinning blade is cumbersome for many tasks other than skinning. Most hunting knife blades are a compromise between these two basic shapes. Fancy blade shapes like drop points and boot points are someone's idea of a better hunting knife shape, but these shapes are also between the two extremes of skinner and fillet knife (Fig. 11.1).

A hunter's personal preferences and uses will determine which blade he or she chooses. If the hunter often goes on backpack hunts for large game and only carries one knife, a blade with plenty of curve for skinning would be preferable. On the other hand, if most hunting will be done from road vehicles and the animal can be field-dressed and then brought back to skin where more knives will be available, perhaps a more pointed knife is what is needed. The wider the blade, the more useful it is as a skinner, but the more difficult it will be in tight spots and in many other situations. Most hunting knives must serve as all-purpose knives and their shape reflects this.

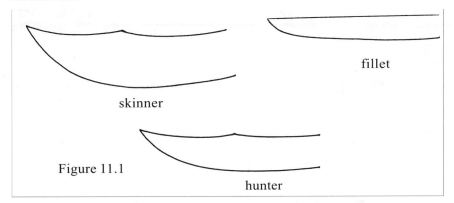

fillet

skinner

Figure 11.1

hunter

The construction and composition of a knife determines its rust and stain resistance, hardness, and strength. Only poor-quality knives show any rust or stains after use. Most knives are made of high-quality steel which won't rust or stain. An important factor for a hunter when choosing a knife is the hardness of the steel used. A suitable hunting knife blade should be hard enough to completely skin medium-size game animals (like deer, sheep or pronghorn) without needing a touch-up. Softer steel is easier to sharpen, but the edge won't last long. A very hard steel blade may keep its edge, but it is very hard to touch up in the field. Harder steel is also brittle and may chip more frequently. Personal choice and demands determine how hard the steel in your knife should be.

The strength of a knife comes from its thickness and composition. Too thin of a blade may break and leave a hunter in a bad situation. Choose a very thick blade, and it will be hard to put a good cutting edge on it. Thick blades are often hollow-ground in an attempt to get the best of both worlds–strength and a fine cutting edge–and this does help. The composition of the steel will also affect its strength; while harder steel is generally stronger, it chips easier. However, chipping is seldom a problem unless a hunting knife is really abused. As before, personal preference and requirements determine how you select for these features.

Some hunters swear by ceramic knives for durability. These knives will keep an edge for several skinning jobs and even several seasons with light use. The drawback is they cannot be sharpened without special tools. They have to be sent in to be resharpened–a nuisance at the least. It seems to me that hunters should be able to sharpen their own knives. I recommend sticking with steel knives.

Another thing to consider when buying a knife is the bevel on the cutting edge. Basically, hunting knives come with two types of cutting edges–general purpose and fine. The tradeoffs between these two edge types involve toughness and cutting ability. A general purpose edge is tougher– it will last longer, but the fine edge will be sharper. The innate cutting ability (assuming it is sharpened correctly) of any knife is predominantly determined by its bevel. The bevel on hunting knives ranges between 15 degress (fine) and 22 degrees (general purpose). See Figure 11.2

15°   22°

Figure 11.2

END VIEW OF KNIVES

The original bevel can probably be changed if desired, but the bevel is somewhat dependent on the knife's thickness. A general purpose bevel (around 22 degrees) is good for many uses and will keep its edge longer. A fine bevel (around 15 degrees) is useful when a sharper edge is desireable (like caping out a trophy), but it will need to be touched-up more frequently. A blade with a bevel between these two extremes will have some of both qualities–toughness and sharpness.

Sharpening Tools

There are literally hundreds of different types of sharpening devices. They can be made of either natural stones or man-made surfaces. The man-made surfaces are generally less-expensive and more uniform in grit size (surface texture). Naturally occurring stone sharpeners have a mystique about them and are still preferred by "traditionalists."

Sharpening stones (including both natural and man-made varieties) are still very common and useful sharpening tools. They come in a variety of grit size from coarse to very fine. The coarser the grit, the faster steel can be removed; the finer the grit, the keener the edge which can be produced. Natural stones usually have one grit size on both sides. Man-made stones may have a coarse and a fine side, and some are even three-sided; each of the three grit sizes used for a different purpose. Stone materials are also made into grinding wheels which are used to remove large amounts of steel quickly.

When using sharpening stones (natural and man-made), oil should be regularly applied to the stone's surface to float away pieces of the stone which fracture off, as well as particles of steel from the knife (or other tool) being sharpened. Honing oils are made for this purpose, but any lightweight oil is suitable. Gun, vegetable or mineral oil and even kerosene can be used. Clean water can be used in a pinch, but oils are better because

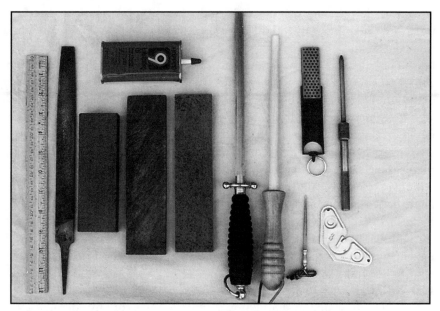

Sharpening devices from left to right: file, man-made stone, natural Washita stone, natural soft Arkansas stone, chef's steel, ceramic rod, diamond-impregnated flip-out sharpener, 3 1/2 inch steel, diamond-impregnated rod, and groove-sharpener.

of their higher density and superior ability to float the stone and steel particles off the surface. New stones should be soaked overnight in a pan full of oil to condition them, then wiped clean. Anytime dirty stones are cleaned—by scrubbing with warm, soapy water—they should be re-conditioned by soaking in oil.

After heavy use, stones will become "bellied," or have a depression in them where most of the contact occurs. This depression must be removed periodically to keep the stone functioning at its best. Simply turn the stone over on 80 grit sandpaper placed on a flat surface. Using a circular motion and a few drops of water periodically, grind the stone until it is once again flat. Wipe it off, re-soak it in oil and it will be like new.

Other materials employed for sharpening knives are grooved steel, diamond and ceramic. Steel files are occasionally used when a lot of material has to be removed quickly, but the result is a coarse edge. For finer work, a chef's steel can be used. The fine grooves and round shape make them good for putting a very keen edge on knives. Diamond is the hardest natural material on earth so it cuts steel quickly and lasts a long time. Diamond-impregnated sharpeners come in several grit sizes and many shapes for rough or fine work. I personally carry a diamond sharpener because my Buck knife has very hard steel and is hard to sharpen with softer sharpeners. Ceramic is also made into sharpening tools, but its fine texture is only good for touch-ups or putting the final edge on a blade. A fine steel, diamond sharpeners and ceramics should all be cleaned regularly with regular household cleanser and water to remove the steel particles that accumulate. This keeps their grooves and cavities from getting plugged–which would greatly reduce their effectiveness.

Some honing aids are designed to help the user maintain the proper bevel on the blade. These can really improve the results for less-skillful sharpeners because a prime requisite of effective sharpening is keeping the blade at the same angle stroke after stroke. Some of these aids are clamps which attach to the blade and make it simple to repeatedly keep the same angle between stone and blade. Other devices are stones or other sharpening materials that are fixed into a "V" shape. The knife blade is simply drawn through the "V" until the desired cutting edge is achieved. Both of these aids make it much easier for even a beginner to put a good cutting edge on a knife.

Knife-Sharpening Procedure

The first step in sharpening a hunting knife (or any smooth blade) is to determine if the bevel is correct for the function. Once the bevel is decided upon, the blade should be examined for proper shape, excess steel, dips, nicks or larger chips. Correcting any of these problems requires removal of considerable amounts of steel. A grinding wheel, file or coarse stone is best for removing steel quickly. The one drawback with using a grinding wheel is the possibility of overheating and losing the temper of the steel. Plenty of water and a light pressure should be used with a wheel. This takes an experienced hand as a knife blade can be overheated and lose its temper in just a matter of seconds. A de-tempered blade will be discolored, soft and won't hold an edge–useless to a hunter.

Coarse stones or files are generally more available and much safer for removing steel from hunting knives. When using a coarse stone, first cover it with a light film of oil. Then, holding the blade at the proper angle, stroke it from heel to tip, tip to heel or in a circular motion. Any of these motions work as long as 1) the proper angle is maintained from heel to tip and 2) the same amount of steel is removed over the length of the blade to retain the proper shape with no dips.

A file will also work to remove steel quickly, but it is hard to use on small blades. Clamping a blade in a fixed position—like in a bench vise—is desireable when using a file. Stroke the file perpendicular to the knife blade with long, even strokes as you move from one end to the other. The proper way to use a file is to push it slowly into the work (the object you are filing) with slow, firm, deliberate strokes. A file which is properly fitted with a handle is easier and safer to use. Remove the same amount of steel from tip to heel to retain the original contour of the blade.

After any visible damage to a blade has been removed, the edge should have the correct bevel with no excess steel (Fig. 11.3). The edge must have the correct bevel before moving on to the next stage of sharpening. Maintaining the same angle between the blade and the sharpening tool(s) during the entire process is the *key* to sharpening any smooth blade (knives, arrowheads, axes, machetes, chisels, etc.). It is the only way to achieve a good cutting edge.

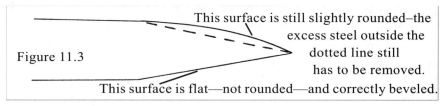

Figure 11.3

This surface is still slightly rounded–the excess steel outside the dotted line still has to be removed.

This surface is flat—not rounded—and correctly beveled.

END VIEW OF KNIFE

The next stages in the sharpening process involve working the blade over progressively finer grit stones or other abrasive materials, always keeping the same angle between the blade and the abrasive surface. The finer the grit of the final sharpening material, the keener the edge on the blade. A circular motion will remove steel faster so it can be used with the coarse grit stones, but a heel to tip motion should be used with the finer grit sharpeners. The heel to tip motion is the most natural for most hunters so it is usually the best way for them to maintain a consistent angle. This heel to tip motion is also best for use at the final stages of sharpening so the grooves cut into the blade by the stone will parallel the cutting motion when the knife is in use. This will reduce cutting resistance and produce a cleaner cut.

The amount of pressure used during this entire process should vary. At first, when using a file or coarse stone, the pressure can be heavy to increase the speed at which steel is removed from the blade. As the grit size of the sharpening material is reduced, the pressure should also be reduced. At the final stage of sharpening, only a light pressure is needed to acquire a very keen edge. Too much pressure and the edge may be removed too fast, it may curl over or an undesireable hair edge may be produced (Fig. 11.4). A hair edge is too thin to last long enough in the field to be useful to a hunter, even though it may be impressive on the back of a fingernail.

After a hunting knife has been sharpened as described, it is ready for field use. To retain a fine cutting edge, a knife should be touched up frequently in the field with any fine-textured sharpening tool. When touching up a blade in the field, the bevel is increased ever so slightly (less than 1/2°). This is because the edge of the blade has been worn back slightly

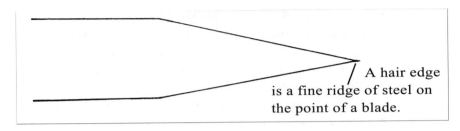

A hair edge is a fine ridge of steel on the point of a blade.

Figure 11.4   END VIEW OF KNIFE

and to sharpen it at exactly the same angle would require the removal of a considerable amount of steel–which is not practical in the field with a fine-textured sharpener (see Fig. 11.5). This slight increase in angle between the blade and the sharpening tool makes a touch-up take less than two minutes. A field touch-up can be done several times while still maintaining a good working edge on the blade. After that, the blade will begin to round, leaving a blunt edge. Before this happens, it should be put through the complete sharpening process again. The actual number of times a blade can be touched-up depends on how much the sharpening angle is increased each time–which depends on how much of a hurry you are in. The steeper the angle, the faster you will get a useable edge, but the fewer times you can touch up the blade before it gets too blunt to be useful and needs a thorough sharpening.

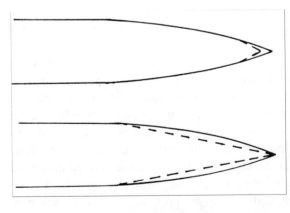

The point of this blade would have a slightly steeper angle (the dashed line outlines this) after a field touch-up.

The alternative is to do a thorough sharpening on the blade, which will take longer, but will restore the blade to its original angle–represented by the dashed lines.

Figure 11.5   END VIEW OF KNIVES

For field touch-ups only the smallest of hones needs to be carried for most hunting trips–and none at all in some cases. I personally carry a small, one-piece Buck Woodsman knife and a small Swiss army knife with two blades. These three blades will last for the duration of most hunts, with the exception of those for the largest game animals in North America. On sheep hunts where weight is important, I never carry a hone. The Buck will keep a decent edge for two or three sheep skinnings without even a touch-up and I have the super-sharp Swiss knife blades to cape with and for backup. If I should someday dull all three blades on such a trip, a rock will put an emergency edge on them until I can properly re-sharpen them. A knife blade can be sharpened with any object which is as hard or harder than the steel in the blade–even a knife blade of harder steel will work (so I could sharpen the soft Swiss knife blades on the back of the much harder Buck knife). This might take some time because most blades are very smooth (like a very fine sharpener), but it may be helpful to understand this concept if such a dilemma arises.

Hunters who are really good at sharpening knives have a feel for the right angle of the blade on the stone. The sound of the steel also tells them when everything is just right. One way to check yourself is to color the knife edge 1/4" back with a felt marker along the length of the blade. Take a few sharpening strokes with both sides of the knife on a stone and then check to see if you are removing steel evenly on both sides and along the entire length of the blade. Then adjust accordingly.

Axes, Hatchets and Mauls

Axes and hatchets are common to many hunting camps where firewood is needed. A double bit axe is the most efficient weapon to attack firewood and it will last twice as long between sharpenings as a single-bit axe. However, for most camps a single bit axe or hatchet is sufficient. For a long-term camp a maul is a faster splitting tool and less dangerous than a double bit axe. The back of these tools will also double as a stake driver or hammer. Whichever tool is chosen, if it has a wooden handle, this should be wrapped with wire near the blade to prevent bruising. Small diameter tie wire is a good material to wrap around the two inches of handle closest to the head. This will prevent any blows from maring the handle and weakening it. It will last considerably longer if this is done.

All of these heavy cutting tools are sharpened to a convex shape to help split wood and not get stuck. Dull axes and hatchets are often the cause of serious hunting camp injuries from glancing blows. File sharpening alone is typically enough for these tools. However, if an axe will be used for fine work—like carving or log cabin work—a stone can be used to achieve a finer edge. Other than maintaining a convex shape when sharpening these heavy tools (see Fig. 11.6), the principles of knife sharpening apply.

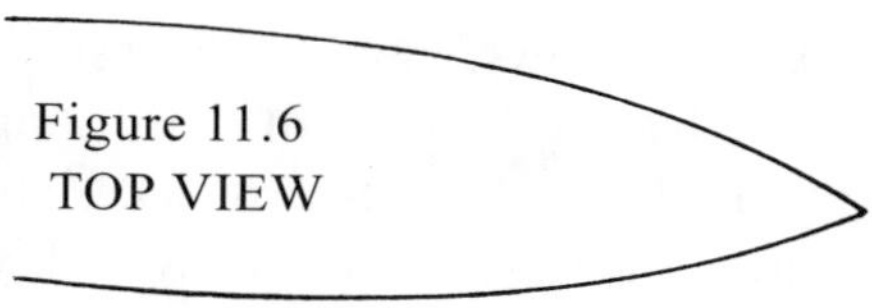

Figure 11.6
TOP VIEW

A slightly convex (rounded) shape is usually best for axes and hatchets. This shape is more efficient for splitting wood because of the wedging effect.

Saws

There are a multitude of wood and bone saws to choose from. Features to consider when selecting a saw include size, collapsibility, weight, cutting speed, strength, durability and function. During most hunting trips only a relatively small amount of wood or bone will be cut, so cutting speed is seldom a critical factor. Size and weight are generally the two most important features to look for in either type of saw, although strength must also be considered. Often a compact, two-sided saw like a Knapp sport saw with wood-cutting teeth on one side and a bone saw on the other is a good choice. I have owned one of these for over twenty years. When it is sharp, I can cut through six-inch logs in a few minutes and through the skull of a bull moose in less than fifteen minutes. More important than the choice of saw is its sharpness. Both wood and bone saws need to have sharp teeth and a proper set (see Fig. 11.7) to work efficiently.

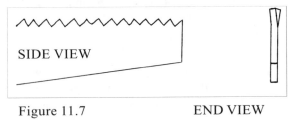

SET= Alternate teeth on a saw blade are bent towards opposite sides so the blade makes a wider cut than the thickness of the blade. This prevents the blade from getting stuck in the material.

SIDE VIEW

Figure 11.7   END VIEW

Sharpening saws takes special tools and more practice than most people will get during their lifetime. The best strategy for the vast majority of hunters is to take their saws to a professional sharpener. They only charge a few dollars and this is usually needed only once a year at most. Sharp saws should be protected with a leather, nylon (lighter than leather and dries quicker) or temporary cardboard sheath. A sheath protects people, other equipment and the blade. Moisture will dull a sharp blade as well as mar the surface and reduce its glide. Saws which are sharp and free of rust will cut ten times faster than the dull, rusty hunks of metal some hunters carry year after year with no maintenance. My lesson concerning dull saws occurred many years ago on a solo moose hunt. After four hours of tiring work—cleaning and quartering a large bull moose—I spent another exhausting hour cutting the horns off the skull. I will never go afield again with a dull bone saw. Like knives, sharp saws are safer, faster and a real joy to use.

All of these cutting tools, from knives to saws, should be kept sharp at all times. With an understanding of the basic principles of sharpening and a little practice, anyone can keep their blades sharp. Sharp blades are immensely safer and faster than dull ones. Successful hunters invariably have *sharp* knives on their belts.

Chapter 12
CLOTHING

There is a tremendous variety of clothing designed specifically for hunting. A good understanding of the how's and why's of clothing's function and design is a prerequisite to making sensible choices between the hundreds of brands, styles and fabrics available. Successful hunters know how to select the proper hunting clothing and when to use each garment to get the most out of it. The proper clothing helps them hunt harder, be more effective hunters and consistently come home with game.

Heat Retention

One basic requirement of hunting clothing is that it keeps the hunter warm. Clothing keeps us warm by slowing down the loss of our body heat. Convection, conduction, radiation and evaporation are all ways we lose heat (these terms are explained in Chapter Eight–"Survival"). To slow heat loss by *convection*, clothing should slow or stop wind currents from reaching the skin. Tightly woven fabrics or coated materials like rain wear are best for this. Clothing slows down *conduction* heat loss by trapping air between its fibers. Since air is a poor conductor, body heat is lost slowly through clothing which holds a lot of small air pockets. Wearing layers of clothing is another way to trap pockets of air to slow the loss of body heat by conduction.

Radiation heat loss is not significantly affected by most types of clothing. However, shiny materials like those used in space blankets do depend on their ability to block radiation heat loss as part of their effectiveness. *Evaporation* heat loss is directly linked to the amount of moisture which clothing repels, absorbs, and/or holds against the skin. Slowing this type of heat loss is best accomplished by staying as dry as possible. Heat loss by evaporation is often the most significant factor in loss of body heat. This is the reason many hunters' top priority when choosing hunting clothing is how dry it will keep them.

Comfortable clothing should not only keep a hunter warm and dry, but also cool the hunter when necessary. In hot weather, the appropriate clothing will help dissipate body heat, yet not put a hunter at risk of hypothermia should the temperature drop significantly at night. Clothing's comfort factor also depends on its feel on the skin. This is mostly personal preference–some people can't wear wool because it irritates their skin, others don't like synthetics and feel natural fabrics are intrinsically better.

Camouflage

Another beneficial function of hunting clothing is camouflage. Camouflage works in one of two ways. One way is to break up the outline of a hunter so he blends in with the background, i.e. it looks like the hunter is not there. The other way is to make the hunter look like something else–usually trees or bushes. The eyes of horned and antlered big game animals are designed to pick up differences in light reflectiveness and not color. This means the camouflage pattern and amount of light it reflects are more important than the specific colors. A camouflage pattern with distinct vertical edges between colors is usually more noticeable to game animals than a pattern with more horizontal or fuzzy edges. Patterns with more contrast between their colors are also better for breaking up the hunter's outline. Patterns with all dark colors tend to blend into one darkish blob at longer distances which is easily discernible to game. Another solution to breaking up the hunter's outline is a ghillie suit. This type of suit is designed with dozens of pieces of odd-shaped material sewn on a base garment. This works so well it is the first choice by our military when personal concealment is a top priority. This approach to camouflage is now used for some hunting clothing which has leafy cutouts that present an irregular outline and even move with slight breezes. In some situations, these new designs can be very effective.

Hunters should also remember to make use of background camouflage. When approaching game, the texture and the light reflectivity of the background are vital to remaining undetected. A background that is noncontinuous like bushes or a broken rock hillside can effectively disrupt a hunter's outline, whereas that same hunter's outline will be obvious in front of an unbroken field of tall grass or a hillside of continuous tundra.

Another camouflage scheme hunters can use is to stick pieces of the local vegetation into their clothing to serve as last-minute camouflage–usually for the final portion of a stalk. This type of hunter camouflage is almost always available and always the right shade and texture for the situation.

Hunter orange requirements vary tremendously in North America. Some states (like Alaska) have no requirements and others require continuous orange over most of the body (no *camouflage orange* allowed). The reason for hunter orange is because it is spotted by humans more often than other colors. In bright light, low light, and wet or dry conditions hunter orange has reduced the number of hunting accidents because it is readily recognized as a human object. Hunters who apply the aforementioned principles of camouflage can deal with hunter orange requirements in the most successful manner. If regulations allow, avoiding orange on body parts which move—arms, hands, and legs—is one of the principles to apply.

Mixing camouflage patterns helps break up the hunter's image into smaller blocks, thus making it less likely animals will recognize the human form.

Another basic tenet which I follow is to mix camouflage patterns for upper and lower body. This prevents my body from being recognized as one large object. Counting hats, gloves and equipment, I sometimes wear seven or eight different camouflage patterns at one time. In most situations, this mosaic of camouflage patterns is much harder to detect than one single color or pattern.

In addition to "sight" camouflage, hunters must also be concerned with "noise" camouflage. This applies to gun hunters as well as bowhunters. Noisy clothing and gear will spook sharp-eared animals at several hundred yards in favorable conditions. I have seen an Alaskan moose pick up his ears at 500 yards after I made a soft bull grunt at a level below that of a normal speaking voice, and I know animals can easily recognize human sounds—which are out of place in the woods—at much greater distances. Noisy cordura nylon or any metallic sound immediately alerts animals to a hunter's presence. Clothing and gear should be carefully selected and then modified to be as quiet as possible. Rifles, bows, pack frames and other metal objects can be protected with liquid rubber, camouflage tape or moleskin at spots where contact may occur. I personally have strips of moleskin all around the shelf and arrow rest of my bow to eliminate noise should the arrow contact these spots. I've also covered the bow limbs and quiver with camouflage tape to reduce the scraping sounds of brush against these hard parts of the bow. A couple friends of mine use liquid rubber all over their bows to reduce noise. Thoughtful planning can prevent errant noises and provide "noise" camouflage.

Other Clothing Considerations

Other factors to consider when selecting hunting clothing are weight, bulk, cost and durability. Many big game hunts require off-road travel by horse, plane, ATV or backpacking. Clothing which is lightweight and compact is always preferable in these cases, particularly on backpacking trips where every ounce is carried on the hunter's back. Hunters who make it a habit to consider weight and bulk will have a more functional wardrobe, useful for a wider range of hunting conditions.

Cost is also a factor for most hunters. By selecting clothing with a wide range of uses, hunters can maximize productivity of their hunting budget. Durable clothing will help cost-conscious hunters reduce replacement costs, plus prevent possible field disasters. Hunters must be able to rely on their clothing (and equipment) to carry them through demanding field situations. Clothing must be tough enough to last for the duration of marathon trips to the mountains of Alaska or the desert canyons of Colorado, where personal safety and hunting success is dependent on tough, functional clothing.

Fabrics

The most definitive aspect of clothing is its fabric. Every material used for hunting clothes has distinctive characteristics. Hunters must understand these traits to make the best choices of clothing.

Fabrics can be evaluated by their insulating value, toughness, comfort on the skin, breathability, wind resistance, and moisture resistance, absorption and retention. All these factors affect how a fabric will function in the field and should be considered when selecting clothing.

This treestand hunter is difficult to see because of his effective use of several camouflage patterns. He has chosen quiet fabrics which are absolutely necessary for bowhunters who want to be successful.

Natural fabrics include wool, cotton and silk. The common characteristic of these natural fibers is their tendency to absorb and hold moisture. This tendency is their biggest downfall for most hunting situations. Clothing which holds moisture next to the skin will cause a significant amount of heat loss by evaporation. Unless they are in very hot weather conditions, most hunters need to be warmed and not cooled by their clothing.

Cotton is the most common clothing fabric because of its comfort next to the skin, quietness, durability and low cost. Cotton's biggest drawback for most hunting situations is its tendency to attract and hold large amounts of moisture. Wet cotton has little or no insulating value. It is very cold when wet and dries slowly. This is the main reason cotton should only be used in hot weather when the temperature does not drop below 60° F. In hot weather cotton can help cool hunters by trapping moisture and holding it next to a hunter's skin. In cool or cold weather, this tendency to hold moisture will put the hunter at high risk of hypothermia. This is why many hunters (myself included) in northern climates wear absolutely no cotton clothing except on day hunts. One of my sheep hunting clients actually discarded his cotton clothing in the mountains after it became soaked and useless after one day—wearing his (water-repelling) synthetics for the rest of the rainy hunt.

Silk also absorbs and holds moisture, but not as much as cotton. Silk feels great next to the skin, is only semi-durable, has little insulating value and is costly. It has little use for hunting purposes.

Wool clothing resists moisture somewhat and has been a longtime favorite of hunters. However, it does absorb a lot of moisture when exposed to several hours of rain or heavy perspiration and then is extremely hard to dry out. In cold weather hunting or when external heat sources are available to dry clothing each night, wool clothing can be a good choice, but not for fall backpacking trips. I did wear wool pants on my sheep hunts here in Alaska twenty years ago, but discontinued that after one rainy trip when my pants got soaked on the first day. For the duration of that backpacking trip, my pants were wet and extremely cold. It still chills me just thinking about it; I ended the hunt early because of it. Wool clothing is also heavy and restrictive during physical exertion–like climbing mountains.

Wool does have some attractive characteristics. Good wool is breathable, tough, quiet, non-reflective and somewhat warm when damp. The abrasive fibers of wool clothing irritate skin and warm the wearer, even when wet. However, this irritating characteristic makes wool unwearable for some people. This is the reason two of the outfits who currently offer high-priced wool hunting clothing suggest wearing non-wool underwear–which defeats one of the purposes of wearing wool in the first place. Another drawback of wool is the difficulty of cleaning it without significant shrinkage and cost.

A great variety of surplus military wool pants are also available at much lower cost than the expensive woolens offered to hunters; and I have found these low-cost pants to outperform those designed just for hunters. Several brands of plaid wool shirts are also available which, again, outperform the expensive models. Allowing for the drawbacks noted, wool is by far the most useful of the three natural fibers for hunters.

Synthetics are the class of fabrics which justifiably makes up most hunting clothing. The most obvious advantage synthetics have over natural fabrics is the way they interact with water. Since our bodies produce about 20 ounces of perspiration per day, our clothing must be able to deal with this moisture and still keep us warm and comfortable. Many synthetic fabrics are engineered to attract body moisture and wick it away from the skin. Moisture which stays next to the skin will cause cooling by evaporation; a little of which is okay when you are overheated from a tough climb, but excessive cooling is what leads to hypothermia–the number one threat to hunter safety. Unlike natural fabrics which actually absorb moisture *into* their fibers, synthetic fabrics absorb moisture *between* their fibers. This allows a much larger percent of excess moisture to be wrung out or shaken out of synthetics than from natural fabrics (like after a mishap around a body of water). Additionally, the remaining moisture trapped *between* synthetic fibers dries much quicker than moisture which gets trapped *inside of* natural fibers. This is very important to hunters who have to deal with rain, perspiration and stream crossings and who depend on their clothing to make them safe, warm and effective hunters.

Synthetic hunting clothing can be comfortable, water-resistant, warm, tough, lightweight and affordable. However, there are dozens of synthetic fabrics to choose from and not all offer the qualities necessary for good hunting clothing. Critical research and scrutiny can uncover the best fabrics for hunters.

Fleece clothing comes in many types of camouflage patterns, useful from the southern hardwood forests to the Arctic–as shown here. Dave Widby used snow camouflage while hunting this musk-oxen.

Fleece (also referred to as pile) is one of the most popular synthetic fabrics used for hunting clothes. Fleece is made of 100% polyester, it is hypoallergenic (nonirritating), a good insulator, comfortable, repels water, absorbs very little moisture and dries quickly; it is also affordable, washable, lightweight, durable, breathable, and quiet. Its drawbacks are: it doesn't block the wind and it is bulky. There are numerous varieties of fleece. Some of the brand names are Polarfleece, Polartek, Polartuff, Polarlite, Microfleece, Arctic Fleece, and Stealth Fleece. Clothing made from any of these has its own mix of the qualities mentioned and must be examined individually by the prospective buyer. Although the bulkiness of fleece garments is a given, wind resistance varies between brands. It is improved in some garments by the addition of a wind-proof layer. However, this does add to the weight, breathability and ability to dry quickly. Most hunters choose to wear a windproof layer outside of their fleece when necessary.

There are many other synthetic fabrics widely accepted for hunting clothes. Base layer fabrics include Thermax, Coolmax, Thermastat, Capilene, polypropylene and many others. Their biggest selling point is their ability to wick moisture from the body and dry quickly. This and their softness make them comfortable to wear. For most hunting situations, synthetic underwear is a far better choice than cotton or wool.

Fabrics for an insulating or protective layer include brand names like Worsterlon, Supplex, Microtex, 3SP and generic fabrics like nylon, polyester and acrylic. Again, their main selling point for hunters is their water repellancy. The main drawback to many of these fabrics is they are noisy. Worsterlon is one that is not noisy, as well as being comfortable, durable and affordable. I use it exclusively for my hunting shirts, but I dislike Worsterlon pants because they drag too much when I am climbing. 3SP is a fabric made by Sporthill which is excellent for hunting pants. I use a pair on almost every one of my hunts. They are warm, tough, wind-resistant, very water repellent, fast-drying, lightweight, compact and comfortable–everything I look for in hunting apparel. As more synthetic fabrics are being developed almost daily, experience by yourself or your hunting buddies is the best way to discover which of the myriad of synthetic fabrics is best for your type of hunting. Personal experimentation is costly and time-consuming so, whenever possible, I suggest soliciting opinions from other hunters who have used different fabrics.

For an insulated outer layer on really cold hunts the choices are down or synthetic insulators. Down has a great warmth-to-weight ratio and is used extensively in cold climates. In below-freezing weather down is a good choice. I have a pair of down pants that I've worn on late season whitetail tree stands and when muskox hunting at -85° F. They are great when there is no chance of rain. However, when I have to buy more extreme cold weather gear I will opt for open-cell polyurethane foam insulated gear from Northern Outfitters™. Their gear is used by many dog sled mushers in Alaska and Canada for good reason. The foam has insulating qualities similar to down, but it doesn't absorb moisture like down. On extended cold weather hunts this becomes a prime consideration. When down gets wet its insulating qualities are reduced to almost zero and it is difficult to dry. Synthetic insulators like Thinsulate, Hollowfill, Qualofill, Primiloft, Lite Loft, Polarguard and the open-cell polyurethane foam are better choices in cool, damp weather, and sometimes even in cold weather because of their water-resistance. Some of the newer insulators like Lite Loft and Thinsulate are able to compete with down's warmth-to-weight ratio and down's compactibility (unfortunately some are also comparably priced). Outer layers of synthetic-filled garments are a safer choice when the temperature may hover around the freezing point and produce rain instead of snow. A hunter with down clothing must be very careful not to get wet in this situation or he may face a real threat from hypothermia (which can lead to death from exposure). Hunters with synthetic clothing may have to carry a few more ounces of clothing, but will be in considerably less danger from exposure.

Head-to-toe rain gear is necessary for hunters to be comfortable in some hunting situations, as this hunter pursuing brown bears on the Alaska Peninsula can verify. Horizontal rain driven by thirty-mile-per-hour winds and temperatures in the low forties are common here during both the spring and fall seasons. A hunter has to have adequate clothing to hunt successfully in these conditions.

Waterproof Fabrics

The outermost layer of clothing for hunters is often rain wear. There are many (supposedly) waterproof fabrics to choose from and more are being offered each year. The only absolutely *waterproof* fabric is rubber. Good rubber rain wear will stop all water from coming in from the exterior, but it also stops any moisture from going out from the interior. Since our bodies produce moisture constantly, this means in a few hours of standing or sitting we will begin to feel damp from the inside. Just twenty or so minutes of vigorous exercise will also dampen the inside of rubber rain wear. Rubber is also heavy and bulky. Rubber rain wear is not very practical for most hunting situations. The one exception is when hunting from a boat where keeping out lots of water is often necessary and weight is not a concern. Otherwise, most hunters need to look to the next best alternative to rubber to stop moisture intrusion into their hunting clothes.

This is one of the best ways to keep moisture at bay on backpack hunts–
dry out whenever possible. Tony Russ is taking advantage of the
sunshine after some rainy weather on a sheep hunt.

The ideal rain-wear fabric for hunters would stop water from getting in from the outside and also let body moisture pass through to the outside. Anything less and the hunter will not stay completely dry. This ideal is the target of the growing number of waterproof-yet-breathable fabrics. Gore-Tex is the best known of this type of fabric (in reality Gore-Tex is a membrane intended to be laminated between two fabrics) and it does an okay job of doing both of these functions. Other brands of this type of fabric (membrane) are Cool Dri, Dry-Plus, and Omni-Tech. Although a hard downpour or prolonged rain will drive some moisture through even the best of these fabrics, they do keep most of the moisture out. The quality of seam-sealing when making the garment, how clean it is and its age all greatly affect the performance of these fabrics. All of these fabrics tend to be fairly quiet (by rain wear standards), slightly bulky and costly.

Other fabrics good for hunter rain wear include polyvinylchloride (PVC) laminates, polyurethane-coated (PU) nylon, and waxed cotton. Waxed cotton is almost waterproof but also heavy, expensive, and needs periodic refinishing to keep performing. Both PVC and PU fabrics are fairly waterproof, fairly quiet, compact, lightweight, inexpensive and tough. I have been using various PU suits for over twenty years for sheep and moose hunting here in Alaska. They are not the perfect fabric, but as close as any I can find.

Regardless of the type of fabric used, there are some features which are necessary for a good rain suit. As with most hunting clothing, large pockets with Velcro-closed storm flaps are always handy. Thigh-length coats are always preferable to waist-length coats, both so they can be worn alone and with hip boots and still keep us dry. The coat should also have a hood with a drawstring and a stiff, projecting bill to keep out driving rain. The coat should be cut full to allow for layers of clothing underneath. There should be adjustable Velcro closures at the wrists and all seams should be factory-sealed. The main zipper should have a protective storm flap with Velcro closures.

The pants should have a drawstring plus elastic at the waist. Any slash pockets to provide access to inner pants should have a storm flap with Velcro closures. Pant legs should be full enough to admit boots; zippers on the lower legs with storm flaps are preferable. Lastly, the suit should be a color or camouflage pattern acceptable for your hunting needs.

Layering

One basic principle to dressing properly for outdoor activities is layering. This refers to using many layers of thin clothing instead of one thicker layer. This approach to dressing makes the best use of different fabric types by using each where they are most effective; i.e. as a base, insulating or protective layer. Layering also allows a hunter to add or remove clothing during the day to remain warm without excessive perspiration.

A base layer consists of briefs, t-shirt and long underwear when necessary. Base layer clothing should be comfortable (soft) against the skin and have the ability to wick moisture away from the skin. Synthetics are ideal for base layer clothing as they wick moisture well and do not hold moisture like cotton will. On one of my bear guiding trips to the Alaska Peninsula I felt unusually cold the first day. That night, I realized why I had been cold when I discovered my cotton "traveling" shorts were still on—they had held perspiration against my skin and cooled me unlike my "hunting" Thermax briefs—which dry quickly.

An insulating layer does just what the name implies, it insulates. The thickness or number of insulating layer(s) depends on the level and variations in temperature expected. Insulating layers may consist of shirts, pants, vests, sweaters and coats in moderate temperatures. In cold weather more or thicker layers of any of these and or an extra layer or two of fleece long underwear may be called for. Except in very cold weather, it is better to add two thin layers rather than one thick layer to permit more temperature control. This is particularly important for a sheep or elk hunter who expects to climb for several hours and then sit on an exposed hillside for another few hours. During any rigorous exercise, a hunter should remove as many layers as necessary to control perspiration. Remaining just a little cool during physical exertion will prevent moisture buildup and keep clothing as dry as possible for the "standing" part of the hunt. A hunter with dry clothes will be able to stay out longer and have a better chance at success.

A protective layer should stop wind and rain when necessary. It may be just a heavy shirt, light jacket or raincoat. In more extreme weather conditions it may be a heavy wool mackinaw, an insulated, synthetic, waterproof parka or a thick down parka with a hood. The number and variety of layers necessary depends on the possible weather conditions and variations in hunter activity. When I hunt whitetail deer and only have to walk a few minutes to a stand where I will sit for most of the day, I sometimes wear just a few thick layers, but when I am sheep hunting I usually have five, six or even seven thin layers which I can add or remove as necessary– depending on my level of activity.

Gloves and mittens are another part of the protective layer. There is an endless array of these in all designs and materials and no one variety will suit all hunting needs. When wet weather is possible it is best to use wool or synthetics, as cotton or leather will quickly get soaked and be almost useless. I find that wool keeps me warmer than synthetics in wet weather. In cold weather when moisture isn't a prime concern, I switch to a synthetic shell with a liner or down mittens. Gloves or mittens with windproof layers are warmer, but also take longer to dry. Those with removable liners make drying much easier. I have a box full of a variety of types and pick and choose depending on the conditions I expect. The best strategy is (whenever possible) to take more than one pair to cover different conditions and always have a dry pair.

The final and most important part of a protective layer is a covering for the head. A bare head may lose up to 50% of the body's heat production at 40 degrees Fahrenheit and up to 70% at 5 degrees. It is critical to a hunter's warmth and safety to always have good head gear available. A good hat should cover the ears and neck when necessary and be windproof for optimal warmth. Watch-cap type hats are better than no hat, but a better style hat is a facemask type or balaclava which covers all of the head and neck when needed. The best varieties of balaclavas now have a windstopper layer included which doubles their effectiveness. Another good hat style is the billed cap with long, fold-down ear flaps that fasten under the chin. These cover most of the head and neck, come in water-resistant synthetics and have a waterproof/windproof layer inside. A simple baseball style hat is okay for mild weather hunting to keep off the sun and a little rain, but it shouldn't be depended on for much warmth. Hat styles with continuous brims (cowboy or river guide styles) are also useful to protect hunters from bright sun or rain in mild weather, and they do provide a little warmth.

For most hat styles synthetics are a good choice because of their water resistance and comfort. Wool is okay for warmth, but it soaks up water and is uncomfortable for most people. Down hats and hoods are good for cold weather hunting when moisture is not a concern. For the warmest hats in cold weather fur is the best. Properly constructed fur hats are absolutely windproof and the first choice of people living in the coldest regions of the earth. The fur also traps warm air around the exposed face and keeps it warm without covering it. My personal beaver hat is so warm that I can only wear it when the temperature is below 0 degrees Fahrenheit, but there is nothing to compare to this hat when it gets really cold.

Layering is more important as the weather gets colder. Here, Tony Russ is dressed for his Nunivak, Alaska musk-oxen hunt when the wind chill reached -85° Fahrenheit, yet he stayed comfortably warm.

One thing for hunters to remember when dressing for cold weather is that the human body's first priority is to keep its core temperature at the proper level. Extremities—like hands and feet—are a secondary priority. When the core temperature begins to decrease even slightly the blood supply to hands and feet is restricted to keep all possible warmth for the core. This mechanism can result in cold extremities if we under-dress, no matter how warm our mittens are. To prevent cold hands and feet, make sure to dress sufficiently from your legs to your head to keep the body core warm. On the other hand, when our core temperature gets too high, more blood is pumped to our hands and feet to cool us. So the first thing to do when you get overheated is to remove gloves and mittens. If you are still too hot, removing your hat for a few minutes will really disperse excess body heat. This cooling/heating mechanism of our body was really apparent on my musk-oxen hunt in Alaska. I was dressed so warmly that when there was no wind my hands would stay warm without mittens or gloves at 30 below zero. My body was pumping so much blood through my hands to cool itself that they stayed warm at this extreme temperature. This mechanism is the reason for the old saying, "If your feet (or hands) are cold, put another coat on."

Clothing Selection

The ability to match garments to the season, weather and hunting style is essential to becoming an effective, successful hunter. Some of the factors which should be considered before each hunt are:

1) Can several changes of clothing be taken, or is weight and bulk a limitation? —as when backpacking or flying to camp when it is necessary to take the lightest combination of clothing which will keep the hunter warm and dry in all possible weather conditions.

2) Will there be a heat source to dry gear out at night or is it a cold camp where moisture will build up over the course of the hunt?

3) Will game be close or at a distance? How important is the "quietness" of the clothing? Are you bowhunting or shooting at long range with a rifle?

4) Will the hunter be moving most of the time, stationary or some mix of the two? How much clothing is needed and how thick should the layers be?

5) How important is camouflage and what type should it be? Because bears have poor eyesight, hunters require less camouflage when hunting them than an animal like pronghorn antelope which rely tremendously on their acute sense of sight. Bowhunters need camouflage which works at close range as well as long range; rifle hunters often need only long-range camouflage.

6) How much hunting clothing can the hunter afford to buy? Will a few clothes have to suffice for many types of hunting opportunities?

Some other strategies to remember when choosing hunting clothing are:

1) Buy clothing large enough to wear layers underneath when needed without restricting movement, and buy it ahead of time to allow for a trial run to test it before the actual hunt.

2) Be willing to make alterations to clothing to suit you. The addition of large billows pockets or pant leg zippers are common alterations I make.

3) Suspenders free up your waistline for added comfort and less perspiration, but make sure and buy synthetic models and not cotton which will retain perspiration and feel clammy for the remainder of a hunt once they get wet.

4) Dark clothing attracts more biting insects than light-colored garments.

5) When tent camping, extra clothing can be put into plastic (Zip-Loc or vacuum-packed) bags within duffel bags to keep them completely dry.

6) A emergency rain poncho can be made out of a large plastic bag with holes cut for the head and arms. It is even a good idea during heavy

*The southern hardwood forests of Alabama have clothing requirements
entirely different than northern areas of the country. Temperatures into
the 80's or 90's are common during whitetail season and cotton clothing
is a favorite among hunters. This is George P. Mann with one of his
Alabama whitetail deer.*

downpours to put one of these over your (almost waterproof) raincoat to
keep out all moisture.

7) Suggestions of hunting buddies, acquaintances, local inhabitants, guides
and outfitters can be invaluable when looking for new garments or hunting
in new situations or regions.

Clothing should keep a hunter warm, dry, comfortable, safe and
undetected. An understanding of available fabrics and designs is helpful—
as is personal experience—to discover what works for an individual in
each hunting situation. The best hunting clothing is that which best improves
the hunter's chances of success. Learning how to select and use a complete
hunting wardrobe is another essential skill for successful hunters.

Dressing to stay warm and hunt effectively can call for some unusual clothing. Here, Tony Russ is dressed to stay warm while glassing for brown bears on the Alaska Peninsula. The snowmachine goggles and overboots are key ingredients in staying comfortable for ten or more hours in cold, windy weather.

Chapter 13
FOOTWEAR

Proper footwear is one of the most important pieces of hunting gear. Hunters must often travel long distances in search of game animals and even stationary hunters must have warm, dry footwear to expect consistent success. Warmth, comfort, safety, effectiveness, durability, moisture resistance, odor reduction and quietness are all qualities to look for in hunting footwear.

Selection of Footwear

The type of hunting is the first thing to consider when selecting boots or shoes for hunting. Stand hunters usually need footwear which will be quiet for a short walk to a stand and then keep them warm during several hours of inactivity. Odor reduction is also an important consideration for most stand hunters, both during the walk to the stand and while on stand. Spot & stalk hunters who pursue animals like sheep and elk have a different set of priorities when selecting footwear. Comfort is arguably the top priority for these hunters who depend on their feet to carry them long distances while carrying a heavy pack. Moisture resistance, durability and safe footing on treacherous slopes or while sidehilling are also important considerations for mountain hunters who pursue sheep, elk, deer, moose, caribou, mountain lion or bear.

The terrain a hunter expects to encounter will determine which type of sole is required. Lug soles (Vibram™ is one common maker of these) are a tried-and-true style for mountain hunters who need secure footing on steep, slippery slopes. For flat-land hunting, smooth soles are often preferred because of their light weight, comfort and noiselessness. Soggy terrain like deer swamps of the southern U.S. or the tundra of Alaska call for rubber footwear. Hunting in wet weather, like any coastal brown bear hunts in Alaska or the rainy season in Washington or Oregon, also calls for rubber footwear; whereas canvas is often used in the hot, dry climate of the Southwest. Quietness is an often-overlooked quality which stand hunters and still hunters require to be successful.

As with clothing, the material footwear is made of determines how it will function in the field. Leather has long been the favorite material for hunting boots because of its strength, durability, support, moisture resistance, and protection it provides. With the addition of relatively new waterproof linings (like Gore•Tex), leather boots are still the best in most

The right footwear is crucial for many types of hunting. These sheep-hunting boots have rock-gripping lug soles, are waterproof, and tough, yet not too heavy for long days of mountain travel.

hunting situations. In warm weather conditions canvas shoes are often used because of their light weight and greater ability to dissipate moisture and heat. Both leather and canvas boots are currently available with scent-absorbing layers. This can be a significant factor when hunting animals like whitetail deer or bears with an acute sense of smell.

Rubber and other water and scent-proof materials (vinyl, plastic) are often used by hunters. The ability to keep moisture out and carry little scent are primary concerns when choosing these materials for hunting footwear. Their biggest drawback is retention of moisture around the feet. The best way to overcome this is to have a way to dry them and/or change socks frequently.

Boots with liners made of materials like felt and Thinsulate are a good option when cold weather is expected. Footwear with liners is often much warmer and comes in a wide variety of temperature ranges. Liners which are removable allow hunters to always have a dry pair to wear on alternating days. Footwear which is simply insulated can be good in cold weather, but is hard to dry if too much moisture builds up. Careful inspection of the boot's components will be necessary to discover if this may be a problem. As before, synthetic insulation will be easier to dry than natural materials like wool. My personal sheep hunting boots have Thinsulate insulation, a Cambrelle lining (both of which dry incredibly fast) and a

Gore•Tex layer to keep out moisture. This combination has served me well in below-freezing weather coupled with heavy perspiration during long climbs, and still kept my feet warm and dry.

For added insulation there are also overboots available from many manufacturers. These (usually) synthetic outer liners for boots are made to be carried by hunters to a stand or spotting location and then placed over walking footwear to keep feet warm. They are often made to be stuffed into small pockets and then fluff up once removed. They can add twenty to fifty degrees of warmth to boots for hunters who must remain stationary for long periods. They are particularly useful for hunters who need rubber boots to travel to a stand location, but must then endure near-freezing temperatures in often windy conditions which surpass the insulating abilities of most rubber footwear.

One more factor to check out when choosing footwear is their weight. The old mountain man's guide is that one pound on your foot is the same as five pounds on your back. Heavy boots do slow down a hunter who has to walk or climb any distance. The validity of this claim was apparent to me while guiding for Dall sheep several years ago in the Talkeetna mountains of Alaska. After losing one boot during a river crossing I had to finish the hunt wearing a pair of tennis shoes. I was amazed at how fast and effortlessly I was able to climb a 2,000-foot slope with the lightweight shoes on compared to my usual heavy footwear. I practically ran up the hill with a full pack. If anything, I would say the one to five ratio is an underestimation of how heavy boots can slow you down.

Once a material is chosen the construction of the footwear should be the next consideration. Quality construction is of utmost importance for demanding hunting situations as well as to protect feet. Inadequate footwear is the leading cause of sore, blistered feet, and hunters who are incapacitated because of foot problems are rarely successful. Footwear must be constructed not only to endure tough hunting conditions, but also to fit an individual's foot. The only way to ensure this latter requirement is to go through a rigorous fitting process every time footwear is chosen.

The Right Fit

Boots should not be purchased from a catalog without previous experience with the identical model of boot. Feet are each unique in their design, boot manufacturers use different lasts and sizing charts, and feet change with age. All of these variables and more make footwear selection a difficult and necessarily personal endeavor. Anyone who expects to consistently select properly fitted hunting boots without investing some time and effort is unrealistic.

First, try both feet when fitting any footwear. Almost everyone has one foot which is larger than the other, so using only one foot will not tell you if *both* boots fit. Second, wear the same socks and the same insoles as

The right footwear depends on the species, the location, the time of year and the method of hunting. Here the author shows off the standard footwear for hunting moose in the Brooks Range of Alaska in the fall by any method–rubber boots.

you will wear in field conditions–for obvious reasons. This means you will buy leather footwear (which has a bothersome habit of stretching) one-half to one full size larger than city shoes. It is easy to add another liner or another pair of socks to boots which are slightly too large after stretching, but perfectly fitting boots which shrink are hard to deal with in field conditions. Try every angle of step and put pressure in all directions in the fitting room to ensure you get a good fit. You will thank yourself for your diligence after every trail mile you travel with your new footwear.

Break-in Process

Many types of footwear currently need little breaking-in to be ready for the field, but it still helps to mold them to your foot under controlled conditions. Leather boots particularly will shape themselves to the wearer's foot when wet. Even old leather boots can be reshaped somewhat. The tried-and-true method of doing this is to get the boots soaking wet and then walk them dry. As the leather dries it molds itself to the foot it surrounds. Of course this may take many hours and miles, but it is worth it if you are about to embark on a once-in-a-lifetime sheep hunting trip to Alaska or an African trip you've dreamed of all your life. Even if the trip is just to hunt elk in a western state you will probably decide the investment was worthwhile after several full days of climbing and sidehilling. Certainly your feet will thank you and you will have a more enjoyable trip if you go through a proper break-in process.

Other types of footwear like canvas or synthetics should also be tested before any hunt. Adjustments like adding or removing the appropriate insoles, wearing two pair of thin socks instead of one thicker pair, or just lacing in a different manner should be tried before a hunt. I have a pair of mountain boots with plastic shells and insulated liners which can be difficult to walk in, but I have discovered that by lacing only the bottom six pair of eyelets I can walk much more comfortably on flat ground. This little adjustment has saved me a lot of time and discomfort over many years of sheep hunting. Now I am very attentive to any new footwear to see just how comfortable I can make them by testing variations in socks, liners, insoles, and lacing patterns. A hunter's feet are too important to ignore any possibilities for improved comfort.

Waterproofing

Manufacturers' recommendations should be followed about how and what to apply when waterproofing new footwear. After paying up to several hundred dollars for top-of-the-line boots it is only sensible to spend a couple dollars for the proper water sealant. Boots which are properly treated will keep your feet drier, conform better to your feet (which means fewer blisters) and last longer. Leather footwear should be warmed slowly to no more than 100° F before applying a waterproofing substance. Placing footwear in direct sunshine for a few hours is one good way to warm them as is putting them in a furnace room. A quicker but riskier method is to place them in a *warm* oven. It is best to leave the oven door open to reduce the chance of ruining a good pair of boots.

Once the boots are warm apply several liberal layers of the chosen waterproofing substance, letting each layer soak into the leather between applications. The more thorough the boots have been warmed and the thicker the applications (1/16th to 1/8th inch) the more waterproof the boots will be. Just thinking back to hunts when you've had wet feet should prompt you to do the most thorough job possible. The first few applications to new boots or boots after a long, wet hunt will be completely drawn into the leather, leaving a dry surface. Applications should be continued until the last one remains on the surface. This can then be wiped off with a clean cloth leaving the leather completely saturated with the chosen sealant.

Other materials like canvas or nylon often require spray-on silicon for water protection. This usually requires cleaning and drying the surface before several applications are applied, with drying periods in between. Again, warm footwear will accept more of the sealant and result in a better waterproofing process. These silicon-based sprays can seem expensive, but not when compared to how much money is invested in the footwear and the overall hunt. A few dollars for dry feet is a small price to pay when it means so much to the enjoyment and success of a hunt.

Field Care of Footwear

The objective of finding appropriate footwear and properly caring for it is comfortable feet. And the most important requirement for comfortable feet is to keep them dry. After proper selection and care of boots before a hunt the next requirement is to keep them as dry as possible in the field. The first thing to remember is to take any opportunity to dry boots in the sun. If you are sitting and glassing for game or just taking a rest during a long climb, removing your boots to take advantage of a warm sun can greatly reduce the moisture buildup during the course of a long hunt. Placing boots in the warmest possible place at night is also a good habit. This usually means a high place in a cabin or tent, but it may mean the engine room if hunting from a boat.

When tent camping an evening fire can be used judiciously to help dry boots. Be careful about getting leather boots too close to the high heat of a fire as it can damage them. A safer way to use the fire is to first heat small rocks, then place them inside a sock which is then placed inside the boots overnight.

One very effective way to dry boots is to use the small, disposable handwarmers. These inexpensive devices last anywhere from five to eighteen hours and produce a safe level of heat to dry any footwear. I discovered this application after years of guiding for brown bears on the Alaskan Peninsula and wearing wet rubber boots for weeks. Now I place one of the small models into each of my rubber boots at night. In the morning 90% of the moisture buildup will be gone and I often have warm boots as a bonus. During the three weeks I annually spend in an unheated tent on this hunt it makes for a much more comfortable hunt; my clients really appreciate me bringing enough for their boots also.

One more thing to consider about leather boots is re-soling them. If you have a good pair which are really comfortable, but the soles round off so they are not as effective on steep slopes you can consider this option. As long as the leather uppers are still in good shape a new sole can be attached to extend their useful life. Plastic mountaineering boots can also be re-soled by a good cobbler.

Socks

Socks are almost as important as boots for hunters. Socks are often a major factor in a hunter's comfort level. Good socks help keep your feet warm, dry, and blister-free.

A sock's material defines many of its qualities. Cotton socks can be comfortable for stand hunters in warm climates, but because they hold moisture and mat after just a little use are not good for most hunting situations. Wool socks do provide a lot of warmth for stand hunters and are a favorite for cold weather hunting. For traveling hunters, even after a full day of sweating wool socks do keep some of their loft to warm and cushion

Left to right are: waterproof socks made with Gore-tex fabric, Thor-Lo's made of high-bulk Orlon with extra padding under the balls of the feet, and lightweight Thermax socks for use as liners. The right choice of socks can be an influencial factor in hunting success–whether the hunter is traveling long distances over rough terrain or just sitting long hours on a stand during cold weather.

feet. However, wool blended with synthetics retains more of its loft, is warmer, and quicker to dry. I prefer 100% synthetic socks because they retain most of their loft to cushion and warm feet even after days of backpacking, they are more durable than wool or cotton, less abrasive than wool and dry quickly. The best socks available (for any purpose) is a brand called Thor•Lo™. They have a patented weave design which massages the foot–and feels very good to foot-sore hunters. They also have cushioning pads under the heel and ball of the feet without any annoying edge where the cushions begins. They come in dozens of varieties for any sport or purpose imaginable. They are made of a blend of mostly high-bulk Orlon with minor amounts of wool or other synthetics. They retain an incredible amount of loft even after days of brutal, sweaty backpacking, hold very little moisture and dry quickly even in unheated tents. They are so good to my feet that I wear these socks almost exclusively 365 days a year. Even in quantity they cost at least $6 a pair, but they out-last any other sock and my feet are worth the extra cost. There are numerous other brands of synthetic socks which are good socks, but, for my money, none are quite as good as Tho•Lo™.

One type of sock a hunter can carry in extremely wet conditions is a Gore•Tex sock. These socks will keep feet dry for at least several hours even when footwear is soaked inside. Under adverse conditions it is very comforting to know you can put on cold, wet boots and have dry feet–at least until your boots warm up in several hours. Although some moisture will eventually seep through these membrane-type socks in extreme conditions, they may be worth carrying for the most physically demanding hunts. Before these socks were available I remember one sheep hunt when my leather boots were soaked and frozen solid each morning. I had to endure one to two hours of excruciating cold each morning until the boots thawed and then warmed up. Having a pair of these socks would have kept my feet dry until the boots were warm and made for a much more enjoyable hunt.

An Effective Sock Strategy

Developing an effective *sock strategy* is necessary for maximum foot comfort. For stand hunting in warm climates a thin sock of almost any material may suffice. For stand hunting in colder weather, one thicker sock or multiple layers of wool or synthetic socks is called for–the thickness and number of layers being determined by the temperature. Stand hunters may also consider wearing one layer to the stand and then putting on a second layer after leather boots have warmed up and stretched; or carrying a dry pair to a stand if a long walk is required which may produce moisture in the first pair. Thick socks are often better for stand hunting or riding ATV's where little walking is required, but two or more layers of thinner socks is better when considerable walking may be required. Wearing two pairs of thin socks will help prevent blisters better than one thick sock because the inner sock will grab the foot tightly and not rub against it as one thick pair of socks often does. Using a layering approach also allows another pair to be added during the day as the boots loosen, as they heat up or as they get damp from sweating or outside moisture. Once feet start to move around inside boots sore spots can develop at rubbing points. A quick stop to add or change a sock layer can prevent rubbing and avoid blistering.

Even when heavy wool socks are preferred by hunters, a synthetic liner is usually best. Thin liners of polypropylene, Capilene™ or Thermax™ are smooth and nonabrasive to feet as wool can be. Synthetic liners also have less friction against an outer sock layer so they can move independently–precisely what they should do for maximum comfort. Silk liners will serve the same purpose, but they retain more moisture and don't dry as quickly as synthetics.

Foot Medicine

Even the best socks and layering techniques will not prevent sore feet under the most demanding hunting conditions. The hunter's next layer of defense is foot powder, Toughskin™ and Moleskin™. Applying foot powder before donning socks helps reduce friction and hot spots which can become blisters. Toughskin™ is one brand of liquid coating which

Packing a load of horns and meat down rocky slopes requires good footwear to prevent injuries and sore feet. Tony Russ is using nylon hunting boots made for mountain hiking.

Late fall hunting requires warm footwear if hunters want to score like these two hunters did on this large, nontypical whitetail. Photo courtesy of Chris McKinnon, McKinnon & Co. Outfitters.

creates a "second skin" over hot spots or blisters to prevent further damage. Moleskin™ is one brand of self-adhesive padding which can be placed over potential or actual blisters to protect them. I have used Moleskin™ over open blisters and backpacked for several days with no further aggravation of these sores. It is amazing stuff and I never travel without it.

The last—and I believe most important—strategy for every hunter to know concerning feet is elevation. Gravity causes fluid to build up in our feet–particularly after a long day of still-hunting or backpacking. The extra weight of packing game meat causes undue stress on our feet which usually leads to soreness and blisters. The best way to avoid this is to elevate your feet for 15-30 minutes at night. Pregnant women are told to do this same thing to drain excess fluids and reduce swelling caused by the extra burden their feet are carrying. Bar none, this is the best solution I have found to caring for my feet during my weeks of sheep hunting I enjoy every year here in Alaska. For anyone with sore feet from any kind of walking or standing, I highly recommend this simple, yet effective method to reduce swelling and discomfort.

In most hunting situations, hunters depend on their feet to carry them through a successful hunt. Only a few, limited types of hunting will not be adversely affected by poor footwear or cold, wet, sore feet. Therefore, learning to buy the right footwear and how to care for your feet properly is an important step to becoming a successful hunter.

Chapter 14
CAMPING & OTHER GEAR

Hunters use all sorts of gear for big game hunting. The most important consideration when choosing this gear is to *choose the right fit*. Backpacks, tents, sleeping bags and other gear must not only fit the person, they must also fit the style of hunting, weather, personal expectations, and hunting terrain anticipated. A tent which is unsuitable for weather conditions is as much a liability to a hunter as an ill-fitted backpack or inadequate sleeping bag.

The first sources of information a hunter should use are friends and acquaintances who have used similar gear. They can often start a hunter on the right path to gear which fits his or her specific needs. Better yet is trying out the gear you are planning to purchase either from a friend's gear cache or a rental room from a local sporting goods store. The minimal option to getting a good fit between hunter, hunting style and gear is careful hands-on inspection or analysis of product description before purchasing. Competent salespeople can often help, but don't rely too heavily on their opinions if you have doubts about their knowledge or sincerity.

A more reliable source for gear information is comparison guides in magazines like Backpacker or catalog comparisons (which may be biased, but at least give relative specifications). One warning when using any gear guide or catalog specifications chart–be skeptical about listed weights. Manufacturers know people are weight-conscious and often fudge in favor of lighter weights. Carrying a scale to stores when comparison shopping is one way to get actual weights, but catalog shopping always has the inherent risk of dissatisfaction with product weights when they arrive. The more a hunter can do to determine the actual specifications and quality of gear by paying careful attention to salespeople, catalog descriptions, and personal advice, the more likely he will be pleased with his gear's qualities and its performance.

Tough Fabrics for Gear

There are several common materials used for tents and backpacks which hunters should be familiar with to make good gear selections. Canvas is heavy cotton fabric commonly used to make wall tents or tepees. When canvas gets wet it swells and closes the small gaps between the threads. As long as the canvas remains taut and nothing touches it, water moves downward along the fabric without dripping through. However, if anything touches the fabric, water will be drawn through it at that point. If the object is touching the inside of a tent while it is raining for example, water will flow through the fabric onto the object and then begin to drip into the tent. Objects which typically cause a canvas tent to leak in this manner include tent frames and inner guy ropes as well as sleeping bags or personal gear. Coated canvas fabric is a little more forgiving, but will still leak in this way during any lengthy rain. Uncoated canvas can be treated with silicon or other commercially prepared sealants to improve its moisture resistance, but it will never be completely waterproof.

Canvas is also relatively heavy and hot during warm weather. Because of these drawbacks as a tent fabric, canvas has been replaced for most uses by synthetics. However, for cold weather camping when weight is not a problem canvas is still popular. Because of its thickness it holds heat well and provides some insulation when internal heaters (gas or wood) are used. It is also relatively inexpensive and durable when properly dried and stored.

Cordura nylon is a heavyweight, stiff, abrasive-resistant, rough-textured, wind-resistant, durable fabric used for packs, footwear, duffel bags and protective gear cases. Plain cordura repels moisture fairly well and coated cordura is virtually waterproof. Packs and duffel bags made of cordura should be checked for a waterproof coating; this makes these items much more serviceable for hunters.

Ripstop nylon is a lightweight, supple, synthetic material with larger threads every 1/4 inch or so—giving it a characteristic checkerboard appearance—which stop small rips from becoming gaping holes. It is used for coat shells, outerwear, stuff bags and lightweight gear coverings. Ripstop is not abrasion, wind or water-repellent by itself, but can be made fairly wind and waterproof with the proper coating. To check for a waterproof coating on any synthetic fabric, look for a shiny side (usually just one side is coated) produced by the coating. This shiny side should always be on the inside of gear bags or garments to prevent abrasive damage to the coating. Polyurethane is the most common substance used for waterproofing synthetics. Rain gear and packs using this coating agent will list it on their labels for conscientious buyers who read labels.

Nylon taffeta is a soft, supple, lightweight synthetic used for linings in clothing. It is not abrasion-resistant or water-resistant. Polyester taffeta is similar to nylon taffeta, but more water and UV-resistant, so colors don't fade as much as they do in nylon taffeta. Both taffetas are often coated for water resistance.

Almost all synthetic materials can be made more water-resistant by applying spray-on silicon. This commonly comes in aerosol cans available specifically for this purpose where sporting goods are sold.

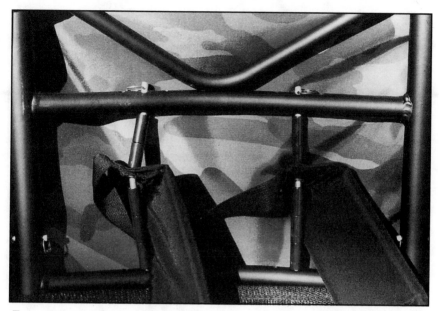

Every aspect of gear should be inspected carefully. The shoulder strap pin on the left bent when the pack was fully loaded with game meat. Gear failures can be critical on backpack hunts.

Following instructions on the silicon spray and any cautions on the gear will enhance the results.

Fasteners come in a variety of forms, each with different characteristics. For outdoor use, nylon zippers are usually much better than metal because they are quieter and less affected by water and cold temperatures. Two-way zippers are useful on duffel bags, long rain coats, and protective cases. Coil zippers are preferable where strength and durability are important.

Buttons are reliable fasteners, but they do come off at inopportune times and are slow. Velcro is much faster for pockets which are frequently opened, rain covers over zippers, sleeve closures on rain coats, and draft hoods on sleeping bags. Experienced hunters often alter gear to suit their needs and adding or changing fasteners are easy ways to change many types of gear to better serve your needs.

Tents

Tents come in an ever-increasing array of sizes, styles and grades. There are three-season, four-season, single-wall, double-wall, triple-wall, freestanding, dome, tunnel, cabin-style, tepee-style, A-frame, floor-less, bivy sacs, modular tents and more. Hunters who use tents should have at least a general understanding of the characteristics and purposes of each tent style to make the proper selection(s).

Canvas wall tents can be comfortable quarters for hunters in areas with minimal wind. Wood stoves can be used inside of these if they have stove jacks—like this one on the lower right panel.

The purposes of a tent are to provide warmth and protect its occupants from sun, precipitation, wind and insects. These qualities along with durability, ease of erection, comfort, size, weight and cost are what to look for when tent shopping. Catalogs often offer charts which allow for quick comparisons between the tents they sell. This is the best place to start for hunters looking for a new tent. However, remember to treat weights and non-measurable descriptions with a little skepticism. Tents described as "three-person" are often a tight fit for two. It is better to rely on the square footage of floor space for size comparisons, but even this has to be balanced against the steepness of the tent wall of each design to see how much *usable* floor space there actually is. As with all gear purchases, use common sense and try to imagine every possible good and bad characteristic before you buy.

Design is a primary consideration. Moisture is a main consideration in tent design. Remember that an average person gives off a quart of moisture during eight hours of sleeping. Any additional time or activity in the tent will dramatically increase the amount of moisture inside. Optimally, all this moisture should be passed to the outside of the tent.

Keeping precipitation and dew out and allowing inside moisture to escape is best accomplished in one of two ways. The most common construction strategy to achieve this is a two-layer tent; the inner tent is not waterproof, the outer layer is waterproof and there is an air space between the two layers. Precipitation falling on the outer layer simply runs along this waterproof layer down to the ground. Moisture inside the tent can pass through the permeable inner layer to the air space—which then circulates and removes the moist air. The better double-wall tent designs with an outer, waterproof fly also have a waterproof floor which extends 6-12 inches up each side wall of the inner tent layer. This keeps any minor collection of ground water from coming in through the walls. Also, since the waterproof fly should not quite touch the ground to allow good air circulation to remove moist air, this "bathtub style" design stops any errant precipitation which may pass under the fly and reach the inner tent walls from coming into the tent.

The alternate construction strategy is using a single layer of one of the newer semipermeable fabrics like Gore•Tex. Small molecules of water inside the tent are theoretically passed to the outside, but larger water drops are not supposed to penetrate the fabric into the tent. The advantage of this tent design is (hopefully) lighter weight since there is only one layer of fabric. However, their moisture transfer performance is not as good as two-layer tents and they generally cost more. Canvas is another example of single-layer tent construction whose qualities have already been discussed.

Large tents with vertical or near-vertical walls and high roofs make comfortable base camps in areas with wind protection or mild weather. These large tents can be heated with properly vented gas stoves or wood stoves with a stove jack through the roof. Single-layer canvas is commonly used for this type of tent. It is relatively inexpensive and durable if properly dried and stored between uses. Single, double, or triple-layer nylon tents are also available in this design—the multilayered models providing more insulation for colder weather conditions. Nylon tents also come in geodesic or dome shapes which provide almost as much room as wall tents, but are often lighter, less bulky, more wind and water-resistant, and easier to erect.

Another possibility for a main camp tent is a tepee. Single-layer tepees shed wind and water well because of their steep walls and rounded shape. Their steep wall design also provides lots of head room compared to floor space. And they are the ultimate design for having an open wood fire inside a tent. The fire's smoke just flows directly out the top hole around the poles. Its one major drawback is its bulk. The long poles needed for construction are difficult to transport as is the large amount of tepee material.

The shape and construction of a tent will determine how well it withstands wind and rain. Generally speaking, tents with lower, more streamlined profiles will shed both wind and rain better. Most four-season tents have rounded or very slowly sloping shapes, low peak heights, more poles and are made of heavier material than three-season tents to withstand the rigors of winter weather. Their drawback is the extra weight, bulk and cost. Three-season tents intended for milder weather often have more vertical sides, higher peak heights and are made of lighter materials. This provides more floor space per pound of weight–which is a critical factor when backpack hunting. Because they often have lighter material and more bug screening in place of heavier fabric, three-season tents usually allow air and moisture to pass out of the tent better than four-season models. The result of all these differences is that three-season tents are preferable when four-season strength is not necessary. Experienced backpacking hunters using three-season tents will allow for their lack of strength by placing these tents in more protected areas (See the section on tent setup in Chapter Nine – "Camping").

Most tent poles are made of fiberglass or aluminum. Fiberglass poles are heavier and less costly than aluminum poles. Hollow fiberglass poles are lighter than solid fiberglass poles, but also break easier. Good aluminum poles are stronger than either types of glass poles. Some tent manufacturers offer both options for their tents and sell replacements. Backpackers usually opt for aluminum poles because of the weight advantage. Also, aluminum poles which are bent in the field can usually be straightened and/or reinforced sufficiently to be serviceable through the end of a trip–at which time replacements can be purchased. Broken fiberglass poles, however, are much harder to repair satisfactorily in the field. A very few tents can be poled with local small trees—like some wall tent styles and tepees—but this is not practical for most situations.

Bivy sacks are small, single-person bivouac tents. They sometimes incorporate one or two hoops to hold tent fabric off the occupant, but others are just large, uninsulated bags which are designed to lay on top of the occupant's sleeping bag or just directly on a clothing-clad hunter. Most incorporate some brand of "waterproof-yet-breathable" material to reduce weight and are more accurately described as water-resistant. They also don't breathe very well so a considerable amount of moisture collects on the inside. The primary advantage to using one of these bivy sacks is their light weight and small size–often under two pounds and sometimes under sixteen ounces. These personal shelters are practical in mild weather and for short hunts, but few hunters are determined enough to use these uncomfortable "tents" for other than an occasional, "Rambo-style" hunt. Their advantage is questionable since standard-construction, one-person tents under two and one-half pounds and two-person tents under four pounds can be found which provide much more protection and comfort for just a couple more pounds; and a hunter will be drier, more rested, and more likely to hunt effectively.

A more practical single-person shelter for weight-conscious hunters is a small, waterproof tarp with several grommets. If there are physical features like large boulders, cliffs, deadfalls or brush in the area a tarp can

This tent has a vestibule for storing boots, wet gear or packs–which frees space inside and makes for more comfortable camping.

be quickly fastened into a comfortable shelter with a little cord or rope. Finding a suitable location to do this takes a little experience, more time each evening and the result may not be as roomy or convenient as a tent. Plus, when there is severe weather or a large numbers of insect pests a tarp may not be a good choice. However, you can purchase a good six foot by six foot tarp for under $20 which weighs under a pound and use it comfortably in more situations than most hunters believe possible. I have been much more comfortable during the nights I spent under a small tarp than the times I have used a small bivy sack–and the sack cost ten times as much!

There are a few other tent pointers to keep in mind when shopping for or using tents. Having a small area (called a vestibule) outside the main tent, but inside the waterproof fly makes a convenient place to store wet gear or cook in inclement weather. The trade-off for this convenience is more weight and higher cost, so balance your priorities and choose accordingly. Also, remember that any tent (or vestibule) must be adequately ventilated to operate a stove inside safely. Many people die from using even small stoves inside a closed tent which rapidly lowers oxygen below safe levels. Tents are also very flammable, so use caution with any fire source which can quickly destroy your only shelter and any gear stored in it, perhaps leaving you suddenly with few clothes and gear in harsh weather–a survival situation.

On warm nights or during rainy weather, tents with *good* circulation are much more comfortable. Better circulation is often accomplished with more insect netting panels in the inner tent fabric. Some tents are designed so these panels are exposed only by opening zipper-operated fabric panels. Others just use insect netting to make up the roof of the inner tent with no fabric panels to cover them. The latter make for lighter weight tents and are common in three-season models.

Freestanding tents are supported by their poles alone. This convenience makes them easy to move once erected for exact positioning. Tents which are not freestanding require fastened guy ropes to hold them erect and are more time-consuming to move. The trade-off is extra weight associated with the poles of freestanding tents and often, extra cost.

Lastly, look carefully at construction and modify if necessary. Seams should all be double-stitched. Rain flys should provide complete coverage of the inner tent. The lower edges of flys should not be too high off the ground if the tent will be used in windy areas. Examine stakes to be sure they are the proper type for the hunt area and there are enough–plus a couple extra in case of damage. Seal all seams before the first use and repeat whenever seams show any signs of leaking. Tent manufacturers or local tailors are often willing to make modifications as well as repairs (zippers?) to any brand of tent for a reasonable price. Carry a little repair tape (duct tape is good for this purpose and many other tasks) in case of field emergencies. Nylon tent flys and floors can also be coated with Thompsons Waterseal™ to extend their life and effectiveness.

Sleeping Bags, Pads and Cots

The second most vital piece of gear for a camping hunter (after a tent) is a sleeping bag. No matter how cold and wet a hunter gets, if he has a warm, dry sleeping bag to crawl into at night he can continue to hunt safely and effectively. Choosing the right bag is another critical decision for a successful hunter.

The two major factors to consider when choosing a sleeping bag are bag shape and the type of fill material. Rectangular bags are roomy, but heavy and bulky for packing. If comfort is a priority and weight is not, this bag shape is okay. Mummy bags are contoured in the shape of the human body to be as warm as possible with minimal weight and bulk. For these reasons, this type of bag is invariably used by backpacking hunters. The top opening in a mummy bag should have a drawstring closure which reduces it to just a small hole for breathing, and gives it the appearance of its namesake. Another variation is a semi-rectangular bag with roominess and bulkiness qualities in between the two basic bag styles.

The type of fill used in a bag determines some of its most important qualities. Synthetic fill materials like Polarguard, Hollofill, Qualofill, Lite Loft and Primaloft repel moisture well. Even after a total submersion,

Regardless of their fill type, all sleeping bags should be stored loosely while not in use–like this one hung in the corner. Leaving them stuffed for extended periods of time will compress the fill material, reduce loft height and lower their insulating abilities.

synthetic bags can be wrung out and still provide most of their dry insulating value. The other common type of fill—goose or duck down—is useless when wet. Down readily attracts and absorbs moisture which reduces its insulating values to almost zero, and then is very difficult to dry. A camper who lets his down sleeping bag get wet when temperatures are below 50°F at the least faces a very cold night, or several, until the bag will provide much insulation. Under some circumstances this camper may be in serious danger from hypothermia if his bag gets wet. This is why synthetic bags are a much safer, more comfortable and more common choice for most

This Ridge Rest™ pad is waterproof, lightweight, inexpensive and easily packed–as shown here. This is a great combination for backpacking hunters.

camping. In very cold conditions down is still a practical choice. This is mostly because down has a better warmth-to-weight ratio than the best synthetics–although the newest synthetic fill materials are coming close. Down also costs considerably more than most synthetics.

The shell material for sleeping bags is almost always synthetic because of the need for a moisture-repellant fabric. Some of these materials are lighter and more abrasive-resistant than others which affects the performance of the bag. There are inexpensive bags on the market made for car or backyard camping which have cotton shells and may even be filled with a cotton mixture. Hunters must be careful to avoid putting themselves in a situation where their lives depend on a bag of this type. These bags can easily become saturated and absolutely useless for providing insulation.

Manufacturers' listed bag weights and temperature ratings are some of the most unreliable gear data there is. Weight is such an important consideration for sleeping bag shoppers that manufacturers exaggerate statistics to sell their products. One thing to look at is the loft of the bag; it is one good indication of how warm the bag will be. Loft is a term for how thick the bag is–the thicker the bag, the warmer it will keep you. There is no sure way to see through manufacturers' false claims, but personal advice and honest salespeople can be very valuable. Comparison shopping and careful study of temperature rating-versus-weight tables can also educate a shopper so unrealistic measurements may be spotted before a bad purchase is made. Simply being aware of this danger will make a consumer a little wiser and thus more likely to make a good choice. For sheep hunting here in Alaska I look for a synthetic sleeping bag which will keep me warm to at least 20° F. I have been able to find several models which do this and weigh in at about three pounds. For colder trips, you should be able to find synthetic bags which are good to 0° F and weigh about four pounds. For details on sleeping warmly in cold conditions see Chapter Nine–"Camping."

Features to look for in a high-quality sleeping bag are full-length draft tubes over zippers; a box foot shape which stands up to keep toes from pressing tightly into the bag and getting cold; and a draft collar around the neck and head for additional warmth. To preserve a sleeping bag's loft and thus its temperature rating, it should be hung up or stored loosely in a large bag which breathes (fabric–not plastic). Storing a sleeping bag in a compacted mode will reduce its loft over time, and synthetic bags are much more susceptible to this loft reduction than down. I store my bags hanging on the wall, but since I use them—and stuff them—up to 100 times a year they lose about 5° of temperature rating each year. I replace my sheep hunting bag every two or three years and use the old one for warmer camping situations.

There are also overbags and liners to improve the comfort and warmth of sleeping bags. Overbags are usually made of water-resistant material, they add warmth and keep the bag clean. Liners are a soft material like flannel or polyester fleece which prevent cold nylon from touching the occupant's skin, make the bag warmer and keep the inside clean. Both overbags and liners are easy to clean compared to sleeping bags which usually have to be taken to commercial launderers or hand washed.

Sleeping pads are used to insulate a person from a cold sleeping surface–the ground or floor. The value of sleeping pads is underestimated by most people who haven't slept on a cold surface without a pad. A cold, dense surface will act as a heat sink and rob a lot of heat from a sleeping

A sleeping pad is particularly important to keep campers warm when the ground is frozen–like at this late-season goat-hunting camp in the Kenai Mountains of Alaska.

person. Conversely, a good pad will stop this heat transfer and also provide a more comfortable surface to sleep on. The best pads do this while being as light as possible.

There are open-cell, closed-cell, inflatable and self-inflating pads. Open-cell foam pads in two to six inch thicknesses absorb moisture readily, so they are seldom used outside of permanent shelters like cabins or lodges. They are comfortable, less inexpensive and less bulky than standard mattresses. Newer versions of open-cell pads incorporate waterproof barriers around the outside to keep out moisture.

Closed-cell foam pads come in many varieties. Traditional models are smooth-surfaced, dense and relatively heavy compared to newer models. Ensolite™ pads are one example of older designs. Newer designs include Ridge Rest™ and Z-Rest™ designs with surface corrugations to add comfort and insulation without adding weight. Full-length models of this type can weigh less than one pound and half-lengths can be under eight ounces for weight-conscious backpacking hunters. These pads provide more comfort and warmth than similar-size flat pads for the same weight. I buy full-length models, cut them in half and then have a spare to use after the first half wears out.

Self-inflating pads do just that. They incorporate an inner open-cell pad surrounded by a waterproof exterior. When a valve is opened the inner pad expands and draws air inside. Closing the valve after the pad is inflated is all that is required by the user. These pads work best when they are left inflated except when transporting. Otherwise, the inner pad loses its ability to expand by itself and the user has to blow air through the valve to inflate the pad. I have one of this type which is twenty or more years old and it still self-inflates because it has always been stored in an inflated condition. There are many thicknesses, lengths and widths of these pads available depending on how much weight and bulk is a allowable. Single-person models can weigh up to four pounds and the half-length versions still weigh close to two pounds, so these are not the best options for serious backpacking hunters. However, they provide more comfort and warmth than flat or corrugated pads so are an option for shorter pack-ins or when weight is not so crucial. Another drawback to these pads is they can be punctured, so more care must be exercised with these than with closed-cell pads which are almost indestructible. The outer covering of self-inflatable pads is also water absorbent, so they should be carried in a waterproof stuff sack—which adds to their effective weight.

Older-style inflatable air mattresses are heavy and provide less insulation than self-inflating designs. They are okay when transportation is available and care is taken to prevent punctures.

Sleeping cots can be both comfortable and a space-saving device. Extra gear can, and should, be placed under sleeping cots to free up tent or cabin floor space. Empty spaces under a sleeping cot allow air to flow freely through the void. If this air is unheated it can cool the person sleeping on the cot tremendously. Packing gear into this space will stop air flow and prevent this unnecessary cooling effect. For the same reason, pads should also be used on cots, rather than sleeping on bare cots. A sleeping person on a cot needs to be insulated from cold air or gear below the cot just like he should be insulated if sleeping directly on the cold ground. Like pads, cots also come in numerous sizes and styles. The proper choice will depend on how much space is available and how important weight is. Taller cots are more comfortable for sitting and create more space for gear storage—assuming there is enough vertical space in the shelter (tent?) to allow for them. Shorter cots with spring steel legs are usually lighter and less bulky to transport and often have rounded legs to protect tent floors. I have one of these models which has also lasted twenty years so far and is still in great shape. Sleeping cots are notorious for breaking and tipping over so remember this when deciding how much you are willing to spend. Most inexpensive models will have to be constantly coddled to last even one trip. Generally, a few extra dollars for a better cot is well spent.

My experience with cots in tents has taught me a few valuable lessons. First, always tie sleeping pads onto cots so they don't continually slip off during the night. Simple loops of cord tied around the cot and pad will usually suffice. Second, always set up cots and then lie in them to settle them into the ground before trying to sleep on them. Jostling around a little helps to find any irregularities in the ground surface below the tent. Then put extra cardboard, tent bags or duffel bags under the cot's legs to level them as well as to protect the tent floor. A few minutes of testing and leveling will be rewarded many times over by better sleeping conditions each and every night of the trip. This simple procedure is one of the habits of an experienced and successful camping hunter.

Stoves and Cooking Gear

Camp stoves come in an assortment of styles, sizes and fuel requirements. Base camp stoves can be as convenient as home ranges *with* ovens—when weight and bulk is not a limiting factor. These large stoves often run on large propane containers and have controls every bit as adjustable as the home variety. Base camp stoves can also be smaller one, two or three-burner Coleman-style stoves which run on bottled gas or refillable tanks of white (like Coleman fuel) or auto gas. There are even range-top ovens for these stoves to allow baking in the field. Relying on wood stoves for cooking nowadays is questionable given the convenience of lightweight gas stoves and the limited supply of available wood in most areas (because of scarcity, wet conditions or restrictions on cutting). Wood-fire cooking also produces more smoke and soot, excess heat (sometimes a desirable by-product), requires a long start-up period, is restricted at times (fire permits) and requires heavy tools to gather the fuel.

Backpacking stoves come in a great assortment depending on your needs and fuel preferences. For mountain hunting where weight is a limiting factor, there are many single-burner stoves weighing under one pound for boiling water and cooking small meals. The best of these will boil a quart of water in less than five minutes and are no bigger than a large coffee cup. Mountain Safety Research (MSR) makes several models of high-quality backpacking stoves to meet a variety of requirements. One significant difference among backpacking stoves to be aware of when selecting one is their ability to be adjusted to a low heat level. Some can only run on high or almost-high while the better ones can be adjusted from low to high heat for all cooking needs.

Camping stove fuels vary almost as much as the stoves themselves. Some fuel cannisters are refillable, some are not. Refillable fuel bottles can use white gas (Coleman fuel), unleaded auto gas, kerosene, or propane. White gas is the most popular fuel because of its wide availability, low cost, clean burning qualities, efficiency and light fuel containers. Its one drawback is that it needs priming. Kerosene is also cheap and plentiful, but less-efficient, smoky and stinky. However, kerosene is more available than white gas on a worldwide basis. Unleaded auto gas is slightly less efficient and clean-burning than white gas, but also inexpensive and widely available. The better models of stoves can burn all three of these fuels,

This MSR Whisperlite stove nestles into a six-cup pot for convenience as well as lightweight and compact backpacking.

although some require changing a fuel jet to burn kerosene efficiently. Propane fuel cannisters come in small to huge sizes. The five to fifty-pound variety are those used to heat backyard grills or even homes and can be used for small camp stoves. Propane is inexpensive and works well at low temperatures. Although one-pound cannisters used for camp stoves are not advertised as refillable, this can be accomplished with the right adapter— rather than discarding each empty container and having to buy new ones at a higher overall cost. One advantage to using propane stoves is the ability to hook them up to large containers when conditions permit carrying the extra weight and bulk. This is much cheaper and more convenient than changing small bottles, particularly when the stove is used to do the cooking for a large hunting party and/or for a long season.

Fuel types which come in nonrefillable cannisters include butane and blended propane/butane. Of these two, the blended fuel is more efficient and runs better at low temperatures. The fuel cannisters are convenient, provide good heat control and work well at high altitudes. Their drawbacks are higher expense, more weight and bulk (empty fuel cannisters to carry). However, newer models have improved weight/fuel ratios which rival white gas stoves.

For heating purposes propane, kerosene or white gas models are commonly used by hunters. Any of these fuels are satisfactory for this purpose as long as safety precautions are observed. These include fire prevention and proper ventilation for both exhaust and oxygen depletion

The lightweight solution in cooking gear for two people on a backpack hunt: one stove, one pot, two cups and two spoons. This is all hunters need to enjoy hot meals and drinks.

reasons. For these reasons many experienced hunters never leave a gas heater on while sleeping. One mistake when using gas heaters can be deadly.

Pots, pans and eating utensils are usually limited by space and weight restrictions for hunters. The rationale is to utilize items which serve multiple purposes. Base camps often have several pots and pans of varying sizes to accommodate cooking for several people. Cast iron, aluminum and nonstick cookware are all used depending on weight restrictions and convenience desired. Camp sets often utilize nestling pots to save space. Camp cookware should be carried in a cloth pouch to avoid blackening other gear with residue soot from pot bottoms. Depending on the size of the camp and duration of the hunt, cleaning items can be as simple as one nylon scouring pad or brush and a small container of dish soap. For more sophisticated camp kitchens, paper or cloth towels are handy if space permits. Eating utensils are most commonly limited to one *nonbreakable* set of a plate, bowl, cup, fork and spoon per person. Hunters should have their own knives. Spares of utensils can be carried for a large hunting party if space is available.

For backpacking hunters cookware often means one pot to boil water along with one cup and one spoon per person. This is the lightest way to go, anything above this is a luxury. Look for rounded-bottom pots for easy cleanup, tight-fitting lids and a size which will accommodate your backpacking stove to save space. Aluminum pots are lightweight, inexpensive and very popular. Steel pots are heavier and costlier, but much more durable. Titanium is very costly, but much lighter and stronger than either aluminum or steel.

Map and Compass

The more remote and unknown a hunting area, the more important a map and compass are to a hunter. Hunters who are hunting virtually in their back yard can often do without either, although hunters do get lost every year within a mile of their own homes. Flat, forested areas with no visual landmarks and watersheds which don't have obvious downhill routes are particularly easy places for hunters to get lost. At the least, most hunters should carry a compass and all hunters should have a map whenever venturing outside their home range. Topographic maps depicting highways, roads, trails, creeks, rivers, lakes, forests, tundra, hills, mountains, ravines, etc. are useful for scouting and planning a hunt as well as finding your way in new country. "Topo" maps are one of the most valuable tools for hunters scouting for new areas or hunting away from home. For hunters in large country like the western U.S. or Alaska, topo maps are almost a requirement for successful hunting.

DeLorme Mapping at P.O. Box 298, Freeport, Maine 04032, (207) 865-4171, produces topographic map atlases for 27 of the 50 states. These map atlases contain topo maps of the entire state. It is not only the cheapest way to get maps of an entire state (about $20 for the atlas), but it can be very educational for hunters wanting to become more successful.

The United States Geological Service (USGS) sells individual topo maps with different scales and aerial photos of much of the U.S. They also have map catalogs and index maps of states for selecting which maps you want. Contact the USGS, Information Services Office, Box 25286, Denver, Colorado 80225, 1-800-USA-MAPS or (303) 202-4700.

Maps should be sprayed with a commercial map waterproofing spray or covered with a light coat of varnish to protect them for years of use. Maps can also be covered with a clear contact paper or shelving paper. This is the method I use to protect them during long backpacking trips in the inclement weather of Alaska's fall. A layer on both sides is best for maximum protection.

At the cost of a few dollars, every hunter should have a lightweight, compact, easy-to-use compass. When compass shopping look for a base plate with an arrow for direction of travel, a movable dial with easily readable markings, a scale index on a base plate for estimating distances and an attached mirror. The mirror is most useful as a safety device for solitary hunters to remove small particles which may get in their eyes. Mine has saved me unnecessary discomfort or worse several times.

The first thing to do when you get a compass is to practice with it *before* going hunting with it. At the least, this will tell you if it is working properly and teach you how its parts are supposed to function. The first thing to remember about using a compass is that it works on the earth's magnetic field, so be sure no objects are nearby which will cause a false reading. Magnets, batteries, electrical appliances, metal zippers or iron are some things which may do this.

The next thing to do is find out what the magnetic declination is for the area you will be hunting. Magnetic declination is the difference between the direction of the geographic North Pole and the direction of the magnetic North Pole. This declination varies depending where you are in the world. Since maps are made using the magnetic North Pole, you should next adjust your compass according to the declination in your current hunting area. This is usually done by turning an outer ring on the compass the desired number of degrees. Consult directions with your compass so you can use it correctly. Relying on improper usage is worse than not having it at all.

The modern alternative to a compass is a device which uses the Global Positioning System (GPS). GPS devices are now available for under $100 which are no bigger than a cell phone (another handy thing to take along when hunting alone or when out of familiar country). A GPS can tell you time, altitude, your heading, your speed, the distance from other locations, the directions back to other locations, draw you a map and tell you elapsed trip time–and probably more as new models are developed. It is a fantastic navigational tool for relocating preprogrammed waypoints anywhere on the earth within 100 feet. However they do run on batteries which run down; so keeping a two-ounce compass on a string around your neck for a backup might be good insurance.

Another valuable device for solitary hunters in remote areas is a personal Emergency Locator Transmitter. This phone-size electronic signalling device can be turned on when a hunter suddenly faces a life-threatening injury or is trapped by weather or equipment failure. For a few hundred dollars and a pound or two it can be a cheap safeguard for hunters.

Packs and Duffels

Most hunter use either backpacks or duffel bags to transport gear. These flexible parcels fit into small airplanes, on horses, into boats or on ATV's better than hard-sided luggage. Duffel bags are a good choice if no actual backpacking will have to be done or packs can be carried inside duffels. Some of these bags even come with shoulder straps for carrying short distances when necessary. It is best to select a duffel bag with more space than you expect to need–there always seems to be one more thing to put in it. However, be aware that most airlines have a 100-inch limit for baggage; this 100 inches is the total of the length, width and height. This

This waterproof duffel can go anywhere and keep gear dry. It also has pack straps for carrying through airports or for short hikes.

restriction is not always enforced and soft luggage seems to get by more than hard-sided bags, but some attendants may enforce this if your bag is too cumbersome. A good strategy is to be prepared to remove items and put them in your carry-on if this happens.

Other features to look for in duffel bags are strong two-way zippers, large rip-proof straps sewn all the way around the bag for toughness and a method of fastening both straps together; this is to prevent baggage handlers from grabbing one strap at a time which is more likely to cause damage. Waterproof material, double or triple-stitching and wide straps for packing are other desirable features. Water bags made for canoeing and kayaking are a good choice if you are going to be traveling around water or sleeping in a tent. These waterbags come in all sizes and shapes just like duffel bags and will even float when properly sealed. It is a good practice to use plastic bags within all bags to ensure dry gear. Even "waterproof" duffel bags and waterbags leak at times. It is a simple, cheap way to guarantee dry gear in even the wettest conditions.

For backpack hunting or hunts where gear or meat may have to be carried long distances during the day, a hunter needs a proper pack. The first decision to make is whether it will be an external frame or an internal frame pack. An external frame pack has a visible frame of aluminum or nylon. Most of these can be used without the packbag as a bare frame for hauling heavy loads like game meat. The greatest advantage of an external frame pack is its ability to haul really heavy loads. An experienced (read this to mean very strong and well-conditioned) packer can haul loads up to 150 pounds all day over rough terrain with an external frame pack. The best internal frame packs max out at 80 or 90 pounds–when they become unbearable to the same experienced packer. The difference is in the way the load is distributed. An external frame will distribute the load well between the shoulders and hips. An internal frame usually has small aluminum bars inside the pack which put most of the load on the shoulders as more weight is added–only a small percentage is placed on the hips. External frames also prevent heavy loads from shifting whereas internal frames allow movement with each step–causing more discomfort and fatigue. External frame packs also allow the packer to walk in a more natural, upright posture, allow the load to be moved up or down on the frame and allow more air ventilation to cool the back. Internal frames also have to be loaded more carefully to prevent hard objects from poking the packer's back, whereas an external frame protects the wearer better from objects in the pack.

Internal frame packs do have some desirable features for hunters who will not have to carry more than about 75 pounds. They catch less brush because of their narrower shape and they are easier to carry in airplanes and small vehicles. They are also more comfortable with lighter loads and are easier to balance because they flex with body movement–like when you are climbing through dense brush, up steep hillsides or on skis or snowshoes–this is where they have a significant advantage over external frame packs. I learned this lesson well on one long ski trip through the mountains many years ago when I wore a internal frame while my companion wore an external frame. I had a much easier time of it while he constantly fought to keep his balance against his stiff external frame pack. His pack made him work twice as hard on that trip as I did.

There are many advantageous features to look for in either of these two basic pack designs. The basic pack material is the first item to examine. Sturdy nylon fabric—often cordura— with a waterproof coating is the standard for most pack bags. However, very heavy material can add unnecessary weight. I buy packs made of medium-weight nylon which weigh

Hunters who expect to carry very heavy loads need external frame packs for their support and comfort. Tony Russ with a full load of sheep meat, cape, horns and gear—well over 100 pounds.

about five and a half pounds and hold up well over several years of rigorous use. I don't feel the real heavy duty packs which weigh two or three more pounds and cost three times as much are worth buying. I like carrying a couple pounds less every step I take as well as buying the newest pack designs every few years. However, the heavy duty packs will last ten years or more and many people choose them for their durability as well as their extra features.

An alternative pack material is one of the newer, quieter varieties often sold to bowhunters. Some of the new packs fabrics are fleece, Saddle-Cloth™ and Stealth-Cloth™. These packs usually have a waterproof lining and come in an assortment of camouflage patterns. They often come attached to one of the narrower nylon frames to reduce noise and catch less brush. They are not capable of handling as much weight as the larger aluminum frames, but may carry up to 100 pounds and are more flexible–thus making brush-busting and climbing easier.

A hunting pack should be the right size to fit your body. Try them on before purchasing and ask if they come in different sizes and if they are adjustable. Packs should have padded shoulder straps, a sternum strap to keep shoulder straps from sliding too far out on your shoulders and a padded hip belt–and all of these should be adjustable to fit you precisely. The pack bag should also be adjustable up and down on the frame to best balance the load on *your* back– every back has a unique design.

Look for a pack with plenty of pockets of the right sizes to fit your needs. A mesh water bottle pocket is handy on the hip belt as are pockets for a spotting scope and a map. When shopping for a pack remember that you can and should customize your pack to fit your individual needs. If you like dividers in the main bag then look for packs with this feature. I like one large compartment without dividers, but I have sewn on extra pockets, an arrow case holder and a climbing pole attachment to my pack. A little material, a few zippers and some thread and you can have a customized pack which fits your needs precisely. A professional tailor can always be found if no one in your household has the ability to do the sewing.

Look for large nylon zippers on pockets rather than small metal ones which are noisier and more likely to break. Also look for storm flaps over zippers. Plenty of tie-on points are convenient for hunters who always seem to have too much gear to fit into their pack. Compression straps to stop heavy loads from shifting are almost mandatory for internal frame packs.

Deer hunters who hunt areas where they are always close to transportation seldom need a full-size pack. They can get by with a day pack or a fanny pack for the few things they will need. Look for many of the same features as on large packs when shopping for one of these. However, hunters who are not certain how large a pack they will need when travelling to a new area might be wise to take a modular pack. These full-size packs commonly have a detachable fanny pack, day pack and pack board which can all be used separately. This is a good way to cover all possible pack requirements when uncertain about an upcoming hunt.

No matter how perfect a pack is for a particular hunt, it must be loaded correctly for optimal use. Packs which are loaded top-heavy or with too much weight to the sides greatly decrease the amount of weight you can carry comfortably. The difference can be as much as 50% for the worst weight distribution. Heavy items should always be put as close to the middle of the back as possible. Meat, food, tents, horns and other heavy items should be put close to a packer's center of gravity. Poor arrangements cause the packer to fight the load with every step. When packing out from a successful hunt with the heaviest of loads (often 140 pounds on Dall sheep hunts) when items have to be tied outside the pack, pick the lightest ones to put the farthest from your center of gravity. Sleeping bags, pads, clothing and capes are typical items which should be placed on top or tied to the back of the pack. See Figure 14.1 for the correct way to load a pack.

Figure 14.1

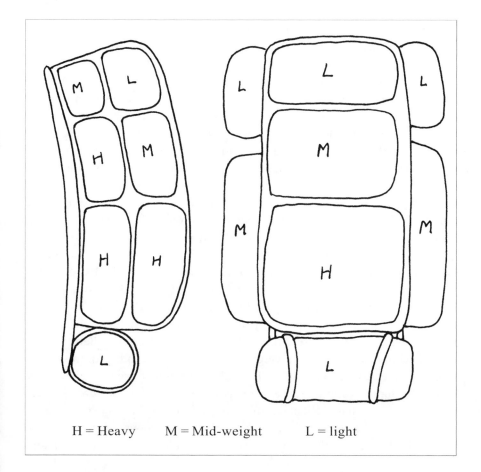

H = Heavy   M = Mid-weight   L = light

When backpack hunting, one of the keys to maximum enjoyment is to pack as light as practical and still have what you need. One way to check yourself at the conclusion of each trip is to spread out everything you carried. Except for absolute essentials like rain gear and your first aid kit, after the second time of doing this and noting an item which was not used, leave it behind the next time. This will weed out unnecessary items and lighten your load. Other ways I have lightened my load are by using only half a sleeping pad and using extra clothing as a pad under my legs and feet; repackaging food to leave behind unnecessary containers; taking only a cup and spoon for eating utensils; and always considering the weight of items I might buy and being on the lookout for lighter gear.

Miscellaneous Gear

One mandatory item for hunters should be a first aid kit. Hunters can get into trouble even a few hundred yards away from their vehicle and backpacking hunters are often days away from help. A first aid kit does not have to be complex or heavy. My kit which I take on week-long backpacking hunts into remote parts of Alaska weighs less than seven ounces. Essentials for me are a few sterile pads, a needle, fire starters, matches, painkillers, antacids and anti-diarrhetics. Remember to include extras of any prescription medication. Each hunter's kit can be as simple or complex as needed. See Chapter Seven– "First Aid" for more details.

A flashlight is as essential as a first aid kit for hunters. Darkness is something we deal with on almost every hunt and it will surely come sooner or later. Having to worry about getting out before dark or getting lost in it are unnecessary burdens to put on yourself. Dependable flashlights or headlights weigh only a few ounces and are very small compared to their value when needed. New batteries should be put in at the beginning of each hunt and extra batteries carried in a pack, vehicle or at least left at the main camp when away from home. Good models also have a spare bulb attached somewhere for the unexpected burnouts. Gas lanterns, candle lanterns and candles are other possible light sources.

Telescoping climbing poles are relatively new accessories which are extremely useful for mountain hunting. These are basically ski poles which collapse to about 24 inches and expand to about 60 inches. They have wrist straps, small baskets which prevent the tip from sinking too deep in tundra or poking too deeply into rock crevices and positive locking rings at the (typically) three joints. They weigh in at somewhere around ten ounces and are worth their weight in gold when descending or traversing steep hillsides with a heavy load. They also let a hunter use his upper body when climbing steep inclines and provide balance on loose scree slopes. As a guide I have had a client tell me that if I didn't provide one of these for my first-time sheep hunting clients I would be an irresponsible guide. Every client who I have introduced to these climbing poles has loved them. There

Bob Kelez with a great Dall sheep. These sheep live in treacherous country, so hunters must have the best gear—for safety and success.

were a few stubborn clients who refused to even try one to my dismay–they were slower and more at personal risk because of it. This is a vital piece of equipment for any hunter roaming open mountain slopes.

Protection from biting insects is mandatory in many hunting areas. On the tundra of Alaska or the swamps of the Southern U.S. mosquitoes, white sox, black flies and no-see-ums can actually threaten an unprotected hunter's health and sanity. Insect repellant sprays and liquids work for short periods of time, but must be applied every few hours to be effective. If several daily applications are necessary for more than a day or two the active ingredients will begin to cause skin problems. A better method of insect protection in these cases is to use head nets, gloves and/or bug jackets–garments made of bug netting which are periodically soaked in bug repellant. For areas where wood ticks are present it is necessary to use a good tick repellant as well as routinely check for ticks on the body. Unlike mosquito bites which cause only a minor irritation for a few hours, ticks can carry Lyme disease which can be deadly. For camp areas bug repellant coils can be burned or devices which periodically release vaporized bug repellant can be used to make the camp area more comfortable. At a minimum, a wise, traveling hunter always carries a small bottle of bug repellant as insurance; unforeseen insect problems have ruined more than one hunt.

One more handy item for hunters to own is a stitching awl. This allows a hunter to repair or modify heavy fabric or leather items. Stitching will often loosen or break on otherwise serviceable gear like packs, tents, gloves, gun cases, etc. A few stitches is often all that is needed to stop any further damage and make the item useful for many more years. If not repaired, the item may jeopardize a hunt or have to be replaced prematurely.

Many hunters compile a gear list after many seasons to remind themselves what is needed, what is unnecessary and what is optional. Making your own gear list can save you from forgetting crucial items which requires either return trips to recover them or will cause a reduction in the enjoyment and/or success of the hunt. My method of packing for a hunting trip is to mentally go through all the possible activities on a hunt and gather items as they come up in this mental rehearsal. For those who prefer a tangible gear list, the following is a fairly complete list of possible items for a hunting trip which can be pared down to fit individual needs. It is meant to be a master list from which other lists can be made. For example, a base camp list, a spike camp list and a backpacking list can each be made from this master list depending on which type of hunt you are going on. Don't overpack or under-pack. If you can stay warm, dry, and well-fed, you have everything you need. The right gear list will be the lightest combination that accomplishes this.

Figure 14.2   **HUNTER'S GEAR CHECKLIST**

CAMPING
__ TENT W/FLY, STAKES, & ROPES
__ GROUND CLOTH
__ TARPS
__ GROUND PAD
__ SLEEPING COT
__ SLEEPING BAG W/LINER, OUTERBAG
__ EXTRA ROPE AND TWINE FOR CAMP
__ AXE, HATCHET & SHARPENING STONE
__ CHAIN SAW, FUEL, OIL & TOOLS
__ SAW, SHOVEL, HAMMER & NAILS
__ CAMP LANTERN, FUEL & SPARE PARTS
__ CANDLE LANTERN &/OR CANDLES
__ WOOD STOVE & WOOD
__ GAS HEATER, FUEL & SPARE PARTS
__ STRIKERS, LIGHTERS & MATCHES
__ FOLDING TABLE & STOOLS
__ PORT-A-POTTI & TOILET PAPER
__ CAMP SHOWER OR SUN SHOWER
__ COMMUNICATIONS &/OR PUBLIC RADIO
       W/SPARE BATTERIES

__ CAMP FLASHLIGHT & ALARM CLOCK
__ LAND USE PERMIT
__ CAMP TOOL KIT & FIRST AID KIT
__ INSECT COILS & REPELLANT
__ TAPE & TIE WIRE

COOKING & EATING

__ CAMP STOVE, FUEL & SPARE PARTS
__ COOK BOX OR STOVE STAND
__ COOKING GRILL
__ COOLER
__ WATER PAIL OR JUG
__ WATER PURIFIER
__ COFFEE POT
__ DUTCH OVEN
__ FRYING PAN
__ BOILING POTS
__ 2-QUART DRINK CONTAINER
__ SPATULA AND LARGE SPOON
__ COOK KNIFE
__ CAN OPENER
__ CUPS AND PLATES
__ TABLESPOONS, FORKS & TEASPOONS
__ ALUMINUM FOIL
__ PAPER TOWELS
__ DISHWASHING TUB
__ POT SCRUBBER/PAD & DISH SOAP
__ PLASTIC TRASH BAGS

FOOD

(TOO VARIABLE TO LIST, SEE CHAPTER 15–JUST MAKE
SURE YOU HAVE EXTRA IN CASE OF WEATHER OR
TRANSPORTATION DELAYS.)

CLOTHING

__ SOCKS; LINERS & HEAVY DUTY
__ SHORTS & T-SHIRTS
__ LONG UNDERWEAR
__ PANTS & SHIRTS
__ VEST; CAMO &/OR BLAZE ORANGE
__ COAT OR PARKA
__ WIND PANTS AND COAT
__ RAIN GEAR
__ GLOVES, MITTENS & HATS
__ BELT &/OR SUSPENDERS
__ BOOTS, WADERS & CAMP SHOES

__ GAITERS
__ BANDANA

HUNTING

__ LICENSES, TAGS & REGULATIONS
__ WEAPONS & AMMO
__ HOLSTER, QUIVER & AMMO POUCH
__ TREE STAND
__ ARMGUARD, TAB, GLOVE & RELEASE
__ GUN, BOW & ARROW CASES
__ CLEANING & REPAIR KIT
__ SPOTTING SCOPE, TRIPOD & BINOS
__ RANGEFINDER
__ DOG, DISH, FOOD, COLLAR, LEASH,
        BLANKET & WHISTLE
__ GAME CALLS, DECOYS & CAMO NET
__ FACE NET & CAMO MAKEUP
__ GAME SCENTS & SCENT SHIELD
__ GAME BAGS AND PLASTIC BAGS
__ BONE SAW
__ HUNTING KNIVES & SHARPENER
__ DISPOSABLE SURGICAL GLOVES
__ SALT FOR CAPES & HIDES
__ PACK FRAME & BAG
__ DAY &/OR FANNY PACK
__ ROPE, CORD &/OR TWINE
__ MAPS, COMPASS, & PERSONAL ELT
__ FIRST AID KIT, SNAKEBITE KIT
__ INSECT REPELLANT
__ SPACE BLANKET & WHISTLE
__ WATER BOTTLE & SNACKS
__ FLASHLIGHT, EXTRA BATTERIES, BULB
__ LIGHTER, MATCHES, & FIRESTARTERS
__ CAMERA W/EXTRA FILM & BATTERIES

PERSONAL

__ TOWEL, WASH RAG & SOAP
__ TOOTHBRUSH, TOOTHPASTE & FLOSS
__ SHAVING KIT & COMB
__ TOILET PAPER & READING MATERIAL
__ PRESCRIPTION MEDICINE
__ EXTRA EYEGLASSES & CONTACTS
__ LIP BALM, ASPIRIN, & ANTACID
__ NEEDLE, THREAD & BUTTONS
__ CLIMBING POLE, EXTRA SHOELACES

Chapter 15
FOOD

Food can be an important factor in a successful hunt for several reasons. The type and quantity of food eaten will determine how hard you can hunt and how long you are able to hunt effectively. Mealtime satisfaction and enjoyment can also add or detract from the overall ambiance of a hunt–affecting the memories of our hunting experiences. Learning to choose the right foods for each hunt will help you improve your hunting success and enjoyment.

Basic Considerations for Selecting Food

Nutrition is the first consideration when selecting food for a hunting trip. Proteins, carbohydrates, fats, vitamins and minerals are all essential for hunters who want to hunt hard day after day. Balancing nutritional requirements with limitations imposed by hunting situations can be difficult, but is a requirement for consistently successful hunters. Chapter Five – "Nutrition for the Hunter" explains the basics of nutrition and how they apply to hunters. Hunters who know recommended Daily Values should be able to make food lists for hunting camps which satisfy their nutritional needs as well as their palates.

The method of transportation used is the most significant factor limiting food choices for a hunting trip. When mechanized transportation is available to carry large, heavy foodstuffs and storage containers to camp, almost any food can be taken. As transportation becomes more difficult, it restricts the types of food suitable for a hunting trip. The most spartan of hunting conditions— backpack hunting over long distances—places the most constraints on food selection. Backpacking hunters must carefully plan food lists to minimize weight and bulk while maximizing nutrition and eating satisfaction.

Whenever transportation is limited, weight and bulk of foods are of utmost concern. Choosing foods with less water content and using proper packaging are the best ways to reduce both weight and bulk. Identifying lightweight foods is the best way to save weight. Learning to discard heavy, bulky packaging in favor of lighter, compact containers is another. Ziploc bags are one very useful item for hunters. They save weight, bulk, reduce odors, protect food and are inexpensive. I once met two sheep hunters returning from their backpack hunt who were carrying a lot of unneccessary weight and bulk. When they invited me for coffee I noticed they were

Good nutrition is necessary for hunters who expect to hunt hard day after day and come home with game. A Coleman two-burner stove is a standard of hunting camps.

carrying enough coffee for an army, and they still had it in its original glass jar! Before a hunting trip with any transportation limits, all food should be examined for possible re-packaging to reduce weight, bulk or improve protection of the food.

Food preservation in the field isn't a concern when refrigeration is available, but many hunting camps will not have this luxury. Usually, perishable foods can only be taken in limited quantities, must be placed in the coolest locations and eaten first. Shady spots, stream banks, snowbanks, rockpiles and holes in the earth are all good locations for perishable foods. Food must also be protected from pests, both large and small. Bears, raccoons, fox, coyotes, crows, magpies, squirrels, mice and insects are just some of the critters which can get into camp food supplies. These pests can be a minor inconvenience at the least, but food lost to scavengers may bring a premature end to a hunt or put hunters in survival situations in remote areas. Plan on storing food out of reach of critters and/or inside animal-proof containers to reduce attractive odors. In bear country this usually involves using ropes to suspend food containers out of reach—at least twelve feet high in brown bear country and away from climbing trees in black bear country. Large, inexpensive, durable, plastic tubs with locking lids are readily available in many sizes for this purpose. Backpacking hunters can take lightweight, waterproof duffel bags or extra plastic bags for storing food.

Available cooking facilities, cooking time, ease of preparation and water availability also affect food choices. Time spent cooking or cleaning up afterward takes away from hunting time, so quick preparation and cleanup are attributes to look for in hunting-camp foods. Ease of preparation is also appreciated by hunters wanting to get out at first light or returning from a tiring day of hunting. Packing water to camp for cooking and cleaning also takes hunter time and effort, so water required for preparation and cleaning should be considered when making a food list.

Aromas produced by cooking should be another consideration when camp is located close to the hunting area. Mobile hunters who camp within their game's home range may want to forego cooking altogether to reduce odors which may spook game. Other hunting situations may just dictate which days you should have cold meals and when it is okay to cook, depending on where camp is that night. Some game animals tolerate human smells and others do not. Generally the closer game lives to people the more they get used to smells. Game animals living in remote country are often alarmed by new odors and hunters should be aware of this and plan their hunting foods accordingly.

The spiciness of foods you eat will sometimes affect the odor you give off. Hunters who use scent eliminators or cover-ups should be cautious about eating terribly spicy foods as this may defeat their efforts at scent protection.

All these food considerations have to be balanced with the length of the hunt. It is one thing to eat a very limited variety of camp food for a few days, but entirely another to do so for two or three weeks. The longer the hunt, the less inconveniences hunters are willing to put up with, so plan food accordingly. On one extreme, a single hunter on a two-day hunt may be happy to throw a few protein bars in his pack to save weight (no stove, fuel, pots or utensils) and time. A hunter in charge of food for a group of ten hunters for three weeks who tries that strategy might end up on the meat pole after the first "meal."

One vital consideration when choosing food is its nutritional *density*. Choosing foods which have high protein and caloric contents will save both weight and bulk as well as improve nutrition on your hunting trips. Since I often backpack hunt, I usually look at caloric content first. I want as many calories per ounce (c/o) to get the most out of the food I carry on my back. Table 15.1 shows how some foods compare in caloric and protein content. These numbers were derived by dividing the calories or protein per serving by the ounces of food per serving. Most foods have these numbers printed on their labels so this simple mathematical calculation can be easily done for any foods you may consider for a hunting trip.

Table 15.1

FOOD	CALORIES PER OUNCE	GRAMS OF PROTEIN PER OUNCE
raisins	83	1
oatmeal (plain)	105	4
Pemmican™ bar	112	5
Tiger's Milk™ protein bar	116	6
granola	125	2
chocolate bar	130	1
oriental noodles	133	3
dried milk	110	10
dried parmesan cheese	129	12
cashews	163	4
freeze-dried chili dinner	160	8
freeze-dried chicken stew	130	5
freeze-dried cheese omelette	150	11
canned chicken	35	7

Except for the raisins and chicken, the rest of these foods have at least 100 c/o so I would call them nutritionally dense. When transportation is not a concern, nutritional density is not so important; but for backpack hunts I generally take only foods with over 100 c/o. I also look for foods with high amounts of protein when weight is important. With these criteria in mind I get as much nutrition for the minimum weight of food. The foods I have found which best satisfy these criteria are nuts and protein/energy bars. These are the foods I take for my lightest backpack hunts.

The values in this chart (fig. 15.1) were derived without the weight of packaging. The addition of heavy containers or wrappers can significantly lower food density values–which is why re-packaging is so important to weight-conscious hunters. By viewing foods from a nutritional-density perspective hunters can improve their nutrition while reducing food weight. The next section uses all the aforementioned considerations to choose suitable foods for hunting situations.

Suitable Hunting Foods

The first meal in a hunting camp should be a hearty breakfast. As explained in Chapter Five—"Nutrition for the Hunter"—a person needs at least 500 calories by mid-morning to replenish glycogen stores after a night of fasting. Without these calories, muscle glycogen will be depleted and a hunter will not be able to operate at 100% efficiency. If this happens regularly over a week-long hunt, a hunter will lose muscle mass and strength.

Oatmeal is a traditional, hearty breakfast which is lightweight, inexpensive, easily and quickly prepared, makes a minimal mess, uses little

Food bars are a standard item for hunters to carry for snacks, even meals in some cases. The Snickers bar is okay for quick energy, but doesn't provide much protein nor stay with a hunter. The Pemmican bar is a complete meal with 400 calories and 17 grams of protein. The Tiger's Milk bar with 7 grams of protein and less sugar than the Snicker's bar and is a good snack for hunters.

water and is easily re-packaged and stored. The instant variety is commonly used, but regular oats can also be prepared by just adding hot water. They will be a little coarser than when cooked for five minutes, but this is preferred by many of us oatmeal fans. Adding nuts, dried fruit, spices and sweetners can add an endless variety of flavors to this staple breakfast food and please most hunters. At 105 c/o and 3.5 grams of protein per ounce before the addition of nutritionally dense nuts and fruits, oatmeal is as close to an ideal hunting camp food as there is.

More complicated breakfasts such as eggs, bacon, pancakes, grits, etc. are also traditional camp favorites. Although these foods are not recommended for backpack hunts, they do provide more variety for a long hunt when mechanized transportation is available. They take considerable more time for preparation and clean-up, which may keep hunters from getting into the field at first light. These foods also present more storage and pest problems. However, they do provide plenty of calories to keep hunters going strong until mid-day and plenty of protein to sustain them over a long, hard hunt.

Hot drinks are another favorite—often necessary—morning food. Coffee, tea or chocolate are common. Instead of these I often just use powdered drink mixes for a hot beverage. By doing this, I only have to carry one item for drinks all day long. Any beverage, particularly caffeinated ones, should be consumed in moderation in the morning for stand hunters who don't want to smell up their stand location. Caffeine should also be avoided by those who get any sort of unsteadiness from this drug—some bowhunters are more susceptible to this and should be aware of the deleterious effect caffeine has on their shooting.

When hunters are pressed for time or just don't want to bother with cooking, they still should eat something with enough calories (carbohydrates are the best source of morning calories as they are easily digested) to keep them going strong until mid-morning. This can be a granola or protein bar, a handful of trail mix, dried fruit, or other dried foods. Then they should plan on another snack at mid-morning to provide more fuel for their hard-working bodies.

Midday meals usually consist of ready-to-eat (rte) foods rather than sandwiches or soups, although these are fine when available. Rte foods include sausages, meat sticks, jerky, cheese, many kind of bars (protein, granola, energy, chocolate, etc.), trail mixes, nuts and candy. These should be chosen carefully to get the most nutrition and calories per ounce, especially for backpacking hunters who count every ounce they carry. Nuts, sausages and many bars provide over 150 calories per ounce in addition to high quantities of protein. Protein and energy bars come in a great variety and some of these have up to 15 grams of protein per ounce. These are great foods for weight-conscious hunters. Most hunters snack on these foods all day to maintain their energy level rather than have one large lunchtime meal. Consuming high-energy drinks like Tang, Gatorade or sports drinks during the day helps provide energy as well as needed liquids.

The evening meal is usually where the day's adventures are related to others and comraderie between hunters is built. More time is usually spent preparing and eating this meal than any other. This meal should provide enough nutrition to restore often-overworked bodies and be satisfying to the palate. Protein, in particular, should be available in enough quantity to repair muscles for the next day's hunt. In many hunting camps this meal is just like any you would have at home—with meat, vegetable, bread and dessert. Game meat is often on the menu if hunters have been successful. Game meat has large quantities of protein, but less fat than beef or pork, so other sources of fat are often added to the meal for additional calories. Extra calories are often necessary because mountain hunting with a heavy backpack can burn up to 7,000 calories per day. Lack of fat is why game meat is darker red and why it cooks quicker than beef. It also dries out more easily while cooking so water should be added to prevent this.

The kitchen is the focal point of most hunting camps. A good cook should be treated well by hunters who depend on the cook for their meals. Here Matt Wolfe prepares what will no doubt be an excellent meal for a camp full of hungry guides and hunters.

In hunting camps where transportation limits the types of food available, the evening meal is still a focal point of the day. There are several types of main entrees which are lightweight and quickly prepared. One type is Ready-to-Eat™ meals which come in vacuum-packed, foil pouches requiring only a few minutes in boiling water before serving. Only one pot is needed, no additional water or ingredients are required and cleanup is a snap. Heater Meals™ are even more convenient–securely packaged with their own heating device. No fuel or pot is required, just start the internal heater and serve when hot. There is minimal preparation and cleanup and no water is needed.

Meals-Ready-to-Eat (MRE's) are a U.S. military invention for troops on the go. They contain drinks, freeze-dried meals, oatmeal, granola bars, chocolate bars, matches, toilet paper, chewing gum, etc.–everything you need for one meal or a whole day, depending on which type you get. Their taste is somewhat lacking, but their convenience is attractive to many hunters who swear by them.

Freeze-dried dinners come in a great variety and their taste has improved dramatically over the past twenty years. They typically require only the addition of boiling water to prepare. They can be prepared in, and eaten from, the package they come in. They are lightweight, fairly satisfying

A typical kitchen on a backpack hunt. Although the food is simple and the accomodations frugal, hot meals can taste incredibly good on backpack hunts.

and their cost is moderate. Breakfasts and desserts are also available. Most backpacking hunters take some freeze-dried meals. The one drawback is they never seem to get completely rehydrated, so some people's digestive systems may revolt if fed a steady diet of freeze-dried food. I try to eat no more than one freeze-dried meal a day and less if possible. I also add extra water and let them sit longer than directed to improve their digestibility. To save weight I sometimes leave behind the outer packages and put several inner pouches in a Ziploc bag. Just make sure to eat these first on the trip because they don't keep well once opened.

Remember to read the nutritional labels on any type of packaged meals. Freeze-dried dinners often have less than 300 calories per serving, which is much less than backpacking hunters need. Examining labels while you are planning food is necessary if you want to get sufficient nutrition for a successful hunt.

Pasta is a good item to take on hunting trips if sufficient water and fuel is available. Pasta contains high levels of carbohydrates to provide long-lasting energy for hard-working hunters. Oriental noodles or noodle cups take less time to prepare than traditional pasta noodles and still contain good quantities of carbohydrates. Couscous is another good pasta which I take on almost all my hunting trips. It is prepared by adding boiling water and waiting five minutes. Although it is bland by itself, a great variety of ingredients can be added for flavor. I add dried vegetables, dried soup mixes, Parmesan cheese and/or seasoning mixtures like Mrs. Dash. It can also be eaten as a hot breakfast cereal with milk, fruit, sugar and/or cinammon. I also add it to my freeze-dried dinners to bulk them up and make them more agreeable with my digestive tract. It makes the dinners more like real food. Couscous is also inexpensive ($1.59/lb.), stores very well and has a good amount of protein. It is the most perfect pasta I have found for hunting camps.

For long, hard hunting trips some hunters take dietary supplements to sustain their health with the often-limited amounts and varieties of foods available in hunting camps. This is a good idea if you will be out more than a week, expecially if you are going on a backpacking hunt which really limits food selection.

Wild foods are another possible source of nutrition for hunters. Using native foods necessitates excellent knowledge to avoid ingesting poisonous or debilitating plants and animals. Hunters who choose to use wild foods must be able to balance the time needed to gather the food against what it saves them in time to bring in food. This means there must be a good supply of natural foods so inordinate amounts of time aren't needed to gather it. After twenty years of hunting sheep in Alaska I have concluded that—with the exception of wild blueberries—wild foods are not in great enough profusion to be useful to mountain hunters. Even our berry crops are not predictable enough to be relied on by hunters. I still take advantage of wild foods which are readily available, I just don't rely on them.

Other suitable foods which I have discovered for hunting trips include powdered honey, powdered butter, and powdered cheeses. Powdered teriyaki marinade is one of the best ways to prepare game meat I have found, even at home. On my backpack hunts where every ounce counts, I always take a package of this powder along with me. Sheep meat marinated in Teriyaki is unsurpassed by any method of preparation.

There are some general guidelines about food and cooking all experienced hunters should know. Always take extra food in case bad weather or mechanical failure extends the hunt. The more remote the camp, the more important this rule becomes. Unwritten rules concerning camp cooking include: treat the cook well if you want to be fed well; anyone who complains about the food becomes the cook; and whoever cooks doesn't have to do the dishes.

Finding a good variety of foods which are suitable for hunting trips is difficult, but worth the extra effort. Meals shared around the campfire or camp stove can be some of the most memorable times of our hunting careers—even more memorable than the hunt itself. The time you spend planning meals for your hunting trips will be doubly rewarded by increased energy and stamina, as well as enjoyment at mealtime–all of which are ingredients of successful hunting trips.

The dinner meal tonight in hunting camp will taste better to this happy hunter than anything an uptown restaurant could possibly create.

SECTION V.
FIREARMS & OPTICS

Chapter 16
FIREARMS

Choosing a firearm should be done with considerable forethought. The choice you make will have a significant impact on your hunting success. It may also affect how, when and where you can hunt. A good bit of knowledge is required for any hunter who expects to choose an appropriate rifle, shotgun, handgun or muzzleloader to fit his needs.

Some of the questions you should ask yourself before buying a firearm are:

1) Will this be used for one species or several species?

2) Can I afford to buy more than one firearm?

3) Should I buy one specialized firearm and use it until I can afford more specialized firearms, or should I buy an all-around weapon for all my future big-game hunting?

4) What is the habitat of the game I expect to pursue; should I have a flat-shooting rifle for antelope and sheep or a faster aiming firearm for close shots at moving whitetails?

5) What is my age, strength and ability with a firearm and how will that change in the near future? Can I handle a magnum? Will I be able to take advantage of an expensive, accurate rifle?

6) How tough is (are) the animal(s) I expect to hunt with this firearm? Do I need a magnum rifle for elk and bear or a flat-shooting weapon for thin-skinned animals?

7) Do I need a lightweight gun (perhaps a handgun?) for long backpacking trips, or will a heavy, more accurate rifle be better suited to my hunting?

8) Do I want the challenge of hunting with a handgun or muzzleloader? Do I want to hunt in muzzleloader seasons?

9) Do I need a shotgun to hunt areas where rifles are restricted?

10) Do I need a weather-resistant gun for wet conditions or near saltwater? A basic understanding of modern firearms will help you answer these and numerous other questions you may have.

Rifles

Rifles are the most productive weapons for hunters. They have the longest effective range and come in a great variety of styles, sizes and price ranges. They provide most hunters with the best accuracy with the minimal amount of practice. Rifles are so named because they have small, twisting grooves cut into the inside of their barrels which are called "rifling." These grooves cause bullets to spin–producing more accuracy and distance.

One basic consideration when selecting a rifle is which action to choose. The action is the device which loads the cartridge and ejects the spent case. Rifle actions include the following styles.

Lever action – The lever action rifle has probably taken more deer in the U.S. than any other action type. The good balance, light weight, short length and quick, easy action allows hunters to shoot quickly and accurately in brush and timber where many deer are hunted. It is also good for quick follow-up shots when needed.

Pump action – Pump action rifles are quick and easy to operate, but not so easy to disassemble, nor as reliable as lever or bolt actions. This is a very popular action for shotguns, but has limited use in rifles.

Break-open – This style of rifle opens at the breech to load one cartridge (two if it is a double barrel). It is strong and reliable, but follow-up shots are slow. There are very few of these rifles being sold to modern hunters.

Bolt action – This is the strongest, most reliable and popular action for rifles today. Because of its strength it is favored for magnum cartridges and by handloaders–who are concerned about excessive pressures. After a little practice hunters can cycle additional cartridges through bolt action rifles without lowering them from their eye; letting them fire follow-up shots as quickly as with any other action type.

Semiautomatic – Although these are sometimes referred to as autos, they are only automatic loaders, not true automatic rifles as seen in the movies. Auto-loaders use the force of their recoil to load the next round, which makes them fast and reduces recoil. What they gain in speed and ease of operation they give up in reliability and strength of the action. They must be kept very clean and rust-free to operate reliably.

In addition to a careful consideration of action types, hunters should also think about what metal finish they want as well as the type of stock to get. Blue steel is the most common metal finish on guns and it will serve most hunters well. Blueing helps the gun resist rust which is the main threat to a gun's useful life. However, guns which are regularly exposed to wet weather for weeks, used near salt water frequently or have to endure any type of physical abuse on a regular basis—like being slid in and out of a scabbard frequently—will tend to lose a blue finish prematurely and rust excessively. For any of these situations a more-resistant finish or metal may be preferable. Stainless steel, Nickel plating, Parkerizing or nylon coating are some of the ways to protect a gun from harsh conditions. The initial extra expense to purchase one of these guns may be justified by the extended lifetime–which can be three or four times that of a blued gun in conditions like we see here in Alaska.

The traditional look in a big game rifle is blued steel, like the upper model in the photo. The lower rifle is made of stainless steel with a matching nickel-plated scope; both are much more resistant to rust for hunting in wet weather or near saltwater.

A synthetic stock may also be a worthwhile investment to improve durability and save weight. Wooden stocks are arguably more esthetically pleasing, but they can crack and swell in wet conditions–which can adversely affect accuracy. Rifle barrels can also be glass-bedded or free-floating to improve accuracy in wet conditions.

When total rifle weight is a major concern, there are many production models and numerous custom gunsmiths who can satisfy this need. It is possible to purchase magnum rifles which weigh under six pounds when fully fitted with a sling and scope for those willing to pay the high price these specialty guns bring. For all but the best of these lightweight models, accuracy suffers somewhat when weight is reduced. In general, heavier rifles are easier to hold steady and shoot accurately than lighter ones. Most hunters will be served well with an average seven to eight-pound rifle which costs less than five hundred dollars, rather than paying several thousand dollars for a custom gun.

Shotguns

When shotguns are used for big game hunting it is typically because their projectiles (slugs or pellets) don't travel nearly as far as those from rifles or handguns. Rifle bullets can still be deadly three, four or even five miles downrange, while shotgun slugs are limited to a mile–usually far less. For hunting in populated areas or when hunter density is high, shotguns reduce the chances of long range accidents. Shotguns are sometimes called smoothbores because they do not have rifling grooves inside their barrels. To compensate for this, slugs used in shotguns are rifled for accuracy. Rifled slugs have small, curved flutes around their edges which cause them to spin when shot out of smoothbores. These flutes perform just like the curved vanes on arrows to spin the slug. Buckshot is sometimes used for big game hunting with shotguns, but this is a very short range combination. For more on shotgun ballistics see Chapter 19 – "Ballistics."

Shotguns come in bolt-action, pump-action, break-open and semiautomatic. All of these are acceptable for big game hunting. Special, interchangeable barrels are often used when shotguns are used to shoot slugs—versus normal shotshell loads. These barrels usually have open sights instead of the bead on most shotgun barrels. Hunters must be careful when using choked shotgun barrels to be sure this is safe. Manufacturer's specifications will identify specific choke types which can be safely used with slugs. Shooting slugs from some choke types can destroy the gun and put the shooter at risk of serious injury.

Handguns

Modern handguns are available which are adequate to hunt almost any North American big game except maybe the big bears—and even these can be hunted safely if there is a heavy backup rifle in experienced hands. There are several magnum cartridges which can be used in handguns made to handle the extreme pressures. The well-known 44 magnum and lesser-known 41 magnum are accurate and effective out to 100 yards using special handgun scopes. There are also numerous single-shot handguns made which can handle magnum rifle cartridges, making them reliable weapons at 175 yards in the right hands. Handgun hunters are often seeking the unique challenge this weapon offers. The light weight and portability are also attractive characteristics for proponents of handgun hunting.

Like rifles, handguns also come in several action types.

Single-action revolvers – Revolvers got their name because they have a rotating cylinder containing several (5 or 6) cartridges. The hammer on single-action revolvers has to be manually cocked (pulled back into a locking position) before each round can be fired; the firing is then done by pulling the trigger.

Double-action revolvers – These look the same as single-action revolvers, but have two modes of firing. They can be cocked and fired in the single action mode or fired by just pulling the trigger, which both cocks and fires the trigger in one motion.

Semiautomatic pistols – These handguns have a magazine which holds extra cartridges. A slide must be pulled back to cock it for the first shot. Single-action autos must be cocked before each round by working the slide. Double-action autos are by far the most common. They only need to be cocked before firing the first round. Thereafter, the recoil from each

Carl E. Brent and Carl F. Brent show off a nice whitetail taken with a double-action revolver. Big game hunting with pistols is a popular sport for those who want the additional challenge of a short-range weapon.

round loads another round and cocks the firing mechanism. Successive rounds can be fired as quickly as the trigger can be pulled. Semi-autos without an external hammer cannot be accidentally discharged (as revolvers can be) if their hammer catches on something and then releases. However, semiautomatic pistols often have a light trigger which is easily discharged accidentally by inexperienced handlers.

Break-open – These can be loaded with only one cartridge each time the handgun is opened. A hammer has to be cocked before each firing. Because of its strength, many of the heaviest handgun calibers are made in this style.

Bolt action – This handgun operates just like a bolt action rifle. These generally hold only one round in the chamber so each round has to be manually loaded. Heavy handgun calibers are also made with this action.

Muzzleloaders

Muzzleloaders are a type of firearm which is loaded through the muzzle end of the barrel rather than at the breech. Hunters choose to use muzzleloaders for the challenge, nostalgia and the special seasons some areas offer. Muzzleloading weapons using conical-shaped slugs have effective ranges of up to 125 yards with proficient operators. Those using ball-shaped slugs can be effective up to 100 yards. Although both types can be shot beyond these limits, most do not retain enough energy at longer distances to be effective on big game animals.

Traditional muzzleloading firearms require several steps to load each round. It is time-consuming and takes practice to do correctly. Only one shot can be fired after each loading so hunters often get only one chance at an animal. However, there are newer designs on the market which load powder, patch and slug all in one motion. This allows hunters to fire successive rounds much quicker, but these new designs are not legal in some muzzleloader seasons because of the advantage they give the hunter.

Cartridges

A cartridge is a complete unit composed of a bullet, a primer, powder and a case to hold everything together. Most big game cartridges have a primer seated in the middle of their base, and they are called centerfire to denote where the firing pin strikes the cartridge. The common .22 caliber is called a rimfire because it is struck near the rim, not the center.

Caliber is the name given to the *approximate* size of bullet—in decimals of an inch or millimeters—a gun shoots or a cartridge holds. Some, like the .243, use a bullet which is exactly 243 hundredths of an inch. Other calibers, like the .300 Winchester Magnum, actually hold a slightly different size bullet than the name indicates–308 hundredths of an inch in this case. The names of calibers are sometimes modified to give additional information about them. The .300 Win. Mag. was developed by Winchester and is a magnum (more powerful) version of this caliber. The popular .30-06 shoots a bullet of 308 hundredths of an inch and was designed in 1906–so the '06 was added to refer to the year of development. Nomenclature of calibers is just one of the many fascinating aspects of firearms which intrigues many thousands of gun collectors worldwide.

There are dozens of different calibers available for modern big game hunters. The ones in common use today range from .243 caliber to .458 caliber. Some are magnums useful for hunting dangerous game, some are known for their long-range capabilities, some are known as brush-busters, some can be handloaded to cover a wide range of hunting conditions, some use inexpensive ammunition, others can be easily made into wildcat loads and some are just old favorites. The mixture of all the possible advantages and disadvantages determines how a caliber performs for a specific purpose. For details about how calibers and bullets perform, see Chapter 19 – *Ballistics*. For serious study beyond what most hunters require, there are literally hundreds of books written on this subject available wherever books are sold or rented (libraries).

Sights

There are several types of sights hunters use. Open sights have a rear ramp with a notch and a front post to align in the notch. Peep sights

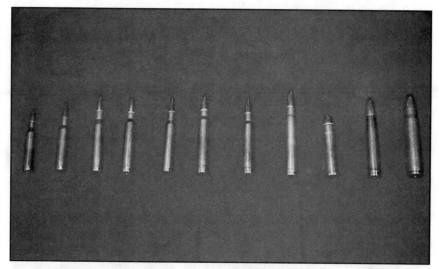

Modern big game cartridges range from the smallish .243 Winchester on the extreme left to the monstrous .500 Jeffrey on the far right. There are so many calibers and loads available to choose from that hunters can have a hard time deciding which to use for their individual needs.

have a circular rear sight with a hole in it and a front post which is supposed to be centered in the rear hole. Both of these sights are made for distances up to 100 yards for the average hunter, although highly trained marksmen can use them accurately well beyond this range. Both open and peep sights are good choices for quick shooting at animals in heavy cover–typical of much of the deer hunting all over the U.S. Their strength and reliability is also appreciated by hunters. Both sight types allow hunters to achieve a quick sight picture and shoot in the few seconds a deer often stands still in hunting conditions. These sights are also good for aiming at a moving deer– another situation deer hunters frequently encounter. For deer and other big game under 100 yards, both of these sight types work well.

However, because of their optical advantage, telescopic sights (scopes) are used by the majority of big game hunters. Gun scopes for big game are commonly used in powers of magnification from 1.5x to 9x. Scopes with powers above 9x are available, but not practical for most hunting. The lower power scopes are generally used for short ranges— like the deer scenarios described above—and for dangerous game. Low power scopes in the 1.5x to 4x range have a wider field of view, gather more light, and are smaller than higher power scopes. Mid-range scopes from 4x to 6x are used when shots may range from 20 yards to 300 yards. Higher power scopes up to 9x are used for the longest ranges on open country animals like antelope and sheep.

The scope mounts better be solid and the hunter must trust his gun/ scope combination when a bear such as this comes out of the brush at forty yards heading straight at the hunter, as this ten-footer did.

Fixed-power scopes are set at one magnification level. They are less expensive than variable-power scopes which can be adjusted over a range of magnification levels. The most popular fixed-power scope is the 4x because it can be used satisfactorily at most hunting ranges. The most popular variable scopes are 1.5x-5x, 2x-6x, and 3x-9x. Fixed power scopes have been more reliable in the past both for accuracy and waterproofness.

However, the better variable scopes available today are just as reliable as fixed-power scopes in both of these areas; but they still cost a lot more, are heavier and bulkier. In addition to selecting the power(s) of your scope there are also choices between heavy or fine crosshairs, wide angle scopes for a larger field of view, 4-plex reticles (sighting marks inside the scope), post reticles or dot reticles. Given all the possibilities, scope shopping takes time and a good knowledge of what's available to choose the right scope for the hunting you have in mind. One thing you should remember when scope shopping is that there is a wide range in reliability in rifle or handgun scopes. Some will fog on you at the worst time and some variables will not hold their zero when magnification is changed. Modern rifles are very reliable and most any model will do an adequate job, but this is not true of scopes. You can scrimp on your rifle, but don't scrimp on your scope, it just might let you down. It is not unreasonable to spend more on a scope than on the rifle you put it on.

When attaching any type of sight it is a good idea to use something like Loctite to prevent screws from loosening after repeatedly firing the gun. Successful hunters remember to do little things like this and they are the ones who don't miss the once-in-a-lifetime chance at the monster buck.

Extras

Other items you may need for your firearm are a sling, shooting stick(s), a gun case, an ammo pouch and a scabbard. The proper sling can help you carry your weapon all day in a comfortable and safe manner. The right sling in the right hands can also help you shoot accurately when no rest is available. I like a wide sling made of a stretchy nylon/rubber mixture. It repels moisture in the wettest conditions and gives slightly when traveling over rough ground, which is easier on my shoulder. I can also slip my arm through it quickly for sudden offhand shots. The old one-inch leather varieties are heavier, less convenient and less comfortable in my experience.

Shooting sticks have been used for years by Europeans, but haven't found many proponents in the U.S. However, both the one or two-leg models are extremely useful in some types of hunting terrain. In brushy areas without convenient trees to use as rests or in open, wet tundra they provide a quick, stable rest for long range shooting—anything over 100 yards. They are not as stable as being prone on a convenient, dry hillside, but they can provide a surprisingly steady base when needed.

Gun cases and scabbards are both necessary to protect guns in transit. One primary consideration is to get a good fit. Otherwise your gun may suffer unnecessary abuse. Gun cases should be made of a breathable material, unless you are worried about salt water corrosion or the gun falling overboard on a raft trip. Then you might choose a watertight case which also floats. For more typical conditions, a quality leather or canvas case made to fit your gun will protect it sufficiently. Cheap cases (vinyl comes to mind) with weak handles always seem to let you down at the wrong time–like when you are handing the gun from the dock to the boat. The same goes for a scabbard. Outfitters are not likely to have just the right size scabbard to fit your expensive or heirloom rifle, so buy one with a good cover before a horseback hunt and you will have it for a lifetime. It will pay for itself even if you only use it once. Leather or nylon ammo pouches which slide over your belt are a convenient way to carry extra rounds of ammunition when hunting. They are made to fit each size of ammo and good models hold eight to ten rounds noiselessly, but securely, on your belt. They have a cover for weather protection which is quickly removed by opening a simple snap or Velcro closure.

Practice, Practice, Practice . . .

Once you have your hunting firearm completely set up, practice is vital to your hunting success. To a large extent, the amount of practice a hunter gets with his weapon—rather than how much he paid for it—determines how successful he is. Practice builds confidence and also gets a hunter familiar with his weapon. This enables a hunter to operate his weapon quickly and reliably when the time comes to shoot. Knowing how to operate the action and safety without looking at your weapon can help you take advantage of many hunting situations and put game in your freezer, rather than just having another tale about the one that got away.

Regular practice with your weapon will also help you determine what you *and* your weapon are capable of in the field so you won't go beyond reasonable limits. Practice is also the best way to determine if any modifications should be made to your gun to best suit it to you and your shooting/hunting style. As a guide I meet a lot of hunters who have paid considerable sums of money to hunt Alaskan game animals. I have been lucky and most of my clients have been very good shots due to a lot of practice. However, I did see one brown bear hunter in last year's camp who I was glad not to guide. He was barely able to hit a two-foot square at 100 yards–with a solid rest. The worst part was, he was happy with that! I can't fathom why most hunters don't practice more often. Just a few hours before the season would improve some hunter's accuracy by 100 or 200% and their chance of success would go up just as much. There is no reason why any hunter with a decent rifle and a good scope cannot put every shot into a ten-inch circle at 300 yards with a solid rest; but I bet a full 50% of hunters cannot do this. For improved hunting success, *practice with your weapon.*

Chapter 17
FIREARM SAFETY

Although hunting is a relatively safe sport there are still many unnecessary accidents each year. Some of these involve firearms. One of the primary responsibilities of all hunters must be to handle firearms in a safe manner. As population and hunter densities increase in North America this is becoming increasingly important. By being responsible with firearms each hunter is not only protecting his own safety, but he is also doing his part to improve the image of hunting and ensure the future of hunting in America.

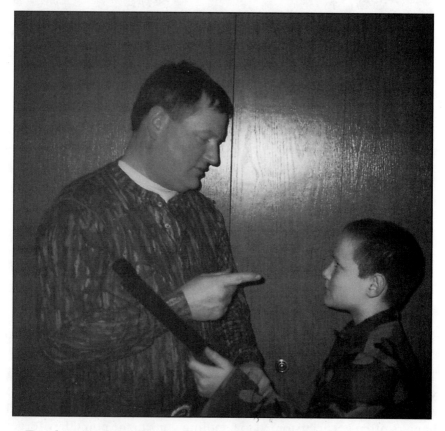

Teaching young hunters the rules of firearm safety rests on the shoulders of experienced hunters and shooters.

Firearms should always be pointed in a safe direction, even when taking trophy photos. Dan Sullivan's smile reflects his elation at taking this forty-inch ram.

Common sense should prevail whenever you are handling firearms. Three basic guidelines of firearm safety are: 1) Never point a gun at anything you do not intend to shoot. 2) Treat every gun as if it were loaded. 3) Always be sure of your target and what is beyond your target. Experienced hunters often get accustomed to handling guns to the point they forget basic rules of safety. These three rules should be so well ingrained in every hunter's mind so they are automatic habits which are *always* followed, no matter how tired or excited a hunter gets.

As a guide I have to be aware of how clients treat their guns around me for my own safety and because I am responsible for their welfare during the hunt. I am very strict about treating every gun as if it were loaded to the point that I have offended some hunters who insist they know how to handle firearms. I never point a firearm at anything I don't intend to shoot even if I've unloaded it and removed the bolt so it can't possibly fire, and I insist that my clients do the same with their weapons. But some clients have been upset when I point this out. My opinion is that these habits of gun safety must never be broken so no matter how tired or excited hunters may be, careless accidents won't happen. I feel anyone who is offended by strict adherence to safety rules should not be trusted with a gun, so I will continue to insist on safe gun handling at *all* times.

The complete list of firearm safety rules is often called the "Ten Commandments of Firearm (or Shooting) Safety." The wording varies between lists, but the following one is fairly complete.

TEN COMMANDMENTS OF FIREARM SAFETY

1) Never point a firearm at anything you do not intend to shoot. It is a tool which is made to kill so no horseplay is *ever* allowed with a firearm. Keep your finger off the trigger unless you intend to shoot, and keep the safety on until you are ready to shoot. Remember, a safety is not a fail-safe device; it is only a piece of equipment–and equipment sometimes fails. Never use a scope on a firearm to determine if something is human or otherwise.

2) Always control the direction of the muzzle so it is pointed in a safe direction. This includes carrying it in a manner so if you fall it will not be pointed at someone. Never pull a firearm toward you by the muzzle. Do not let a gun point at you or a bystander when you are cleaning it.

3) Treat *every* firearm as if it were *always* loaded.

4) Be sure of your target and everything beyond it within range. Be positive about the appearance of the game you are hunting and always have a sure backstop whenever you fire a gun. Remember that rifle bullets can kill up to five miles away and shotgun slugs can kill up to a mile away. When hunting with other hunters, agree on everyone's location, route and safe angles of fire.

5) Make sure the barrel and action are clear of any obstructions. Always check your ammunition for proper fit and only carry the proper ammunition for your weapon. The wrong ammunition can destroy your gun and cause you or bystanders serious injury. Make sure your weapon is in safe operating condition and you know how to operate it correctly. Wear hearing and eye protection whenever possible.

6) Unload firearms when they are not in use. It is best to leave the action open. Firearms carried in vehicles should be unloaded and in cases. Unload

firearms before taking them inside a house, and don't load them inside a house. Don't carry a loaded firearm unless you are ready to shoot.

7) Never cross over, climb up or under any fence, tree, ditch, log, etc. with a loaded weapon. Don't lean firearms against trees, logs, cars, boats, walls, etc. where they may fall and point in an unsafe direction.

8) Do not shoot firearms at hard, flat surfaces nor at water.

9) Store firearms and ammunition in separate locations in locked containers. These should be beyond the reach of children and out of sight of unauthorized handlers.

10) Avoid alcoholic beverages and drugs before or while handling or shooting firearms.

Handguns must be treated even more carefully than rifles for three reasons. They are shorter and more easily pointed in an unsafe direction; they often hold many rounds of ammunition which can be loaded into the chamber quickly; and they are often treated like toys by kids and adults alike.

Muzzleloading weapons have some special safety guidelines, mostly having to do with proper loading. These firearms must be loaded exactly as directed and with the proper components. People who try to experiment with amounts or types of components can create dangerous situations.

Muzzleloading firearms require more skill and care when loading than standard firearms to prevent accidents.

Explosions and injury can result from this type of careless behavior. Hunters wanting to use muzzleloaders must be willing to learn more about their weapons and exercise extra care when handling them.

All hunters should learn about their firearms and how to handle them safely. It is essential to both their safety and success as hunters.

Chapter 18
FIREARM CARE & MAINTENANCE

The three basic reasons to take good care of your firearms are personal safety, to protect your investment and to improve your hunting success. Firearms which are not functioning properly due to neglect are not safe even when handled carefully; it only takes a few minutes of time after each use to maintain an investment of from several hundred to several thousand dollars; and a clean, well-functioning firearm is much more likely to shoot accurately and reliably when you get one of those rare chances at a trophy animal. The combination of these reasons should be enough to convince hunters that it is in their best interest to learn and practice proper firearm care and maintenance.

Firearm maintenance varies somewhat depending on whether it is for home storage, transportation to and from the field or for actual field use. Before learning the differences between these three strategies, the basic causes of firearm deterioration and methods of protection must be understood.

The Enemies of Guns

The enemies of guns are rust caused by moisture, corrosion caused by chemical action and mechanical damage caused by physical abuse. Proper and thorough cleaning of a gun can reduce the first two effects to the bare minimum and extend the useful life of most guns to fifty or more years. Gun metal is susceptible to rusting and pitting due to moisture on its surface. Most guns are blued on the outer surface to help them resist moisture's effects, but the inside of the bore is just bare steel and must be scrupulously cared for to last a reasonable amount of time. Rusting or pitting can ruin the accuracy of a barrel in a just few years. Chemicals like salt in ocean air, substances in perspiration, blood, saliva or other body fluids, and acidic or basic foods all promote corrosion of gun metal. While these rust and corrosion-promoting agents cannot be entirely prevented from contacting our guns, how often they contact them and how much time they stay there can be limited by preventive care and timely cleanings. There are 100% stainless steel firearms and nickel-plated firearms available which are much more resistant to both rust and corrosion. However, even these high-price firearms still rust and corrode, albeit at a much slower rate. Proper maintenance is necessary to preserve all rifles, shotguns, muzzleloaders and handguns–no matter what type of steel they are made of.

Most mechanical damage can be prevented by careful handling and using protective cases during transportation. Using aluminum cleaning rods rather than steel can also help as hard metal can damage a barrel's crown and ruin accuracy. To further prevent damage, cleaning should be done from the breech end rather than the muzzle end whenever possible.

Cleaning for Home Storage

Following are the fourteen steps necessary to prepare a firearm for long-term storage in your home. Steps one through eight are applicable when cleaning a gun for any purpose. Steps nine through fourteen may vary depending on future plans for the gun.

1) Wash your hands to remove any substances which may be destructive to gun metal or stocks.

2) Empty the magazine and chamber.

3) Wipe entire gun—stock as well as all metal parts—with a dry cloth.

4) Warm the gun until completely dry.

5) Run one or two patches through the bore to remove any powder particles, dirt and moisture. Always use cleaning rods from the action end of a bolt action rifle to minimize damage to muzzle–other action types have to be cleaned from the muzzle end.

6) Run solvent-soaked patches through the bore next. Let solvent sit and soak a few minutes to help dissolve fouling.

7) Next, run a solvent-soaked brass or bronze brush through bore at least ten times to physically remove rust and fouling. Plastic brushes won't get all of the fouling out.

8) Use dry patches next to remove the solvent and fouling residue.

9) Run oiled patches through the bore to coat it with *light oil* if the firearm will be stored for a short time. The thickness of the oil coat varies from very light for a gun which is about to be used to a thick coat if the gun will be stored for more than a few days. If any residue still shows on patches, repeat steps five through seven. If the gun is to be stored for several months, it is better to use a *light grease* like Rig which has more viscosity than oil so it will not flow and leave exposed metal over time. Caution: do not touch oil or grease to any optics, this can ruin their fluorescent coating.

10) Wipe outer metal surfaces with oil or grease rag. Be sure to cover all surfaces of action, clip, bolt and metal sights. However, be careful around the firing pin hole. Oil or grease which gets in there can become gummy with dirt or cold temperatures and prevent the firing pin from striking a cartridge with enough force to detonate the primer. This can ruin your chances at a game animal at the least. If oil is suspected on the firing pin, soak the entire area in a good solvent like white gas and then be careful to

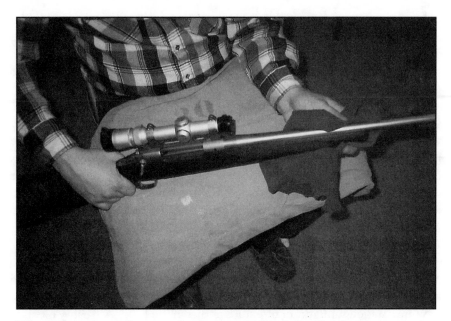

When cleaning a firearm for home storage, the final step is to wipe the metal parts with an oily rag so no fingerprints remain to cause rust.

not get more in there when re-oiling.

11) Wipe wood surfaces with boiled linseed oil–if compatible with finish.

12) Close action and magazine; release firing pin before storing.

13) Do not touch metal parts with bare fingers just before storage; use greasy fingers or gloves if the metal must be touched. Keep an oily rag handy to wipe off any fingerprints which may get on stored firearms when they are handled.

14) <u>Caution</u>: remember to run a clean patch through the bore before any use to remove excess oil or grease which could cause dangerous overpressuring if fired.

Long guns are best stored horizontally. If the muzzle is up during storage, oil is likely to run down into the action and gum it up. Oil may also run into the stock and weaken it. When storing guns for more than a few weeks and grease is used, the length of storage will determine how thick a coat of grease is needed. Always remember to store ammo separately from firearms.

Firearms should not be stored for any length of time in cases which can trap moisture inside. Any guns which are stored in cases should be muzzle down. Guns in storage should be given a periodic check for moisture and cleaned again if necessary.

Transportation

In addition to a good soft case for transporting firearms, more-protective hard cases are usually preferred for long distance transportation. Hard plastic or metal cases with locks are best. Guns should fit snugly to avoid scuffing or physical damage from the case itself during transit. Waterproof cases are often preferable, but since these cases can also trap moisture inside, guns left inside these must be checked frequently.

Guns should be cleaned for transportation just like for home storage with the possible exception of the grease coating, unless of course they will be inside a container for more than a few days. A good layer of grease is always good insurance in case humidity changes or travel mishaps prevent you from attending to your firearms. Grease inside and outside can easily be removed when you reach your destination. For short trips, a layer of light oil on a clean firearm is all that is needed. Just remember to remove any excess oil before firing the gun.

Field Use

Firearms suffer most of their damage from rust, corrosion and physical abuse while in the field. The first step to eliminating this is to always take clean guns into the field. A thorough home cleaning will remove anything which will attract moisture or dirt in the field. A freshly cleaned gun will also have a uniform coating of protective oil over all surfaces. Any heavy buildup should be wiped off the outside to avoid attracting dirt and to make the gun suitable for handling. Prior to any intended field use, the bore must also be cleaned of all grease and all but the lightest coating of oil to prevent overpressuring when it is fired.

For proper field care of firearms, some sort of maintenance should be continued for the duration of the hunt. A full-sized cleaning kit with a solid rod, a brass brush, patches, solvent and oil should be taken whenever possible. When weight and bulk limitations don't permit this, there are many small kits available. Some are small enough to fit in a pocket and come with a flexible rod. They often have all the basic components of larger cleaning kits–but in less quantity. For extreme cases of lightweight backpacking I sometimes get by with just an oil-soaked rag and a string in a Ziploc bag. I can wipe the exterior of the gun down daily with the oil rag, then tear off small pieces to pull through the bore with the string each day. This is the minimal amount of maintenance which should be done for a gun and then only on hunts of a week or less. Longer hunts really call for a flexible rod, brush and solvent to provide adequate protection for a valuable firearm.

In an emergency, field removal of debris can be done with any type of string and a piece of fabric. Simply tie a small piece of fabric or paper towel on one end of a short length of string, fishing line or shoelace. Unload the gun, open the action, drop the string down the bore by way of the breech and pull it through the muzzle. Tying a small button or other object on the free end of the string can sometimes help draw it through the

Hunters who frequently hunt in wet weather must be conscientious about oiling their firearms each evening to prevent rust–particularly if they hunt near salt water.

bore. Check the bore for cleanliness and repeat if necessary. If the muzzle is completely plugged, first use a twig, grass stem or other thin object to open the blockage; then use the string and patch to clean the bore.

Another item I sometimes carry in the field is a small rag soaked with boiled linseed oil. I have removed my rifle stock's excessively shiny finish and replaced it with this protective oil for the purpose of camouflage.

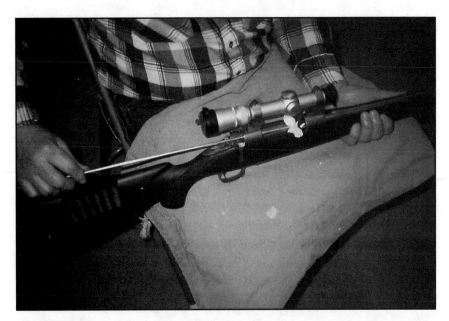

The most important part of the cleaning process is protecting the bore of a firearm. Pitting and rust inside the bore can ruin a firearm's accuracy in just a few years.

However, over the course of a long hunting trip in Alaska's extremely wet weather the oil finish can be diminished, so I use the oil rag to maintain the stock on longer hunts. Even for guns with a factory finish which has only worn off in a few spots, a linseed oil rag can be used in the field to help protect the wood in wet conditions.

During the course of any hunt, especially in wet weather, it is a good idea to run an oily or greasy patch over all the external metal surfaces of a gun once a day. This is particularly important when hunting near salt water to prevent the corrosive action of salty air or water. The bore should be cleaned and lightly oiled each night for the best protection. Then, each morning a dry patch should be run through the bore to remove any excess oil.

When hunting in cool or cold weather be alert for condensation when bringing guns into warm tents or cabins. All cold metal surfaces will produce condensation if they are brought into warm places each night and this can lead to rust. To avoid this, firearms can be wrapped tightly in coats or blankets before bringing them into warm tents so they will warm up slowly and not cause condensation. Firearms can also be left in an unheated tent or in a covered area outside to avoid this.

In very cold conditions hunters must be careful of snow or ice getting into a gun's bore, melting and then refreezing. This blockage is not very noticeable to a casual observer, but it is a very dangerous situation which must be watched for and completely removed before firing the gun. A similar thing happened to me on one brown bear hunt as I was following a wounded bear along a shallow creek through dense alders. I slipped and fell, not noticing that I had splashed water into the action of my rifle. It wasn't until a few hours later that I discovered the firing pin had frozen in place. Luckily for me I didn't run into that bear at close range with a nonfunctional rifle.

Excess oil or grease should be scrupulously removed before any cold weather hunt. Thickening of these lubricants can cause guns to malfunction in cold temperatures. Use a solvent like white gas to completely remove oil or grease. However, you must remember that the gun will be unprotected from moisture after doing this, so be conscientious about quickly removing any moisture that touches the gun or gets in the bore.

To prevent rain, ice, snow or any debris from going down the muzzle of a firearm in the field a short piece of black electrical tape can be placed over it. A short piece of tape like this will immediately be forced off when the gun is fired before excessive pressures can occur. It is a common habit in areas with a lot of rain. There are also disposable, rubber muzzle covers available which serve the same purpose.

Other enemies of firearms in the field are rodents which like to chew on gun stocks. Human perspiration leaves salt on stocks which entices porcupines, squirrels and mice to chew on them for this highly desirable mineral. Cleaning gun stocks and keeping them out of reach of gnawing rodents are two ways to help prevent this.

Proper firearm care for home storage, transportation and field use requires regular investments of time and energy and attention to detail. One obvious reward is the longer life and better appearance of your firearms. More important is the improved safety you will enjoy from properly maintained firearms. If these benefits aren't enough, the greater chances of hunting success you have with a perfectly functioning firearm should be a driving force to learn and practice proper firearm care and maintenance.

Proper firearm maintenance is one of the many ingredients of successful hunting. Chris McKinnon with an Alberta whitetail.

Chapter 19
BALLISTICS FOR THE HUNTER

For our purposes, we will define ballistics as the internal and external processes and results which occur when a firearm is discharged, i.e., what happens when a gun is shot. Most hunters do not need to know the physics behind the propulsion of a bullet down a gun's bore or the ensuing aerodynamics of the bullet in flight after it leaves the muzzle. However, a basic understanding of how caliber, bullet and load selection affect velocity, energy and accuracy will help them make better selections for their hunting needs. Hunters with a good understanding of ballistics can also make better decisions about which shots are reasonable–passing on low-percentage shots and knowing when to take the shot.

Ballistics Tables

Ballistics tables are an excellent source of information and a good place to begin. They can be found in reloading manuals or rifle/ammunition reference books. Each table will commonly give muzzle velocity, downrange velocities, energy at each distance, time of flight for each distance and bullet path information for a specific caliber with a specific bullet and powder charge. By looking at these tables it is fairly easy to compare different calibers, bullets and loads to find one for your specific needs. Thoughtful comparison will also reveal how bullet weight and powder charge affect velocity and energy in general, or for specific loads you use.

Here are two examples. The first is for a .30 caliber, 180 grain, spitzer bullet with a ballistic coefficient of .44.

Table 19.1

RANGE		MUZZLE	100 YDS	200 YDS	300 YDS	400 YDS
velocity, in fps		3000	2781	2572	2373	2183
energy in ft. lbs.		3596	3091	2644	2250	1904
time of flight, seconds		0.0000	0.1039	0.2160	0.3375	0.4693
bullet path	100yds	-1.5	0.0	-3.0	-11.3	-25.7
(inches) +/-	200yds	-1.5	1.5	0.0	-6.8	-19.7
line of sight	300yds	-1.5	3.8	4.5	0.0	-10.7

The second one is for a .338 caliber, 275 grain, semi-spitzer bullet with a ballistic coefficient of .46.

Table 19.2

RANGE		MUZZLE	100 YDS	200 YDS	300 YDS	400 YDS
velocity, fps		3300	3075	2862	2659	2464
energy in ft. lbs.		6650	5772	5000	4318	3707
time of flight, seconds		0.0000	0.0942	0.1953	0.3041	0.4213
bullet path	100yds	-1.5	0.0	-2.2	-8.6	-20.0
(inches) +/-	200yds	-1.5	1.1	0.0	-5.3	-15.6
line of sight	300yds	-1.5	2.9	3.6	0.0	-8.5

*(Speer Reloading Manual Number Ten, pp. 535 & 538)

Looking at these two tables illustrates a few important principles for hunters. Since bullet velocity times bullet weight equals bullet energy, a fast, heavy bullet has more energy (also called knockdown power by hunters) than a slower, lighter bullet. The first table shows that a .30 caliber, 180 grain bullet traveling at 3,000 feet per second (fps) has 3,596 ft. lbs. of energy at the muzzle; the second table shows that a .338 caliber, 275 grain bullet traveling at 3,300 fps has 6,650 ft. lbs. of energy at the muzzle. This is 85% more energy for a 53% heavier bullet traveling only 10% faster. The reason for the big jump in energy is because it is a result of a *multiplication* of the two factors. This is an important principle to remember for hunters who are looking for more knockdown power in their own gun or looking for a new gun for this reason. In fact, bullet weight varies more than speed between calibers so it is the more important of the two when energy is a concern. And since firearms kill by shock and tissue damage, bullet energy is a primary ingredient for quick kills.

The next aspect of a ballistic table to notice is how much the energy decreases as the bullet travels downrange. The .30 caliber bullet loses 47% of its energy between the time it leaves the muzzle and the time it travels 400 yards downrange. This can be significant when you are hunting tough animals like goats, elk, bear or whenever your gun is barely adequate for the animal you are hunting. Energy loss is another reason why experienced hunters shy away from shots which, although are within their accuracy range, are beyond the effective killing range of their weapon. Taking long shots when you are less likely to make a perfect shot is compounded by the fact that the bullet will have less energy to make up for a poor bullet placement.

Another fact which is apparent from ballistics tables concerns how we sight in our rifles. Hunters who zero in their rifles at 100 yards have probably never looked carefully at a ballistics table. Looking at the .30 caliber table shows that the bullet will drop 11.3 inches below the line of sight if zeroed in at 100 yards; but only 6.8 inches below the line of sight if zeroed in at 200 yards–a 4.5 inch difference. The only thing you have to give up to gain this advantage is your bullet will be 1.5 inches over line of sight at 100 yards–which is of no real consequence. By zeroing in your rifle at 200 instead of 100 yards, you can just shoot dead-on at (most) big game animals from 0- 300 yards without concerning yourself with holdover (how much higher you have to aim to hit your desired point of impact). And beyond that, your holdover will be significantly less than if you had zeroed in at 100 yards. If you zeroed in at 100 yards and had to shoot at 300 yards, an 11.3 inch drop would be too much for average-size big game animals and you would have to decide how much higher to aim than normal. Not having to calculate holdover is a tremendous benefit under actual hunting conditions when excitement runs high. The fewer judgement calls you have to make and the less to remember, the more likely you are to make a good shot under pressure.

These are three of the most obvious points hunters can glean from ballistics tables. There are literally hundreds of tables like this for every big game caliber, each with a different combination of bullet weight, bullet shape, and velocity. Further inspection of tables can assist hunters who either want to improve their general knowledge of available calibers or need to know more for handloading purposes.

Of course, most hunters will not need to study dozens of ballistics tables to make a wise cartridge choice. Many hunters will hunt with one group of hunters most of the time, so a caliber recommendation from them will be sufficient–as long as it works when they test it at the range and then in actual hunting situations. However, the minimum contact a hunter should have with ballistics tables is to have a copy of (or know by heart) the one which applies to the cartridge he uses regularly. This one table will give hunters the exact trajectory (bullet path) of their bullet so they know how to sight in their gun and how much holdover is necessary at any given range in the field. Just following this one rule will eliminate most missed shots at game.

Ballistics Concepts

For those hunters who wish to understand ballistics and its terms a little better there are a few commonly used terms to know. Velocity is the speed of a bullet measured in fps. Ballistic tables list muzzle velocities as well as downrange velocities at specific distances. Both are useful for energy calculations. The energy of a bullet is calculated by multiplying velocity by bullet weight and is listed in foot-pounds. The ballistic coefficient is the ratio of the sectional density of a bullet to the coefficient of its form (this ratio is stamped on bullet boxes so you do not have to figure it out yourself). The ballistic coefficient affects how a bullet flies through the air. The sectional density is a bullet's weight in pounds, divided by the square of its diameter in inches (also stamped on bullet boxes). The sectional density is also a factor in how a bullet flies.

Bullet refers to only the missile—usually made of lead plus other metals. Remember that a cartridge is composed of a case, a primer, powder and a bullet. The jacket of a bullet is the outer layer—which is designed to control expansion. The core is the inner, softer portion of the bullet. The bullet becomes a projectile when it is in flight. Expansion refers to how quickly and how much a bullet widens after striking an animal. Mushrooming is another term for this, used because this is the desirable shape of the bullet after it expands. Bullets which don't mushroom correctly often break up and don't penetrate as well as a perfectly mushrooming bullet. Penetration is how far a bullet goes into an animal. Penetration and expansion are trade-offs. A bullet which expands too quickly may not penetrate far enough to reach vital organs and produce a quick kill. A bullet which penetrates too far, i.e., completely through an animal, may not transfer *all* of its energy before exiting. This is important with large, dangerous animals which need to be slowed or knocked down so follow-up rounds can be fired if necessary.

Bullet styles include hollow point—which has a hollow front section for quick expansion; round nose soft point—used for penetration before energy transfer; spitzer soft point—which is fairly pointed and has better penetration and flight characteristics than round-nose, but still transfers energy well; boattail—which has a tapered rear portion and the flattest trajectory; spire point—a conically shaped bullet used for its good flight characteristics and good penetration; full metal jacket—which provides maximum penetration on large, tough game animals; and partition bullet—containing a layer of jacket material crosswise through the core which helps it retain weight during expansion, thus delivering more energy. There are also rifled slugs which are used in shotguns and are short-range projectiles. Shotgun slugs used for deer are usually around one ounce (437.5 grains) in weight and have a muzzle velocity of less than 2,000 fps. These two factors make them a short-range weapon. For comparison, a typical rifled slug shot from a 12 gauge slug barrel loses about 40% of its velocity in the first 100 yards—whereas a .30-06 bullet typically loses only 12% of its velocity. Slugs are also less accurate—100-yard groups of six inches are common versus under two inches for most .30-06 rifles. For these reasons slugs should only be used at distances under 100 yards.

The debate over which bullets are better brush-busters does not have clear-cut answers. In the past, common belief was that heavy, round-

There is such a wide array of firearms currently available that hunters must know basic ballistics concepts to choose an appropriate caliber and style to suit their hunting requirements.

nose, slow-moving bullets would not be deflected as much as faster-moving, pointed bullets. Newer evidence indicates just the opposite is true. What is clear is that no bullets are good at going through more than a few twigs and retaining their direction and shape—they mushroom and change course—so don't try to shoot through anything but the smallest amount of light brush, and this should only be attempted if absolutely necessary and at close range.

Magnum cartridges have more power than most cartridges of the same caliber. They provide more velocity for long distance shooting and more knockdown power for hunting dangerous game. Magnum cartridges are usually belted–meaning they have a visible, additional strip of metal around their base to hold the extra pressures these cartridges develop. Magnum cartridges produce more recoil and noise when fired, and are disliked by some shooters for these reasons.

Recoil is the backward "kick" felt by a shooter as energy from the firing of a cartridge is sent back through the gun stock. This can be reduced with the use of a recoil-reducing device on the muzzle, sometimes called a muzzle brake. Muzzle blast is the noise and shock wave sent forward and to the sides of the muzzle as a round is fired. More of this energy is redirected to the sides when a muzzle brake is used, so bystanders should be careful and stand behind the muzzle to avoid getting more of the shock and noise from the rifle.

Hunters pursuing open-country game like Dall sheep must understand the trajectory of their rifle/cartridge combination to expect success. Kelly Stevenson with a nice ram.

Trajectory is the bullet's path as it flies. A flatter trajectory is preferable for hunters because their bullets will drop less and holdover will be less. Line of sight refers to the straight line through the sights to the aiming point. Holdover is the amount of vertical distance the aiming point has to be raised to allow for bullet drop in order to hit a target at a long distance. Windage is the amount of horizontal correction of sights or sighting point to allow for wind deflection. Wind deflection is the amount of horizontal distance a bullet deviates from its original line because of the affects of wind. This can be significant at longer distances. Accuracy is the measure of a gun's or bullet's ability to consistently group all shots close together. A group is a cluster of bullet strikes resulting from aiming at one point on an intended target. Minute of angle refers to 1/60th of one degree in angular measurement. At 100 yards this equals approximately one inch. A gun which shoots minute-of-angle groups will shoot all shots in a group into a one inch circle (measured from the centers of the bullet holes) at 100 yards. Only high-quality rifles are capable of doing this.

Proper application of ballistics to hunting can help hunters choose the correct calibers and cartridges and then shoot them better. Most hunters will choose to shoot factory-loaded ammunition because it is more convenient than handloading their own. There is plenty of variety in factory loads to meet the needs of most hunters. Handloading allows interested hunters to produce less-expensive ammunition, make a greater variety of loads for a greater range of hunting situations, and get more accuracy out of their firearms by tuning cartridge components to suit each gun. And some individuals just get more satisfaction out of their hunts by being more involved in the details of their firearm's performance. There are also custom loads available for hunters who want more performance from their firearms, but don't want to handload themselves. Custom loads can also improve accuracy, increase knockdown power, and provide more variety for single firearms, just like handloading does.

Sighting-in

Proper sighting-in of a firearm is crucial to hunting success. It is advantageous for three reasons: it gives the hunter practice with his shooting skills; gives him familiarity with his weapon so he can function successfully under pressure; and, most basically, aligns the gun's bore with the sights so it will shoot where the hunter points it. A careful consideration of ballistics will help hunters make good choices of caliber, bullet and load before even going to the firing range. Knowing the effects the point of zero you choose has on your field shooting (which has already been discussed) is also a useful preparation for the sighting-in process.

Bolt action rifles (or pistols) should be bore-sighted before ever firing a round at the range. This can save unnecessary sighting-in rounds by ensuring the point of impact is close to where the sights point and not completely off the paper (or whatever target you will use). By removing the bolt (using an unloaded gun, of course), and placing the rifle on a steady rest, the point of impact can be seen by looking down the bore and estimating where the very center of it points. Select an object at least fifty yards out for best results. Then, without moving the gun, look through the sights and find the point of aim to see if these two line up. Adjustments are made to the sights until the two points are as closely aligned as possible. By bore-sighting in this manner, the first round fired should strike within ten inches of the desired point of impact for even a novice at this procedure. I can bore-sight my own rifle to within four or five inches every time. I often use bore-sighting in the field for a quick check on my rifle's sights if there is any chance they may have been knocked out of line. Only taking a few minutes, it is a comforting thing to do whenever you are in the field anticipating a shot of great importance to you and want to be as sure as possible of the outcome. Unfortunately, bore-sighting is not possible with other action types.

The actual sighting-in process should be done with sand bags, or other stable pads to place the rifle on—which are all on top of a bench rest. A bench rest lets the shooter sit comfortably so he does not exert unwanted pressure in any direction which will cause the gun to move before or during the firing of sighting rounds. Whenever shooting a firearm from a rest the barrel should not touch anything. Barrel contact may change the gun's point of impact for that shot, and throw off your attempt to sight it in or, worse yet, cause you to miss a game animal. Gun stocks are meant for your hands to hold during firing, barrels should not anything.

When a bench rest is not available, a stable platform for the gun which also allows the shooter to be relaxed will do. If the gun is expected to be close to zero already from previous shooting or bore-sighting, groups of three shots should be taken with several minutes in between groups for the barrel to cool. A hot barrel will usually have a different point of impact than a cool one. Use the center of these three-shot groups as a reference point to fine-tune the sights. A spotting scope is useful for this so groups can be checked without walking up to the target each time. When you do walk up to the target, tape or a dark marking pen can be used to mark all bullet holes so they won't be confused with any additional shots you may take.

If the firearm has not been sighted in with the present sight attachment or cartridge selection, the first thing to do is to find out where it is striking. It may strike the target on the first shot, in which case you can continue as the above procedure outlines. If it does not strike the target, the point of impact must be found to proceed with the sighting-in process. It helps to have a bystander to spot your bullet impacts and tell you which way to adjust the sights so your bullets will strike the target. If no one is nearby to help with this, you need a backstop like a dusty dirt pile to shoot into so you can see where the bullet strikes. Once the rifle is close enough to zero to strike the target, then you can proceed with the fine-tuning process by shooting successive three-shot groups as described in the previous paragraph.

There are some basic rules of marksmanship to follow which will help you at the range as well as in the field.
1) Get a good sight picture.
2) Take a normal breath.
3) Relax your muscles.
4) Let out about half of your breath, then slowly squeeze the trigger.
5) Apply a steadily increasing amount of pressure until you fire.
6) Hold the sight picture and your position as much as possible after the shot; this follow-through is vital to good shooting and to avoid flinching.
Most rifles can be safely dry-fired. Check with a gunsmith if you are

Confidence in your rifle's knockdown power and your own shooting ability are necessary before hunting large, dangerous game. Dan Manny with a ten-foot Alaskan brown bear.

unsure about yours. Dry-firing can be a great way to practice your technique without going to the range, or to tune up just before a hunt. Your trigger finger will become "educated" with practice and develop a feel for the trigger. All good shooters have an educated trigger finger.

When you feel the rifle has been zeroed at your predetermined distance (a 200-yard zero is best for most hunting situations), be sure and shoot a few single shots with cooling time in between. This will assure you that a cool barrel—which is most likely what you will have in field conditions—will shoot where you want it to.

After your firearm is zeroed in, you should also practice with it in shooting positions you may have in the field. Prone (lying on the ground, across a mound, or across a log), sitting, kneeling or standing—in order of shooting accuracy—are the common positions to practice. All of these are more likely positions than a bench rest to be used in a hunting situation. The two keys to shooting well in all these positions is to find a *stable* position that you can *repeat* each time you use it. Knowing exactly how to get into each position in the field saves time and gives you confidence–two important ingredients of successful hunting.

Shooting practice and the sighting-in process are also times to assess the fit of your gun's stock and the trigger pull. Your gun's stock should feel

Tony Russ used a .30-06 and 220 grain bullets to down this paddle-horn moose in 1976. Firearms for moose hunting must be fairly heavy to put down these large creatures.

comfortable—not too long or short, nor with too much or too little drop in it. The weight and the length of the trigger pull should also feel comfortable to you. Test both stock and trigger pull in all positions first, and then decide if they need adjustments. Find a good gunsmith if you want any work done on these components to make your rifle fit you. Adjustments can help you feel more comfortable as well as shoot better. I adjust my rifle triggers to a three-pound pull weight because I shoot better with this light trigger weight. However, most gunsmiths will not set a trigger that light because they have too much liability in case of an accident—and most hunters do not like their triggers this light anyway. Find out what best suits you and set up your gun in that manner. These adjustments, along with a good background in ballistics, are good ways to improve your hunting success.

Chapter 20
RANGE ESTIMATION

Accurate range estimation is vital to a hunter's marksmanship. The ability to accurately guess longer distances for stalking purposes or time planning can also have a positive or negative effect on hunting success. There are several simple ways to learn and practice this skill, so there is no reason why every big game hunter should not be fairly proficient at it. There are also some very precise rangefinders on the market for hunters willing to spend the extra money. Even the most expensive, flattest-shooting rifles and the most innovative bow designs available today are more effective weapons in the hands of a hunter who can accurately estimate range.

Methods of Estimation

There are several methods of estimation which should be learned, practiced and used in appropriate situations. Each method is best suited for a particular range of distances and will be most accurate within that range. However, after making a range estimation, experienced hunters will often use an alternative method to determine if the first guess is plausible. Often, extremely poor guesses can be detected and corrected in this manner.

The first thing a hunter should learn is how to step off 100 yards. This is a common distance which forms the basis of many range estimation methods. At 5 ft. 9 inches, I need 103 steps to cover 100 yards on flat ground. I check myself regularly at shooting ranges which have 100, 200 and 300 yards marked off. I have also noticed that the telephone poles in my neighborhood are set 100 yards apart, so I check my step length whenever I walk down my street. Uneven ground, up and down-slopes, snow and cumbersome clothing will all affect the length of your step, so adjustments have to be made whenever these—or other—adverse conditions are present. Practice will teach each individual how much to compensate for each condition.

Once you have determined your step length and know what the first 100 yards of distance looks like, you can practice with the 100-yard intervals method. This method is most useful for distances of 100-500 yards. First, pick an object you think is within this interval. Next, imagine how many 100-yard intervals will fit in the distance between you and the object. Of course, the last interval may be only a portion of 100 yards. Realize, too, that each succeeding 100-yard interval after the first will look shorter than the previous one, i.e. the second interval looks shorter than the first, the third interval looks shorter than the second, etc. As you would expect, each succeeding interval after the first will also be harder to estimate accurately. Regular practice is the best way to improve accuracy. A good way to practice this method is while walking down a long, straight road. Select objects within 500 yards, guess the distance, step it off, and then look back to where you were when you made your guess. If you are lucky enough to have telephone poles with 100-yard spacing like I do in my neighborhood, you can use these to check your estimates without walking to the distant objects. Simply block the telephone poles out of view and guess a distance. Then look at the poles to verify the accuracy of your guess.

I often practice this interval method while walking during the summer to get ready for hunting season. As a sheep hunting guide I need to be able to tell my (firearms) clients how far they are about to shoot. But, since I am also a bowhunter as well as a bowhunting guide, I need to be able to guess shorter distances from 10 to 70 yards. To do this, I use a modified form of this method using ten-yard intervals. Except for the size of the interval, I employ the same principles as the 100-yard interval method.

The next method is most useful for distances from 100 to 1000 yards. I call it the <u>halfway</u> method. I often use it to check an estimate I have made using the 100-yard intervals method. To use the halfway method, first pick the halfway point to the target to which you are estimating the distance. Then estimate the range to the halfway point and double it for the final range estimation. This method is a useful check for any length of range estimation because many times it will quickly point out when gross errors have been made.

The next method, called the <u>appearance of objects</u> method, also works within 1,000 yards and serves as a good check on other methods of range estimation. This method requires that the hunter knows how specific characteristics of his target look at given ranges. It is only useful to someone with experience at observing the specific target at different ranges. Practicing this method requires actual field time, which is one good reason to get into the field during the off season. Game animals are the obvious targets to practice recognizing features of at different distances, but common vegetation which is a uniform size will also work.

Range-finding rifle scopes with two horizontal reticules work on this principle. They rely on the constant spacing between their two reticules to use as a guideline. By knowing the average size of the animal you are looking at, a comparison to the reticule spacing will tell you how far away it is. These range-finding scopes aren't used much anymore, but the principle is still valid. Experienced hunters can still get an idea of the distance of a

Accurate range estimation is vital to bowhunters. A miscalculation of only a few yards will often mean the difference between a clean kill and a clean miss. This is George P. Mann with a large barren ground caribou.

well-known animal by looking through their scope (with a normal reticule design) and mentally comparing the image to past images at known distances. I often do this in an offhand position to see how much the crosshairs are moving on the animal. I know I can just barely hold the horizontal crosshair within the outlines of the back and brisket of a sheep-sized animal within 300 yards, so the amount the crosshairs waver gives me a rough idea of the distance. This is just one more way to check your range estimation from one of the other methods already outlined. The more experience you have with your scope and rifle setup, the better this method will work.

The <u>bracketing method</u> is most useful for ranges over 500 yards, but it can be used for short distances as a good check on other estimation methods. Because it is best at ranges beyond shooting distances, its real value is not so much for estimating shooting distances as for estimating how much stalking still needs to be done to get within a reasonable shooting range. To use this method, a hunter estimates two distances—first estimating that the target is no farther than x distance, then estimating it is no closer than y distance. The average of these two is the estimated range. This method is helpful when terrain or conditions make other methods unreliable. Sheep hunters often use this method when looking over ridges and canyons or through fog or rain—conditions which distort normal estimation methods.

This method is often used to estimate longer distances to plan how much time will be needed for a stalk. Making good estimates in these cases can save hunters from stalking animals which are too far away to reach within remaining daylight hours or, conversely, passing up a stalk on an animal which is reachable before dark.

Another check to use on a range estimation is to walk toward the object and reassess the guess. This works best at ranges within 500 yards. Even taking three or four steps toward the object—while watching closely for how much closer the object appears—can often tell you if your estimate is reasonable. If you are uncertain about the distance to an animal and have reached the last patch of cover, a variation of this test is to backtrack twenty yards and estimate again. This can either support your first estimation so you can go ahead with the shot, or make you adjust the first estimation and perhaps avoid a missed shot.

Another good practice for hunters is to make distance estimations while in motorized vehicles with odometers. Automobiles, ATV's and snowmachines can all be used to help hunters learn what one mile, two miles or even greater distances look like. Off-road vehicles are particularly useful to hunters since we are typically guessing distances over countrysides and not down roadways. Trying to guess distances of a mile or more will help hunters gauge distances in the field where accurate estimations can affect their success. Spot & stalk hunters often depend on their ability to accurately assess long distances to determine feasibility of stalking a distant animal. It can be particularly helpful for backpackers who travel long distances on foot. Accurate distance estimation for them can save hours of walking after too-distant animals or help them make good decisions about when to camp—instead of being caught by darkness with no campsite nearby.

Practicing all these methods will be useful for most hunters. There are times when even the best range estimators are uncertain about their own guesses or are challenged by hunting partners. In these cases, using additional methods can instill confidence in an estimation or persuade a partner. Hunters who practice all these methods can use them quickly in hunting situations when time always seems to be crucial to success.

Factors Affecting Accuracy

There are many factors which affect the accuracy of range estimations. Knowing what these are and how they affect estimations can improve a hunter's precision at this skill.

Light is the first factor to consider. Anything other than full daylight with the sun overhead and clear skies can affect range estimations. Dim light early or late in the day makes objects look farther away than they really are. Bright sunlight from your back shining on objects will make them look closer, while sun shining in your eyes from behind an object will

Distances in open country can be deceiving even to experienced hunters, but practice with the help of ATV's with odometers can improve estimation accuracy. Stan George with a caribou taken by Kevin Keene in the Talkeetna Mts. of Alaska.

make it look farther away. Rain, snow or dust in the air makes objects look farther away. Fog also does this, sometimes to extremes. On one recent bowhunt for deer as my partner was beginning a stalk, I reminded him the heavy fog would make the deer look much farther away. As I sat there waiting for my partner to return, another buck appeared behind me within bow range. Even though I realized the deer was closer than it looked in the heavy fog, I still shot over it three times in a row.

The nature of the object also affects your judgement about distance. Objects with a distinct outline look closer than other objects at the same distance, but with a fuzzy or irregular outline. Objects with a contrasting color or higher light reflectivity than the background will look closer than they are. Objects which blend into their background seem to be farther away. A partially hidden object looks farther away than if it were completely exposed.

As many hunters can tell you, the terrain over which you are trying to judge distance will also affect the precision of your estimations. Objects which are uphill look closer than they are; those which are downhill look farther away than the actual distance. Objects look much closer than they are in flat, open country; a little closer than they are in open, irregular terrain; and farther away than the actual distance in timber or brushy areas.

Rangefinders

Range estimation is useful when deciding whether to shoot, attempt to stalk a little closer or hope the game comes closer. Not knowing the correct distance may cause you to make the wrong decision, so range estimations must be accurate to help—not hinder—your hunting success. For those who can't make good range estimations and those who want more precise estimates, there are rangefinders. These devices use one of two methods for distance calculations. The relatively low-cost models, called coincidence rangefinders, rely on the user's ability to bring two images into focus as one image, using a set of lenses much like an SLR camera. This type of rangefinder is most often used by bowhunters for distances of up to 100 yards, but there are models made for distances up to 1,000 yards which are useful for all hunters. These are accurate to within 5-10%, depending on the brand *and* the operator.

The other, much more expensive type of rangefinders use a laser beam to measure distance. A fine laser light is sent out from the rangefinder, reflects off the target and is picked up again by the rangefinder. The elapsed time is used to automatically calculate the distance–which is displayed on a digital readout. These rangefinders are quick, easy to use, lightweight and accurate to within a few yards. There are lower-priced models useful to 400 yards and top-end models which work out to 4,000 yards. I am able to use my 600-yard model successfully with only one hand and get a good reading within four seconds of pointing it at an animal. One-hand use is vital for us bowhunters so we can quickly get an accurate distance without setting down our bow or moving unnecessarily to spook our nearby quarry. After using mine for the first time this year, I never want to go bowhunting (or guiding) without it.

Some manufacturers have also built laser rangefinders right into their binoculars and rifle scopes. These make handy dual-purpose units for those hunters with enough money (several thousand dollars) to purchase them. In addition to the prohibitive high cost, another drawback to these ranging binoculars or rifle scopes is their excessive weight, but they may be worth the extra weight to some hunters–particularly if they are not traveling far or have motorized transportation.

Besides finding distances to game you are about to shoot at, laser rangefinders have other worthwhile uses for hunters. One use is to find both the distance to a game animal and the distance to a possible shooting location. By calculating the mathematical difference between the two, the result can be used to decide if the position will be close enough to shoot from–or if you need to look for another spot. This can save you from wasting time sneaking to a poor shooting position, which is especially important for bowhunting when as little as ten additional yards can mean you are out of range.

This laser rangefinder by Bushnell weighs just 9 1/2 ounces, measures ranges from 20 to 600 yards, sells for about $300 and can be operated with only one hand.

Laser rangefinders are also a great aid when practicing range estimations. With one of these handy devices you can sit in one spot, make dozens of guesses out to several hundred yards and then find the actual distances–all within a few minutes, and without walking to each target you've chosen. Estimates can be checked quickly from any location, even sitting inside buildings or automobiles because most laser rangefinders will work right through glass.

Laser rangefinders can also measure distances which otherwise, we can never know for sure. Some examples of these are distances over ravines, gorges, or rivers which we cannot step off, but we often encounter while hunting. Other examples are when you are looking over very uneven ground with shallow gullies or boulders which must be walked around. In these types of terrain, it is very hard to be accurate when stepping off the distance, so you can never really be sure of the range. There is also the unique case of looking up into the tops of trees and estimating distance, or looking out of treestands. Many bowhunters as well as gun hunters use one of these devices to range several spots around their stand each time they climb into one. If they have time they can still range an animal which walks within shooting distance, but if time is crucial they may just rely on their memory of the predetermined ranges and quickly take the shot. All of these circumstances present immeasurable ranges without a rangefinding device. Laser rangefinders, in particular, can give reliable distances for

To successfully hunt deer in open fields like this often requires good range estimation for long shots. Photo courtesy of McKinnon & Co. Outfitters

these and other situations—either when actually hunting or when practicing range estimation. The results can be unbelievable for hunters who have been guessing at these immeasurable ranges for years without any reliable feedback (their hunting partner's vociferous disagreements don't count since he was only guessing, too). When I used a laser rangefinder for the first time in the mountains of Alaska this year I realized I had been habitually underestimating many distances over 200 yards. Now, I will learn what distances within my rangefinder's 600-yard range look like—in the most difficult types of terrain. Knowing what I do now, I don't think any hunter should be without one of these devices.

Range estimation is a part of good marksmanship as well as effective stalking and planning during a hunt. Practice at this skill is necessary for accuracy and confidence. Rangefinders—the laser variety in particular—can greatly improve a hunter's range-estimating skills and marksmanship; both of which will lead to more hunting success.

Chapter 21
OPTICS

Binoculars, rifle scopes and spotting scopes are some of the most important pieces of gear for hunters. Since we basically hunt with our eyes, hunters without good optics are at a severe disadvantage in the field. Optics have literally hundreds (maybe thousands) of uses in the field. A few of the uses I have employed them for are: spotting game, judging antlers & horns, verifying my target, shooting at game, looking for possible stalking or hiking routes, looking for water, looking for my partner, looking at other hunters, looking for my tent, looking at animals in my camp, looking for berries on a distant hillside, looking for game trails, watching wildlife, watching wounded game, watching to see if game can sense me, looking for wind direction and velocity, looking at the size of a possible river crossing, looking for rising fish and looking at bullet holes in a target. This list can be added to almost indefinitely because optics are so useful to hunters for many parts of a hunt.

Basic Characteristics of All Good Optics

There are some basics to look for whenever choosing hunting optics. Poor optics are almost useless to hunters, so high-quality items should always be used. Some hunters balk at paying hundreds of dollars for binoculars or spotting scopes, but this is a mistake. Good optics will last for ten, twenty or even thirty years with a little care. Even a five-hundred dollar set of binoculars amortized over twenty years is only twenty-five dollars per year—which is less than most hunters spend on gas each season. Viewed this way, expensive optics aren't really that costly—particularly when their value to a hunter is considered. Although the initial outlay of cash is daunting, purchasing high-quality optics is one of the best investments a hunter can make in his future success.

There are some characteristics to look for when shopping for any type of optic. Look through the optic to check for clarity of the image. The quality of the lens helps determine this as does the anti-reflective coatings on them. The best optics are multi-coated on every lens surface to reduce reflections and improve light transmission. Single-coated lenses should be avoided by serious hunters who want the most from their optics. A thorough in-store comparison of optics will show a hunter which ones are brighter and clearer. Brightness is important for hunters who need to see in low light conditions—a common situation. Brightness is also affected by the size of the objective lens, which is the one farthest away from the viewer. The trade-off for larger lenses is increased bulk, weight and cost.

Another critical feature of optics is their water-resistance. Optics which fog inside when used in wet weather are worse than useless to hunters who depend on their optics. Losing the use of his optics during a hunt can easily prevent a hunter from being successful had the optics functioned properly. I suggest always buying waterproof optics to limit the chances of this happening. This is no guarantee the optic won't fog, but reputable manufacturers will replace them if they do. High-quality, waterproof optics are the best way to minimize chances of a field failure, and they are well worth the expense.

Binoculars

A pair of good binoculars is second only to a hunter's rifle on the list of the most essential pieces of hunting gear. It is not unreasonable for them to cost more than a hunting rifle. Trying to use a rifle scope in place of binoculars is poor hunting strategy in almost all situations. A rifle scope is usually of less magnification, more tiring to use, creates more movement which can spook game and may result in pointing a rifle at another hunter while verifying a target. In some cases when a spotting scope is carried, binoculars may not be necessary, but both optics should be taken on many types of hunts.

The size of binoculars you buy depends on the intended use. Magnification of seven to ten power and objective lenses of from 40 to 50 mm are good ranges for most hunters. If you will only buy one pair, 8x X 42mm are a good all-around choice. In binocular descriptions, the first number indicates the magnification and the second number is the size of the objective lenses. For most uses, 8 X 42's aren't too large to carry all day, but have enough magnification and brightness to be used for hours of glassing without eye strain. Binos with over ten-power magnification can be hard to hold still enough to get a clear view. Several hours of looking in this manner will tire out the hunter's eyes and diminish his ability to see clearly. Binoculars with objective lenses above 50mm may bring in more light, but they can be bulky. Size does not necessarily mean more brightness, so don't buy on this criterion alone. Quality is always the most important thing to consider.

Compact binoculars can be useful for many hunting situations. Sizes of 8x X 25mm or 10x X 30mm are commonly used by hunters. Ten-power compacts may have too much magnification for some users, but others like them. Brightness is often reduced in the compacts, but good glasses will still gather a lot of light and brighten the view. Compacts' biggest selling feature is their small size and weight—often less than 10 ounces and small enough to fit in a shirt pocket. I carry a pair of 10x X 25mm's when sheep hunting in Alaska. I also carry a 45-power spotting scope for serious looking,

*Binoculars are one of the most important items of gear for hunters.
By using optics which enhance visual acuity, hunters can see
several times as much game as they would see with their eyes alone.*

but the compacts are handy for frequently checking mountainsides while hiking. Having to stop, take out a spotting scope, and set it up is time-consuming and bothersome, so the bino's 10 ounces are worth carrying.

All binoculars should have a center focus ring. It is quicker and just as reliable as individually focusing rings on each barrel. A strong, wide carrying strap is mandatory for binos which are often carried for hours every day. Rubber armored binos are a little heavier, but quieter and more durable for those willing to carry the extra weight. Binos should also have eyecups for keeping your eyes the correct distance from the lenses and to reduce glare in bright sunshine. I'll never forget one bespectacled brown bear hunter I guided who didn't know what these were for. He complained that during his twenty-odd years of hunting he never had much use for binoculars because the aperture was so tiny. He had never pushed in the eyecups, so his eyeglasses kept his eyes too far away from the lenses to see well. When I pushed them in for him, he was flabbergasted at how well he could see.

Spotting scopes are invaluable for most types of open-country hunting. Variable scopes of 15x - 45x are a good choice for most hunting situations. Larger scopes are heavier, bulkier and not useful in many conditions. Unless there is full daylight and no heat waves, 30 power is about all that is practical to use. The 60x scopes can only be used at their maximum in perfect conditions in the field. Spotting scopes are so useful for seeing more detail in situations where binoculars are frequently used that I seldom go hunting without mine.

Rifle Scopes

Rifle and handgun scopes are used almost universally in place of open sights because of the tremendous advantage they give hunters. With the exception of only a few circumstances when open sights are preferable—like when following a wounded brown bear into thick alders—there are scopes from 1x to 24x which are suited to almost every type of hunting.

The most popular and useful sighting reticles are duplex reticles. These consist of fine crosshairs in the middle of the scope's view plus four thicker sections on the outer portions of the crosshairs. The fine crosshairs allow precise aiming in normal light and the heavy crosshairs are still visible in low light conditions, and useful for quickly aiming at moving animals. Fine crosshairs, crosshairs plus posts, aiming dots, and other reticle configurations are also available for hunters who prefer these.

Most hunters choose variable scopes because of their versatility. Now that the unreliability of variables—their biggest drawback in the recent past—has been overcome, there is no reason hunters should not use a variable scope. The 3x - 9x is still the most popular size, although it is larger than most hunters really need. 1.5x - 6x or 2x - 7x are the best choices for most big game hunting as 9x is seldom necessary. A magnification of six or seven power will let most hunters see well beyond ranges at which they, or their guns, can shoot accurately. Handgun scopes are typically 1x - 4x because they are a short-range weapon.

The drawbacks to having a larger scope than necessary are extra cost, bulk and height. Larger scopes are harder to pack safely, carry quietly and tend to bang on objects more often—thus getting out of alignment more often. They also offer a narrower field of view—making it harder to locate animals quickly in the scope (this has cost *many* hunters their chance at an animal). Field of view (f.o.v.) can be increased in any size variable by choosing wide-angle models. This is a good way to get an increased f.o.v. without increasing scope height and minimizing weight.

Although objective lens size helps determine light gathering ability of the scope, 40 to 50mm is enough for most hunters. This range of objective size will be bright enough to be used in any low light conditions a hunter will encounter. Lenses larger than 50mm will not be appreciably brighter except in absolute darkness—which is after normal shooting hours.

Compact scopes are lighter and smaller than normal and, when combined with wide-angle objectives, can still be quite bright. They are very popular with hunters who carry their guns for many miles.

Both very small, and very large, rifle scopes may pose mounting problems on average-length rifle actions. Extension rings can solve some

Spotting scopes are invaluable for hunting animals with great eyesight. Tony Russ is using a spotting scope to observe sheep on the distant mountain while staying safely out of their visual range.

of these problems, but avoiding extreme sizes is easier. When mounting scopes be sure and check tube size to get the correct mounting rings; both one-inch and 30mm tubes are common. Also remember to use Loctite or a similar substance to secure the mounting screws, so they don't loosen after repeated firings and cause a missed shot.

Whichever variable a hunter uses, in most situations it should be set on the lowest power until game is sighted. Having a scope set at the lowest power will give the hunter the widest f.o.v. if a moving animal suddenly appears at close range and time is crucial. If the animal is not moving quickly, even if it is at a great distance, there should be time to bring the scope's magnification up to the desired power and make the shot. Of course, in some situations a hunter expects an animal to appear at long range for just a few seconds. At these times, a hunter should have his scope set at a higher power beforehand.

Cleaning optics correctly can preserve their usefulness for a full twenty or more years. Any dust or grit will scratch a lens surface if it is rubbed. To avoid scratching lens coatings or even the glass itself and damaging your optics, treat them as carefully as an expensive camera. The first step is to blow off dust with an air brush like those used for cameras or by lightly blowing on the lens. The next thing to do in optimal conditions is to flood the lens with distilled water, roll it around a little, pour it off and air dry. If this doesn't remove all the smudges, use lens tissue

Optics must be handled and cleaned with care to prevent damaging their glare-resistant coatings. The coatings reduce glare and allow hunters to use optics much more effectively in bright sunshine.

with a small drop of lens cleaning fluid on it. Rub gently in a circular motion with as little pressure as possible to clean the lens. One option for field cleaning is to carry a lens-cleaning pen made specifically for hunters to clean their optics. Since these pens place a solid surface on the lens, be as gentle with these as possible to avoid damage.

If you have nothing else when you need to clean a lens, a soft, clean tissue or soft, clean piece of fabric will do. First blow on the lens to remove dust or water. Then gently brush the lens surface with the clean material using as little pressure as possible. This is the most common way optics are scratched, so keep this practice to a minimum and be very careful to preserve your optics. Proper cleaning products and gentle handling will keep your optics in top condition and provide you with bright, clear images for many years.

Optics are essential items on a hunter's gear list. A basic knowledge of the various types of optics and their applications will help hunters make good choices and spend their money wisely. Although the initial investment may seem high, good optics are durable, so their cost is not really that high when looked at on a yearly basis. Experienced hunters know that high-quality optics are indispensable to successful hunting.

PART VI.
ANIMALS
& THEIR SENSES

Chapter 22
GAME BEHAVIOR

The general behavior of a game animal is determined by its species; more specific behavior is determined by the unique environment of each individual. Each species has its own behavior patterns and temperament which must be understood to hunt the species successfully year after year. Whitetail deer are successfully hunted with treestands because of their predictable movement patterns. Elk and mule deer are seldom hunted with treestands because they move more randomly and have larger home ranges. General behavior patterns like these are influenced on a yearly basis to some degree by changes in available food crops, weather patterns, wind patterns and vegetation. In addition to typical species' behavior, individuals of each species also exhibit behavior patterns defined by their unique environment. Many of these individual behaviors are determined by how much human contact individual animals have (hunting pressure is often a major part of this), what type of terrain they live in, how profuse and reliable their food supply is, how much competition they have, and how many predators are present. Hunters who want to successfully hunt several species in different habitats need an understanding of both general and individual behavior patterns.

Behavior Patterns

Animals' behaviors are shaped by their need for food, safety/shelter and sex. The priority of these three needs depends on the species, the sex of the individual and the season. Within one species, the seasonal changes have the most significant effect on priority. Each species has adapted to a niche in their environment which best fulfills these needs. Caribou have adapted by traveling endlessly to avoid over-browsing their main food supply–lichens. Lichens grow at such a slow rate—as slow as one inch per fifty years—that caribou would soon destroy this food supply if they didn't follow this behavior pattern. Musk-oxen instinctively form a defensive ring to protect themselves from their chief predator–wolves. This behavior has seen them through thousands of years of coexistence with wolves.

Unfortunately, this safety-induced behavior did not protect them from subsistence hunters in Alaska who took advantage of this defense mechanism and wiped them out of Alaska by the mid-1800's. After being reintroduced in the 1930's, the herds are now managed for sustained yield to prevent this from happening again. The rutting season has a profound effect on whitetail deer, making even the largest bucks change their elusive habits and act uncharacteristically bold as they seek sexual partners. This is often a whitetail's most vulnerable time and hunters often take advantage of this.

Game animals learn to evade humans in two ways. They learn by contact with humans and from other individuals of the same species. The more generations of a species which has regular contact with humans, the better that species becomes at avoiding us. This is one of the prime reasons whitetail deer—which easily adapt to living in close proximity to human populations—are so good at evading hunters. Whitetails have been living in close proximity to humans for many generations and passing on accumulated knowledge to each new generation. Additionally, many current populations of whitetails have almost daily contact with people from the day they are born and learn even more. By the time most deer are old enough for hunters to shoot at them, they are well-educated about our habits and can avoid us the great majority of the time. Although moose are not generally thought to have good hunter-avoidance abilities, this is at least partly due to the amount of contact past generations of moose have had with humans. In areas where several generations of moose have had regular contact with people, moose readily learn to avoid us–specifically during hunting season. Given enough contact, all game animals can learn to avoid hunters and pass this ability on to their offspring, just like whitetails do.

Among North American big game animals, the sexes are usually separate during most of the year, coming together only around their mating season. This separation is influenced by their main priorities in life. Adult males often desire safety first and food second. Adult females' first priority is good food for their growing offspring, so they take more risks to provide this. In general, the result is that males are found higher, farther away from human development and in denser cover than females–the larger males being the most reclusive. Males also come out to feed later in the evening and go back to cover earlier in the morning than females with young because of this difference in their safety/food priorities. In most species of game animals, the largest adult males usually bring up the rear when they do travel in a mixed-sex group. When entering an opening the males will usually be the last to enter and the first to leave a feeding area. This habit developed from generations of living with predators. Since predators usually find their prey by scent, a prey species' chances of survival were improved when the largest, strongest members traveled at the rear

Most whitetail deer populations have had regular contact with people for generations which has taught them many effective ways to avoid humans. This whitetail was outsmarted by a hunter.

to protect the herd from a following predator. For the same reason, the largest bucks also leave an opening first on their way back to a bedding area in order to check the herd's backtrail for danger. If any danger is present, the bucks change course. The other herd members follow the buck's scent trail to safety. This is possible because many game species have scent glands which give off a specific odor when the animal is alarmed. Other members of the same species traveling the same route within a 24-48 hours will be alerted by the odor given off by an alarmed animal—often running away as if they had sensed the danger themselves. Although the historical predator-prey situations no longer exist in most of North American game's populations, many prey species' habits associated with predator evasion still exist. This traveling order habit is still advantageous to them, but in a different way. Man is now the main predator and he usually selects the large males as his prey, rather than any member of a group like predators do. However, man uses his eyes and not his nose, so he waits in openings for his prey. Females which enter openings first will often detect hunters before the males get into the open—thus protecting the most sought-after members of the species.

    Most of our North American big game species live in or near timber or brush—elk, whitetail deer, and black bears are some examples. They use this cover for safe bedding areas and to escape predators or hunters. They spend a majority of their non-bedded time on the edges of terrain within their habitat. Edges where forest meets meadow, brush becomes timber or grass meets brush provide both food and safety simultaneously. These species also travel the edges frequently to see possible danger while keeping close to the safety of heavy cover. The biggest obstacle when hunting species which use cover for safety is trying to find them.

Open-country species like sheep and caribou don't typically try to hide. They escape danger by running long distances. They bed, eat and travel in ways which afford them a good view of their surroundings–ridges and promontories are favorites of these open-country animals. This also puts them in full view of hunters most of the time. Hunting them successfully depends not so much on finding them, as not being seen by them first.

All game species bed in locations where they can see, hear or smell danger coming from as many directions as possible. Beds should also provide concealment, shelter from bad weather and escape routes to other, nearby cover. Animals typically slow down, look constantly and zigzag or fishhook on their trail just before bedding. Fishhooking back along their trail allows them to watch their backtrail for predators who might be following them. On one bowhunt for bison near Delta Junction, Alaska, I noticed the trails of five bulls I was following started to zigzag back and forth. I immediately slowed down and began to look for them in the heavy brush. Almost simultaneously, I spotted the bedded bulls just forty yards ahead–just before they would have spotted me. Without their telltale trail to tip me off before I walked into them, I probably would not been able to arrow one of those bulls at seventeen yards–the same bull who now graces my trophy room wall.

While hunting any big game species it is prudent to remember the danger they present to us. Both black and brown bears are commonly encountered by hunters. Each year a few of these encounters are deadly for man or beast. A little understanding of these and other dangerous animals and some forethought can prevent some of these tragedies and make hunters more comfortable while in the field.

Brown, grizzly and black bears have poor eyesight and keen noses. They often have a hard time determining what you are, so they stand up to get a better look. The vast majority of the time, once they sense that you are human, they run. If a bear does come toward you, unless there is a tall, climbable tree nearby or a bear-proof shelter you can get to before the bear gets to you, do not run. Bears are very quick on their feet and you cannot outrun them. Running just indicates to them that you are afraid, so they will chase you to check if you are food or a smaller predator they can chase away. If you try to run and they catch you, the least they will do is slap you around a little to show you who's boss. If you resist, they will continue until you stop and they get tired of displaying their dominance. If there is no safe retreat nearby and a bear comes toward you, the best

Bears are the most common threat which hunters worry about in the field. However, the great majority of the time, brown bears like this one are only interested in getting away from humans. Automobiles pose a much greater threat to us than bears.

thing to do is stand your ground and face the bear. Walk back and forth a few steps and yell to show the bear what you are. Usually when a bear determines you are human, this is all he needs to know to decide that he should leave. If the bear still comes your way, you must stand your ground. Showing dominance among wild animals involves a lot of bluff behavior. Bears will often come within thirty feet and sometimes closer to test if they can bluff-charge you into backing down. If the only other option you have is to run, don't. I once had a brown bear run at me through heavy brush several times and then swerve away within thirty feet each time, trying to get me to run. He finally gave up and ran off. I had a rifle but wasn't about to use it until absolutely necessary. Whether or not it's true that *all* brown/grizzly bear charges are bluffs as some experts claim, I can't say for sure, but certainly the great majority of them are.

The most serious threat from a brown/grizzly bear comes if you get too close to its kill or its young. In these cases there is often no time to react before the bear is upon you. For whatever reason, if a bear does attack you, the best thing to do is drop, curl into a ball and lie still. The bear may still hit you a couple times, but you have no choice at this point. Just wait until the bear leaves before moving. Conversely, if you are attacked by a black bear, the best action to take varies with the situation. Black bears have been known to eat humans much more often than brown/grizzly bears. The accepted strategy with them is to stand and fight them off, making them go elsewhere for easier prey. There have been several cases of people fighting off black bears with only their fists by hitting their sensitive noses. A large stick would be much better if one is available. However, if the bear is very large and you think it is only trying to chase you off, the best thing to do may be to lie still until it leaves—as you would if it were a brown/grizzly bear. The specific situation would determine your best course of action.

Attacks by mountain lions have to be treated entirely different than bear attacks. Like most wild cats, mountain lions often attack people and even regard them as suitable prey. Therefore, cougars have to be treated as a real threat. They aren't so large that they cannot be fought off with any sort of club or even large rocks. Making yourself look as big as possible (holding your coat open may help) and yelling loudly can scare them off. If attacked, stand upright to keep them away from your head and neck which they commonly target. The threat they pose is increasing dramatically in places like California where hunting has been stopped. Hunters should be aware of these cats and the threat they pose.

Wolves are still found in great numbers in Alaska and Canada, but pose little threat to hunters. Because of their fear of humans and ability to stay out of sight, they are seldom seen even when abundant. However, coyotes and fox are common camp pests and steal whatever food they can. The only serious threat to hunters that any of these canines pose is their tendency to carry rabies. Any unusually friendly or strangely acting canine should be avoided and shot if it gets too close. Rubber gloves should be used to dispose of the body and the head should be sealed in plastic to be sent to a lab for a rabies examination.

Anytime you get between a big game animal and its young there is an element of danger. All females will defend their young vigorously, and large species like elk or moose can easily kill humans which threaten their young. Moose have been known to kill humans while defending their calves and any adult will kill a dog which gets too close. All big game animals should be treated with the respect that large, powerful animals with sharp hooves or claws deserve.

Daily and Seasonal Movements

Animals move in their search for food, safety, shelter and sex. There are daily movements between feeding and bedding grounds as well as seasonal movements adapted for avoiding harsh weather, finding food or in response to sexual urges. Daily movements in normal weather may be as little as a few hundred yards for whitetail deer with small home ranges and seasonal movements may be as large as several hundred miles for migrating caribou herds.

This barren ground caribou bull is on its annual northward movement typical of the species. Hunters can see thousands of these animals during a week-long hunt if the migration is in progress.

Each species is unique in both daily and seasonal movements. Whitetail deer often have home ranges as small as 100 acres in areas of good food and cover. Whitetails prefer to stay near their familiar escape routes and cover when pursued, so hunters seldom push them out of their home range. Unless they are in very open country, these deer will rarely go more than 200 yards after being spooked. Even when pushed out of their home range, they will usually return within a few hours. However, elk will often line out and go five to ten miles after being spooked, and not come back for a week.

Each species has unique patterns of when it rises, goes to feed and returns to bed. For instance, deer usually go to their bedding area while morning thermals are still carrying scent along their backtrail so they can walk nose-to-wind and detect any danger. Then they wait until the thermals have reversed before they lie down, so any predators following them to their beds would be scented. In some species—like Dall sheep—the feeding/bedding cycle is repeated two or three times each day.

Dall sheep use thermals in a similar way to detect predators which may get above them. A sheep's defensive strategy is to stay above predators near the safety of steep cliffs, so preventing predators from getting above them while feeding in the lower pastures is of utmost importance. Sheep end their morning feeding while the thermals are still going downhill. They can then walk uphill to the safety of steep cliffs, always going into the wind to check for predators above them. In the evening, they wait until the thermals go downhill before going down to feed, so they will be able to scent any predators which get above them while feeding.

This pattern of going uphill in the mid-morning to bed and then descending in the evening to feed is typical among big game animals which live in or around hills or mountains. By moving uphill with their own scent in the morning and then downhill with it in the evening most of their scent is kept close to them. This means less scent is spread around for predators to locate and follow. This movement pattern also helps them get the better feed at lower elevations, as well as escape the heat and insect pests by going higher during the day. Being able to escape insect pests is beneficial and sometimes crucial for animals to get sufficient rest and be able to feed properly. After one very wet spring near Aniak, Alaska, the biting insects were so numerous some of the young, inexperienced moose were actually dying from insect harassment. They weren't able to feed or rest much. The moose which survived knew where to find breezes and would actually stand in the middle of the rivers to escape the biting insects.

Many species of big game animals with large home ranges move constantly during the year to find food, escape predators, insects and parasites. Most predators do this as do larger prey species like elk and moose. Some species also migrate each year to escape heavy snows and to find food. Among a species which does migrate, there may be some populations within the species which do not. Most caribou herds in Alaska and Canada migrate several hundred miles each spring and fall. However, there are some small herds which don't move at all. When caribou do migrate they move en masse; thousands of animals can appear and disappear in several hours. Like most open-country animals, their walking speed is much faster than a human's, so cutting them off or ambushing them are the only viable options for hunters. Mule deer migrations are entirely different. Muleys exhibit more of a gradual drifting between summer and winter ranges, sometimes as much as a 7,000 ft. elevation difference. Mule deer migrations involve small groups of does and fawns, followed by larger bucks a few weeks later, whereas migrating caribou herds often contain animals of all ages and both sexes. In areas where elk migrate, once the large bulls are finished with the rut they often travel ahead of the cows and fawns so they can get at the good food. Once a hunter understands the nuances of a species' movement and migration patterns in a region, it is necessary to balance these with each year's weather pattern to make necessary adjustments.

Weather and Climate Influences

Daily and yearly weather patterns have different effects on game

Hunters who understand an animal's daily movement patterns can hunt it more successfully. Dave Widby waited at a waterhole for this buck antelope to come within bow range.

movements, as do any extreme variations in these patterns. There are differences in how weather affects each species and sometimes even different populations of the same species. There are also some generalities which apply to most big game animals.

Daily movements are tied to thermal air movements related to normal weather patterns. Any wide variation in the weather can change the normal thermal direction or timing and affect daily game movements. Strong winds or rains can cancel the pattern of thermals and have animals moving in uncharacteristic patterns to try and keep air movements in their favor. If winds or rains are strong enough, they may keep animals from feeding at normal times. In these cases, there will be a sudden flurry of activity when the wind or rain subsides. The animals will be hungry and go to feed whichever time of the day the weather lets up. At these times, game animals will often feed all day long to catch up on nourishment. After a heavy rain I often see moose come out of their favorite timber retreats to escape the dripping vegetation. Heavy rain is common in moose

This group of bowhunters took a week-long hunting trip to Kodiak Island at the peak of the Sitka blacktail rut. These deer are much more active and less wary at this time of year.

country during hunting season so this is a great time for hunters to be out looking in earnest.

Another time when game animals often move more is ahead of an approaching storm, so this is also a good time for hunters to be watching in earnest. Elk seem to predict storms up to 24 hours in advance and will spend more time feeding. This ability may be associated with barometric pressure and humidity. This may be the same reason hunters with a lot of experience in one area can also predict some storms–the air actually feels different.

A sudden cold spell can have the same effect as rain or wind of slowing game movements temporarily, with a similar burst of activity when temperatures return to normal. Animals often seek slopes or meadows where the sun first hits after such a cold snap and, if snow has fallen, will try to find snow-free places to feed and bed. If the cold weather continues beyond a few days it will cause game to feed more than usual to take in more calories, sometimes feeding all day and night.

In times of unusually warm temperatures, animals will often feed earlier in the morning and later in the evening to avoid the heat of the day.

During bright phases of the moon on clear nights, most game will feed all night and be less active at normal daylight feeding times. Because they get to bed earlier than usual in the morning after bright, moonlit nights, they will often be more active at midday than usual–stretching and feeding a little to break up the long bedding period during the day. Strong winds or heavy precipitation can reduce the nocturnal activities during a bright moon just as these weather extremes can reduce daylight activity.

Periods of drought may also cause some animals to become nocturnal. Since drought increases their need for water, this allows them to go to watering places under the cover of darkness and avoid predators who try to ambush them in daylight hours.

Behavior During the Mating Season

During their mating season, adult males of most big game species are easier to hunt successfully. The increased sexual drive makes bulls, bucks, rams and boars less wary of danger as they focus on finding and keeping sexual partners. The exact timing and ritual of the rut varies for each species and sometimes, for each population. In general, the timing of the deer rut at their northernmost ranges in Canada is two to three weeks earlier than in the Southern U.S. This is a result of both the differences in the amount of daylight and climate. Local weather patterns can also affect timing of the rut, as can each year's weather. A population which lives near the top of a 5,000 ft. mountain may rut earlier than one which lives only a few miles away, but several thousand feet lower, because of the temperature difference. Unusually cold weather often advances the start of the rut; warmer weather delays it.

The mating season draws males and females of a species together more than any other time of the year. With some species the mating involves one female and one male together for a short time; for other species the largest males gather huge harems and try to defend their mating rights against other males. Bull moose and elk commonly gather large harems and fight vigorously to keep other males away from the cows. Most deer just look for one doe at a time, abandoning the previous doe when they go looking for the next one. The rut may be the only time that the largest males of a species have any interaction with others of its species, living a solitary life for the rest of the year.

The mating area within a species' range also varies. Some species have a specific mating grounds within their home range, others mate anywhere within their home range. Dall sheep populations use the same mating grounds each year. As the rut draws near, the males and females start drifting toward these mating grounds from their respective summer ranges. The older animals which know the locations of these areas pass this knowledge on to younger animals. Whitetail deer and moose usually mate anyplace within their home range they happen to meet. In general, animals with small home ranges do not have specific mating grounds. Game animals which are also predators–bears and cougars–also do not congregate in large numbers on specific mating grounds–for obvious reasons.

Mating rights are usually earned by physical battles among adult males. Horns and antlers are the most common weapons, and size is the most important factor in success. Antlers are rubbed against small trees or saplings to remove velvet and outline the territory of a buck or bull. These "rubs" are used to remove velvet and help harden antlers, strengthen neck muscles for fighting and leave the male's scent for other deer to find. Bucks also use their hooves to scratch slight depressions in the ground called scrapes. These are used by adult males to leave their scent to advertise their readiness to mate. Wallows are used by elk and moose to intensify their scent and broadcast it over a greater area during the rut. Although the use of scents by many game species is most noticeable during the rut, scents play an important role in communication between members of many species all year. Deer have four sets of scent glands they use to identify each other in addition to communicating sexual readiness, dominance, safety and danger to other deer.

During mating season there are minor and major changes in behavior patterns. At the peak of the rut males may stop eating altogether and devote all their waking hours to the pursuit of females. Their most active hours may also change significantly during the rut. The rut may bring some males out earlier in the evening and keep them out later in the morning. Some adult males caught up in the fever of the rut may be out all day long in search of females. Rutting fever can cause bucks to do incredibly stupid things. On one deer hunt after I had missed a nice buck at close range and scared it off, my buddy shot the doe which the buck had been following. We had forgotten about the buck and were cleaning the doe, when the buck walked back up to within 30 yards of us and the dead doe. His mating urge drove him to ignore us and come back for the female. During the peak of the rut adult males can become easy targets as they ignore their normal instincts about avoiding humans. The behavior of females is also affected by the rut, but not nearly as much as that of males.

Effects of Hunting Pressure

Game animals' behavior often changes significantly with the onset of hunting season. The more "educated" the animal and the heavier the hunting pressure, the greater the changes in their behavior. If there is significant pre-hunt activity in preparation for the season, this can precipitate the changes in experienced animals even before the start of the hunting season. Large whitetail bucks who have experienced heavy hunting pressure in previous seasons have learned to change their behavior as soon as hunting activity starts. These deer may be very visible during daylight hours in open fields in summer and fall, but quickly change their habits when pre-hunt activity starts. After living through two or three hunting seasons these

Carl F. Brent and Tony Russ with a whitetail that was harvested during the rut. Whitetails change their habits dramatically when hunting pressure is heavy.

large bucks know to stay hidden as much as possible–some even become nocturnal for the entire hunting season. Large bucks also learn to approach their bedding grounds from downwind during hunting season.

Depending on the hunting pressure and the length of the hunting season there may also be changes in animal behavior during the course of the season. Some of these changes are hunter-related, some are natural changes associated with changes in weather, food supply, and the rut cycle. Because of these changes, game sign found before the hunting season may be useless after the season starts. On the Alaska Peninsula, the largest brown bears often become nocturnal as soon as pre-hunt activity starts in preparation for the two-week season. Large bears are typically ten or more years old, so they have learned from experience to avoid humans during the hunting season. The most productive times to hunt them in the fall season are very early and very late–hoping to catch one during the few minutes of daylight they may be visible each day. The really large, old bears seem to know they should not be out when there is any daylight. During a hunt several years ago, I saw a huge ten-footer drop a salmon in mid-bite and suddenly bolt for cover as dawn approached one morning and he realized he had made a serious mistake.

The pressures of hunting season will often make experienced males change their daily travel routes. These animals may no longer use major trails which are too exposed and used by too many hunters. Although most

Large Kodiak brown bears like this one taken by Bart Schleyer are difficult to hunt because they are often nocturnal during the fall hunting season. Using a bow makes this feat truly remarkable.

of the females, young animals and smaller males may still use major trails, the larger adult males will switch to using minor trails. These minor trails may be hard to detect because they are used so little and, in some cases, only during the hunting season. The older, wiser whitetail deer will even remember hunters' stand locations from year to year and avoid them when hunting season begins. This may cause only a slight adjustment in their daily routes to stay just out of range of the stand. The deer know where the stand and hunter are and, although they can see it and the hunter while they travel, stay just far enough away to feel safe. New stands put up during the season can also be identified quickly by hunter-wise bucks. It is no more difficult for some bucks to identify hunters in tree stands than if they were on the ground.

Each species of game animals has identifiable behavior patterns. Some are constant from year to year and some change depending on weather, climate, food, hunting pressure, population density, predation, etc. Understanding the patterns of a species of big game animal, the differences which a population in a hunting area may exhibit, and any unique habits of the individual being hunted are all indispensable to successful hunters.

Chapter 23
GAME SENSES: SIGHT, SMELL & HEARING

North American big game animals all have better sensory awareness of their environment than humans. This is understandable since they need acute senses to survive. We rely on our senses to a lesser degree, depending on our superior intellect to help us perceive, comprehend and control our environment. Animals detect hunters by sight, sound and scent. Each game species has a unique blend of strengths and weaknesses in these three areas. A thorough understanding of the abilities and limits of each animal's senses is one of the ways hunters can improve their success.

In general, the size of an animal's external sense organ indicates the strength of that sense. Bears have large noses and small eyes. This indicates they have an excellent sense of smell and poor eyesight–which is true. Using this same logic, since moose have vary large ears and noses, they should have great senses of sound and smell–which they do. Relatively speaking, humans have large eyes, but small noses and ears, so it makes sense that we rely on our best sense—our eyesight—to perceive our world.

The big game species of North America generally rely on their sense of smell more than any other. The first reason for this is that most of them have relatively large noses and all have at least a good sense of smell–and most have an excellent sense of smell. The second reason has to do with the reliability of this sense. Their world is full of sights and sounds which are not always interpretable for even the keenest of eyes or ears. Both predators and hunters have learned ways to camouflage their bodies and reduce sounds which would give them away to prey species. Therefore, prey species cannot be sure that their eyes or ears will detect danger (mountain sheep and antelope which depend more on their eyes are possible exceptions to this rule). However, their noses are very discriminating and seldom fooled. As all predators and hunters have discovered, a downwind animal will smell you. The exception to this rule is when hunters use scents or scent-blocking clothing, both of which are discussed later in this chapter.

Sensory Acuteness

Table 23.1 is a chart which rates the sensory acuteness of North American big game animals. There is also a column which rates the wariness of each species. The order in which these species are listed indicates the overall difficulty in hunting a large, adult male of each species. The difficulty in bagging a particular species can vary tremendously between location and certainly between weapons used, so this order is just an average. For example, caribou are relatively easy to take with a rifle, but moderately difficult to take with a bow. However, their sheer numbers is a factor which pushes them down on the list. The order also takes into account other factors like difficulty of terrain (which is why sheep are listed so high) and weather obstacles (which accounts for polar bear's high listing).

Table 23.1

NORTH AMERICAN BIG GAME SPECIES' SENSORY ACUTENESS

Game Species	Sight	Hearing	Smell	Wariness
whitetail, mule, blacktail, & coues deer	E	E	E	E
all sheep species	E	G	G	G
polar bear	F	F	E	G
all elk species	E	E	E	E
brown/grizzly bear	F	F	E	G
all moose species	E	E	E	F
Rocky Mountain goat	E	F	G	F
pronghorn antelope	E	F	G	G
black bear	F	F	E	G
cougar	G	G	E	G
Sitka blacktail deer	E	E	E	G
bison	E	G	E	G
all caribou species	E	G	E	P
musk-oxen	G	F	G	P

E=EXCELLENT   G=GOOD   F=FAIR   P=POOR

Sight

The eyes of game animals are similar to humans, but not exactly the same. All mammalian eyes contain two types of light receptors–rods and cones. Rods are more sensitive to light than cones, so they work better in low light intensities. Cones are best for distinguishing colors in bright light, but don't work well at all in dim light. Ungulate species have more rods than cones in their eyes so they can see well in dim light, but don't distinguish colors well. Human eyes contain more cones than rods so we can see colors well in bright light, but cannot see color or shape in dim light. However, we have a greater concentration of rods near the edges of our eyes, so looking next to an object—rather than directly at it—in dim light can help our eyes detect it. Prey species (deer, elk, moose, sheep, etc.) also distinguish outlines and edges better than we can in daylight or dim light–an adaptation which helps them detect and elude predators.

In addition to the advantage they have in distinguishing light intensities, ungulates also have a wider field of view than we do. This is a direct result of the placement of their eyes to the sides of their heads. This gives them a view of about 270°. The placement of our eyes to the front of our heads limits our view to about 180°. This side placement lets prey animals watch for predators in a wider area around them. Although they only have good depth perception for approximately 90° directly in front of them, they easily spot motion in their entire range of view–which is crucial for prey animals. Motion is a sure indicator of danger to prey species and the most important factor for hunters to consider when hunting any species. Predators (and humans) have eyes in front and very good forward depth perception so they can strike effectively at prey species. Predators are only slightly handicapped by having a limited side view since they are not usually preyed upon, and they still can see to the side somewhat and pick up quick movements in their entire 180° range. Just last fall I was stalking a black bear with my bow and got within 30 yards when he moved unexpectedly and caught me between two pieces of cover. As he stepped out from behind a bush with his head down and pointing 90° to the side, he froze for about two seconds. Although I was motionless and in a crouch, his peripheral vision noticed my shape protruding above the ankle-high berry bushes. Without ever moving his head toward me, he bolted for cover and I never saw him again. Even his front-positioned predator eyes were able to detect me directly to the side and escape the plans I had for him.

Both game species' eyes and our own are better for looking below than above. This is because of the bony protuberance above most mammalian eyes which protects them from rain, snow, dust, etc. Game also looks for danger from below far more than from above–and they position themselves to see below rather than above. Ungulates also see their world as a horizontal mural where vertical lines are cues to danger.

Because game animals' eyes have more light receptors than color receptors, they do not see the range of color vision that we do. Most can distinguish between colors which reflect different amounts of light. They can see that a shiny orange is different from a dull brown for instance, but most can't tell that a shiny orange is different than a shiny yellow–if they reflect the same amount of light. Most cannot see any difference between the muted browns, greens and yellows on many camouflage patterns. Many of the camouflage patterns hunters use look like they are made of only one hue to these animals, so it really doesn't break up a hunter's outline as it is

The hunter in the center of this photo is well-camouflaged because his hands and face are covered, he has used several camouflage patterns, and the patterns contain large, light-colored patches.

designed to do. To effectively break up a hunter's outline, camouflage patterns should have (contrasting) light and dark colors which reflect different amounts of light. Additionally, the borders between the colors should be fuzzy and not sharp to imitate an animal's natural world. Sharp outlines are out of place in the woods. Animals quickly notice them and become alerted. Hunter orange is a neutral color to animals (unless it is shiny) and is okay to use as long as you don't move. Skin color is noticed by whitetail deer, so cover all of it when hunting them.

Animals' eyes also see ultraviolet (UV) light which our eyes can't detect. Chemical dyes in clothing and brightening agents in detergents often reflect UV light. Animals will see UV-brightened clothing as glowing, so any hunter dressed in these clothes will be detected quite easily. Hunters' clothing should be colored with organic dyes or washed in UV-free detergents to prevent this.

Because animals' eyes are even more sensitive to bright light than ours, hunters should take advantage of a bright sun in their quarry's eyes by keeping the sun at their back whenever possible. Hunters should also cover all bare metal or shiny gear with tape, dull paint or felt-tip marker.

But, above all else, hunters' top priority should be to reduce movement to a minimum whenever game is in sight or may be looking, because game will detect movement more than any other visual cue, and they will run faster and farther from it than from any non-moving image which alerts them.

Hearing

In general, game animals can hear a wider range of frequencies and a lower level of sounds than we can. However, the difference in hearing among game animals and the way they treat sounds varies greatly. Ear size among North American big game animals varies from two-inch black bear ears to twelve-inch moose ears. Additionally, bull moose have four to six-foot antlers which can be directed toward sounds—acting as huge antennae to bring in soft sounds as far as a mile away, making their sense of hearing one of the best among animals anywhere.

Forest dwellers like moose, deer and elk have good to excellent hearing and are constantly filtering noises in their world. They know the sounds which belong in their environment and which ones are out of place. They rely more on their sense of hearing than their eyesight because it usually detects danger at a greater range with more reliability. They only flee if a sound is identifiable as dangerous—saving energy by ignoring "safe" sounds.

Mountain-dwelling animals like sheep and goats place much less importance on sounds because there is so much inconsequential "noise" in their world which is similar to predator sounds. Rocks are so frequently falling off cliff faces or rolling down slopes that it is not practical for these animals to become alerted each time they hear these sounds. They would be a nervous wreck and never get any rest. Instead, they take notice

This moose's horns can be directed like an antenna to reflect sound to his ears. Hunters can use the same principle to hear better by cupping their hands behind their ears.

of the closest sounds and may stop eating or focus on them briefly, but go back to what they were doing if it isn't reinforced within a matter of seconds by sight, smell or repetition of the same sound in the same location. They will be alerted if they hear footfalls which come closer, but hunters can usually get away with occasional noises and not alert these mountain-dwellers.

Animals can also direct their ears independently or together toward sounds to amplify them. Hunters should always watch an animal's ears for cues about what they've heard or haven't heard. Once the ears stop scanning for noise and both point one way for more than a few seconds, the animal is alerted to a sound; if they are pointing independently and/or still moving around, the animal is not alerted.

Even though we do not have large ears or the ability to move them (without using our hands), there are ways to increase our hearing abilities while hunting. First, make sure your ears are clean before a hunting trip—it does make a difference. Next, learn to use all of your ears' innate abilities. The human ear is capable of a far greater range and acuity than most urbanites give it credit. One way to learn to hear better is to go out into your backyard, a park or your hunting area; then close your eyes and listen. Learn to hear all the sounds that game animals hear daily. Also, watch animals to learn what sounds they make and what they mean. Train yourself to listen for and recognize important sounds. Scolding birds or chattering squirrels may mean a predator is approaching or another animal is near. Learn to distinguish wind or water from footsteps. Also learn to listen to the noises you make and how to minimize them as much as possible. Hearing loss due to noise pollution is common in people of any age from music, machinery, airplanes, firing guns, etc. Protect your ears whenever practical with plugs or ear muffs. Lastly, by facing soft sounds and cupping your hands behind your ears you can effectively make your ears larger and increase the sensitivity of your hearing. It is very simple, but vastly improves your hearing.

Contrary to the popular image of the perfect hunter, there is no such thing as a moving hunter that is "silent." Although hunters should make stalks without being heard whenever possible, when still-hunting or traveling–the goal of hunters should be to avoid loud noises and make only proper noises. Avoiding loud, incongruous noises requires practice and a slow pace. Proper noises fit in according to the time of day, the place and the animals found in the area. An example is a moose hunt I went on many years ago on the Kenai Peninsula of Alaska. I knew moose regularly traveled through an area I was walking through one morning. I paced myself to walk at the same speed as a feeding moose–taking a few steps every minute or so, then pausing as if I was a relaxed moose slowly feeding along. One hour and fifty yards later a bull appeared at about 70 yards, doing the same thing. He had heard me and looked in my direction, but was not alarmed–until I put a well-placed bullet through him. The only reason I even saw that bull was because I made noises just like a moose slowly feeding in the early morning in the right location. Other moose around me also heard me, but were convinced I was just another moose.

Walking along with an occasional soft swish of hunting clothing against brush–just like fur against brush, moving at a relaxed animal's pace, and even breaking an occasional twig is "proper" noise for hunters. The phrase "Quiet as an Indian" does not mean absolutely silent, it means making just a little noise and all of it the proper kind of noise. A hunter moving through the woods being absolutely silent (which isn't possible under any conditions) is unnatural and deer would be as alarmed by this movement without sound as they would be by loud, uncommon noises. There is a narrow range of acceptable noise in the woods–above or below this range and you arouse suspicion. Learn what this range is and then develop a hunting style of walking which makes only the proper noise within this appropriate range.

Think about moving like a prey animal and not a predator when hunting. Un-alarmed prey animals meander slowly and stop frequently to look, listen, test the breeze for danger and eat—if appropriate to time and place. Predators often go in a direct course, quickly covering a lot of ground as they search for prey. Making prey-like sounds will alert far fewer animals than if you make predator-like sounds.

Be aware of the weather and how it changes noise in the woods. Leaves on trees will absorb considerable noise and soften what isn't absorbed. Once leaves fall off, noise will travel much farther and be easier to distinguish—not a good thing for noisy human hunters. Soft snow on the ground can certainly allow careful hunters to travel within the proper noise levels, but snow covering trees also absorbs a lot of sound. On one snowy day on a deer hunting trip to Kodiak Island, Alaska, I was able to walk by a bedded deer at 15 feet without alerting it. Only when it stood up to look at my buddy following me at twenty yards did I even see it and make the fifteen-foot shot with my recurve. Six inches of fresh snow on the ground and the trees made for as quiet conditions as possible, yet the deer still heard my buddy's careless footsteps. Even in the best conditions you have to make the proper noise because you are never absolutely silent.

The last thing to keep in mind about sound is the way it bounces around in mountains and canyons. It is very difficult for animals (and humans) to determine the direction of loud noises in these types of terrain. If they are uncertain, animals in the mountains will instinctively run uphill whenever they hear loud noises. Gunshots are a good example of this. If the first shot at an animal misses or causes a slight wound, the animal will often go uphill. This is one of the reasons hunters prefer to get above animals in steep terrain—animals will usually run uphill toward you if the first shot isn't fatal.

Smell

Game animals depend heavily on their acute sense of smell to warn them of danger from predators and humans. They also use this sense, along with scents they produce, for communication about gender, dominance, direction of travel, fear and sexual readiness between other members of their species. Animals typically have several glands to produce scents. The highly scrutinized whitetail deer have Sudoriferous, Pre-Orbital, Nasal Sebaceous, Vomeronasal, Salivary, Interdigital, Metatarsal and Tarsal glands to produce these scents. Just like other species, whitetails use their scents to pass specific information in appropriate places at proper times.

Hunters can often take advantage of a species' complicated use of scents. Doing so requires a thorough knowledge of the intricacies of scents and their usage for that animal. Using scents at the wrong time or place will not only fail, it may fail miserably by alarming animals. Sex scents are the most popular and useful scents used by hunters, and the ones most often used incorrectly. Careful study and research into a species'

The size of the external sense organ indicates the relative strength of that sense in the animal. One look at this bear's nose indicates just how good his sense of smell is. Our eyes are (relatively) our largest external sense organ and our eyesight is our best sense.

habits is necessary to use these properly. Attractive scents are commonly used around bedding areas, feeding areas, rub or scrape lines, travel corridors and near tree stands or blinds. Stand hunters often use urine drags to bring animals within their shooting range. Whenever scents are used, one rule to follow is to use clean rubber gloves when handling them. Contamination with human scent is a common, yet easily avoidable mistake of many hunters.

Ungulates like caribou and deer have interdigital glands between their hooves which enable them to trail one another. Secretions from these glands are also capable of communicating alarm or fear to other animals for as long as 48 hours. These same glands produce scents used in scrapes to indicate dominance and sexual readiness.

Most game animals pattern their daily activities around the prevailing air movements to take maximum advantage of their acute sense of smell. Animals living in timber or brushy environments prefer to travel nose-to-wind to smell any danger ahead of them. Game animals living in open country typically rely less on their sense of smell and more on vision to spot predators. This reflects the unreliability of wind direction in open areas more than the animal's lack of ability to smell. Open-country species like sheep and pronghorn antelope do have a good sense of smell–hundreds of times better than humans. They will easily smell predators (or hunters) at great distances when conditions are right. I've been scented by Dall sheep at over one-half mile.

There are some generalizations about wind directions and how they pattern game animal movements. Thermals are winds caused by temperature differences in localized areas. They are sometimes just a slight drifting of air rather than a noticeable wind. Thermals generally go uphill soon after the sun comes up and change to downhill after temperatures cool off in the evening. Some of the ways prey species use thermals are: they head into thermals when going to bedding areas; they choose bedding areas where thermals will bring any trailing predators' scents to them; they follow thermals during the day to minimize their scent distribution; and they keep thermals at their backs when they can use their eyes in front of them. The ways animals use air movements is complex. Each species, population and individual has its nuances which can only be understood by careful study of the animal and its habitat. Simple explanations will not predict all behaviors–careful study and thought is necessary. One example is: whitetails often feed downwind in open areas for two reasons. Their attention is focused on feeding so their heads are down and their eyes' range is limited, and they are making chewing noises so their ears are distracted. By traveling downwind they are able to smell any predator following their scent trail and, even with their heads down, they can still see directly in front of them for nearby danger.

Timber and topography have variable effects on thermals and prevailing wind directions. Ridges, tall stands of trees, and creek/river drainages commonly alter air movements as much as 90°, and sometimes as much as 180° in some situations. One clue to normal air flow in an area is game trails. Trails will often indicate how topography affects air movements in that area by their meanderings. Game will make these directional changes as they try to keep their nose into the wind as much as possible. They particularly do this when confronted with dense vegetation where their eyes can't warn them of danger. They will often create trails which allow them to travel downwind of visually impenetrable vegetation to scent any possible danger before entering. In open areas where animals' eyes are more useful to locate predators and scenting them is not so vital, game trails are more direct.

Although hunters cannot eliminate their scent entirely nor have absolute control where it goes, there are ways to reduce it considerably and have some measure of control over where the remainder goes. Reducing our scent by even 50% can have a tremendous effect on how often we are detected. Any strong smell which our noses can detect—like urine, sweat

Whitetail deer have excellent senses and are usually quite wary. Chuck Eisenhower took this North Dakota whitetail by spotting it at a distance and shooting it in its bed.

or foot odor—must be terribly powerful to animals (and smelled at far greater distances and in far more circumstances than weaker odors) and must be eliminated whenever possible. This lesson had to be taught to me twice. In both instances, the extra smell I produced when relieving myself was too strong and my quarry scented me at close range—even though I was downwind. Hunters should think ahead and keep strong odors as far away from game as possible. Digging holes and then covering human waste is a good habit to get into whenever in the field.

The best approach concerning scents is to leave a hunting area as unchanged as possible. Remember you are in an animal's home and it will detect any strange smells you leave there. Even minor odors left by hunters will be noticed by animals up to 48 hours later. Strong odors may last for weeks. Wearing rubber boots and rubber gloves are good ways to reduce human odor—a method which has been used successfully for decades by trappers. It is not guaranteed to eliminate all odors, however. I discovered this on one bowhunt for a Kodiak brown bear. After walking two miles upstream through a creek in hip boots, my partner and I spotted a large bear heading our way. We backed off fifteen yards and waited in the tall grass as the bear approached and crossed the creek to our side. As the bear started up the near bank, he suddenly smelled the spot we were

Bowhunting bears on the ground requires careful attention to scent and wind direction. George P. Mann with a large grizzly bear.

standing when we spotted him, whirled, and ran off. Our boots were clean, we had walked through water for two miles and the breeze was blowing from the bear's backtrail, yet he still scented the water which had dripped off our boots. Hard to believe, but it just shows how good an animal's sense of smell can be and how important it is to control odors in the field.

There are several ways for hunters to reduce human scent to a minimum. Daily or even twice-daily showering with unscented soap is a great benefit when possible. When daily bathing is not possible, an alternative is to take chlorophyll tablets to reduce body odor. These tablets have to be taken 3-7 days in advance and then continued for the duration of the hunt. Additionally, activated charcoal tablets should be taken to counteract the gas the chlorophyll tablets produce. Some hunters swear by this routine, claiming their week-long, shower-less hunting camps are considerably less odoriferous when everyone uses these two substances.

There are also scent-reducing sprays on the market for hunters. These can be used directly on skin as many times per day as necessary. Even if a hunter bathes in the morning, these sprays can be used during the day to counteract any sweating which has occurred. These same sprays are also useful for reducing odors on clothing, footwear and gear. Concentrates are available to reduce weight for backpacking hunters.

Hunting clothes should be washed in scent-free soap without UV brighteners. A slightly cheaper, more available alternative is baking soda.

In addition to, or instead of this, clothing can be placed in a scent-free bag with local vegetation. (Plastic garbage bags often have fungicides with a distinct odor and should not be used.) Using a common vegetation from the hunting area imparts a cover scent to clothing. There are even special containers made to do this with hunting clothes. These come complete with an internal fan and a scent bag to impart the cover scent. Fir or spruce boughs are good, pungent types of vegetation for this, as long as they are common to the area. Alternately, these containers come with a charcoal mat to eliminate odors—rather than add them—to clothing.

As another alternative to adding a cover scent, baking soda can be placed in a bag with clothing to draw out unwanted odors. By far the simplest method to rid hunting clothing of odors is to hang them outside at night to air out. Whenever possible, clothes should not be brought into a tent or cabin to absorb food and other odors. It is best to avoid cooking or eating odoriferous foods while wearing hunting clothes. Foods like beans, onion, garlic or any spicy foods will add strong odors to clothes and hands. Washing hands and brushing teeth can help if these are eaten. Having a set of camp clothes will allow hunters to keep hunting clothes away from food or other camp odors.

Hunters should also avoid fueling automobiles or ATV's while in their hunting clothes. Spills or even fumes will add a strong smell to clothes which alarm animals at great distances. This can be avoided by having an attendant or non-hunter in the group fuel vehicles, or by fueling rigs the night before the hunt.

The most complete scent protection comes from using one of the scent-blocking suits made for hunters. These suits utilize charcoal to absorb organic odors and then hold them until the suit is heated in a home clothes drier. They can be used for up to three weeks at a time before the charcoal is saturated and has to be cleansed by the heating process. A hunter who bathes, takes precautions to keep his clothes clean and uses one of these suits can often come within ten yards *upwind* of game animals and not be scented. Backpacking hunters who don't have the facilities to keep themselves or their clothes clean can use these suits to drastically reduce their odor—it only has to be worn during the last quarter-mile of a stalk to perform its function. Other scent-blocking items available to hunters include hats, gloves, packs, boots and over-boots.

The one thing all hunters should have is a wind direction indicator. It is vital to hunters that they know which way their scent is moving; to determine this, they have to know which way the air is moving. A wind direction indicator should show a hunter the direction of the slightest air movement. A feather or a thread tied to a rifle or bow is a good device for this. A small squeeze bottle of cornstarch or other fine, odorless powder

Fred Gonzales with a good elk. These animals also have excellent senses, but their size and vocalizations during their rut make it more difficult for them to escape detection as easily as whitetails can.

can also be used. Although strong winds are easy to identify, there are many times air movement is slight and variable. When thermals are changing direction or when hunting in dense brush or timber, wind direction may change 180° in the space of a few seconds of time or a few yards of distance. Hunters in the final moments of a stalk have to watch for any wind changes and one of these indicators is the means to know this information.

A thorough understanding of a game animal's senses and its habitat will allow hunters to see the world from the animal's point of view. Most forest-dwelling animals depend heavily on their sense of smell to alert them to danger. Others, like mountain sheep, goats and pronghorn antelope which live in open country rely more on their eyesight to spot most predators. The animal's sensory strengths and weaknesses will also affect its behavior in everyday as well as extraordinary situations.

Hunters also need to consider their own sensory strengths and weaknesses. By doing this, hunters can use their abilities to the fullest and improve their effectiveness. The combination of knowing a game animal's sensory abilities as well as their own will allow hunters to create the most favorable hunting situations and the best chances for success.

PART VII.
THE HUNT

Chapter 24
TRACKING SKILLS

The ability to identify and gather information from big game tracks is essential to consistent hunting success. Tracking skills are necessary for preseason scouting and the actual hunting, as well as recovering wounded animals. Tracks can tell a detailed "story" to hunters who know how to "read" them. At the least, hunters need to know what their quarry's tracks look like and be able to distinguish them from similar tracks. There are often several species of big game in an area which have tracks of similar size and shape—even livestock tracks can confuse inexperienced hunters.

Reading Tracks

The more savvy hunters become at the art of tracking, the more information they can glean about activity, mood, sex and size of the animal making the tracks. One basic rule is to study several tracks closely before making decisions. Individual tracks are sometimes misleading, so using several for confirmation of any conclusions is a good habit. Another rule is to use any other relevant information. The best trackers use confirming evidence like feeding sign, droppings, or hair and combine it with carefully observed track information before drawing logical conclusions which affect their hunting decisions.

The fundamental information to gather is the species which made the track. Sometimes this is obvious if there is only one hoofed animal in the area. For situations where there are several species which make similar tracks, hunters need to know the characteristics of each of these. Figure 24.1 depicts tracks of North American big game animals plus a few domesticated animals. Every hunter should know the tracks of any species he may encounter while hunting. Since during the course of a lifetime of hunting in North America a hunter may encounter all of these, it may be wise to learn them all.

Important characteristics of individual tracks to remember are length, width, overall shape, shape of each half of the hoof (or pad), whether dewclaw (or claw) marks typically show, and the normal gap between the hoof halves. Hunters should either commit this information to memory or carry some sort of fact sheet whenever more than one species may be present in the hunting area. Common associations of species are: moose and caribou, moose and elk, deer and antelope, deer and elk, sheep and goat, domestic sheep or cattle with any of these, and black bears and brown/grizzly bears. One thing to remember about hoofed animals is that the front hooves are usually larger than the hind hooves. Measurements should be taken using the front tracks for accurate comparisons.

The pattern of an animal's tracks indicates what it was doing at the time. Single, evenly spaced, walking tracks indicate an animal searching for food or companions. Meandering, walking tracks indicate an animal looking for food. Multiple, evenly spaced, walking tracks indicate migrating animals. Tracks which depict an animal stepping on its own tracks also indicate feeding activity. Running tracks with bounding leaps are from a spooked animal. Running is evident by the deep impressions toward the front of each print, sprayed soil to the rear of prints and the large spaces between each set of four prints. Each species has slightly different patterns when involved in each of these activities. Field experience is the only way for hunters to know the little nuances of each species. A good time to get this field experience is in the off-season when animals are not evading hunters. Animals are often most visible during summer and winter months outside the hunting season. Hunters can make a lot of associations in a short time by observing track patterns with the animals present to demonstrate what activity produced the tracks. There is no better training for a hunter than to see an animal make a track and watch this track as it ages for the next week. Doing this with tracks under different weather and soil conditions will provide invaluable training for beginning and experienced hunters who haven't had the opportunity to learn good tracking skills.

One consideration when interpreting track patterns and what they mean is the angle of the ground–if any. Tracks going uphill will be closer together than they would have been on flat ground. Those going downhill will be farther apart than on flat ground. Hunters can easily misinterpret tracks which go up or downhill unless they remember to allow for the slope. Animals also tend to bound on steep uphill or downhill slopes for no apparent reason. This should not be interpreted as a spooked animal unless the bounds continue once the tracks come to flat ground. Individual track size is also affected by steep terrain. Tracks going uphill appear shorter and more rounded. Tracks going downhill often appear longer.

The number and arrangement of tracks can indicate sex and age of the animals. Large, old males often travel alone in a deliberate manner and stick to dense cover. Mixed sizes of tracks usually means a group of females and young animals of various ages. However, if the species is migratory, a group like this may be composed of large males as well. A single, medium-sized track indicates a female if it travels deliberately, and a young male if it travels a little more haphazardly and changes speed

In the absence of rain or snow, this wolf track looks several days old because of the roundness of its edges.

frequently. A group of medium and large tracks—especially after the rut—indicates a group of males.

Tracks can give other clues about sex and size if hunters know what to look for and have some experience with their quarry's tracks to make valid comparisons against. Most of these are not infallible signs, but just additional indicators to be used in combination with other factors. The validity for each species varies; field experience is required with each animal for practical applications. In ungulate species, large males' hooves are often more rounded in front than females or small males because of the males' greater weight. In most species—particularly bears—the width between left and right footprints is a good indicator of size and sex. Large males are much wider of body, thus, they leave a wider track. Large males also tend to drag their toes and leave drag marks more than females–who are more dainty walkers. Male deer usually urinate farther forward than does and sometimes to the side. The heaviest males of a species also make the deepest tracks.

The sharpness of tracks is the main clue to their age when other factors are equal. Fresh tracks in moist, firm soil or clay have sharp edges. The edges begin to round the minute the tracks are made. Precipitation and wind will round the edges faster than dry weather. Heavy rain or strong wind will often make a track only a couple hours old look a week old. Temperatures which waver around the freezing point will also break down the sharp edges on a track much quicker than normal. Tracks in the sun will dry and age much quicker than those in shade. Cracks appearing in tracks as they dry are a good indication of their age to the experienced eye–cracks appearing and widening with time. Accurate aging of tracks is very helpful when scouting to determine the number of animals in an area. It is easy to overestimate the animal population in an area if all tracks are thought to be made at the same time when, in reality, they were made by a few animals going back and forth on the same trail. In these cases, the ability to tell which track is the freshest may also indicate where a hunter should look for the animal(s).

Even when fresh, tracks in sand or dry soil are not sharp and are difficult to age. They do not age quickly and often look the same whether they are fresh or several days old. In these cases, tracks should be followed for a while. They will usually cross better soil conditions for aging them. Following a set of tracks over different soil types is actually a good practice for all situations. The additional evidence will produce better evaluations in almost all tracking situations. Debris which collects in prints is a good indicator of track age in any soil type.

Game Tracks (measurements don't include dewclaws) Figure 24.1

Antelope - 3" long by 2" wide; no dewclaws, splayed (pointed outward) toes, outer edges of hooves are straight—not heart-shaped, front and rear hooves make separate prints when walking.

Goat - 3" long by 2 1/4" wide; splayed and pointed toes, more rounded outer surface than sheep.

Sheep - 3" long by 2 1/4" wide; toes spread and rounded from weight on front and from rocky terrain, dewclaws almost never show unless two-inch mud or snow.

Deer - 3" long by 2" wide; rear portion of hooves often don't make distinct impressions, dewclaws sometimes register, front and rear hooves are on top of each other when walking.

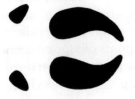

Caribou - 4" long by 5" wide; very rounded outer surface, halves like two crescent moons with very large space between them, as wide as long, dewclaws almost always show.

Elk - 4 1/2" long by 3 1/2" wide; roundish outer edge, narrow gap between halves, dewclaws show in soft mud or snow only.

Musk-oxen - 5" long by 5" wide; squarish overall shape, large, oval gap between halves, dewclaws seldom show, hooves blunt in front and back.

Bison - 6" long by 5" wide; roundish outer edges, overall shape is oval, slightly splayed toes, dewclaws often show.

Moose - 7" long by 5" wide; oval space between hoof halves, dewclaws show—particularly of large bulls, weight farther back on hooves rather than on toes like elk.

Domestic sheep - 3" long by 3" wide; blunter tracks than either deer or pronghorn and halves more widely separated.

Cows/cattle - 6" long by 6" wide; larger tracks than elk, much more rounded than moose and never with dewclaws.

Black bear - usually front print is less than six inches wide, small, sharp claw marks on front only.

Grizzly bear - front claw marks often show and may be slightly curved, also larger and farther out from pad marks, rear claws may show.

Brown bear - larger than grizzly but basically same animal, hind claw marks don't show, front claws may show—straighter than grizzlies' if present.

Cougar - roundish overall shape, tend to be wider than long, no claw marks, wider than canine tracks.

A ruler or other device for measuring tracks is useful when hunting where unfamiliar animals will be present. Trying to decipher a mixture of tracks from wild and domesticated animals can be frustrating. Livestock like cows and sheep have tracks similar in shape and size to those of big game animals so every advantage is necessary—particularly when tracking wounded game. Even experienced hunters may want to measure game tracks to learn more about their quarry or to identify the track of a specific animal they are hunting.

When there is no soft soil or mud to leave obvious tracks hunters must look for other, logical signs. Leaves which are turned over, bent, or have frost or dew missing are some of the more subtle signs to look for. Dew, rain, snow or frost missing off tall grass or brush is often visible and usually easier to pick out if looked at as a long trail and not an individual track. Many times, by lowering your eye near the ground, these trails are easier to line up. A line of depressions made by animals walking over gravel or rocky ground is also easier to pick out from a low angle.

Trails of bent grass or broken spider webs are other signs to look for. In some areas, hundreds of webs are made each night, so broken webs are a good indication of game traveling on trails in early morning. Muddy water in creeks, rivers or standing water can indicate where game has crossed as well as how fresh the trail is.

A knowledge of animal behavior patterns can help when tracking animals. When tracks disappear on hard surfaces the experienced tracker uses logic based on typical behavior to predict which way the animal went. The continuation of the track can often be found this way. Behavior patterns can also help hunters make logical inferences about the time of day a track was made. When hunting a species which feeds early or late in the day, a track found around midday is probably not hot, but made several hours ago. However, a fresh-looking track going into a feeding area found at first light may be worth following very slowly because an animal may be just ahead. A good tracker who recognizes this as a hot track will slow down immediately and have a good chance of sighting the animal before being spotted. However, realizing that bears often travel a dozen or more miles each night and make circuits rather than returning on the same trail, it probably wouldn't pay off to follow fresh morning tracks unless they are steaming hot. Of course, a hunter who finds a hot track must always be attentive enough to check that there is not a hotter set from the same animal on top of the first set and going the other way. A thoughtful combination of track characteristics and typical animal behavior will often determine a hunter's best course of action.

A combination of knowledge, close attention to detail and logic is necessary to fully understand the meaning of game tracks and get the most benefit from them. Knowing the characteristics of a big game animal's tracks is a fundamental requirement of being able to track it. Hunters who are the most observant and pay attention to detail can glean the most information from animal tracks. A logical combination of track information with any other factors will determine the best course of action for the hunter. Hunters who are adept at all these facets of tracking will greatly improve their chances for success.

The ability to read tracks and sign is a necessary part of scouting and locating game. Carl E. Brent and large brown bear tracks on a Kodiak Island beach.

Chapter 25
SCOUTING
AND LOCATING GAME

The most significant ingredient in consistent hunting success is finding an ample game population. Likewise, a "great" hunter who regularly bags the big one, can only do so by hunting in areas containing quality animals. Some hunters just happen to live in areas with dense populations or record-book animals, but even these hunters have to do some scouting if they want to find the best locations to hunt in their areas. To some degree or another, all hunters can improve their hunting success by some level of preseason scouting. Many of these same scouting skills can also help hunters locate game during the hunting season.

Thorough preseason and in-season scouting can be more important to success than hunting skills. The best hunters will not score if there are no legal animals present, yet even beginners have a good chance when legal game is abundant. Knowing where to hunt is often the biggest factor in a hunter's success. Time and effort spent scouting will pay off in hunting success.

"Paper" Scouting

There are three types of scouting for hunters: paper scouting, preseason scouting and in-season scouting. Paper scouting refers to research which is done before ever setting foot in the field. Paper scouting can begin the day after the end of the hunting season. Good paper scouting can save hours of unproductive field work by directing hunters away from low-density game habitat. Hunters can then spend their preseason scouting time in areas which will satisfy their hunting needs—whether that means trophy animals, lots of animals, different species, easy accessibility, low cost, new areas, remote areas or little competition, etc.; paper scouting can uncover all these factors.

Hunting statistics are the first paper resource to examine. Local, State and Federal wildlife agencies usually summarize these by year and region and they are often available to the general public. Hunters can find out where the highest harvests, largest animals, highest success rates or fewest hunters were in past seasons.

Biologists can also provide other valuable information like animal migration routes and timing or the management goals in an area– whether it is large animals or lots of them. Nonresident hunters, in particular, often benefit from visiting these biologists. It is also a good idea to get a copy of hunting regulations from these agencies to learn open seasons, bag limits and general hunting regulations.

The record books are the next paper resource to consult. Most hunters would prefer to take a larger animal, although a "book" animal may not be necessary. The record books will at least give hunters a general idea where large animals have been taken in the past. Nutrition, population density, weather and genetics are all important factors in trophy production, and all are fairly stable. Thus, in all but the most unusual cases, geographic regions tend to produce similar-sized trophies from year to year.

Other valuable sources of information are hunters, landowners, mailmen, milkmen, bus drivers, etc. Although hunters can be tight-lipped about their favorite spots, many can be talkative if approached correctly. One of the best times to do this is immediately after a hunter has been successful and wants to inform others (brag) of his hunting prowess. Most hunters feel this at times, it is part of the euphoria of success. Local or regional sports shows are one place to meet other hunters and hunting "experts." It may take a little detective work to uncover exactly where a large trophy was taken or where a highly successful individual hunts, but this can be a very productive scouting skill.

Landowners and/or farmers can also be useful and willing sources of advice. Living on the land as they do gives them tremendous insights into game populations and habits. They can also tell you which landowners are involved in quality management of game species to produce larger trophies. Workers like mailmen and bus drivers who spend time in an area can also be good sources of information about populations as well as large animals. All these people can direct hunters looking for numbers of animals as well as those looking for large trophies.

There are also hundreds of local newspapers, dozens of periodicals and thousands of books with hunting information. Local newspapers often publish photos of residents' hunting successes. Watching for these and reminding friends and relatives to do the same for you can bring in valuable information not available anywhere else. Of course, there are dozens of magazines covering all types of hunting and regions of the country. Their stories and articles often contain information about where to go and how to hunt

Hunters should do plenty of paper scouting before choosing guides or outfitters. This should include talking to unsuccessful clients of the guides or outfitters as well as successful clients. This is Chris McKinnon of McKinnon & Co. Outfitters.

the specific area. And there are always new hunting books—like this one—coming out with good information for scouting hunters.

Periodicals and books also provide vital information about the different species of game animals. Hunters need to know the life history of each game animal they hunt for scouting, as well as hunting purposes. Details about tracks, droppings, beds and how to identify these signs made by large males are vital for effective scouting. Some of the best whitetail hunters measure tracks, droppings and beds to identify those made by large bucks and avoid wasting time scouting deer they aren't interested in hunting. Even while paper scouting, the more a hunter knows about his intended quarry, the better inquiries he can make. Books and magazines can give hunters general information about an animal's habits as well as the latest discoveries and hunting techniques. A typical example of this is that all North American deer have slightly reddish coats in summer and grayish fall coats. Since hunters need to know where deer are in fall rather than in summer, finding gray hair is more valuable than finding reddish hair. This type of basic information will help determine the general area to hunt.

The final step in paper scouting is gathering land ownership maps, topographic maps and aerial photos of the area(s) selected.

Land ownership maps are not always available, so hunters may have to learn about land ownership from counties or states and make a map of this type. Hunters can use land ownership maps along with the hunting regulations to determine where they can hunt without permission (public lands) and where they will need permission from private landowners. Then they can ask for hunting permission on the private lands before spending any scouting time on areas which cannot be hunted.

The next step is to narrow down the hunting area to the most likely hunting locations. This will save time in the next step, which is to draw in roads, buildings, large crop fields and other important features on topographic maps and aerial photos (if available). Once these features are added, the maps can be studied to determine the most likely spots game will be. For this step, hunters must use all their knowledge of the species they are hunting so they can focus their efforts in the next scouting step—preseason scouting. Making good guesses about where the intended quarry lives can save huge amounts of time and mean the difference between finding good sign or no sign at all. Big whitetail bucks, for example, use ridgelines for travel corridors whenever possible. Topographic maps will show where ridges are and hunters can then put these high on their list for field scouting.

Aerial photos can give an overall, detailed picture and help identify likely feeding, bedding and trail locations. When available, these photos contain a tremendous amount of detailed information which can save hours of scouting time.

Preseason Scouting

The time for preseason scouting—actual field work—also begins the day after the previous hunting season closes. This can be a great time to scout because the animals are typically exactly where they will be during the next hunting season and acting in the same manner, so it produces very valuable information. Also, there are very few, if any, other hunters in the field, so you can have the woods all to yourself. Of course, in order to begin this early, a hunter must have done any necessary paper scouting steps and have already decided where to hunt during the next season. Otherwise, any preseason scouting may be directed at the wrong area and be a waste of time. Many hunters are in the same location from year to year, so this is not a problem. At this point, a hunter should have learned the life history of his quarry, received permission to hunt if necessary, selected his hunting area, purchased maps and/or aerial photos and pinpointed some potential hot spots to scout. Paper scouting may

This moose-rubbed tree indicates bulls are in the area at some time around the rut, but knowing the exact timing is crucial for this information to be of optimal use to a hunter.

not be as interesting as field work, but it is a vital part of a thorough approach to big game scouting.

There are some general guidelines to follow for preseason field work. The most basic one is to scout where game will be during your hunt. Since many animals move during the year, scouting efforts must be directed at the ranges they will use during your upcoming hunt. Scouting elk or mule deer on their winter range does little to tell hunters about their locations and habits during the fall hunting season. For many species, winter food is different, feeding times change and animals have different associations—males often bunch in winter, but rarely during fall hunting seasons. Depending on the

This whitetail scrape is a common indicator of a buck marking its territory and looking for does.

species, scouting winter ranges can still be useful for learning about population sizes, herd compositions and large trophies present. Looking at elk or mule deer herds in winter can be useful from these aspects because the animals are so much more visible at this time of year. Assuming this is done before antlers are dropped, this may be the best or only time of the year trophy animals can be seen and scouted. Scouting mountain sheep or goats on their winter ranges is always useful since their horns are never shed. However, since there is always the possibility that large individuals may winter-kill, winter scouting is best used for a general estimation of the possible trophy production of a herd. Keeping tabs on the herd's health over the winter will indicate how many of the large males survive and thus, help determine where to hunt. Winter scouting is only useful if the hunter knows where these animals will be during the hunting season.

The way a species' population varies from year to year also affects the reliability of preseason scouting for herd size and trophy content. Many northern animals like Dall sheep, Sitka deer and some whitetail deer populations are mostly affected by weather. These populations can drop suddenly over a winter due to harsh weather conditions. Caribou, on the other hand, are most susceptible to wolf predation and overgrazing. Their populations display classic boom and bust cycles which are somewhat more predictable. All of these species can have sudden population declines from these factors. Bear populations, however, are fairly stable over all of their ranges. Hunters must keep these variables in mind when devising their scouting plan(s) and determining the reliability of winter scouting.

Winter scouting on deserted fall ranges can be informative if animal sign is visible. Deer rub lines and trails along with general topography can be used to identify their fall patterns. The lack of vegetation in winter can also help a hunter see the habitat more clearly to understand game patterns.

Hunters also have to make allowances when scouting during the summer months. Game animals often change their feeding, bedding and movement patterns from summer to fall. Summer scouting can still be useful for determining herd sizes and the numbers and sizes of large animals. This is in part due to the fact that game is typically more visible in summer than fall. Hunters should look in the upper portions of animals' ranges in summer because they try to avoid heat and insects during the hotter months. The largest males of a species are often found at the upper edges of their range in all seasons, except during the rut.

When scouting game, hunters should look at the habitat as the animal's home. Habitat is never uniform throughout. There are preferred places for animals to feed, bed and make trails depending on the characteristics of the land and the weather patterns. Look for the animal's bedroom, kitchen and highways and imagine where each is best located. Remember that an animal's needs are food, shelter, safety and sex. By doing this, hunters can better understand the animal's habits and get the most from their scouting time. It is a good habit to carry a small notebook when scouting to keep track of details and to make sketches when needed. Simple drawings can add a tremendous amount of meaning to scouting results. They will often help hunters "see" an animal's home with better clarity.

Animal sign to look for while scouting varies with species. Figure 25.1 lists the important signs for North American big game animals. Meticulous scouters who pay attention to detail can identify all these animals by their sign and learn the most from it.

Figure 25.1

COMMON SIGNS OF NORTH AMERICAN BIG GAME ANIMALS

Species	Signs to look for
Black Bear	Tracks, dung piles, turned-over or torn-up logs and stumps, berry patches.
Brown/Grizzly Bear	Tracks, trails, dung piles, salmon carcasses, dug-out squirrel holes, hair on trees.
Polar Bear	Tracks, activity around seal holes with blood, beds in snow crevices.
Cougar	Tracks, droppings, carcasses, hair.
Deer	Tracks, trails, droppings, rubs, scrapes, beds, shed antlers, feeding sign.
Pronghorn	Tracks–particularly around waterholes, droppings, sheds, feeding sign.
Caribou	Tracks, trails cut into tundra & across hillsides, droppings, feeding craters in snow.
Moose	Tracks, trails, rubs, beds, droppings, wallows, sheds.
Elk	Tracks, droppings, beds, sheds, wallows, rubs, scrapes.
Sheep	Tracks, trails, droppings, sheds, hair.
Rocky Mt. Goat	Tracks, trails, droppings, hair.
Bison	Tracks, trails, dung piles, feeding sign.
Musk-oxen	Tracks, droppings, feeding craters in winter, hair.

Trails are year-round signs of game habits and presence. They must be interpreted with the specific animal's habits in mind. Major trails mean different things depending on the species. Some are migration routes and only used for a brief period during the year. Caribou migration trails are only used for a few weeks each year. Hunting them at other times is generally a waste of time. Major trails made by whitetails may be used mostly by does and young animals; the only time bucks may use them during the hunting season is after dark. In these cases, barely distinguishable minor trails may be the main highways of bucks during hunting season. Bucks may only use these minor trails for a few weeks of hunting season so they might not even be visible until *after* the season starts. Other reasons buck trails often look little-used in comparison are that mature bucks tend to be solitary most of the year, there are fewer mature bucks than does, fawns and yearlings, and bucks choose more secure trails once hunting season opens. The *minor* trails are often the *major* buck routes during the season.

When hunting coastal brown bears in Alaska, a similar logic applies. Large males have their own trails which sows often avoid to protect their cubs from cannibalistic males. These trails are identified by the wide spacing between the left and right tracks, often twelve inches or more. In this case, another thing to consider is how easily the fragile tundra is marred and how long it takes to recover. One large male can make a deep trail in the tundra during his lifetime (10-25 years) which may be visible for decades after his death. Unless there are fresh, large tracks on this trail, hunters can easily be deceived into hunting for a large bear that is long gone. Each species is different, so their behavior and their habitat must be understood to scout for—and hunt them—successfully.

Droppings or dung are also informative signs to look for while scouting. Size and numbers can be used to locate large animals and determine population numbers. Droppings and dung piles of each species have characteristics which indicate what they have been eating and when they were made. Moose droppings in winter are mostly made of sawdust-like material from the wintertime browse they eat. Summer-time droppings are flatter, softer and contain more dark green vegetation. Seasonal traits of a species' droppings are important to know since this type of sign can easily persist for twelve months. Hunters who don't know the differences can be fooled into hunting parts of an animal's range that are devoid of game during hunting season.

Rubs and scrapes are signs of bucks' and bulls' presence in an area. Since deer and moose rub in August, they are not necessarily around their rubs later in the fall. Last year's rubs must also be distinguished from this year's for pertinent scouting information. Scrapes and wallows indicate the presence of bucks and bulls–deer make scrapes, moose and elk make wallows. Large scrapes in the presence of large sheds are a good indication of large whitetail bucks. However, mule deer may be fifty miles away from their scrapes or rubs when they shed. Since moose and elk also move considerable distances in winter to escape heavy snow and find food, their sheds are usually far removed from their rutting activities–including their wallows. Rubs are seldom revisited by any antlered species, so their use is mostly for scouting for the presence of these animals, and only occasionally useful for stand locations.

Feeding sign is useful when it can be found. Animals can be grazers, browsers, carnivores or omnivores–or a combination of these. Grazers eat grasses and low-growing vegetative plants. Sheep are a classic grazing animal, but because of the remoteness of their habitat and difficulty in finding this sign, it is not very useful. Deer, elk and moose are grazers at times and browsers at other times. Browsing sign is easier to identify than grazing sign. Unfortunately, the animals are usually grazing during hunting season, turning to browsing in winter. Still, browsing lines are easy to spot and do indicate where good numbers of animals winter–which does have some use for scouting hunters–as previously mentioned.

Escape terrain and cover should also be looked for while scouting. Most animals use some type of escape terrain–sheep use cliffs, deer and bears use dense cover and wetlands, and pronghorn and caribou like wide open country. While the presence of any one of these by itself doesn't indicate that a certain species lives nearby, it does indicate where animals that are there will run when threatened. Escape terrain and cover should always be noted by scouting hunters, particularly when animals have already been located. It is part of an animal's home which will be used frequently after hunting season begins.

The results of paper scouting and field scouting for sign will outline animal hot spots where there is much more game than in surrounding areas. As previously mentioned, habitat is not uniform. There are some spots which have warmth, shelter and food–with plenty of game, too. Other areas close by without one or more of these qualities may seem devoid of game. This dearth of animals may also be noticeable in small game and bird populations. Many times these differences in animal populations can be directly related to temperature differences. Cold spots often have little food so

Aerial scouting can be useful to learn herd composition and look for large bulls–perhaps for the next season. These bison are in Alaska's Farewell herd.

animals don't stay long and just pass through. The temperature differences can often be related to the way the land slopes. North-facing slopes are often windier and colder than south-facing slopes. This pattern is recognized again and again by attentive hunters who spend time in the field. It is useful to remember when mapping animals' habitat and when looking for game in unknown territory.

When patterning animals, it is much more reliable to use sign rather than sightings alone. Sightings are usually brief and only tell part of the story. Sign is fairly permanent and can tell the whole story to conscientious scouters. One trick to create fresh sign to read is to find a patch of soft dirt or mud on a creek bank or dirt road and brush it clean of all old tracks. New tracks you find on subsequent days will be easy to age and will help identify animal movements.

Patterning animals requires an intimate knowledge of their behavior and habitat. The last step in preseason scouting requires the use of all a hunter's experience along with adequate paper scouting and field work. This is the final map work using the previously created map with the added features. Using this map, hunters should add the details of the animal's habitat including feeding areas, bedding areas, escape cover, travel corridors with important major and minor trails, rub and scrape lines, wallows, sighting locations and sheds which were found. Predominant winds can be included, as can known or expected stand locations. In short, it should include everything hunters know about the animal(s) and its habitat which will help them hunt it. This type of map can be made of a large area to use for overall hunting strategy or of a smaller area to pattern one specific animal. Creating these maps will give hunters a visual image of their hunt area which can be invaluable during days in the field.

In-Season Scouting

Hunters who cannot scout before the season can use the first few days of their hunt as their information base—if they haven't already taken their animal by then. For this type of scouting it is even more important for hunters to be alert, pay attention to details and carry a note pad to jot down thoughts and make sketches. Even hunters who have done a year's worth of thorough scouting should pay close attention to animal behavior during their hunt because it will probably be changing in the presence of hunters. During many short hunting seasons, hunting pressure is very high, so this time of year is like no other—with respect to animal behavior. Hunters can only observe this behavior for a short time, so they must make the most of it to learn as much as possible.

Locating game rather than just their sign now becomes a top priority. All of a hunter's knowledge of animal behavior will now be tested as he tries to anticipate where and when game will appear. Two of the most significant factors hunters need to consider are the weather and the rutting cycle. Weather often affects animals' daily schedules as well as the beginning of yearly activities like the rut and migrations. Both the rut and migrations are often delayed by warm weather and advanced by cold weather. A spell of warm weather can create a lull in the rut or cause reverse migrations in extreme situations. In cold weather, animals usually look for warm, sunny slopes to bed, unless it is still hot during hunting season. If snow is present, animals prefer to bed on the lower edge of it. During the rut, bucks and bulls will often cruise long distances in search of females. Passes in hilly or mountainous areas are good places to watch for these cruising males.

On moderately windy days, prey animals often stay amongst trees and don't move much. On very windy days, deer will sometimes get nervous because they cannot hear or smell danger very well. They will move more to escape the errant smells and to stay ahead of danger they cannot hear. Stand-hunting can be good at these times, as can still-hunting, since your noise will be covered. I've often come

Good sign can indicate where an animal is, what it is eating and when it came by a location. Alert, educated hunters can determine all these factors from this fresh black bear dung full of berries.

upon deer on windy days which hadn't sensed me because of the conditions, yet were looking around frantically–trying to use their eyes to make up for what their ears and noses couldn't tell them under the conditions.

Whitetail deer have many subtleties of behavior during their rut which can direct a hunter's strategy. Before or after the rut the best time to see mature bucks is early or late in the day; during the rut bucks may appear anytime. When rutting, bucks are likely to be moving more than usual just after a rain to freshen their scrapes. Bucks visit their scrapes more before does come into heat; afterward, hunters should stand near natural travel funnels to intercept bucks chasing does. A buck's runway of rubs is typically on a minor trail in heavier cover, from 30-100 feet off a major trail. Each rub in the line is just visible from the last one. Hunters looking for large bucks should hunt large rubs in late October.

An area can also be over-hunted. Remember that your scent stays around for days. Animals may be scenting you as they come by your stand or vantage point at different times than when you have been hunting. If your scouting has shown there is game in the area, give it a rest for a few days, then come back and try different hunting hours.

Finding fresh elk sign like this rub is always good for a hunter's confidence, and a confident hunter is usually more alert and conscientious about doing all the little things which add up to success.

A thorough scouting job will identify the best locations to find the animals you want. Paper scouting is the most time-effective part of the process—narrowing down a nationwide base of land to the specific spots which meet your needs. Preseason scouting in the field is best accomplished by hunters with good knowledge of their quarry's behavior patterns and life history. Any final in-season scouting which can be done will help direct a hunter's action during the season. Hunters with confidence in their scouting are more likely to hunt effectively in the best locations, and improve their chances of success.

Chapter 26
PLANNING THE HUNT

Hunt planning is one of the crucial steps in successful hunting. Hunters must use knowledge gained from scouting as well as from past hunting experiences. Planning will set the stage for the hunt—determining the species, how, when, where and with whom you hunt.

The first decision to make is what species to hunt. The most common animal for U.S. hunters to pursue is the whitetail deer, and most do so year after year. Those who want to pursue a different species should carefully analyze each one with respect to the following criteria. First, determine which species are available near your home. Do you want to hunt one of these or is there another, distant species you would rather pursue? If the latter, are you willing and able to spend the money to hunt this other species? The answer to this second question often determines what to hunt and where to hunt it. Your physical condition may also limit what and where you can hunt. To participate in some hunts, there is some minimum level of conditioning you will need to have a reasonable chance of success. The hunting season of a species is another consideration. The season must fall within a time period when your entire hunting party is able to hunt.

The goal of the hunt should be considered when choosing the species to hunt. Is it a trophy hunt or a meat hunt? How big of a trophy is desired? When considering possible hunting locations or times for one species, are you willing to settle for a fair trophy if the odds are good, or would you rather have a chance at a really big one even though the odds are low? Are both meat and trophy potentially important? Except for a few species during their rutting period, all wild game can be quite tasty, so good meat is generally possible in addition to nice trophies. Is a hunt in your old stomping grounds what you want, or do you want to see new territory or have a new type of adventure? Is a quality hunt with little competition important? Maybe a remote hunt is desirable or maybe a multiple-species hunt would be fun.

Another facet of choosing the goal is deciding how many hunters will be in the group. In general, the bigger the group, the less chance you have of getting a large trophy, but a larger group usually means you have a better chance of getting at least some meat. The most productive hunter is one who hunts alone–particularly when it comes to getting a large trophy. One hunter makes only one-fourth the disturbance as two hunters. He also gets first crack at the largest animals and best hunting spots. The benefits of a large group are cost savings, more camaraderie, increased safety, better chances at limited permits, sharing of (possibly expensive) equipment, sharing of personal contacts and sharing of information about a new area– both before and during the hunt.

Plan Early

You can never plan early enough for a big game hunt. For one thing, anticipation of the hunt is a large part of the enjoyment, so early planning increases the pleasure of the event. Some enthusiastic hunters even plan their wedding dates and (try to) plan their children's birthdays so they don't occur during any major hunting seasons–or at least not on opening week.

The next thing to do is learn the hunting regulations and relevant laws for the species and area you will hunt. It is surprising how many hunters don't bother to do this. It can not only save you from getting an unnecessary citation, it can improve your chances at success, too. On one deer hunt in Wisconsin many years ago, I missed a chance at my first whitetail buck on opening morning because I didn't know the regulations. I let a large forkhorn pass by my stand at 70 yards and never raised my rifle because I wanted something bigger. Later, my hunting partners—cousins who had grown up in the area—informed me I could have shot the buck and had one of them within earshot punch his tag, so I could keep hunting. I had never heard that party hunters could punch a tag for each other as long as they were close enough to talk between themselves. I missed my only chance at a deer that season because I hadn't learned all the regulations. Legal hours, open seasons, legal game, legal weapons, tagging requirements, trespassing laws, age limits, etc. are highly variable between states and even counties, so it is advisable to learn the regulations and laws in every location you hunt.

Information sources to contact about general hunting regulations as well as additional laws on public lands are state wildlife agencies, the Federal Fish & Wildlife Service, the Forest Service, the BLM, state parks departments and Federal Park managers. These agencies have information about hunting opportunities as well as regulations and laws you will need when hunting on these lands.

*Planning early for a remote hunt—like this one for musk-oxen—
which involves guides, outfitters or other services is a must.
George P. Mann with a Northwest Territories' bull.*

Other information sources for hunt planning include booking
agents, guides, outfitters, local biologists, personal contacts, sporting
goods stores, lodges and outdoor equipment rentals. Most of these
have a vested interest in helping hunters and many just like to talk
hunting. Some factors to question people about are any unusual
regulations in the hunt area, the chances of the season being closed
unexpectedly, pending regulation changes, and how extreme weather
may affect the location of the game herds or the likelihood of success.
When hunting unfamiliar areas, surprises can be averted by a
thorough investigation into all aspects of the hunt.

Some hunting areas are restricted to drawing permit holders,
limited license holders, trespass fee permit holders, those with
permission from landowners, first-come applicants, residents only
or nonresidents only. Looking into the licensing or permit process
early will uncover any of these situations in time to plan accordingly.
Some permit hunts require applicants to apply for two or more years
in advance to get enough preference points to have a reasonable
chance of drawing. Once preference points are earned, some permits
have almost a 100% chance of being drawn. Other hunts are first-
come registration hunts, so early arrival is necessary. In some states,

USGS maps are essential when planning a hunt to a wilderness area with which hunters are unfamiliar. A few minutes' worth of looking at these maps can help hunters focus their efforts on the most likely hotspots to hunt rather than spend days of field time accomplishing this chore.

nonresidents aren't eligible for some permits, but in others, nonresidents have a better chance than residents. The situations are quite variable, so hunters should investigate early enough to ensure the best chance of getting a license.

If you hunt on private land where permission to hunt is required, there are some basic rules to follow when dealing with landowners or land managers. Remember, you are representing the hunters to landowners and the rest of the public. Whatever you do will reflect on all of us and impact the future of hunting. Treat landowners and their property as you would want people to treat you.

—Always get permission to hunt private land.

—Ask where to park your car.

—Ask if you should identify your vehicle in a special way.

—Leave gates and fences as you found them, unless there is obviously a problem—then fix it and/or contact the landowner. Do not block any gates or barways (animal gates) with your car.

—Never drive across fields, pastures or crop lands without specific permission.

—Bring out any garbage; do not burn or bury anything on the property. If you must smoke, do it on roadways—never in fields, crushing it out completely and bringing it out with you.

—Never cut living plants, or any brush or trees without specific permission.

—Use portable tree stands—do not build permanent ones. Never use wire or drive nails into trees.

—Basically, ask permission for anything you aren't sure is okay.

—Stop and visit the landowner at other times of the year to say hello, but avoid his busy times like planting or harvesting periods.

Another part of planning is determining if any special gear, special weapons, physical conditioning or shooting practice is required. These considerations are mostly for hunters traveling out of their area to hunt a different animal and/or hunt in a different type of terrain. Advice from experienced hunters or locals from the hunt area is helpful, but should be confirmed by more than one source. Magazines or books tend to be more reliable sources of general hunting information if this is all that is needed, but reliable local advice can be very specific and invaluable. Physical conditioning is crucial to some types of hunting (see Chapter Four) and usually improves hunters' chances for any type of hunt. Practice with your weapon (see Chapter Sixteen) can also be crucial to success, depending on the animal and terrain. Early planning will give hunters enough time for any necessary preparations.

Timing of the Hunt

Scheduling will be determined by the specifics of the hunt as well as the hunter's goals. The year of the hunt should first be determined. Biologists and locals should know about the current population of a game herd and possibly the future trend for the next few years. If a herd's population is peaking, maybe this year is the time to go. On the other hand, when populations are lower and on the upswing, the trophy quality is usually much higher than when the habitat is at its maximum carrying capacity. Personal considerations such as work schedule, necessary preparations, and financial considerations are also a large part of the scheduling equation.

After the year is chosen, the time of the season to hunt must be considered. In some areas, up to 50% of the whitetail deer are taken on the first day of the season. With many species, the first day or week of the season is a good time to hunt. This is because of the high number of legal animals, their relative complacency after a break in the hunting pressure and their constant movement due to hunting

Timing is crucial when hunting migratory species like barren ground caribou. Tony Russ took this early season bull before it migrated out of the mountains where it had spent the summer.

pressure. Of course there are some hunting situations where the early part of the season is not good at all. Spring bear season in Alaska and Canada usually opens before many bears are out, so hunters who begin too early can spend weeks without seeing any game. Migrating species should be hunted according to their migration schedule, wherever that may fall within the season. The end of the season may also be appealing, depending on the species. The rut of many species just begins as the hunting season ends, so the last few days may have more buck or bull activity because of this. This is typically the case during the early moose seasons. In the case of Dall sheep, the first snows of winter and the early stages of rut often bring huge rams out of their unreachable, mountain retreats as their hunting season draws to a close. Some of the serious sheep hunters wait until the last week of this season to hunt for these large rams, even though the weather is colder and wetter than earlier in the season.

Weather is another consideration because it often changes considerably as fall turns to winter during the course of a big game season. This can have both good and bad connotations, varying with the species being hunted. Winter often brings animals down to more accessible areas, but can also make hunting, traveling and camping more difficult–and certainly colder. The number of hunters may also be down later in the season as they get discouraged and go home.

Another consideration is the phase of the moon. Some animals' daylight activities are affected by the amount of moonlight each night. Planning a hunt to coincide with the darker phases of the moon may be prudent depending on the species being hunted and the time of year.

Guides and Outfitters

In some locations, for some species, a nonresident is required to hire a guide or outfitter before hunting. This typically means more cost, but results in a higher success rate. In Alaska, where the law requires most nonresidents to hire a guide when hunting Dall sheep, they enjoy a 65% success rate–compared to a 30% success rate of residents without guides. Besides higher success rates, guides who know the terrain and the dangers of hunting an animal also provide a good measure of safety. In fact, one of the primary reasons for requiring nonresidents to hire a guide to hunt brown bear, mountain goat and Dall sheep in Alaska is to protect hunters from the dangers involved when hunting these three species.

Even if hiring a guide is not required by law, it often pays to do so. They can provide gear, lodging, food, horses, transportation and expertise which many nonresidents do not have. Just the cost of the gear necessary to hunt in some areas is prohibitive for a one-time hunt. Here in Alaska where transportation is a major cost, paying an outfitter or guide to use his gear and field transportation is sometimes less expensive than the cost of buying and transporting the gear one-way into the field–let alone getting it back. Additionally, a good guide will have the best gear to improve your odds of success as well as comfort. Hunters who try to put together all the gear and necessities of a remote hunt often cut costs and end up lacking some essentials or working with inferior equipment. Other benefits of having a guide are the reduced work load in the field and a minimal amount of logistics to work out.

If you do decide to hire a guide or outfitter, check them out thoroughly. They can make or break your hunt. Friends or relatives are good places to start for recommendations. Reputable booking agents are available to help find the right professional at no extra cost to you. Always get some references so you can talk to past clients and get their views. Ask specific questions from a detailed list you make for comparing different outfits. Try to talk to the person who will be your personal guide to get a feel for a match in your personalities and goals for the hunt. As in any service industry, there are good ones and bad ones; it is up to you to find the right match for your expectations.

Some animals are best hunted with a guide. Mike Traub (r) shows off his Dall sheep taken with guide Tony Russ in 1998.

If you do choose a guide, you have to trust his judgement. I often compare notes about bear and sheep hunters with a Master Guide I work with here in Alaska. It is incredible how some neophyte bear or sheep hunters "know" more about how to hunt these animals than guides with twenty or thirty years' experience hunting in Alaska. Even more incredible is the story this same Master Guide related to me about his experience on an African Safari. As he was following his professional hunter on foot through the brush one day, my guide cut across a patch of grass—which the head tracker and professional hunter had gone around—and promptly stepped on a poisonous snake. As my guide said after this experience, there is usually a reason guides do what they do, so follow their lead exactly to stay out of trouble. This same rule applies to guides in North America–if you select them for their competence, let them do the guiding and follow their lead.

Planning for a big game hunt is an exciting and important part of the experience. Adequate research and thought is necessary to produce consistent satisfaction with the results. Time and effort on this phase of the hunt will be rewarded with greater success.

Chapter 27
HUNTING TECHNIQUES

There are several effective techniques which can be used to successfully hunt North American big game animals. The most successful hunters know how to be an efficient hunter/predator in whichever technique they are using. They are able to slow down, leave their everyday worries behind, use their senses of sight and hearing to "see" the quarry's habitat and become a part of the outdoor world. This is not easy for many of us to do because most of our time is spent apart from the natural world in which game animals live. It helps to begin thinking like a hunter as you travel to your hunting area, pausing for at least a few brief moments as you step into the woods. Then, begin your hunt, as you step into the role of the hunter/predator.

Choosing the Appropriate Technique

The basic techniques for hunting big game in North America are stand or blind-hunting, spot & stalk hunting, still-hunting, driving, calling, and baiting. The most successful hunting technique in any situation will be determined by the species, their current behavior patterns, the abundance of animals, the location, which part of the hunting season it is, the time of day, the weather, the amount of hunting pressure, the size of the hunting group and the skill level of the hunter(s). In addition to personal skill level, personal preference will also affect which method a hunter chooses in a hunting situation.

Stand or blind-hunting refers to the use of a stationary location where hunters wait for animals to pass within shooting range. These can be tree stands, ground stands, ground blinds, pit blinds, floating blinds or any spot where hunters wait to ambush animals. Driving, calling and/or baiting are often used in conjunction with stands to bring animals within range of standing hunters.

Spotting and then stalking game is useful wherever game can be seen from sufficient distance to allow the hunter to remain undetected. Hunters typically use optics from a vantage point to watch for game. When a suitable animal is spotted in a good location, the

Using the most appropriate hunting technique is the mark of an experienced hunter. George E. Mann used the spot & stalk method to take this caribou.

stalk begins. Cruising shorelines is another form of spot and stalk hunting where animals are spotted from a boat, then hunters are put ashore to stalk them.

Still-hunting is the most difficult of all these hunting methods. To use this technique, a hunter moves slowly through moderately dense–to dense cover while searching for animals at close range. It is basically one long stalk without knowing the location of your quarry. The name of this method has two meanings. First, it refers to the speed of the moving hunter–so slow that he appears to be still. Second, hunters who use this method are most likely "still hunting" when others are done, because it is so difficult to do successfully.

Driving involves using moving hunters to "drive" animals to stationary hunters. The moving hunters should be basically still-hunting, while the other hunters are basically on stand, waiting for animals to come within shooting range.

Calling includes any noises—grunting, rattling or calling—made to lure animals within range. It is usually done during an animal's mating season, however, some—like fawn bleats to call in deer and predator calls used to bring in bears—can be used at any time of the hunting season.

Baiting usually involves placing food and/or food scents where animals will smell them and then come within range of a hunter waiting near the bait. Bears are the most common game hunted this way, but deer are also baited in some states. Baiting includes using animal decoys to lure in game–often accompanied by the use of scents.

Figure 27.1 is a list of North American big game species and the most common methods used to hunt them. The different species of moose, caribou, sheep or elk have been listed together because they are hunted with similar methods all across their ranges. The deer and bear species have been listed separately because each is hunted using different methods. Hunting techniques have only been listed when they are used on a widespread basis for that animal, even though every method could be used to hunt each species in the right situation.

Table 27.1

HUNTING METHODS COMMONLY USED FOR NORTH AMERICAN SPECIES

Whitetail deer – Stands, calling, spot & stalk, still-hunting, driving, baiting.

Mule deer – Spot & stalk, still-hunting, calling, driving.

Blacktail deer – Spot & stalk, still-hunting, calling, driving, stands.

Coues deer – Spot & stalk, still-hunting, stands, calling, driving.

Black bear – Stands over bait & stands-ambush, spot & stalk, calling, floating/still-hunting.

Brown/grizzly bear – Spot & stalk, stands-ambush, floating/still hunting, calling.

Polar bear – Spot & stalk, stands-ambush.

Caribou – Spot & stalk, stands, floating/still-hunting.

Elk – Spot & stalk, calling, still-hunting, stands.

Moose – Spot & stalk, calling, still-hunting, stands.

Goat – Spot & stalk, stands.

Pronghorn – Spot & stalk, stands, driving, baiting.

Sheep – Spot & stalk, stands-ambush.

Cougar – Driving with dogs, spot & stalk.

Bison – Spot & stalk, still-hunting, driving, stands-ambush.

Musk-oxen – Spot & stalk, driving.

All animals on this list can be hunted with the spot & stalk technique. It is a basic predator response—we see the animal, then we try to catch it. The other techniques are more specialized and used less often—mostly by humans and not other predators. Stand-hunting in one form or another can be used for all these animals, too, because anytime hunters get in front of a moving animal and wait they are stand-hunting.

After species, the next most important factor for determining which hunting method to use is terrain. Wide open country is ideal for spot and stalk hunting because hunters can use vantage points to look for animals at long distances without too much concern about being spotted themselves. Heavily wooded or brush-covered terrain should be hunted with stands or by still-hunting—depending on the species being hunted. Each area should be examined for any unique characteristics when deciding on the best hunting method to use. A large, impassible physical barrier—like a body of water or a gorge—will funnel animal movements significantly and will influence your hunting decisions. Stand-hunting would probably be a good technique in this case.

Every factor which may affect animal movements—the distances, directions and predictability—should be considered when selecting a hunting method. Recognizing these factors and correctly assessing their effects are two of the most important skills a hunter can possess. They are also skills which every hunter can and should continually improve upon.

Spot & Stalk Hunting

Spotting game is a skill which hunters learn by practicing. Although spotting is most important for this particular hunting technique, it is a necessary part of all techniques. Good game spotters anticipate where to look for game and know what to look for. Hunters need an accurate mental image of the animal they are seeking so they can pick out the animal or part of the animal from the surrounding cover or background. Even game in wide-open terrain is often hard to see because animals are naturally camouflaged. Caribou and bighorn sheep are two good examples of animals which can be very difficult to spot against their typical background unless they are moving.

Every hunter overlooks some game, but the better spotters know to search for parts of animals–in addition to the whole body. The horizontal line of an animal's back is the part of an animal which hunters most frequently spot first. It stands out because few other objects have such straight, long horizontal lines in typical

Spot & stalk hunters are more effective if they have a partner who can direct them during a stalk. Here, Chris Watchus is using a signalling device to direct his hunting partner.

habitat. Distinct vertical lines are often legs and should also be looked for by hunters. The color of an animal's body is another good clue which should trigger a scanning hunter to look more carefully. Horns and antlers have both unique shapes and unusual colors, so they are another good clue. Bull moose can often be spotted for miles by looking for their distinctly white antlers, even when in moderately dense cover. At closer ranges, head, neck or ear outlines of many animals can be picked out by alert spotters.

The best game spotters know the animal they are looking for in great detail. They have memorized the exact hue of the animal's coat and know the size and shape of animal to look for. Hunters who pursue the huge Kodiak brown bears for the first time often don't understand that even the biggest bears are short when on all fours. The hump on a big male is no higher than four feet off the ground, and most are shorter. Experienced hunters who realize this know to look in short cover which neophytes will pass up as too little to hide a big bear. An inaccurate mental image can severely handicap a hunter's spotting efforts. Studying photos before a hunt can vastly improve a hunter's spotting effectiveness during the hunt.

Spotting typically calls for the use of binoculars and, sometimes, spotting scopes. Hunters using binoculars or spotting scopes must understand that our eyes can only focus on a small portion of the view we see through these optics. Small portions of the field of view (the total view we see through optics) have to be examined carefully for our eyes to see everything clearly. Otherwise, animals can easily be overlooked.

The typical strategy for spotting game is to get on a high vantage point where large areas can be visually searched. Hunters should always approach ridges or knolls with caution, so they are not spotted by game. Going slowly, removing hats or reflective glasses, covering shiny faces and hands and peeking over the tops carefully will prevent game from spotting hunters in these elevated locations. Advantages to getting above game are: animals look for danger from below most often; when game is spotted, hunters can travel downhill faster to get to it; the largest males of many species are usually in the highest portions of their habitat; and the highest hunters often have game pushed to them by hunters below. Hunters can also climb a tall tree in flat country or use the middle of a valley as a vantage point to scan the side hills–as long as caution is used and game is far enough away to avoid detection. The degree to which hunters have to be concerned about alerting game depends on the animal and the situation. Game which is accustomed to seeing people will sometimes let hunters travel in full view–if the animal feels it has not been spotted. During hunting season though, this may change dramatically, with the slightest sign of people making game move out.

Spotting game is the most important aspect of some hunts. This brown bear hunter is sitting in a bunker for wind protection while he looks for bears—for up to twelve hours per day.

Good hunters look for game in effective patterns. The first thing to do from any new viewpoint is to quickly scan for obvious animals without any optics, noting the locations of any animals or objects which need further inspection. Next, binoculars (or spotting scopes) should be used to examine the quality of the visible animals, the suspicious objects for verification and then the whole area in a slow, meticulous pattern. It is helpful to have an inspection pattern to examine every bit of the area in view. This pattern can be as simple as top to bottom and left to right, or more complex, depending on personal preference. The important thing is to use some sort of pattern to avoid missing animals.

Knowing where to look for one game species comes from a familiarity with its unique behavior patterns (Chapter Twenty-Two). However, there are a few generalities which pertain to almost all animals. Animals seek warmth, so sunny slopes in cold weather are always good spots. In general, south-facing slopes in colder climates are better than north-facing slopes. Heavy snows will concentrate animals in areas which have less snow—like beaches, riverbeds and windswept ridges or pastures. Open-country animals like caribou and sheep often skyline themselves to get a better view. Animals which live in dense cover usually stick to it, seldom coming out into open area during daylight hours in a hunting season.

Plan on looking in an upwind direction so animals won't scent you. If you do have to look downwind, stay back a reasonable distance for the species you are hunting. Bears have excellent noses so you should be at least one mile away from them when looking downwind. However, whitetails in many suburban habitats are so used to living with human scent they aren't spooked unless you smell closer than 200-300 yards.

In addition to looking in the right spots and from the right location, you have to look at the right time. Since animals are much easier to spot when they are active rather than when bedded, spotting for many big game animals is most productive early and late in the day—their most active times. However, this is not true of the antlered males of many species during their rut when they are out all day looking for females or of brown bears which seem to travel all day during the spring season in search of food. However, in the fall hunting season, large male brown bears are seldom seen in daylight—some becoming completely nocturnal. Species, sex and age must always be considered when deciding when to spot.

If a hunter is spotted by game, there are a couple ways to convince the animal it is in no danger. Act disinterested by looking in another direction—don't act like a hunter who focuses his attention toward the animal. Look down, kneel for a while, walk back and forth—anything to bring out the natural curiosity of the animal and

By listening for their bugling and homing in on these sounds, hunters can spot & stalk elk audibly in addition to visually. This bowhunter is obviously pleased with his 5x5 bull.

make it relax. Meander to a location where you can get out of sight, then stalk the animal while staying behind cover.

There is another ruse to try on animals which are accustomed to seeing humans in a nonthreatening activity–like photographing or berry-picking. This method is to slowly angle toward the animal while acting disinterested. Hunters should never walk directly at an animal which has seen them. It may also work with very curious species like caribou or young animals of any species. Sometimes hunters can actually get within shooting range with this method.

If you have hunting partners, you can all walk out of sight and then you can drop off behind some cover as your partners come back into the animal's view and continue to hold its attention. This ruse depends on the animal's inability to count in order to be successful. It doesn't work nearly as often if you only have one partner, since animals seem to count to two okay, but if you have two or more companions who can stay in sight while you continue the stalk, it often works.

When there are two or more hunters in a group, there are some responsibilities of each member, depending on whether they are the leader or a follower. Hunting groups should not travel en masse like a pack of dogs. Organized hunting groups will scare far less game and be far more productive. There should be only one leader at any one time. The *leader's* responsibilities are: 1) Allow for the followers' physical and emotional limits when setting the pace. This keeps the group tighter which spooks less game. It also improves safety and allows for quieter communication. 2) When pausing to rest on steep slopes, stop where there are enough level spots for everyone in the group. 3) Make less noise than the followers. 4) Don't let branches whip back and hit the followers. 5) Warn followers if any rocks are falling toward them. The *followers'* responsibilities are: 1) Follow the leader's trail exactly unless otherwise discussed and agreed upon. This also keeps everyone in a tight group. 2) Step in the leader's tracks to reduce noise–when noise is critical. 3) Don't crowd the leader, but stay close enough for necessary communication. 4) Make less noise than the leader. 5) Let the leader know if you want to stop.

The *Stalking* phase of this technique begins right after you spot an animal you are hunting. The decision to wait or go after the animal immediately is a crucial one and should be preceded by careful study of the stalking route and the animal. First, is the animal worthy of a stalk? (Field-Judging is covered in Chapter Twenty-Eight.) If it is worthy of a stalk, can you successfully complete a stalk to a suitable shooting position before it moves out of range, before nightfall, without spooking other animals, with the current wind directions and given the intervening terrain? Hunters must perform a quick, careful inspection of the stalking route(s) to the animal–imagining every step of the way to foresee any obstacles. Physical obstacles like impassable rock walls when sheep hunting or areas of noisy brush when deer hunting will prevent a successful stalk.

The species you are hunting is a major consideration when planning a stalk. The species' behavior patterns must be understood to accurately predict what it will do in the time it takes to complete the stalk. Goats rely on their noses to sense danger and will go to the closest, steepest cliffs to escape; bears also rely on their noses to sense danger, but they will run to the nearest dense cover to escape; and sheep rely on their eyes and will run toward the top of the mountain and often go over to escape–each responds differently, even though all three may be spotted on the same mountainside within a few hundred yards of each other. Each game species must be understood and treated differently to be hunted effectively. Sheep can spot you at three miles, goats will seldom see you beyond one-half mile and bears can sometimes be approached in the open within three hundred yards–if they can't smell you.

Because of their keen senses and extreme wariness, whitetail deer are the ultimate animal to take using the spot & stalk method. Photo courtesy McKinnon & Co. Outfitters.

Because all species of North American big game trust their noses to alert them to danger more than any other sense and because air movements are so unpredictable, the most difficult aspect of stalking is keeping hunters' scent away from their quarry. First of all, except for during wind storms (which are usually poor times to hunt), air movements do not flow in only one direction for very long in either time or space. Trees, brush, bodies of water, hills, gullies, valleys, mountains, etc. can all have minor or major effects on the direction and velocity of air currents. During a typical stalk a hunter will cross several of these vegetation or topography changes which may affect the way his scent moves. Thermals and new weather systems may also change air movements between the time a hunter begins a stalk and when he finishes it. Therefore, wind direction and possible changes must be a prime consideration when planning every stalk. Executing a stalk around the time when thermals will change is risky and usually futile except for highly experienced stalkers. Hunters can sometimes use an intervening gorge or ridgeline to keep their human scent away from game when thermals change, but nothing is certain when considering air movements. In addition to careful consideration of current and predictable wind directions while planning a stalk, hunters must constantly monitor the air movements *during* a stalk. Knowing that scent is a major reason stalks don't succeed, the best hunters pay strict attention to air movements at all times.

Another consideration when contemplating a stalk is how far the animal will go if it is spooked. Sheep and bears often run over or around a mountain–a distance of several days travel for hunters. Whitetail deer seldom go more than 300 yards before slowing down and hooking back toward their home territory. Older, larger individuals of any species will often go much farther than the average animal of that species–that's probably one of their habits which allowed them to grow larger in the first place. Also to be considered are the chances of getting another opportunity at this or another animal before the end of the hunt. If you think there are numerous animals of the same quality nearby, your decision will be different than if you've seen only one in a week.

A decision to wait until the animal moves into a better position or even until the next day is sometimes difficult, but often the best one. If weather like fog or rain—which may be advantageous to stalking—may be coming or the animal is about to bed down for (what you predict will be) several hours, waiting may drastically improve your chances of success. Waiting until the sun drops lower so it will be at your back is also a good ploy at times.

Whenever possible, a complete analysis of the stalking considerations and options should be performed before a stalk. Sometimes, when there are numerous if's and but's to consider and it is late in the day or late in the hunt, experienced hunters will just go for it. These hunters hope they can overcome any obstacles which come up or, better yet, the animal's movements will put it into a great stalking position before the stalk is finished. This is great when it happens this way, but more often it fails. Carefully planned stalks produce much higher success rates.

One of the vital skills of a good stalker is the ability to remember the stalking route. It must be committed to memory by picking out easily identified trees, rocks, gullies, or pastures–anything which will be recognized during the stalk. A stalker who loses his way during even a short stalk will either spook his quarry, spook another animal which will then spook his quarry, or fail to find his target animal entirely and waste his time. Drawing a quick map of complicated routes is one alternative to memorizing it. Another is working out hand signals with a partner who stays in a visible location to signal the stalker. This is also a good idea if the animal is moving

Planning a route carefully and remembering landmarks to keep on track are very important when spot & stalk hunting for bears because they often live in very brushy terrain with low visibility. Guide Tony Russ with client Craig Wazzer and his grizzly bear.

about and not bedded. In these cases, a partner can keep a stalking hunter informed about his quarry's movements as well as the movements of any other animals which may ruin the stalk or provide alternative targets.

In general, the speed of a stalking hunter slows down from beginning to end. Stalkers can often move very quickly at first—if there is plenty of cover and noise is not a factor—then slow down as they near their quarry. Moving as quickly as possible will reduce the amount of time the animal has to move into a poor or unknown position—both of which may ruin the stalk.

Some general stalking pointers are:

–Use topography (physical features of the land) to remain out of sight as much as possible.

–Don't silhouette yourself on the skyline or against contrasting backgrounds.

–Cover all skin—especially your hands and shiny face (camo paint is better for this than head nets which restrict a hunter's view and hearing).

–Move when conditions are best to avoid being spotted—like when the wind comes up, animals are feeding and have their heads down, antlered animals are rubbing their horns or fighting, and any other times animals are distracted.

–Remove squeaky footwear as you get close, or use quiet overboots made specifically for hunters.

–Don't go directly at game when covering any open ground at long range–angle toward it just in case it does see you.

–Many prey species do not detect red light, so it can be used to travel at night without spooking game.

–A bush or small tree can be carried and used to hide behind when crossing openings at a distance from game and sometimes to move within shooting range.

–A man on a horse is usually not considered a threat unless game has learned to fear this combination.

–Antlered game in rut—moose and caribou in particular—will sometimes come toward a set of their species' horns either by itself or carried over a hunter; but don't risk this ruse if other hunters— who may shoot at you—may be nearby.

–Many open-country animals (brown bear and caribou are good examples) will feed on the move faster than a man can walk. Hunters can seldom catch them from behind, but have to be in front or to the side to ambush them or angle in front to cut them off.

Stalking hunters can often get clues about their quarry's attitude by watching it closely. Casually meandering animals are un-alerted and generally don't move very fast. Those walking in a direct line are moving toward or away from something. An animal's head and neck posture often indicate its state of mind–up and directed is alert, lower and moving side to side is relaxed. An animal's ears indicate what it can hear. If they are both up and pointing in the same direction, it hears something. If they are both swiveling independently at a lower angle, the animal is in a casual, but watchful mode. An animal's tail is also indicative of its mood: down and wagging means at ease, a flicking tail means slight alarm and a horizontal tail means it is about to run. Snorting, sneezing or foot stomping also means an animal is alarmed and will probably flee soon.

Most herd animals also use their companions' moods for signs of danger. However, depending on the species and the situation, sometimes a hunter can get away with being sensed by one member of a herd by stopping immediately. If the one member which sensed the hunter cannot confirm his suspicion of danger he may relax. This commonly happens in a species with a strong social hierarchy when a low-ranking member senses possible danger. Unless this animal

Stalking hunters should learn to move when an animal is busy eating, it is distracted or its head is down for any reason. This sheep is busy licking soil for the mineral content, a distraction which allowed the author to get within 30 yards before shooting.

gives a definite alarm signal, the others will often ignore it. On the other hand, in most locations, nervous species like whitetail deer run at the slightest hint of danger sensed by any member of the group. Even a long stare by a fawn can cause all deer in the vicinity to become alarmed and run for cover. In the case of Dall sheep, a sheep which suddenly runs uphill will usually alarm any other sheep which can see it–even if they are two miles apart.

Stalking skills are learned from experience and practice. One of the best ways for hunters to improve these skills is to practice in the off-season. Stalking animals with a camera or just to observe them is an excellent way to become a better hunter and learn more about their behavior. It is also fun and exciting for hunters to try to get as close as possible without being detected. It increases confidence and reduces anxiety for stalks during an actual hunt.

Stand-Hunting

There are many types of stands which hunters use to wait for animals to come within shooting range. Tree stands, ground stands, natural blinds, waterhole blinds, bait stations, floating blinds and snow blinds are all types of stands commonly used by hunters. Most stand-hunting is based on a hunter's knowledge of the game and its habits in a certain area. Hunters use their knowledge of the animals' tendency to use certain trails, crossings, feeding areas and bedding areas at regular times each day and lie in wait in one type of stand or another. Bowhunters frequently use stands because of their need to get within close range before shooting.

One type of stand-hunting involves simply spotting and then setting up an ambush in front of animals on the move–like migrating caribou or mule deer. These stands may be as simple as large rocks or small trees which the hunter can hide behind. Hunters must be able to interpret sign and recognize game funnels to select this type of stand. Geographic features which funnel animals through narrow spits of land, long-used river narrows or centuries-old crossings through mountain passes or saddles are all good places to use as stand sites.

Other stands are very carefully chosen after months or even years of observing and hunting individual animals. Sophisticated tree stands or waterhole blinds used in conjunction with life-size decoys and natural animal scents are often preferred in these cases. Tree stands have several advantages over ground stands: hunters have more visibility from their elevated position; their scent is not spread around as much at ground level; animals don't look up as much as they search at ground level; hunters are more likely to stay put and see more animals; and tree stands don't change the animal's habitat as much as a ground blind so there is less chance the animal will notice the stand. Waterhole blinds are commonly used for pronghorn antelope or desert deer which need to drink water daily– usually early and late in the day.

Stand style is also dependant on individual preference and opinion. I have a friend who is very successful at hunting whitetails in Alabama and doesn't use tree stands. He claims the whitetails there will hear a hunter put up or climb up a tree stand, and every deer which walks by will be looking up to find the hunter to avoid him. After hunting there and noticing that those whitetails are more nervous and spooky than any other animal I've seen, I can believe his claims. He hunts exclusively from the ground, using natural blinds most of the time.

Although the majority of stand hunting is done for our most popular game animal—the whitetail deer—much of what hunters learn about hunting this animal can be used to hunt other species. Whitetails have learned more tricks to evade hunters than any other species. Hunters, in turn, have learned more ways to outsmart whitetails than any other big game animal. Even hunters who haven't–

Stand-hunting is a very popular and effective technique for whitetail hunters. A hunter should always practice drawing his bow or aiming his rifle and taking practice shots if possible.

and don't expect to hunt whitetails can learn a lot of useful hunting information by reading about how these animals are successfully hunted.

Stands can be pockets of vegetation which give a hunter enough
concealment to sit unnoticed and shoot without alerting game.
Dave Widby is practicing his drawing motion in a ground blind.

Stand-hunting is probably the best technique for suburban
hunting typical of much whitetail habitat–unless hunters have enough
space or permission to cross property lines. In many locations, up to

one-half of the deer taken during the firearms season are taken on the first day—and most of those are taken from stands. The high volume of hunters on the opener keeps animals moving all day, so even novices can connect if they stay on a good stand all day. It is also safer to sit still on stand when so many hunters are in the woods— hunters who might mistake your movement for a game animal. Stand-hunting also works very well when deer are rutting since this also keeps them moving much of the day.

Hunters who use stands must choose locations where an animal will pass within shooting range. Choosing the stand sites is, therefore, the most difficult part of this type of hunting. Stands can be near feeding areas, bedding areas, scrapes, rub runways, major trails, minor trails, escape terrain, perimeter trails, creek bottoms, ravines, saddles or any corridor that is a natural traveling route and has adequate cover to make the animals feel safe. To select the correct stand site among the numerous possibilities, hunters must first learn animal habits in the area. Animal habits are tied in to the lay of the land as well as weather patterns, so these must also be learned.

It is important to consider animal behavior rather than human preferences when selecting a stand site. A common beginner's mistake is to put a tree stand on the edge of timber near an open field for the view it provides. This site may allow hunters to see deer and decide where to place their next stand, but it will probably not produce many shots. If deer are seen in open fields during daylight hours, they are usually does and small bucks. The large bucks will not go into a field before dark. Instead, they will stay in the fringes, nibbling on whatever they find until dark. A better stand selection in these cases is a few hundred yards into cover where a trail junction comes near an acorn or fruit tree, or some other food source to attract the large bucks before they can enter the field under the cover of darkness. It is better for buck hunters to see one good buck at this type of site than one hundred does in the open field.

Bucks spend most of the daylight hours in some type of cover, so this is where most productive stands are located. One place to set up a stand is along narrow strips of cover which funnel bucks as they travel from bedding areas in heavy cover to feeding areas in open fields. Of course, these stands have to be far enough into the cover so bucks will go by before dark. Areas of dense cover are not the easiest places to set up a stand, but this should not deter hunters from considering these sites. Successful sites are not chosen for a hunter's convenience. For example, few whitetail hunters (except in more open country in the West) go more than one-quarter mile from their vehicle, so one way to get away from hunting pressure and find more relaxed deer is to go farther than everyone else. One-quarter to one-half mile is not that far to walk to have a successful hunt.

Dominant buck bedrooms, which are often found in dense cover, are some of the best stand sites. Bucks choose their bedrooms primarily for security. Bedrooms are usually one to ten acres in size and located where—under normal conditions—no predator can approach without being detected. Escape routes are only a few jumps away in the form of a steep ridge, a swamp, downed trees or low brush—all of which will slow the predator and let the longer-legged deer get away. Rubs often reveal bedroom areas and old rubs reveal traditional buck bedrooms—used for many generations. Buck bedrooms are the least variable parts of their home ranges and have the most activity—two characteristics which make them good stand sites. Plus, if bucks become nocturnal, these are the only places to find them during shooting hours. For nocturnal bucks, hunters must go into their bedrooms very early (well before morning's first light) and set up their stands right in the bedroom to wait for returning bucks. This is only practical for species like whitetail deer which are very habitual animals and have small home ranges.

During the whitetail rutting season, the increase in animal movement makes stand-hunting a good choice of hunting techniques. Stands near trails which females habitually use are good choices since males will be searching for does on these trails. Deer scrapes are also good stand sites, particularly early and late in the rut when only a few females are in heat. During the intense part of the rut when many does are in heat, bucks will be chasing them rather than checking scrapes. Since bucks often check scrapes by scent from a downwind trail, stands should be set up downwind of this trail so hunters aren't scented. Stands can also be used effectively for Coues deer, pronghorn, caribou, moose and elk during these species' respective rutting seasons.

When selecting stand sites, hunters must remember that animals prefer to travel nose-to-wind. Knowledge of an area's typical storm winds and thermal patterns should be used to select sites downwind of animal travel routes. In case of variable wind directions, two stands can be set up, one on each side of a trail so the hunter can always have a downwind site. Another way to prevent being scented is to select a site with a barrier—like a lake, river or impassible terrain—on the downwind side of the stand. For additional scent protection, stands (particularly those on the ground) should be set up several days before use to reduce hunter odor in the area.

More whitetails are taken by stand-hunting methods than by any other technique.

In most whitetail habitat, there are almost always deer within 300 yards of any place a hunter chooses for a stand site. This means hunters have to be incredibly quiet when setting up the stand to avoid ruining the site. Scouting ahead of the season and setting up the stand at least two weeks ahead of time is one way to prevent this.

Older, wiser whitetail bucks often remember traditional stand sites from year to year if they've seen hunters there. These bucks may be taken by stands a hundred or so yards downwind of the traditional sites which overlook the trails bucks use to scent-check the old site. Bucks also learn to avoid stands during the season once they locate them and this knowledge can be passed on to other animals by scent communication (see Chapter Twenty-Three on game senses). One way to find bucks avoiding stands or eluding hunters for any reason is by mobile-stand hunting. This tactic is where hunters continually move their stands during the season to thwart animal avoidance patterns and to take advantage of knowledge gained from day to day. Mobile-stand hunting works best for heavily hunted whitetail deer populations. This type of stand-hunting can create more noise and scent problems every time the site is changed, so it is mostly used by experienced hunters who are very careful about placing and using stands.

Site design is another important factor. Sites should be prepared with consideration for early construction, minimal disruption to the habitat, safety, silence, comfort, height, stand camouflage and odor minimization. Stand height is dependent on the terrain and the animals being hunted. In hilly terrain, stands have to be higher to get hunters above animals' normal sight patterns. Heavily hunted populations also call for higher stands if animals have learned to look up for stands. Hunters should be concealed if possible, but good background camouflage is almost as good as cover-up camouflage. Shooting lanes must be cleared without unnecessary alterations to the appearance of the area. All clippings should be removed from the area to reduce the amount of visible change to the site.

Cover scents, animal decoys and attractive scents can all be used to improve the site's productivity. Attraction scents can be laid out like the spokes of a wheel from the stand to lure any passing animals within range. Small dabs of scent can also be placed at strategic locations around the site to get animals to pause long enough for the hunter to shoot.

Walking lanes should also be cleared when hunters have the opportunity. These will enable the hunter to get to the stand quietly and stay off game trails. This may just require raking leaves to one side or may entail the use of pruning shears to clear noisy brush.

The decisions to stand-hunt, which stand to use and when to use it are almost as important as site selection and preparation. Rutting activity, heavy migrations, mild weather or any other times when animals are moving well are good times to hunt from stands. Heavy snows or winds which restrict animal movements reduce the productivity of stand hunting in most situations, so it is better to try another technique. The most productive times of the day for stand hunting are generally in early morning or late afternoon—when most animals are moving. However, hunters going after really large animals must remember that these are often solitary creatures and may move at different times of the day than other animals, so they must be hunted according to their individual schedules.

The time of day to use a stand may also depend on the typical thermal wind direction at the site. Thermals will often determine when a site is downwind or upwind of animal movement patterns. This is why many stands are either good morning producers or good in the evening, but not both. Normally, the most productive pattern is to hunt high in the morning when the thermals are rising and low in the evening when the thermals are going down-slope. This pattern is most likely to keep hunter scent away from animals around the stand site.

An elk wallow like this one may be a good stand location if there are plenty of bulls in the area. Hunters must know wind directions near a wallow to hunt it effectively.

Hunters must also consider wind direction and visibility when approaching a stand site. Depending on the species, hunters should stay from 200-2,000 yards away from feeding areas if they are approaching from an upwind direction. Approaching hunters must also stay out of sight of animals. This is a greater concern in open country where animals often bed where they can see long distances. When possible, the optimal time to approach a stand is when animals are elsewhere and have no chance of detecting hunters–even if this means going several hours early.

When leaving stands, hunters must wait until all animals are out of sight. Animals which see you leave a stand will remember and pass this on to other animals by their subsequent behavior whenever they come near the stand site. Hunters should avoid being patterned by their quarry. If there is a possibility that unseen animals know the hunter's normal standing times and the stand is a good site, a change in the timing may be all that is needed to spot them the next time.

Animals may also be alerted to hunters going to their stands by pre-hunt noises. Automobile or boat engines suddenly stopping, doors closing or voices—even a half mile or more away—may all be clues for animals which are accustomed to hunters to be extra-cautious. This problem can be avoided if hunters park more than one-half mile away or have a driver let them off near their stand without coming to a complete stop.

Another way to avoid alerting animals to where a stand is located is to have another person accompany the hunter. Both go to the stand, but the hunter stays while the other person continues on as a decoy. Two people are usually enough when only sounds are giving away the hunter, but if sight is involved, there has to be at least three people traveling to the stand, with two continuing on to fool an animal. Many can count well enough to discern when only two people are involved, but three may fool them.

Depending on the situation, there are two more strategies to use when attempting to travel to a stand without being detected or identified as a possible danger. First, it is often okay to be identified as a human if the hunter acts casual and not like a predator—neither sneaking along nor walking quickly and directly. The hunter should walk slowly and steadily until he is within 100-200 yards, and then be very quiet getting to and into the stand. To avoid alarming any nearby animals hunters should: stay on trails, walk steadily at a medium pace, avoid loud noises, keep their heads pointed ahead, and not stop or appear to be listening for game. Because animals prefer not to flee unless it is necessary, they will often let hunters pass close by if they think they have not been detected and are not being hunted. The alternative strategy only works if the hunter is skilled enough to pass for a nonthreatening animal or can avoid detection altogether. For the hunter to escape identification as a human, he can only make sounds like another nonhuman animal. This can be done by experienced hunters going at the right pace in the right situations. Of course, the hunter must not be sighted or smelled for this to work. Avoiding detection altogether works when no animals are nearby and/or conditions are right for very quiet traveling. When traveling to, from, or between stands, hunters should always be alert for animals traveling or bedded—basically still-hunting whenever they are moving.

Tree stand use requires caution and practice. Studies indicate that as many as one in three tree-stand hunters have fallen. Hunters should always read instructions with a stand, climbing stands, ladders, tree steps, and safety belts and observe any weight or capability limitations listed. Safety belts should always be worn and stands periodically checked for wear and loose parts. Tree stands must be treated with as much respect as guns, since they are both deadly weapons.

Bowhunters often use stands near waterholes to hunt antelope because of their open-country habitat and their excellent eyesight.

For the greatest effectiveness from a tree stand, hunters should climb into them as quietly as possible. Gear should be left on the ground with pull ropes attached while the hunter climbs into the stand, slowly applies weight to the platform to avoid unnecessary sounds and fastens his safety belt. Screw-in hooks for packs, gear and weapons should be put in next. Camouflaging netting—if applicable—should be brought up and attached next. These work great to hide hunters and cover their sounds, unless there are winds—when netting makes noise, moves and can alert game. Next, all gear items are brought up on pull ropes and hung on hooks or attached in predetermined locations before the hunter's weapon is retrieved. Knotting the pull ropes will prevent having them slip through the hunter's fingers. Weapons should be unloaded when lifting or lowering and in a muzzle-down position. As an extra precaution, ropes should never be attached through the trigger guard.

Gear for stand-hunting should be selected carefully to reduce noise, smell and visibility. Warm, quiet clothing—including raingear—is a top priority to keep hunters comfortable, as noiseless as possible, and on stand as long as planned. Scent-blocking sprays or clothing can really improve a hunter's chances if used properly. For best results, sprays can be carried to the stand and then used on everything to eliminate as much odor as possible at the site. To prevent excess perspiration during the walk to their stand, hunters can carry extra clothes in a noise-free pack. Soft material and quiet zippers are both necessary on packs for stand-hunting. Camouflage matching the background can also reduce hunter visibility considerably. This may require owning several different camouflage styles to use as vegetation changes during the season or as various stand sites are used. Weapons, and other possibly noisy or shiny gear, should also be lubricated to reduce noise and covered with non-reflective, noise-dampening tape. Padded, warm seat cushions and hand or body warmers will also keep hunters comfortable, motionless and alert for longer periods. Unscented insect repellants or headnets should be carried when biting insects are about. An air and water-tight portable "P" bottle keeps hunters comfortable and stands scent-free. Hunters should never leave body wastes near stands.

Hunters should prepare themselves and act appropriately when stand hunting. They need adequate rest to stay alert and shouldn't eat or drink heavily prior to hunting. They should not eat or drink smelly foods while on stand nor chew fragrant substances. Hunters can chew non-aromatic substances like grass or twigs if necessary to fight boredom. Watching the natural world of animals and birds is one way to stay alert and enjoy the long hours on stand. Hunters should sit or stand depending on which reduces the chances of being identified by game on the particular stand. Hunters can change position very slowly to reduce fidgeting, but not when animals

When on a stand, hunters must be ready to shoot with minimal movement. Here, Kris Widby has an arrow knocked and is ready for any deer which comes by her ground stand.

are present. Periodically flexing muscle groups slowly with little movement and without changing positions will often suffice to keep hunters warm, loose and alert.

Animals do look up—particularly those which have previously been hunted from tree stands—so hunters must be as quiet as possible. Hunters using ground-level stands need to be even more cautious about making as little noise or movement as possible. If animals do look their way, hunters should close their eyes most of the way, as their eyes will give them away when nothing else is recognized.

Still-Hunting

Still-hunting means moving through the home area of an animal at a snail's pace, trying to locate and get a shot at the animal before it detects you and/or leaves the area. Still-hunters need to know their hunting grounds more than any other type of hunter to be effective. It is the most difficult hunting technique so hunters need some advantage if they expect to be successful. By knowing where the animal is likely to be at a certain time of day in certain types of weather, the hunter can slow down and approach these spots very carefully. Deer often choose one bedding area to use on very windy days which gives them a better view of approaching danger. If a hunter recognizes this, he can still-hunt there on windy days, knowing to be very careful because of the likelihood of bedded deer in the area. Still-hunting is sort of like stalking an animal without knowing exactly where it is located.

The best times to still-hunt are mostly determined by weather conditions. A primary consideration when still-hunting is, of course, the wind direction. Hunters must go either into the wind or at least across it. The weather should, therefore, be stable and predictable enough to do this.

Of secondary importance for still-hunters is preventing their noise from alerting animals. This is accomplished by hunting when the weather will cover or reduce noise. A gentle rain which dampens noisy forest litter and makes a little noise of its own is perfect still-hunting weather. A light breeze also covers hunter noise and makes some of its own. However, very windy days make game very nervous so they seek very dense cover or open areas–both of which are difficult to still-hunt in successfully. Fresh, wet snow makes walking almost noiseless and provides sound baffles–particularly if branches are also covered with snow. Fresh snow also provides good tracking conditions which improve a hunter's chances of locating an animal– as long as there few other hunters to spook or shoot at the animal they are tracking. Crunchy snow makes still-hunting virtually impossible. Although dry fall conditions are typically poor for still-hunting, dewy mornings may soften noisy leaves enough to use this

Although still-hunting is not a typical method of hunting Dall sheep, this one was taken by walking along a canyon rim and occasionally peeking over. Guide Tony Russ poses with his client's sheep.

method before the heat of day. If walking conditions are okay, immediately after a day or two of stormy or windy weather is usually a good time to still-hunt because animals which have been sitting out the weather are hungry and moving around a lot. By still-hunting during the best weather conditions for this technique, hunters can learn more about the animals they hunt by seeing them in various situations and locations. More than any other type of hunting, still-hunting will improve a hunter's all-round abilities.

Even more than other hunting techniques, still-hunting is generally more productive when animals are active. Bedded animals are difficult to sneak up on because they are very attentive–not distracted by feeding or walking. Bedded animals are also lower to the ground which not only allows them to see under the lowest tree branches, it also makes them harder to see.

Many experienced hunters and some hunting books recommend leaving animals alone during midday when they are bedded in dense cover. The theory is hunters will only spook animals and ruin their hunting odds in the long run. This logic states that it is better to wait until the animals move around again in the afternoon to resume hunting. This is true for 95% of the hunters. However, knowledgeable and skilled still-hunters can hunt in many situations during the midday period with good results. This is the advantage of having still-hunting expertise.

The optimal habitat to still-hunt in is a mixed terrain of hills and draws with varying densities of cover. A variety of terrain and cover like this often holds plenty of game, helps baffle hunter noise and usually permits hunters to see any animals within shooting distance. Hunters can carefully peek over ridges to scan for game and go very slowly as they approach dense pockets of cover which may hold bedded animals. Hunters can still-hunt a ridgeline effectively by alternately moving along one side 10-20 feet below the top for 100 yards, then crossing the ridge and doing the same thing on the other side for 100 yards, then repeating this pattern. Moderately open cover also allows hunters to move without excess noise. Although dense, continuous cover often holds more bedded animals, it is difficult to sneak up on these animals and even more difficult to shoot in this type of cover.

Still-hunters can use game trails, dirt roads or cleared utility easements to travel as noiselessly as possible. Optimally, still-hunting should be linked to predictable behavior patterns of game—going toward bedding areas in the morning and toward feeding areas in the afternoon—so the hunter is more likely to be taken for an animal if game senses him. Trying to pass for another animal requires a good knowledge of animal behavior and of the habitat. Hunters can sometimes benefit by carrying a small-scale topographic map, so they know what is ahead of them and move accordingly.

Still-hunting can be used by stand hunters to stalk an animal they have seen go into a bedding area. Stand hunters don't have to be exactly sure about an animal's whereabouts or even the bedding area's location. If an animal repeatedly goes by their stand out of range, but in the same direction after the morning feeding period each day and is likely headed for its daytime bed, skilled hunters have a good chance of taking the animal with still-hunting methods. Still-hunting can be used for any animal which a hunter knows the approximate location of within some kind of cover–fog or dust cloud included.

Still-hunting speed must be adjusted to match the conditions–faster when visibility is good or there is no sign of animals, slower when visibility is poor and animals are likely to be nearby. Experienced still-hunters also adjust their tactics–peeking under trees when in dense timber or tall brush. Both speed and dense timber

Kodiak Island Sitka blacktail deer are plentiful and lack the extreme wariness of most deer. These factors allow hunters to successfully still-hunt them. Todd Fisher with a nice buck.

were factors when I was trailing a group of bison bulls on a bowhunt several years ago. I was barely moving because of the thick cover and I suspected they were nearby, so I crouched to peer under the evergreen limbs and spotted their legs. This was the only way I could have spotted them before they sensed me, so now I regularly peer underneath vegetation for animals when still-hunting in these types of cover.

In general, the proper still-hunting speed is slower than most of us can make ourselves move. "Still" is the key word—as in being motionless. The less you move, the more you will see and the fewer animals will see you first. Still-hunting at 100 yards per hour may be too fast in heavy cover. You may have to crawl in some types of cover to avoid busting brush and scaring all the game within 300 yards. Covering about one to one and one-half miles per day is about right. Think about how slowly animals move through cover most of the time. We have to go slower than that because we are relatively inept at observing and at being quiet. Hunters need to step out of their role as modern, hustling and bustling humans and slow down to be an effective still-hunter/predator. It is a good idea to just stop and stand still each time you step into the woods and begin a hunt. Let your senses awaken and take a backwards step to the predator we were just a few generations ago.

In order to understand your quarry, you must think about what you would do if you were being hunted and your life was at stake. You would stay in cover, lie low, stay on the fringes of trees rather than walk through openings and suddenly angle off course to evade following predators. Once you have a feel for the animal's state of mind, you can hunt it more effectively. This state of mind can also help you recognize how we hunters are identified by our sounds. Hunter movement is identified because it is: off-trail, directly across cover, faster-paced than animals' and loud and persistent.

To avoid producing hunter-like noise and being identified as such, practice traveling quietly. It helps to: keep your legs bent to maintain your balance; feel objects with your feet before you put your full weight on them—placing your feet elsewhere when necessary; push loose, noisy material aside with your toes when possible; take small steps; place your toes first and slip them underneath forest debris as deer do—then set down your heel; learn to look for your next five foot placements at one time, then keep your eyes ahead scouting for game while you take the steps; avoid brushing your legs together which makes unnatural noises; use an animal sound or call (a fawn bleat works well) to cover any obvious noise you accidentally make; wear quiet fabrics and remove or alter noisy gear (I remove my gun sling so it doesn't hang up on brush); and practice these things by trying to sneak up on your hunting partner or animals during the off season.

Float-hunting is a variation of still-hunting where hunters float down a river or creek in hopes of coming upon their quarry along the waterway. It worked for these two caribou hunters.

Hunters using the still-hunting technique must be confident that an animal is close by and will be spotted at any moment in order to maintain their caution and alertness. A moment's lapse will sometimes cost the hunter his only chance to take an animal. I remember a perfect example of this several years ago while moose hunting with my bow. As I followed a small creek surrounded by tall grass—fully recognizing that the creek noise covered my own— I sensed it was a likely spot to see a moose. Just as I came to the end of the grassy patch and could see a good distance into the open forest ahead, I relaxed–a little disheartened because I hadn't seen any moose there. My next step was careless and noisy–and up jumped a young bull at fifteen yards out of the last bit of grass. I still kick myself to this day for missing that great opportunity because of my lapse in concentration. Complete confidence is necessary to remain alert, always poised and ready to shoot.

Still-hunting success depends on always keeping the wind in your favor, so a thread or feather on your bow or rifle is even more important than it is to stand hunters. When coming to heavy cover where deer may bed, it is best to move to the downwind side as you approach. Deer often curl to the downwind side of cover so they can watch and smell their back-trail, so hunters should be looking for animals which have done this.

If there is a lull in the thermals during stable weather conditions, still-hunters should stop and wait until the thermals pick up again. This lack of air movements between the morning and daytime thermals usually lasts less than sixty minutes, so hunters should wait for them to resume before continuing to hunt.

Two partners still-hunting together can be more effective than a single hunter, but it requires cooperation. Partners should agree ahead of time that only one will move at a time while the other watches for game. Partners have to keep track of each other at all times and it helps to have predetermined hand signals for noiseless communication. Partners can travel single file with 20-100 yards between them or parallel each other 50-100 yards apart. Either method works well in the right situation as one hunter can spot animals which try to elude the other partner—a common occurrence for several reasons. Some species circle out of curiosity to get a better look. Deer often circle back on their trail to stay on their home range when they reach its edge. Many animals typically look back from high points or after they've just crossed openings to check for trailing predators. Watching for these animals takes a single hunter's eyes away from the trail ahead and also causes more movement as he continually swivels his head around, but cooperative still-hunting partners are better able to watch their surroundings and spot more animals. We commonly use cooperative hunting partners when we hunt a portion of the Alaska Peninsula for brown bears by using one partner as a decoy and one as a watcher. When we think our quarry is bedded in one of the many alder patches, one of us quietly goes to the upwind side and walks back and forth while the shooter quietly waits on the downwind side. When the hunter's scent reaches any bear in the brush, it will quickly wake up and try to exit on the downwind side to get away. The waiting hunter typically sees the (unknowing) bear moving through the brush and gets a clear shot as it comes out.

Still-hunters should always carry a set of binoculars to see detail in heavy cover. Many times the hunter will only be able to see parts of an animal and will need the optics to pick out the parts, as well as to identify the animal. Binoculars can help pick out naturally camouflaged deer which often hide at close range and let hunters pass by if they think they haven't been detected. On Kodiak Island, Alaska, we've seen large bucks actually crawl through heavy brush on their knees as they were sneaking away from nearby hunters.

Still-hunting for bears along salmon streams in Southeastern Alaska takes skill and nerve as bears may be sighted at close range. George E. Mann with an Alaskan black bear.

Still-hunters should also use face camouflage or a camouflage head net. Our faces are shiny, the highest point on our bodies and they give us away more often than any other part of our body. Camouflaging it at least prevents animals from determining if we are looking at them or which way we are facing. At the best, face camouflage can fool animals and let hunters walk up within range, and at the least it can give still-hunters a few more seconds to shoot.

There are many sounds still-hunters hear and must interpret correctly. Upon hearing an alarm sound from any bird or squirrel, hunters should stop, look, and listen for the animal which prompted the alarm. It may be the hunter's quarry. If the hunter causes such an alarm, it is also a good idea to stop and wait until the alarmist loses interest and the woods settle down before proceeding. Hunters who spook their quarry should also stop and wait before continuing. If the hunter stops immediately the animal may not be badly spooked and may only go 100 yards or so and settle down. After waiting 20-30 minutes, the now-alert hunter can continue and may have another chance at the animal.

Float-hunting is another form of still-hunting where hunters use a canoe or boat for transportation on (usually) moving waterways.

This brown bear was seen sleeping in the brush, then was driven to this waiting hunter by a guide who walked upwind of the bear. The fifteen-yard shot was exciting for guide Tony Russ as well as this client.

This is sort of like stand-hunting in that hunters must arrange everything in the watercraft to be as noiseless and motionless as possible and have their weapons ready. It works best with the shooter in front and his partner in the back controlling the craft. Moose, caribou, bears and deer are often hunted this way. Large whitetails often use tiny islands in rivers or swamps to escape hunters and still-hunting with watercraft is one of the few effective methods to hunt them.

Driving

Driving game is a technique which is a combination of still-hunting and standing. Deer drives are really deer moves where the animals decide which way to move and hunters have to anticipate where to be to intercept them. Deer are seldom driven away from their security cover–they just move from one secure spot to another. Hunters have to pick the route the deer will take. Drives are typically used to hunt species which use cover as an escape mechanism.

When a game drive is planned, the first step is to select the drive area. This should be a relatively small area, depending on the species. Successful deer drives are typically in a plot of land of 2-20 acres. Since deer resist going out of their home ranges, the best drives do not cross range boundaries. Good locations for drives are known bedding areas with only a few strips of cover leading to other secure areas. Dense, continuous tracts of cover may hold plenty of deer, but cannot be effectively watched—no matter how many hunters are involved.

Drives are often planned for midday when few animals are moving. Deer hunters who use stands in the early morning and late afternoon use drives to fill in their hunting day. Drives are also used to move a specific animal out of a small patch of cover.

The next step is to divide the hunting group into drivers and standers. A drive can work successfully with only one stander and one driver, particularly if the hunters are after one animal and they know where it typically beds. Four hunters are a good number for deer drives and a group of ten hunters is about the largest practical size for most deer drives. Larger drives are generally ineffective, dangerous and just spook game.

Drives are the most dangerous of all hunting methods because several hunters are facing each other across heavy brush where game is moving. Since hunters can't always keep track of one another, it is difficult to determine safe shooting directions. For safety reasons, it is best to appoint a manager for a drive who can determine safe shooting angles for each hunter. The manager's first priority is safety, the second is effectiveness of the drive.

Next, standers are quietly placed in position downwind from the cover which holds the animals. Standers are lined up and ideally, can see the stander on either side of them—although they should not be too exposed to game's eyes. Each stander should arrange his spot just like he would at a normal stand, removing noisy vegetation and finding a position where he can be quiet and still. Stander locations are not necessarily chosen for the most visibility, but for the most logical routes animals will take. However, they must have some sort of view and at least one shooting lane. A stander's first priority is also safety. The manager will instruct each stander about the safe shooting lanes, but standers must be alert and not shoot any direction unless they feel it is safe at the time. If appropriate, standers can be placed on deer trails, logging roads, clearings or in tree stands where they will have a good view. They must stay on their stand until the drive is over as signaled by the manager.

Drivers still-hunt into their positions upwind of the cover to be driven. Their positions should form a v-shape with the open end toward the cover and no more than 100 yards apart. This shape is meant to keep animals from slipping out and around the drivers, which driven deer typically try to do. Animals will also try to slip between drivers if they are not spaced closely enough. A driver's first priority is also safety. The manager will instruct each driver if he has any safe shooting lanes and where they are. Of course, drivers must be alert and refrain from shooting in any direction they feel is unsafe. Some of the drivers may be instructed not to shoot for safety reasons.

When the drivers and standers are in position, the manager gives a signal to begin. The drivers move slowly toward the standers. Drivers should not be noisy or fast, but rather move as if they are still-hunting at the drive manager's predetermined speed. They should also try to keep track of the drivers on either side of them and know where the standers are located.

It is helpful and safer if small maps are distributed to everyone involved in a drive. Maps need the basic outline of the drive area, standers' and drivers' original positions, likely game positions, likely escape routes, and drivers' expected routes. A basic map will improve safety immensely by giving every hunter a visual guide to locations of every other hunter, as well as their likely movements. This prevents a lot of misunderstandings which are the reasons for most accidents.

The most successful drives are really nudges, where the animals are very slowly moved from one security cover to another. Running animals make poor targets for the best rifle shots and no targets at all for bowhunters. Hunters need a good knowledge of the area and the animals' escape routes to position the standers and drivers in good locations. Proper driving is like cooperative still-hunting where some partners—the drivers—do all the moving, while the standers do most of the watching.

Calling

There are several forms of calling used to hunt North American big game species. Hunters bugle for elk; grunt, rattle and call for deer; call, rattle and dribble for moose; and call bears. Each method takes skill and knowledge of the species and its habits. Generally, calling is used during the mating period of antlered game to bring in males looking for females. Bears may be called at any time of the year.

The sounds necessary to call in animals are very specific and must be imitated fairly well to attract animals, rather than alarm them. There are commercial products available to hunters for imitating all these sounds. They must be used properly and at the right time of the year for good results. The correct time frame is

Calling game requires practice to be effective. Bugling for elk is a favorite hunting method of bowhunters who hunt during the rutting period of these animals.

often only a few weeks each year and the proper sounds change as the mating season progresses. The best ways to learn how to imitate the sounds are either by having an experienced hunter demonstrate or actually listening to the animals during their rut. Actually hearing the animals is a rare occurrence for most species as they are not very loud and don't occur that frequently. Bugling elk are an exception, and many hunters have learned to successfully bugle elk. However, because many hunters do this, elk in many areas have learned to be very suspicious of bugling sounds. In some areas, hunters now just use bugling to locate other bull elk and then move toward the elk, rather than wait for the elk to come to them.

Calling naturally works best on calm days when sounds will carry the farthest. Hunters should call softly at first so as not to alarm nearby animals—most naturally occurring rattling or grunting sounds are not very loud. Calling usually works best on one animal—especially one the hunter can see. Animals often come in out of curiosity rather than to fight. Two or more animals together will often ignore the calling or be driven away from it.

Males at the peak of the rut are the most likely candidates to call and some will come in running. Calling in an area with a high buck to doe ratio is usually more successful. Fawn bleats for deer can be used at any time to call in does and yearlings.

Calling bears with predator calls may work at any time, in any location. These are useful to bring bears out of heavy cover or to get them in a better shooting location. Hunters need to be careful when calling bears because of the possibility of cubs or sows with cubs coming to the call.

Calling, rattling or grunting can also be a form of cover noise used by moving hunters to confuse game. A few soft calls or grunts can sometimes make an animal wait long enough for a hunter to get within range. Calling can also be used to stop a fleeing animal long enough for a hunter to shoot.

Baiting

Most baiting in North America is done for black bears, but some states allow baiting for deer. Baiting is not as simple as throwing out food anywhere and waiting for game to arrive. Baiting bears is a very skilled, time-consuming procedure. Deer baiting is less demanding, but generally not successful for large bucks except in isolated areas. Scents, a form of baiting, are used for many species, usually in conjunction with stands.

Bait stations have to be selected carefully for good results. Animals have to feel secure enough to come to the bait during legal shooting hours for it to be a useful technique. The bait also has to be placed in an area with a high animal density and with limited amounts or types of natural foods. The longer the bait station is maintained, the more chances that game will remember and continue to come to it. Of course, game which is spooked by hunters at or near the site will usually avoid it for at least a few weeks. In the case of whitetail deer which are alerted to hunters at a site, they may only come in after dark for months afterward. In some areas, bears are so drawn to bait sites they will come in even with hunters in plain sight. However, some bears can be just as nervous as whitetails around bait sites.

The food used at bait sites should be chosen for its smell, low cost, durability, and difficulty to remove quickly. Smell and low cost are obvious benefits to attract animals and keep expenses down. Durable foods are those which don't rot, mold, or turn sour so that animals don't want them. Grain products, sugary substances and mineral licks are durable foods. Foods which are difficult to remove last longer between baitings. Liquid sugars like syrup and honey, or even granulated sugar, will penetrate soil or tree stumps and linger after repeated visits from bears. Concentrated food scents are good

Baiting for black bears is a favorite method of hunting this species because it allows the hunter to inspect the animal for sex, size and coat condition before shooting. Todd Fisher took this bear on a natural bait–blueberries.

ways to distribute odors and maintain a constant food smell at bait sites. Grain spread around on the ground takes longer to remove to the last kernel than grain in a convenient bucket, which deer can clean up completely in a short time. Distributing the food so animals keep coming back for the last little bit prevents the site from ever being completely cleaned out and being deserted by game.

Food should always be handled with clean rubber gloves to eliminate human odors. Rubber boots should also be worn whenever re-baiting or traveling to the site. Any containers used at the site should first be thoroughly cleaned to remove as much human scent as possible. Containers should also be securely attached to immovable objects (trees, boulders, ground anchors) to prevent animals from carrying them off. Bears can smell the slightest human odor for days after it is left on anything. I once watched a black bear at a bait site walk up the trail I had used on the way to the stand. He suddenly stiffened when he passed a bush which had lightly brushed my pant leg six hours earlier. That was all he needed to decide to get out of there in a hurry.

The stand site for hunters at a bait station should be chosen carefully for its view as well as its concealment. Tree stands are often used for this. Shooting lanes have to be cleared and hunters should practice aiming to check out the entire setup. Scent awareness is critical at these sites because animals often come from a downwind direction after smelling the bait. Animals which detect hunters will often never be seen and the bait station abandoned prematurely. Hunters on stand at bait sites have to be every bit as cautious as those on trail stands. Hunters should also remember that bears can climb trees and prepare for this in case it happens. Magnum handguns are a common preparation.

Field baiting for deer with hay bales to hide hunters can be successful, but it is hard to lure bucks in to bait sites of any kind during daylight hours. In most areas, does and young deer come in readily to bait.

Using a naturally killed animal or animal remains from a hunter kill for bears is another option. The hunter has to set up a stand or blind just as he would with a bait station, paying particular attention to the wind direction and staying away from the kill. On one of my guided hunts in the Brooks Range of Alaska, five moose hunters in camp all filled out their grizzly bear tags in two days by sitting over their moose kill sites and watching for bears. My client and I only had to sit for three hours one day to get a bear. The bear came right by the moose gut pile and looked directly at us as if to challenge us for the goodies. I doubt he had seen many humans and wasn't sure about us. He was a typical Brooks Range grizzly, blonde and about seven feet squared.

Bait sites allow hunters a close-range examination of animals for size, sex, coat condition and whether it is a female accompanied by young. Baiting typically gives hunters short, definite shots, too. Good sites also permit hunters to look over a large number of animals and enjoy watching and learning their behavior. Good sites also take a lot of work to set up and maintain.

All six hunting techniques described can be used to successfully hunt big game in North America. Each technique works well when applied properly under the right circumstances. Consistently successful hunters have learned when and how to use at least one of these techniques, and often can use several proficiently.

There is not one or even several "big secrets" to successful hunting, but rather, a lot of little factors which add up when used together. Understanding the behavior patterns of game is one of the most useful "secrets" to know when using any hunting technique. Successful hunters pay attention to many little details every time they hunt, which pays off in the long run. Simple, but effective factors

All hunting methods can be used successfully for most species, if applied in the right way. Dave Widby with a tasty-looking elk he successfully brought within bow range by bugling.

like using the sun at their backs and wearing clean rubber boots with cover scent applied make a difference in their long-term success. All good hunters also cause as little disturbance as possible whenever

The only practical way to hunt cougars is with dogs. In some areas of the western U.S., they take a tremendous amount of wildlife and are threatening some populations.

in the field. This enables them to enter the home range of their quarry day after day and still have un-alarmed animals to hunt each time. Poor hunters often alert all the animals in their hunting area the minute they enter it and reduce their chances of success for the entire hunt. Any hunter can improve his or her success by paying attention to detail, practicing hunting skills and applying the proper techniques at the right time.

Chapter 28
BOWHUNTING

Bowhunting is gaining popularity each year in North America. Of the fifteen million hunters in the U.S., twenty percent are bowhunters during some part of the hunting season. The attractions of bowhunting are the additional challenge, the long seasons and the liberal bag limits. In many states, bowhunting seasons for whitetails are several months long with multiple tags available to each hunter–while firearms seasons in these same states may only be one or two weeks long with a limit of one buck. The bowhunting seasons for other species are also longer than most firearms' seasons in most states. The justification for this disparity is the relatively low success rates of bowhunters compared to firearms hunters. However, bowhunters can—and do—bring home plenty of venison when they have the right gear, adjust it correctly, get sufficient, high-quality practice and learn effective bowhunting skills.

For beginning bowhunters or those who want to learn about this sport, the International Bowhunter Education Program organizes training classes to teach bowhunting fundamentals. The IBEP's goal is ". . .to provide bowhunters with the fundamentals of good, safe bowhunting, and appreciation of and respect for the environment in which they hunt, and a desire to maintain the highest standards of sportsmanship." (Wadsworth 65)

Safety

There are a set of safety rules for bowhunters just as there are for firearms hunters. Bowhunters should learn and understand these to prevent unnecessary accidents and uphold the image of hunting in general.

1) Arrows are as deadly as bullets so only aim them at safe, non-deflective targets and never in the direction of anyone.

2) Be sure of your arrow's path; never shoot one over a hill or ridge were you cannot see its destination.

3) Archery gear, including bows, arrows, and bowstrings can be damaged easily and be very dangerous to the user or bystanders when weakened. Always check gear for wear or damage before shooting.

4) Always have an adequate backstop for targets. Many archers don't realize that arrows have more penetrating power than bullets.

5) Slide bows and arrows under a fence before crossing. Leave them on the ground when climbing trees and use a pull rope to bring them up after you.

6) Check quivers regularly to be sure they are covering all broadheads and none are loose to cut you.

7) Carry bows and arrows in protective cases, preferably in the trunk when traveling in an automobile.

8) Use properly designed and maintained stringing aids when stringing bows and keep your head back from the limbs in case anything slips or breaks.

9) Be careful to watch for broken arrows, broadheads and broadhead blades when cleaning bow-killed game.

10) Use care when sharpening broadheads and always use sharpening strokes directed away from your body.

11) Never shoot an arrow up into the air—it will have enough force to penetrate a man's skull on the way down.

12) Be sure bow limbs have enough clearance from tree limbs or brush when shooting. Limbs can break if they strike anything and cause serious injury.

13) Do not carry arrows on the nock unless you are about to shoot. Broadheads are razor-sharp and can cause serious injuries.

14) Tree stands are dangerous and the cause of many bowhunter injuries. Treat them with respect by observing all safety rules, always wearing a safety belt and pulling up bows and gear *after* climbing up and connecting your safety belt.

15) Bows are designed to always have an arrow on the string when they are released. No bow should be dry-fired (no arrow on the string) for the sake of personal safety and to protect the bow.

Bowhunting Gear

The selection of suitable archery gear is a function of the bowhunter's physical abilities. Drawing and shooting a bow accurately is dependant on the size, strength and temperament of the archer. Bows, arrows and other archery essentials come in different sizes and shapes to fit the corresponding variations in archers. The components of an archer's gear must also be suited to each other for safe, accurate shooting. Even after collecting all the necessary components of archery gear which are suited to the archer and to each other, these elements still have to be adjusted correctly for optimal—and safe—operation. Because of the complexities of completing these tasks, plus the additional hurdles of becoming a

Good gear, knowledgeable help and plenty of practice are necessary to become a competent bowhunter. Bart Schleyer with his bighorn ram.

good archer and then a competent bowhunter, a beginner should have qualified help during these efforts. An experienced bowhunting friend, a local archery pro-shop, or members of an archery club can assist aspiring bowhunters and get them headed in the right direction.

One of the major decisions to make about archery gear is whether to use a compound bow or a traditional bow (longbow or recurve). The main advantage of a compound bow is the relative ease of becoming proficient with it compared to a traditional bow. Because of the mechanical nature of compound bows, they can be held at full draw while the hunter uses sights to aim. Traditional bows usually have no sights and are aimed by pointing the arrow shaft. A beginner can acquire enough skill to hunt with a compound bow in a fraction of the time it would take with traditional equipment. Experienced compound shooters can also return to good shooting form in a matter of weeks, after going months or years without shooting. Traditional shooters have to practice consistently for several months before hunting season to keep up their skills, and year-round practice is recommended. Even with regular practice, most traditional shooters can only shoot with hunting accuracy up to twenty or twenty-five yards, and many should limit shots to under fifteen yards. Experienced, proficient compound shooters can shoot with the same accuracy to at least thirty yards with three or four weeks of regular practice before the season. One hunting advantage of traditional equipment is the shorter time required to draw and release the bow, which can be crucial to success at bowhunting ranges. Traditional shooters also claim their bows are more fun and satisfying to shoot. Most hunters will not invest the time to practice enough to become proficient with traditional equipment. Those who do choose this gear are driven by the personal satisfaction they get from bowhunting the "traditional" way.

There is an endless variety of archery equipment available. Most of it can be functional for bowhunters when used properly in the right situations. Some of the most useful guidelines concerning equipment are:

—Bowhunters should determine their master eye before choosing a bow—pro-shops can help with this.

—Bowhunters need simple, rugged bow designs which will hold up under tough field conditions. Bowhunters who make toughness a requirement of their bows will have an advantage from the start.

—Bow pull weights should be matched to the strength of the owner. Bowhunters who use too-heavy of bows will limit their accuracy as well as their overall hunting success. Heavy bows also tend to wear out shoulders in the long run.

—Overdraws usually increase speed for flatter trajectories, but with a sacrifice in stability, quietness, ease of tuning and accuracy under less-than-ideal field situations. Bows with rounder wheels are often slower, but more stable because there is less bow jump.

—A good practice for bowhunters is to carry an extra string whenever in the field. This string should be put on the bow—complete with nocking point and string silencers if applicable—and used for a few days. Then, it can be taken off, folded and wrapped in a waterproof Ziploc™, and taped to the quiver or other location where it is always available.

—Bows should be carried in hard or soft cases to protect them.

—Nocks should fit snug on the bowstring, but not so tight they affect accuracy or make too much noise. Nocks can be sized after submersion in boiling water for 10-20 seconds to soften them.

—Bowhunters should understand how their bow functions; this may prevent a spoiled hunting trip when mishaps occur in the field far away from a pro-shop.

—Choose gear suited to you, your hunting goals and the area you are hunting. Wood arrows and feathers may be more aesthetically pleasing, but both are susceptible to damage from wet weather.

Bowhunters typically work much harder for their trophies than rifle hunters, so hunting with a bow can be frustrating at times, but the successes are very memorable. Todd Fisher with a Sitka blacktail deer taken on Kodiak Island, Alaska.

Aluminum arrows and vanes are much more resistant to wet or very cold weather.

–Check your arrows for straightness before and during a hunting trip.

–Single-colored arrows are easier to see in flight and find in the field to check for blood.

–Feathers can be steamed to fluff or to straighten them out.

–The most common archery/bowhunting accidents occur when pulling arrows and when handling broadheads.

–All styles of broadheads should be checked regularly for straightness and sharpness.

–Learning to tune your bow well is the most important aspect of accuracy–particularly when shooting broadheads.

–Broadheads should be lightly coated with Vaseline™ or light grease to prevent rust.

–Razor-sharp broadheads are a big advantage–greatly improving a bowhunter's chances of success.

Practice

Bowhunters need to practice much more than rifle hunters to shoot well enough to hunt–the more proficiency they gain with their bows, the more success they are likely to have. Bowhunters with minimal practice time and skill may be limited to very short-range shots at game–fifteen yards or less. Bowhunters with excellent shooting and range estimation skills (or a good rangefinder) may be able to shoot at distances of forty yards or more. This difference in effective range can be a significant factor in a bowhunter's chances for success.

Practicing regularly throughout the year and increasing the amount of shooting time just prior to hunting season is a good way for a bowhunter to improve his shooting abilities and his chances of success. In addition to getting enough practice, a bowhunter needs to get the right kind of practice to become a good shot on game. A game animal typically does not stand still at a predetermined yardage and allow a hunter to shoot several arrows at it from a standing position. Bowhunters usually get one shot at an animal from a unknown distance using any other position except standing. Bowhunters' practice should reflect the realities of hunting to be of the highest value to them.

The first necessity for bowhunters is a well-tuned bow– whether it is a compound or a traditional bow. Hunters should either learn how to do this well themselves (the best alternative) or seek help at a pro-shop or a shooting range. Proper tuning is absolutely necessary for bowhunters who want to be good shots at game. A poorly tuned bow may shoot arrows with field or target points fairly well, but arrows with broadheads shot from an out-of-tune bow will not fly straight nor group well. This will also result in loss of arrow speed, poor arrow penetration and poor hits on game animals. This is exactly what happened to me during my first year as a bowhunter. After practicing with field points for six months, I switched to broadheads–only to see my groups triple in size because of a poorly tuned bow. Instead of getting experienced help, by trial and error I discovered that small, three-bladed broadheads tightened my groups to respectable sizes. However, this solution only fixes the grouping problem, not the loss of arrow speed or poor penetration. All three problems can be solved by proper bow tuning.

After proper bow tuning is accomplished, a bowhunter can begin improving his shooting for hunting conditions. Shooting from a standing position is still the basis of practice because this is used for sighting in, learning proper form, and testing new equipment or adjustments. Practice for hunting conditions involves shooting from likely hunting positions as well as a standing position. Bowhunters should practice from sitting, kneeling, crouching, leaning, twisting and any other positions they expect to use when hunting. All of these

Having a backyard practice range will allow a bowhunter to practice at any time and improve much faster than if he has to drive to a distant range with limited open hours.

positions will cause the shooter to apply different pressures on his bow and arrow hands and affect the point of impact of the arrow. Bowhunters need to know how to minimize these changes in pressure as much as possible in each position so their arrow's point of impact is as similar as possible from every position. During practice, the bowhunter must determine any position in which the point of impact is still significantly different and allow for this when shooting at game.

A bowhunter should also practice with the exact same gear he will use and in similar conditions expected during an upcoming hunt. Bulky clothing must not get in the way of the bowstring or affect drawing of the bow. I find that by tugging on my hunting jacket in a certain way just before shooting, it flattens against my chest and doesn't interfere with my bowstring. Any pack or pistol belt carried during the hunt should also be tested for interference with shooting during practice sessions. If possible, practicing under similar weather conditions to those expected during the hunt is another good habit. Before I went on a musk-oxen hunt to Nunivak Island, Alaska, I practiced outdoors in minus 20° F temperatures in preparation for the very cold weather I expected on the hunt. I had to adjust my twenty-yard sight about twelve inches up and to the right to make up for the affect of the cold temperature. Had I not done this, I most likely would have missed the bull I shot when the temperature was minus 35° F. Bowhunters should test their gear under all conditions of the hunt whenever possible.

It is also important to learn to shoot at one spot on an animal and not the whole animal. Bowhunters who instill this habit during practice are more likely to make good shots under the stress of hunting conditions. One of the best ways to practice this is by shooting at 3-D animal targets regularly. These life-size targets do not have obvious bulls-eyes, just as live animals do not have them. Attending 3-D matches will add a little pressure to your practice. The pressure to shoot well with other bowhunters watching is good training for the pressures of a real hunting situation. Bowhunters can make 3-D shoots and practice sessions even more realistic by moving slowly and deliberately during each shot to further mimic the conditions of a real hunt.

A necessary component of useful practice with 3-D targets is a good understanding of animal anatomy. The first step is to recognize the lungs, liver and heart as the main targets of a bowhunter. These organs are all in the chest area of game animals, but partially protected by the spine, scapula (shoulder bone) and leg bones. Most hunters who take up bowhunting have to learn these organs' locations and how to get an arrow into them without striking nearby bones. It is vital that bowhunters know and practice the best angles to shoot arrows into the animals they hunt for clean kills. Figure 28.1 shows the anatomy of a whitetail deer, the animal most hunted by bowhunters (all hunters, in fact) in North America. Well-placed arrows into any of these three organs typically kill deer quickly— they die within 100 yards of where they were shot. Bowhunters (all hunters, in fact) should study these and other animals' anatomy diagrams and commit them to memory. Chapter Thirty, "Shooting at Game" has anatomy drawings of additional game animals.

Stump shooting is another practice routine which mimics actual hunting conditions. Bowhunters walk through fields or woods like those they will hunt and shoot at stumps, logs, hummocks, etc., at various distances and from different positions. Blunts, field points or old broadheads can all be used for this type of practice, but whichever type of points are used, they should be the same weight as hunting broadheads so they will have the same point of impact. Another form of this is to carry a blunt-tipped arrow in the quiver during the actual hunt. Whenever opportunities arise during the hunting day, the bowhunter can take practice shots to keep loose and confident.

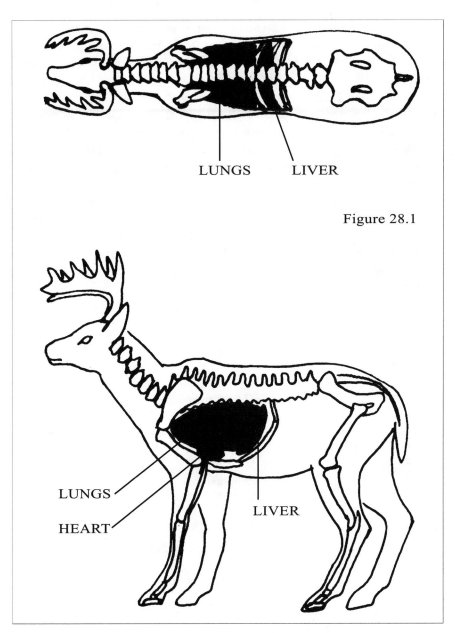

LUNGS   LIVER

Figure 28.1

LUNGS

HEART

LIVER

Figure 28.1 shows a top and broadside view of the internal anatomy of a deer. The lungs, liver and heart are shown in their respective locations in the chest area. The spine, scapula and front leg bones all can stop an arrow directed at the vital organs if the arrow is not placed correctly–which depends on the shooting angle. Bowhunters should study these diagrams and memorize the locations of these organs as well as the major bones of the body.

Bowhunters also need to learn the trajectory of their bows at various ranges. Arrow trajectories are much more curved than those of bullets. The result is that bowhunters need to estimate range within a few yards to make killing shots on game (or do well in a 3-D match). Figure 28.2 shows several arrows' flight paths from when they leave the bow until they strike a target. The greatly increasing curve of an arrow's flight path as it travels further from a bow is why bowhunters' effective ranges are so limited. The decreasing accuracy of range estimation by bowhunters at progressively longer distances is more significant than the actual distance. For a typical bowhunter, estimating a twenty-yard target as being only eighteen yards might mean a perfectly shot arrow would strike two inches low—still within the kill zone of a typical big game animal. The same hunter who estimates a forty-yard target as being only thirty-eight yards would see his perfectly shot arrow strike five inches low—below the kill zone of most big game animals.

Figure 28.2

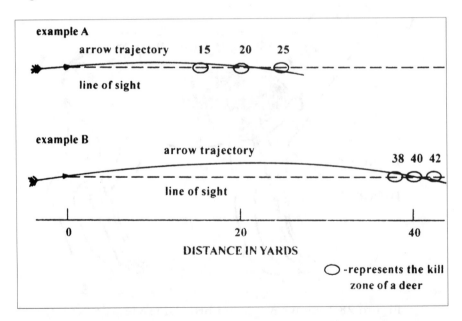

Figure 28.2 illustrates why range estimation becomes increasingly important to bowhunters at longer ranges. Example A shows the trajectory of an arrow aimed at the center of a deer's kill zone twenty yards away from a bowhunter. The oval represents the average size of the kill zone of a deer. In example A, if the deer was any distance from fifteen to twenty-five yards—a ten-yard span—

from the bowhunter, the arrow would still strike somewhere within the kill zone. In example B, the arrow is aimed at the center of the kill zone of a deer forty yards away from a bowhunter. Notice that the trajectory is much higher in this example because of the distance. In example B, the arrow would strike the kill zone of a deer from thirty-eight to forty-two yards–only a four-yard span. At closer ranges a bowhunter has a fairly long span of distance where his arrow will strike the kill zone of a deer. At longer ranges, the span is much shorter, so range estimations have to be more accurate to ensure a killing shot.

Another practicing strategy is to shoot only one arrow per target, just as bowhunters will only get one arrow at an animal. A very experienced bowhunting friend of mine takes this to the extreme and he only shoots one arrow per day in his normal routine. This way, he is shooting under the same conditions of a hunt–no warm-up and only one shot at an unknown distance. For the greatest benefit, bowhunters should practice under these types of conditions. The more realistic practice sessions are, the better bowhunters will perform in the field. This will build both skills and confidence for actual hunting situations.

Hunting Considerations

Arrows kill by hemorrhage, not by tissue damage and shock as bullets typically do. Therefore, good penetration is much more important when bowhunting than when hunting with a firearm. Arrows which pass completely through game also leave a better blood trail because there is no arrow plugging the holes, so more blood can drip out. These facts emphasize that a bowhunter should use a well-tuned bow which produces good arrow flight (the most important factor in good penetration), understand animal anatomy so he can aim arrows correctly, take only high-percentage shots which aren't likely to strike bones and stop, and use razor-sharp broadheads for maximum cutting ability. These are all taught during bowhunter education classes and written in every book on bowhunting for good reasons–they are very important to the effective use of bows and arrows to kill big game. They should be fully understood—and believed—by those who aim to be successful bowhunters.

Before a bowhunter goes afield with new equipment, it should be carefully modified to hunt with–not for just shooting at targets which don't have functional eyes, ears and noses. Hunting modifications should eliminate any sight, sound, or smell from the equipment so these don't alert animals in the field. A good way to find any visual giveaways is to look at a bow from the game's point of view. This can be done by propping up a bow and looking at it from the front—as an animal would see it. Any shiny or colorful areas which stand out to the bowhunter's eyes should be covered with camouflage tape or paint. Next, an assistant can be enlisted to draw the bow <u>without an arrow</u> while the bowhunter stands in front, but slightly to the side for safety's sake. By watching this person draw the bow in several positions, with different drawing motions and at different speeds, a bowhunter can see how an animal views these variations in shooting style. This is a very enlightening exercise and will help any bowhunter choose the best way(s) to draw their bow to reduce observed motion from the animal's point of view.

Next, a bowhunter should draw the bow using several motions and speeds to check for noise. Then he should shoot the bow to check for noise. String silencers, padding on rests, rubber washers under screws, quiver padding, and liquid rubber or beeswax on any bow part can help reduce noise. Pro-shop owners/employees or other bowhunters are good sources of ideas as they are always coming up with new products and methods to silence bows.

Bows and arrows—as well as other gear, clothing, and bowhunters themselves—can also be treated with products which remove or cover-up human scent. Odor-blocking sprays for bowhunters and their clothes can be used before and again during a day's hunt to keep human scent to a minimum. Cover-up scents imitating natural foods or other animals (fox, skunk, coyote, etc.) can be used to confuse game animals and give bowhunters more time to shoot or sneak closer.

Bowhunters commonly use tree stands to get above game and help them escape detection by the animals' senses. There are even specialized stands for attaching to limbs, in tree forks and for two hunters. These can give bowhunters a hunting advantage over animals and their fellow hunters who may be limited by using standard tree stands. Bowhunters must be extra cautious about clearing shooting lanes around stands because even the smallest twig can deflect arrows way off course. I once hit a buck broadside just behind the front leg at seven yards which I thought was a perfect shot. To my chagrin, it wasn't. When we caught up with the deer and finished it off about a mile away, we discovered the arrow had been deflected and angled to the rear when it struck the animal. The arrow must have struck a stalk of the tall grass in the area and been flying almost sideways when it hit the deer. It is almost impossible for arrows which touch any vegetation to maintain their original flight path and characteristics. Since penetration is vital to clean kills, bowhunters must always check for a clear flight path before shooting.

*Bowhunters must take every precaution when hunting wary
whitetail deer. George P. Mann with one of the whitetails he has
taken, in part, by being conscientious about his bowhunting gear.*

Bowhunters using stands should also make range estimates—with a rangefinder if possible—to several spots around their stands. By doing this when they first get settled each day, they will have distances predetermined if an animal appears suddenly and gives them only a few seconds to shoot. It is also a good idea for bowhunters to shoot a practice arrow from any type of stand upon arriving to check their form and accuracy. Shooting this arrow away from likely animal pathways will prevent them from smelling it and ruining the hunt. When the time comes to shoot at an animal, bowhunters must be sure and identify their target and the backstop. Arrows are deflected much easier than bullets and can travel hundreds of yards if they go over hills or ridges.

One of the necessary attributes of a good bowhunter is patience and the ability to determine the right moment to shoot. When a bowhunter gets within bow range of an animal, the hunt is far from over. Getting a good shot off without alarming the animal is half the challenge of bowhunting–getting within range being the other half. A bowhunter's decisions about when to shoot are crucial to success. These decisions depend on the distance, the angle, if the arrow's flight path is clear, the wind, the animal's position, its alertness, its eye and ear orientations, the bowhunter's steadiness or nervousness, and his body position. These and other factors should be considered before any shot is taken. Assessing these factors becomes instinctive as bowhunters gain experience at shooting at game.

Deciding when to shoot also depends on the general behavior of the species and the specific behavior of the animal you are hunting. A nervous species like the whitetail deer will typically spring into motion at the slightest noise or movement within fifty yards–bowhunting range. Sitka deer, on the other hand, will often let a bowhunter within this distance draw and release his bow in plain sight if he does so slowly. The individual animal also has to be considered. There are some unusually calm whitetail deer and some unusually nervous Sitka deer. Bowhunters must examine each animal to detect its mood when deciding when to shoot. Any animal with its ears straight up is alert and will probably move suddenly at the slightest noise–like releasing an arrow. If that same animal let its ears flop down into relaxed positions, a bowhunter would then have a better chance of releasing an arrow without alarming the animal.

A successful bowhunter must take several steps on the road to success. First, equipment which suits the bowhunter's size, strength and hunting needs is chosen. Next, this equipment must be set up

Bowhunters after bears like this ten-foot Kodiak bruin must be confident in their gear and their abilities. Bob Ameen took this monster with one arrow.

and tuned correctly for it to function properly. Then the bowhunter must get adequate amounts of the right types of practice to prepare for hunting situations. Lastly, and maybe most importantly, a bowhunter must learn how to get within bow range of an animal as well as learn to draw and release an arrow without alerting the animal. Bowhunters who can do all of this, plus have the patience required to wait for the right moment to release an arrow, will enjoy the challenge and satisfaction of successful bowhunting.

Bowhunters must match their gear to the animal they are going after–just like firearms hunters. When Carl Brent took this bull bison from the Farewell herd in Alaska he turned up the draw weight on his compound bow and used heavy arrows.

Chapter 29
FIELD-JUDGING
GAME ANIMALS

Field-judging animals is certainly important for trophy hunters who are always looking for the biggest rack, but even the average deer hunter should be able to judge the approximate size of his quarry. And most deer hunters occasionally go to another state to hunt another species, so they should have sufficient field-judging ability to choose an acceptable trophy when they do. They can avoid going home with an animal which should have been passed on, or going home empty-handed after passing on good-sized animals they later regret not taking.

A "trophy" animal is in the eyes of the beholder–usually this is the lucky hunter. A "trophy" is defined by each and every hunter who sets foot in the field. Some hunters have high expectations for large horns and some take mostly "meat" animals. Each hunter has his own set of reasons for hunting. All ethical hunting is perfectly legitimate and has a place in the world of hunting and conservation.

For those hunters who seek the additional challenge of trophy hunting, there are the "Record Books." There are three clubs which keep records of outstanding North American big game animals taken under fair chase rules. These are the Boone and Crockett club, the Pope and Young club, and Safari Club International. These clubs periodically publish books listing their records of the 27 species of North American big game animals. Each club has geographic guidelines for where each species must be taken to qualify for its record book. This is necessary to ensure records represent a fair comparison within each species.

The Clubs Behind the Record Books

The oldest of these three clubs is the Boone and Crockett Club (B&C), established in 1887. B&C keeps records of outstanding animals taken with any legal weapon under their guidelines of fair chase. The Pope and Young Club (P&Y) was started in 1967 to tabulate the largest animals taken legally and ethically with bow and arrow. Safari Club International (SCI) keeps separate record books for animals taken with each major type of legal weapon—rifle, handgun, muzzleloader, and bow & arrow.

Properly practiced, trophy hunting is the challenge to take an outstanding representative of a species under a strict set of ethical guidelines. Many hunters who take up this challenge do not wish to enter their trophies into any record books. They hunt for exceptional animals for the personal satisfaction it brings them. They have their own size minimums which qualify animals as trophies in their eyes, and ethical standards they must live up to for personal reasons. Their trophies are not represented in any record books.

The three record-keeping clubs all have trophy minimums established for each of the 27 species listed in their record books. Animals must meet these minimums after being scored with a strict set of measuring guidelines. Both B&C and P&Y use the same set of guidelines which B&C developed and copyrighted in 1950. Both clubs require a 60-day minimum drying period prior to scoring. SCI has its own set of measuring guidelines and does not require any drying period. In addition to the drying period requirements, another major difference between the scoring systems are B&C and P&Y scores reflect deductions for unsymmetrical measurements between the left and right sides of horns and antlers, whereas SCI does not deduct for lack of symmetry between the sides.

All three record books require hunters who enter trophies to have taken them under a rigid set of ethical standards. These standards go beyond legal hunting regulations. Hunters must meet more demanding rules of sportsmanship and fair chase or their trophies are not accepted into these record books. Any hunters who are caught falsely claiming to have met these standards will have <u>all</u> their records removed from the books and will be banned from entering any future trophies. Also, hunters who maliciously break hunting laws will have all their trophy records removed. Clubs may also remove convicted felons' trophies from their record books, depending on the circumstances.

These actions by the clubs demonstrate one of their goals—to require hunters to meet a higher set of ethical standards than required by law. The challenge of trophy hunting is not only to take large animals, but to do so under a stricter set of rules—one without the other is not acceptable. These clubs have other goals beside keeping records. The money they raise is used for conservation and funding of wildlife projects. The record books are just one way these clubs raise funds to help wildlife restoration and enhancement programs.

The ability to field-judge animals quickly is important because of the nature of animals–they often don't stick around and give hunters a lot of time to decide. Is this moose good enough to shoot?

Each animal must be judged on its species' merits and not hunters' misconceptions. These caribou antlers look huge compared to a deer's, but this is only a good bull and certainly not Boone & Crocket quality.

Principles of Judging

Estimating the size of an animal's horns, antlers, or skull is a challenging task, even for experienced hunters. The first step to becoming a good field-judger is to acquire a basic understanding of how these scores are calculated. Next, the hunter can practice on mounted trophies which have already been scored. After practice and subsequent feedback about the actual scores of mounts and the characteristics which influenced these scores, hunters can move on to live animals with, hopefully, an experienced field-judging friend to tutor them. Along with practice, the more serious students of field-judging should carefully examine recorded information about trophies to arrive at detailed guidelines to use for judging each species in which the hunter is interested.

Hunters must know how scores are calculated before they can make accurate estimates in the field. Within a group of similar species—like the four species of sheep or the three species of moose—the measuring instructions are the same. Skull sizes of the bears and the cougar are also measured the same way. All three record books contain precise instructions for measuring each species for hunters who want this information.

The characteristics used to score animals are symmetry, mass, length, width, and number of points. Symmetry refers to balance between the left and right sides of a set of horns or antlers. For typical classes of animals, the more symmetry, the higher the score. Nontypical categories do not take symmetry into account. Mass is measured by measuring the circumference around a horn or antler at predetermined locations. Lengths and widths are also measured at predetermined locations on horns, antlers and skulls. Numbers of points are counted on antlers and added to the scores. A complete understanding of how these measurements are taken for each animal can only be achieved by a thorough examination of its score sheet and measurement rules.

The score of horned animals does not include a width measurement. Their score is calculated by adding the length of the two horns to the circumferences at four locations spaced evenly along the horns–a total of ten measurements. The result is: mass is more important than length to get a high score for a horned animal. When field-judging the species with horns, first look at overall mass as an indication of its score, then look at the length as a secondary indicator.

More measurements are taken to arrive at the score of antlered animals than the ten used for horned animals. There is a width measurement as well as lengths, circumferences and point counts used to arrive at their total score. All four of these measurements can significantly affect the total scores of antlered game, making them harder to field-judge than horned animals. A typical eight-point whitetail has 16 measurements, a well-developed barren-ground caribou may have 29 measurements.

All four bear species and the cougar are scored with only two measurements–the width and length of the skull. Since the totals of these species' scores are so small—just over 30 inches for the largest brown bears—there is little room for error when judging bears or cougars. Most hunters find that bears are the most difficult animals to field-judge accurately. Recently, I was guiding a brown bear hunter on the Alaska Peninsula when we spotted a large bear which I couldn't judge with enough certainty for the client who wanted nothing less than a nine-foot bear. Finally the bear crossed a river and walked in front of us. I immediately ran up to check the track size—which confirmed my estimation, so I told the hunter to shoot. When we examined the bear, its neck and head were unusually large in proportion to the body, which had made the bear look smaller than its size of nine and one-half feet. Field-judging errors are more typical with bears than any other animals.

Some helpful keys to making accurate field estimates are:
1) Your first impression of the animal is probably a good indication of its size—unless you see it for the first time through your sights at close range, then you may be too excited and think it is bigger than it really is. Good optics will help hunters avoid this pitfall and improve their field-judging accuracy in general.
2) Field estimates made before anyone gives you their opinion are better than those made afterward.
3) Really large animals of most species are often solitary animals. [On my bison hunt, we spotted a lone monarch (the name given to large, solitary bison bulls) which ran off. In looking back, I should have pursued it because the tracks were huge.]
4) Really huge animals are *usually* found in areas which normally produce large trophies.
5) The best years to hunt for trophy-size antlered game animals come immediately after an easy winter, an early spring, and a good summer for growing lots of high-quality food.
6) On antlered and horned game animals, there is more than one characteristic which can make them large trophies. Know these characteristics and look carefully for them when in the field.
7) Depending on the species—horn, antler, or skull size can be compared to: height of the body at the shoulder, breast to shoulder height, body width as viewed from the front or back, length of the body, distance between the ear tips, length of the face, head compared to body size, neck compared to body length, and shoulder height or width compared to hip size. Before using any of these comparisons, ascertain if the animal is of normal size and shape. (Sheep in Alaska are sometimes misjudged if an individual sheep has a short face— which makes the horns appear much bigger.)
8) Body shape is an indication of maturity and size in some species. Old goats of both sexes have pronounced humps, sway backs and long faces; big bears have large hips and small heads; and a mature

First impressions are usually good when trophy judging. This antelope looks huge at the first look—and it is.

bison bull has a bonnet (hair on top of the head) higher than its horns.

9) There are always exceptions to generalities—like the ones I just mentioned—about trophy animals. Always consider each animal very carefully on its own merits before shooting or passing it up. Some of the biggest trophy animals ever taken were in unexplainable locations, spotted at unexpected times or field-judged as mediocre trophies.

    After a hunter understands the basics of how a trophy is scored he should practice estimating scores of mounted trophies and photos of trophies. If the trophies have been scored, the hunter should not know the score before making an estimate, but wait until after the estimate has been made. This kind of practice will force the hunter to develop confidence in his own field-judging abilities. After comparing his guess with the actual score, a hunter should examine the trophy and readjust his mental image to match the actual score.

It is extremely helpful for hunters to look at mounted trophies to acquire a mental image of what trophies of different sizes look like. Scrutinizing a mounted trophy from all angles can create a detailed image in a hunter's mind which can be compared to animals later seen in the field. This can be extremely helpful for those times when hunters have only a short time to decide whether or not to shoot—a typical situation when whitetail deer hunting. If no mounts are available to look at, good photos are the next best thing.

The next phase in learning to field-judge animals is field practice. Preseason practice is possible if the hunter lives near the animals he will hunt and if he can get some kind of feedback. Feedback can be in the form of an experienced friend who accompanies the hunter to critique his estimates. The best type of practice is experienced during the season when the field-judged animals are later harvested, and then scored, for the most accurate feedback. Both types of feedback can help the hunter make corrections to his mental images for scoring and create a set of guidelines which help him make good field estimates.

An In-Depth Analysis

For the hunter who wants to be as good as possible at field-judging one species, a large group of scores from that species can be analyzed in detail. This can show the hunter the general rules to follow for field-judging as well as any idiosyncrasies the species may have. Chart 29.1 is an example of this type of analysis. It is a chart of possible scores of Dall sheep. The chart is based on the longest horn and largest base of a set of sheep horns. The numbers within the chart are total scores in B&C or P&Y points (remember—B&C and P&Y scores are the same).

There are three parts to field-judging a set of sheep horns. The first part is guessing the length of the horns. The second part is estimating the mass of the horns. Hunters typically use the circumference of the bases when estimating horn mass, although the other three circumferences are definitely part of this estimate. The third segment of field-judging is combining the two numbers to estimate a total score. This third aspect is what this chart addresses.

Estimating horn length and mass with accuracy and consistency takes a lot of practice. There are many variables to take into account when doing this. They include relative size of the sheep (for establishing a baseline to compare the horns against), the rise

16.0	156	160	163	166	168	**171**	173	175	178	180	182	184	186	188
15.5	154	156	160	163	165	168	**171**	173	175	177	179	181	183	185
15.0	151	154	156	159	162	165	167	**170**	172	174	177	179	181	183
14.5	147	151	154	156	158	161	164	167	**170**	172	174	177	179	181
14.0	144	147	151	153	155	157	160	164	167	**170**	172	174	177	179
13.5	142	144	147	151	153	155	157	160	164	167	**170**	172	174	177
13.0	138	141	144	147	151	153	155	157	160	163	166	**170**	172	174
12.5	135	138	141	144	147	150	152	155	158	160	163	166	**170**	172
12.0	133	135	138	140	143	146	149	152	155	158	160	163	166	**170**
11.5	131	133	135	138	140	143	146	149	152	155	158	160	163	166
11.0	128	131	133	135	138	140	143	146	149	152	155	157	160	163
10.5	125	128	131	133	135	138	140	143	146	149	152	155	157	160
	32	33	34	35	36	37	38	39	40	41	42	43	44	45

Largest Base Circumference in Inches

Longest Horn Length in Inches

Table 29.1

and drop of the horns compared to the jaw, the degree of curl, the size of the inner hole, and the shape of the horns. After considering all the factors and making length and mass estimates, it is quite simple to approximate the total score.

Each combination of length and mass indicates a somewhat narrow range for the total score. For example, the chart predicts that a (Dall) sheep with a horn length of 41 inches and a base circumference of 14 inches would score about 171 B&C points. While researching, I found ten officially scored B&C Dall sheep with these length and base measurements. These ten sheep had total scores of 170, 170, 170, 171, 171, 171, 171, 171, 172, and 175 points. In this case 171 points is the mean, median *and* mode of these numbers—which means it should be a *very* predictable (average) number to use.

This chart is not perfect of course. I used 264 official Boone and Crockett or Pope & Young scores to come up with these numbers. I had to extrapolate for some combinations of length and base circumference because not all were represented in my data base. Also, not all of the final numbers were averages of my data. I inspected the initial chart numbers and made minor corrections when scores seemed too high or low. But, given enough scores to calculate all the averages, I think the numbers in this chart are very close to average scores of Dall sheep—over the complete range.

Inspection of the chart will show that the average increase in total score due to a one inch increase in length is *three points*. The average increase in total score due to a one-half inch increase in base size is also *three points.* This is a good rule to remember when field-judging Dall sheep. All other factors being equal, *a one inch increase in length or a one-half increase in base size will cause the total score to increase by three points.*

Corrections should be made to the chart's predictions when there is anything out of the ordinary. The chart predicts scores for *average* Dall sheep horns. Average Dall sheep horns do not carry mass well out to the tips. They have a fast taper and narrow tips. Dall sheep horns are usually *not* broomed. The final scores for horns that are abnormally heavy, unusually thin, or broomed on one side should be adjusted. If one horn on a Dall sheep is broomed back five inches, simply deduct five points from the chart's predicted score to get the final estimation. For horns which are broomed on both sides, estimate how much heavier the overall horn shape is compared to normal Dall sheep horns and adjust accordingly. If they are only slightly broomed off (an inch or two), the addition of three to four points to the chart's predicted score should be sufficient.

By using this chart, you can eliminate some of the guesswork in field-judging total score. You don't have to memorize the chart or even carry it with you. Just remember one set of numbers—length, mass and score—in the general range of the size of sheep you intend to hunt. When you are in the field looking at a sheep, estimate the length and mass. By comparing these to the length and mass you have memorized, you can arrive at total score by doing the aforementioned three-point adjustments for length and mass differences. For example, you could memorize the set of 41, 14 and 171. If you then estimate a sheep to be 38 inches long with 13-inch bases, you would subtract nine points for the three-inches shorter length and six points for the one-inch smaller base. This would result in 171 minus 15 points = 156 points. The chart actually predicts the score at 155 points, which is close enough for most sheep hunters.

This chart and explanation of field-judging Dall sheep is an example of what can be done for any species. Hunters who do make such a chart or similar analysis will have a much better understanding of what it takes for a high-scoring animal of that species. This will also give them an awareness of how different variations in length,

After only a glance, this elk is an impressive trophy. In general, the really big trophies are easy to spot. If you have to talk yourself into shooting a trophy, it is probably too small for you.

This sheep's horns drop almost to the bottom of the jaw line and the unbroken tip is well above the eye. Both characteristics indicate long horns and in fact it is over 41 inches–a very good ram.

mass, width or number of points can add up to the same total scores. To be of the greatest applicable benefit, an analysis of this type should be done with scores of animals about the same size as what the hunter expects to see.

Field-judging is a necessary skill for any hunter who wants to predetermine what size animal he is shooting. It is also a necessary skill for preseason visual scouting. The steps to becoming a good field judge of trophy animals are: learning the rules of scoring, learning guidelines for field estimations, practicing on mounts, photos and live animals, and analyzing a large group of scores to get the best understanding of a species' typical and unusual characteristics. Hunters can achieve the level of expertise they want by choosing to take the necessary steps along this progression.

Chapter 30
SHOOTING AT GAME

The ability to shoot at game skillfully is the single most important trait of a successful hunter. All aspects of the hunt leading up to the moment when a hunter pulls the trigger or releases the string pale in comparison. A hunter can have the best pre-shot hunting skills and the most complete knowledge of his quarry, but if he does not shoot well at game, he will not harvest many animals. However, good shooting skills can make up for a lot of deficiencies in hunting skills and knowledge of game behavior. Hunters can ignore some hunting skills which they don't rely on, and still be successful, but shooting at game is one skill which all hunters should master.

The first requirement of shooting at game skillfully is for hunters to know their weapons. This requires regular practice and a working knowledge of the weapon itself. Next, hunters must learn how to shoot, where to place their shots and when to fire for the best results. How, where and when they shoot will affect not only how often and how cleanly they kill, it will also affect the quality of both their trophies and the game meat they take home.

How to Shoot at Game

Hunters should be knowledgeable about their weapons' abilities and limits. This is necessary to sight them in properly at the best distance to fit the current hunting conditions. Hunters must know the trajectory of their bullets or arrows and their personal, effective range with the weapon. (See Chapters 19, 20 and 28 for complete discussions on these topics.) Regular practice simulating field conditions is a vital part of learning to shoot well at game. Hunters should practice shooting from sitting, kneeling, standing, and prone positions. Wearing the anticipated hunting clothing and gear is crucial to bowhunters for the most productive practice sessions and is often useful to firearms hunters who need to learn if bulky clothing or gear will hinder their shooting accuracy.

Good shooters also understand the rules for shooting uphill and downhill. Actually, only one very simple rule has to be remembered: "When shooting uphill, downhill or over flat ground, the *horizontal* distance to the target is used to determine point of aim." The *vertical* distance is not important except to help figure out the horizontal distance. Figure 30.1 shows five different shot angles—0°, 15°, 30°, 45°, and 60°—and how the horizontal distance is affected by these angles. The horizontal distances are used to determine how much drop will occur in bullets traveling the different distances and angles–as illustrated.

As the graphs and explanations of examples A, B and C reveal, when shooting either uphill or downhill at a target a certain distance away, the shooter would allow for less bullet drop than when shooting over flat ground at a target the same distance from the shooter. Also, the steeper the uphill or downhill slope, the less horizontal distance the bullet will travel, so the less bullet drop which will occur compared to shooting over flat ground. These same principles apply to all projectiles–bullets, shotgun slugs, arrows, etc. More hunters make holdover miscalculations on uphill or downhill shots than on any other shooting situation. Good game shots learn these principles and can apply them quickly and correctly.

The difficulty of shooting on slopes is compounded because uphill targets look closer than they are, while downhill targets look farther away. This is a perception problem and it should be solved by using rangefinders or by sufficient range-estimating practice to overcome erroneous range estimations.

In addition to quickly assessing holdover after determining horizontal distance to the target, good shooters also monitor their mental state. Stress can make the best target-range shooters poor shots at game. Hunters can monitor themselves for quick, shallow breathing–which is a common stress-related symptom. One way to improve hunters' concentration and control is to have a practiced pre-shot routine to go through each time they shoot at the range or in the field. Additionally, concentration and deep, slow breathing can help hunters manage their excitement just before shooting. Deep breathing is a method used by people in every facet of their lives whenever stress becomes a hindrance to performance. Taking several deep, slow breaths from the stomach area—not the chest—while concentrating on breathing will calm nerves and improve hunters' performances under stressful field conditions, of which shooting at game is one.

It is best to avoid unnecessary noise or movement immediately before and after shooting at game. Bowhunters are specifically taught to be careful to not alarm animals after shooting at them. Since arrows often strike fatal areas of game without alarming them—often passing all the way through the animal—it is

TRAJECTORIES OF UPHILL AND DOWNHILL SHOOTING
Figure 30.1

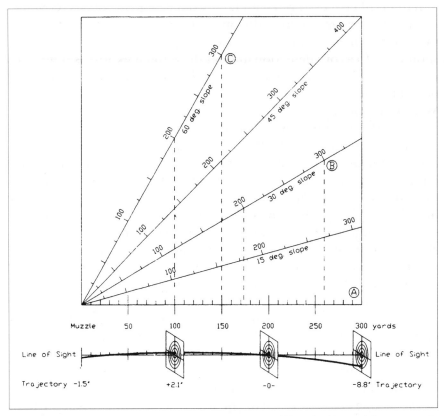

*This graph is based on a 165 grain, .30 caliber bullet with a muzzle velocity of 2700 ft./sec., zeroed at 200 yards.

Example A - 300 yards over flat terrain – When shooting across flat terrain at a target 300 yards away, the point of impact will be almost 9 inches below point of aim.

Example B - 300 yards on a 30° slope, either uphill or downhill– When shooting up or down a 30° slope at a target 300 yards away, the point of impact will be the same as if shooting 260 yards on level terrain, or about 4 inches below the point of aim. This point of impact is about 5 inches above what occurs when shooting 300 yards on level terrain.

Example C - 300 yards on a 60° slope, either uphill or downhill– When shooting up or down a 60° slope at a target 300 yards away, the point of impact will be the same as if shooting 150 yards on level terrain, or about 1 inch above point of aim. This point of impact is about 10 inches above what occurs when shooting 300 yards on level terrain.

better to keep them in sight until they expire, rather than scaring them off and then having to try and find them. Highly excited animals will run farther and—even with fatal wounds—may not be recovered. Also, the increased adrenaline and exhertion will adversely affect the quality of the meat. All hunters, regardless of their weapons, should try to avoid detection and let the animal expire as quietly as possible. This practice will greatly improve recovery times and percentages.

Where to Shoot

All hunters need to learn the vital areas of game to make clean kills. Figures 28.1, 30.2 and 30.3 show the vital organs of deer, bison and black bear. All animals have distinctive body styles with slightly different locations of their vital organs. Hunters need to learn the exact locations of these vital organs in each species they hunt for maximum shooting efficiency. This is necessary to be able to hit the vitals when shooting from all possible angles. Studies have shown that fully 75% of deer hunters cannot accurately point to the heart and lung area of a deer. In Alaska, where over ten thousand people annually apply for 100 bison permits, there are several rifle hunters each year who lose their (most likely) one chance in a lifetime to take a bison by not knowing the kill zone on these oddly shaped creatures. They commonly shoot them in the hump—way too high to hit lungs or heart.

The three most common ways which bullets or arrows kill big game animals are by striking the lungs—which kills by loss of oxygen to the brain, hitting a major artery—which produces significant blood loss and pressure, or by striking the heart—which stops blood flow to the brain. The best target for hunters on a big game animal is the heart/lung area. This target is fairly large, it produces a quick kill and meat loss is kept to a minimum. Good hits in this area will kill the animal in less than two minutes and ruin only a couple pounds of rib meat.

The best shot angle to hit the heart/lung area on a big game animal is when it is broadside or quartering away from the hunter. From these angles the vitals present the largest target and are least protected by large bones (See figures 28.1, 30.2 & 30.3). On a broadside shot, bowhunters are taught to line up their shot slightly back of the front leg and one-third the distance up from the brisket to the top of the back. This shot would strike the center of the lungs on most animals. On a quartering away shot, the aiming point is the same height, but several inches behind the line of the front leg. In addition to producing a quick, clean kill, hitting the heart/lung area will also cause considerable blood loss which improves the quality of the game meat.

INTERNAL ANATOMY OF BISON

Figure 30.2

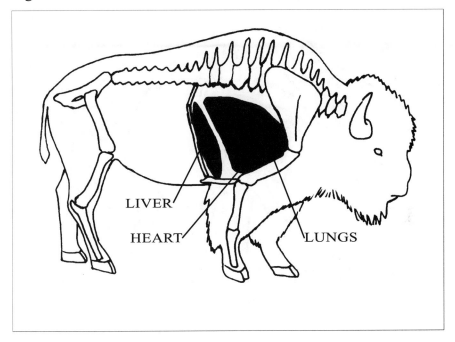

LIVER

HEART

LUNGS

Many hunters—particularly rifle hunters—shoot too high on the body and just clip the top of the lungs, or miss them entirely. A slightly high—but solid—lung shot will kill the animal, but the chest cavity will have to almost fill up with blood before any drips out to form a blood trail. A slightly low—but solid—lung shot will also kill, but it produces a blood trail quicker because of the hole location. In dense cover the difference in the blood trail between these two shots may mean the difference between recovering or losing the animal. Additionally, a low chest shot—as little as two inches above the brisket—may hit the heart–causing a quick death.

High chest shots may also pass through an animal without touching the lungs or the spine–actually piercing only the skin and a little rib meat. There is a gap within the chest cavity below the spine and above the lungs, which enlarges significantly when an animal exhales. Arrows with sharp, clean broadheads passing through this gap will often do no damage to an animal and it will heal completely in a short while. Because of their tendency to cause tissue damage, bullets passing through this gap—although they won't cause quick death or blood loss for tracking—may eventually kill the animal by infection. High chest shots above the spine strike only flesh and hide and are seldom fatal. Hits by either bullets or arrows in the

INTERNAL ANATOMY OF BLACK BEAR

Figure 30.3

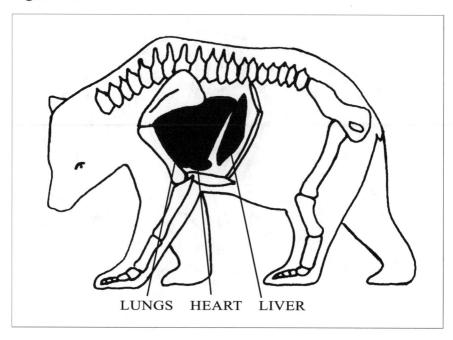

LUNGS   HEART   LIVER

spine are either quickly fatal or paralyzing–depending on where the spine is severed. Spine hits in front of the shoulders usually kill immediately. Spine hits behind the shoulders paralyze the hind legs and the animal goes down immediately, but it is still fully alert with its head up and should be killed quickly with a follow-up shot. However, the spine on even the largest big game animals is less than four inches high–a small target. Hitting high or low will only wound the animal and it will run off–perhaps to die of infection.

Evaluation of the results of high and low chest shots (by bullets or arrows) leads to an obvious conclusion. Hunters should aim low rather than high–one-third up from the brisket or less. Any hit in the lower half of the animal will kill it quickly the great majority of the time. The only non-vital area in the lower chest is the lowest two inches or less of hide and brisket, and a non-fatal, broadside hit there will not likely do any serious damage. If the hunter shoots below the body entirely, the animal may stay put for another shot. On the other hand, shots too high in the chest can have a variety of results from clean misses to minor flesh wounds to immediate kills, with no way for the hunter to know how badly, or if, an animal which runs is hit. And animals hit high—unless spined and they drop quickly—will probably run and not give hunters an opportunity for another shot. Shooting low in the chest gives the hunter the best odds for success.

Bowhunters must be careful to avoid the large upper leg bone or shoulder bone on most animals because these will stop all but the heaviest arrows shot from the most powerful bows. Hitting these bones with an arrow typically produces an audible "crack," the arrow stops after only a few inches of penetration, and the animal is only slightly wounded and runs off. Figures 28.1, 30.2 and 30.3 can be examined to determine the best aiming points to avoid these bones, depending on the shot angle. Bullets are seldom stopped by these bones, so firearms hunters don't have to observe this rule. However, bone fragmentation will ruin more meat, so by avoiding these bones as bowhunters must do, firearms hunters will have more useable game meat.

Head, neck, or shoulder shots are generally not good targets on game animals because of the sizes of the first two targets and the meat loss associated with the third. Although a brain shot kills the animal on the spot, it is only about three inches across on a deer—a very small target. What makes this target even less appealing is that a hit anywhere else in the head will make the animal run—usually at full speed—which hinders effective follow-up shots. These animals often die over the course of days or weeks, as they are seldom recovered. Another problem with taking head shots at bears is their thick skulls can deflect even the heaviest bullets.

Neck shots have similar outcomes to head shots on most animals. Hitting the spine in the neck area will kill the animal quickly, but shots elsewhere in the neck will only wound the animal—which will immediately run off to die days or weeks later. Also, neck-shot animals often drop on the spot from the shock—convincing hunters they are dead—and then get up unnoticed and run off. Shoulder shots—with bullets, not arrows—are likely to slow an animal enough for a follow-up shot or kill it outright if the heart or lungs are also hit. The drawback to shoulder shots is the considerable amount of meat loss possible.

The exceptions to aiming at the shoulders of a game animal are when hunting bears or when any animal needs to be stopped quickly—but this does not apply to bowhunters who should not try to shoot through heavy bones. As a brown bear guide I instruct my clients to shoot for the shoulder bones to slow or stop the bear for follow-up shots. The first shot should be angled to strike heart/lungs as well so it is fatal, but it must hit either the near or far shoulder or upper leg bones. The rule for bears is to keep shooting until they stop moving. Bears are extremely tough, they immediately run for the closest cover at the sound of a shot, they are short targets which get out of sight quickly and tracking them into heavy cover is dangerous and should be avoided. When other species need to be stopped before going over cliffs, into rivers, into dense cover, etc., the shoulder shot can be used to stop them or slow them for quick follow-up shots just like with bears.

Although it is not a recommended aiming point, arrows through the thick portion of the upper, rear leg will usually kill within 200 yards. It can be used to finish off wounded animals which present only this shot angle. Unless they strike bone, bullets striking broadside in this area will usually go completely through, the animal may travel quite a distance and, because of the fat in the area, the hole may seal and drip very little blood for tracking. The differing results are because the hemorraging caused by the larger arrow pathway bleeds much more—inside and outside—than a small bullet hole. A bullet in this area will kill the animal, but not quite as quickly as an arrow, and it will have to be tracked successfully to be recovered, which is not always an easy feat.

When to Shoot

Knowing when to shoot game animals is the third part of the successful shooting equation. For safety reasons, the first thing to consider is the backstop. There must be no possibility of anyone in the direction of fire. Other hunters' locations should be considered as well as houses and roads. Remember that rifle bullets can travel up to five miles and arrows up to several hundred yards and still kill. The safest shots are taken when there is a large, definite backstop (like a large hill) which will also stop any possible deflections. It is also much safer to shoot downhill, rather than uphill.

The best time to shoot at an animal is when it is standing, broadside or quartering away, relaxed, and with its head down. It is also preferable to have the animal's eyes out of view, so it will not see any of the hunter's shooting movements. If possible, hunters should wait until a feeding animal walks past their position and the animal's eyes are directed away or somehow blocked from view (behind a tree or bush) before attempting to shoot. This is particularly important to bowhunters who must get close and whose arrows don't travel as fast as bullets–about one-tenth the speed. An animal who sees or hears the releasing sound of a bow can actually move before the arrow arrives. This frequently happens with habitually nervous animals like whitetail deer who are ready to run at the slightest indication of a nearby hunter. Their first reaction is to crouch slightly as they prepare to spring away. This can lower a deer's body several

Arrow placement is vital to bowhunters who chase dangerous game like this polar bear. George P. Mann is pulling back the upper lip of this bruin to expose its impressive teeth.

inches so that even well-aimed arrows will strike too high in the chest to produce clean kills. This can also happen with other species when they are extremely nervous or alert, so bowhunters should avoid shooting at an agitated animal whenever possible, waiting until the animal relaxes to shoot. Even gun hunters are better off shooting at relaxed game when the range is over 100 yards as nervous animals can move slightly before a bullet arrives–causing a poor hit.

Firearms hunters should always get a solid rest whenever possible. Whenever anticipating a shot, hunters should constantly be looking for a good rest from which to shoot. A solid rest will easily allow a hunter to shoot three or four times as far as from a standing position, and with more accuracy. The next best thing to a good rest is firing from a solid, practiced kneeling or sitting position. From experienced shooters, these positions can produce two or three times the accuracy as offhand (standing) shots. A standing position is also the most vulnerable to wind, so on windy days it should be avoided on all but the closest shots. In open country, hunters should consider carrying shooting sticks for rests if they expect to shoot over 100 yards. These have been used used very successfully by Europeans for centuries, but Americans are just catching on to their advantages. This pair of four or five-foot long sticks attached together at one end are available from specialty shooting retailers.

Game animals which are running or even walking at longer ranges do not make good targets. Few rifle hunters can consistently hit running animals outside of fifty yards, and even the best shooters cannot place shots in the kill zone on these animals with any regularity. An animal walking at a slow pace is a reasonable target out to moderate ranges—about 200 yards—for very good rifle shooters with a good rest. Snapshooting at running game is sometimes justified for the best rifle or shotgun shooters at very close range, with positive backstops, when game is wounded and this is the only opportunity to down the animal. In general, snapshooting is a dangerous practice which leads to many wounded animals and should be avoided. Bowhunters do not take any running shots as a rule. Running animals also have low blood sugar and more lactic acid in their muscles which produces darker, tougher, off-flavor meat with a low PH leading to faster spoilage.

Wind drift of arrows and bullets is another important consideration for accurate shooting at game. Mostly because of their fletching, arrows can be directed off-course by even slight winds at distances over thirty yards, and any wind over twenty miles per hour (mph) will deflect arrows within ten yards. I once shot a musk-oxen at fifteen yards in twenty mph winds, only to see the arrow dive hard left and strike twelve inches off my point of aim. Bullet drift must also be considered. When winds are over twenty mph and the range is over 200 yards (or forty mph winds at 100 yards) a correction may be needed–depending on the bullet and its speed. Hunters can either look up these corrections in a shooter's manual (best) or test their weapons and loads on non-living targets in field conditions. When wind is gusty, it is best to wait and shoot between gusts to minimize its affects, or arrange to shoot directly upwind and not crosswind. At the least, hunters should be aware that wind drift can be significant.

Other times to avoid shooting animals is when they are near water or cliffs. Hollow-haired animals like deer, sheep, moose, pronghorn, elk, caribou, and musk-oxen will typically float if their chest cavity does not fill with water. However, they may still be unrecoverable if in a fast-moving river, floating out into a lake or pulled out by ocean surf–don't scoff, the surf once took one of my bow-killed deer out to sea, although we did recover it hours later with a boat. An additional consideration, even if hunters can get to large game animals which die in water, is being able to move them. Moose, elk and caribou are often too large for one, two or even several hunters to drag out of the water—especially if the bank is steep and

Knowing when to shoot is sometimes as important as knowing where to shoot. Stan George is holding Kevin Keene's 60" moose as he ponders what to do with the huge beast.

slippery. Cleaning a large animal in water is not easy, fun or good for the meat. It is better to wait until animals move away from water before shooting. When animals are within running distance of water, hunters can anchor them with shoulder shots.

With animals like bear or cougar which typically sink if they die in the water, hunters have to take even more precautions. Shooting them until they stop is always adviseable whenever they are anywhere near water. On another of my Alaska Peninsula brown bear hunts, one of our clients shot a nine and one-half foot bear which rolled into an eight-foot deep stream. The guide had to dive down and tie off the bear, then get four more of us to help him with the 1,000-pound bear. Luckily, the stream was slow-moving and the guide had more help close at hand or the outcome may have been tragic.

Goats and sheep are two animals which typically live around steep cliffs and this must be considered in the decision of when to shoot. Goat horns are extremely fragile and can break during even a twenty-foot fall. Sheep horns are much tougher, but—like goats or any other animal hunted around cliffs—they should not be shot when there is a high risk they will die on unreachable ledges. Goats are often passed entirely by experienced hunters even when their location may permit the hunter to place a killing shot, but it is likely there would be only hamburger and hair left when the goat finished bouncing down the cliffs. Responsible hunters should pass up shots at animals in high risk situations of this nature. Frequently, within a few hours the animal will move into a much better position where it can be killed and then recovered in good condition.

Hunters must also know when to fire follow-up shots. [Of course, with bears the rule for firearms hunters is to shoot until the bear stops moving. Bowhunters should shoot only once under most circumstances.] Proper follow-up technique takes concentration. The hunter must pay attention to the final sight picture as the bullet or arrow was fired and careful attention to the animal's reaction. Unless the hunter is sure of a clean miss, he should wait as long as practical before firing follow-up shots. Animals may take up to two minutes to die from a perfect heart/lung shot and may seem unfazed until they drop. Tough animals like elk and goat commonly show little sign of lethal hits even to the best hunter's scrutiny. More shots may be unnecessary and only ruin more meat, or may cause the animal to run harder and farther. One shot—even a fatal one—doesn't alert an animal as much as a volley of shots. Dying animals will often stand in one spot while looking for the source of the shot—until they drop.

However, if the animal is moving and will soon go out of sight into dense cover, over a hill, or onto private land, the hunter has a tougher decision. The lay of the land, the species, the individual animal, the hunter's confidence in the shot, his ability to hit the moving animal, the presence of other animals and any other factors must be quickly considered when deciding whether or not to shoot again. Many times a moving animal will pause to look back toward the hunter, presenting a good target. The only way to predict this happening is by knowing the behavior of the species and interpreting the situation. Sheep often do this to get one last look at the danger just as they are going over a rise which will put them out of sight. Looking ahead in the animal's likely route to find spots it may reappear or stop gives a hunter the chance to get ready and make a better shot. Sheep also die easily, unlike goats which are tough, so a good hit on sheep may not be enough on a goat. Hunters who know their quarry's abilities and limitations can make better decisions about when to shoot—both initially and for follow-up shots.

Another important consideration about follow-up shots is the chance of hitting another animal. This frequently happens with herd animals like caribou and bison, but can occur with any species, particularly when the first animal goes out of sight and reappears.

Because bears are tough and so dangerous to follow when wounded, they are shot until they stop moving. This spring grizzly was headed over the top of a mountain in Alaska's Talkeetna Range when Johnny Graham stopped it.

Hunters often shoot a second animal when their initial target runs out of sight and another look-alike reappears in the same general area. Deer hunters are often put in this situation because of deer's ability to remain hidden. When a hunter loses sight of a deer he has just shot at suddenly sees a deer appear, he can mistakenly assume it is the same animal because no others were in sight. So, he takes another shot, only to find two dead deer when he goes to recover his animal. Waiting on follow-up shots until absolutely necessary can reduce the chances of this happening.

Deciding when to shoot is also a function of the species being hunted. Species which travel in herds usually have a predictable order of sex and size within the group. The largest ram almost always leads a group of rams, but large caribou bulls often come at the rear of large caribou herds. Both bull moose and bull elk with cows are also typically in the rear of the group. Hunters who know their quarry can be prepared to shoot at the first or the last in line depending on the species' habits. This kind of planning is very important to bowhunters because they need to be so close, but it is still helpful to firearms hunters in many situations.

Hunters must also be careful of shooting through animals–particularly in the case of herd species. Caribou are thin-skinned and even the smallest big game cartridges and slowest arrows can—and often do—pass through them and out the other side with enough energy left to wound or kill nearby animals. This can happen whenever there at two or more animals, so hunters need to look carefully before shooting. Whenever possible, it is safer to shoot at lone animals to the side of a herd rather than try to shoot between several herd members.

A species' behavior patterns can also be a determining factor in the timing of a hunter's shot. Musk-oxen typically form a defensive ring when confronted by danger, so there is seldom a need to take long running shots on them–just wait and they will stop. Caribou have evolved in the presence of their constant predator–the wolf. They have learned that anything within their wolf distance—about 70 yards—is dangerous and they run immediately if they see sudden movement inside this distance. Caribou which haven't been hunted much by man will often circle a hunter outside this wolf distance, but within rifle range and even stop occasionally–giving the hunter an easy, standing target. (Of course this doesn't help bowhunters who need closer targets.) Caribou will also come toward hunters from long distances out of curiosity–as will young animals of many species. Hunters who understand and apply animal behaviors to decisions about when to shoot will often get better shooting opportunities.

Shooting at game is usually the culmination of a hunt. The how, where and when to shoot are important aspects of every shooting decision. As with many other hunting skills, shooting decisions should be heavily influenced by the hunter's knowledge of animal behavior. The most successful hunters have mastered the skill of shooting at game.

Chapter 31
RECOVERING GAME

    After a hunt has gone as planned, the hunter has done all the rights things to get in position to make a shot, and then made a good shot, there is just one more task to complete before the hunter celebrates–that is to recover the animal. Even hard-hit game animals seldom drop in their tracks. As was pointed out in the last chapter, spine or brain shots are the only ones which stop an animal immediately. Most fatal shots take from ten seconds to two minutes to kill the animal. And only about one-half of the mortally hit animals drop in sight of the hunter. The other half will have to be trailed to be recovered, which is never a sure thing. There are numerous steps hunters can take to increase the percentage of animals which drop while still in view as well as to increase the total percentage of recovered animals.

There is no better feeling for the hunter than to find his animal soon after the shot and know it died quickly. The proper after-shot routine will improve recovery time.

The Hunter's Response after the Shot

The recovery stage begins immediately after the hunter shoots. His actions from that point on will help determine the final outcome of the recovery process. The best procedure when follow-up shots are not necessary or possible is for the hunter to remain as quiet, motionless and out of sight as the conditions allow. There is no need to further alert the animal to the hunter's presence. Wounded animals who do see or hear hunters will likely run farther than those who don't. Bear hunters—especially bowhunters—in close proximity to their quarry do not want wounded animals knowing their whereabouts for reasons of personal safety. Also, hunters who remain quiet are more likely to hear clues to their wounded quarry's direction of travel or actually hear a dying animal drop. Hunters who can escape detection after the shot will have a better chance of seeing a fatally hit animal drop while still in view. And seeing where a dying animal falls will greatly improve a hunter's chances of recovering the animal.

From the moment of the first shot onward, the hunter also needs to pay close attention to the animal's reactions to the shot(s). The animal's reaction will help the hunter determine where and if the animal was hit. An animal which looks up–then runs, or which stops often to look back is probably not hit; an animal that suddenly jerks or jumps at the shot probably was hit; a bear sometimes roars when hit and they often bite at the bullet or arrow wound; a hard-hit deer usually drops his tail flag and keeps it down while running; an animal which lays its ears down was probably hit hard; an animal which immediately runs flat-out was probably hit in the heart– possibly the paunch; hunching at the moment of the shot usually means a heart or liver shot–occasionally a paunch shot; if an animal's back end goes down immediately, but the head stays up, it was hit in the spine behind the shoulders; an animal which stands while holding one leg up or walks with an obvious limp was hit in the leg. Hunters should pay attention for the sound of the bullet striking dirt, rocks, trees or the animal–these all make different sounds which can identify where the bullet struck. These sounds are usually distinguishable from the noise of the cartridge firing if the target is over 100 yards away; there is not enough elapsed time between the firing and impact sounds if the target is closer.

After their quarry is down or has gone out of sight and earshot, there are several critical observations hunters should make before moving from their shooting location. They should first mark the time of the shot and their shooting location–by memorizing surroundings, breaking branches, piling rocks, draping tissue paper, etc. Then they

Knowing exactly where an animal was standing when the shot occurred is vital to finding clues about the type of wound and the animal's condition.

should mentally note exactly where the animal was at the moment of the shot(s). Both the hunter's and the animal's positions can be later used to establish the shot angle. The shot angle can lead the hunter to arrows, bullet marks, hair, blood, tracks, and other clues to the type of wound, the animal's condition and its location.

Hunters should also create a mental picture of the area from the point of the shot–which is often a good vantage point. This can help hunters find their way to the location where the animal was hit and to where it was last seen. It is easy for hunters to get disoriented once they start toward the site of the hit because their point of view changes, which makes everything look different. Picking out visible landmarks and estimating distances before leaving the shooting location will vastly improve hunters' chances of finding the location where an animal was hit or where it went down.

When to Start Tracking Wounded Game

Unless an animal has fallen in sight and is obviously dead, hunters should wait from ten to thirty minutes before following a wounded animal. Even firearms hunters should wait before following a wounded animal. This will give the hunter time to settle his nerves and think clearly and it will allow the animal time to die if mortally wounded. If the animal does not die quickly and it is not pursued immediately, it will go slower, stop more often and lie down sooner– all of which will make recovery by the hunter easier and more likely.

Bowhunters are taught to wait at least 30 minutes to follow an animal which has been hit and goes out of sight. Bowhunters have less chance than rifle hunters of finishing off a wounded animal which jumps up and runs, or even walks away at any distance over fifty yards, so they must be more cautious about pursuing game too quickly. However, firearms hunters frequently push game too fast and too hard and end up losing wounded animals because of their haste. Even solid hits can take up to ten minutes to kill in some situations. Except in special circumstances, hunters should avoid hasty pursuits and only follow wounded animals after careful consideration of the situation.

There are some special circumstances when a wounded animal should be followed immediately. Most of these occur when hunters have already made a judgement error, often due to excitement. If it is raining or snowing, or about to start doing either of these, and a wounded animal's tracks or the blood trail will not last, hunters should begin tracking almost immediately. If the animal has definitely been hit in a non-vital area like a leg, the back above the spine or another non-vital area, but it can still move well, the alternatives are to follow immediately or let it go. In the right situation, animals with these types of non-vital wounds can be pushed until blood loss kills them outright or slows them enough that the hunter can get in a

Tracking animals after the shot is an art all in itself. Adults can start young hunters off right by showing them every step necessary to recover game. This proud young hunter has taken, and then helped recover, his first deer.

finishing shot. If the animal was shot with a clean broadhead, it most likely will recover. Unfortunately, bullet wounds don't heal as often.

    If approaching darkness is accompanied by another negative factor like warm weather which will spoil the meat, the presence of numerous bears or coyotes, or if the area has cliffs making it dangerous to track at night, the hunter may choose to start after only ten minutes. A ten-minute wait will at least give a hard-hit animal time to lie down and perhaps die, rather than being pushed immediately and possibly escaping.

    After the waiting period at the site from which the shot took place, the hunter should go to the site(s) where the animal was hit.

Information the hunter gathers from a close scrutiny of the hit site is vital to recovery efforts. Careless work on the part of the hunter at this point often determines if recovery efforts will be successful or not. The first important step is to locate the hit location(s) through adequate orientation by the hunter before leaving the shooting position–as discussed previously.

When the hunter has found the hit location, he should first mark the spot, unless it is obvious. Then, the area must be examined very carefully for the arrow, bullet marks, blood, hair, fat and tracks. These are all clues about if and how the animal was hit and will direct the hunter's next actions. Bleeding is sometimes internal or very minor, so a close scrutiny of the area is necessary. Sometimes there is no evidence at the site of the hit, so hunters should check at least the first 100 yards of the animal's trail for any signs it may be wounded. Because blood is not always obvious from a distance, it is important to find the exact spot where the animal stood and not just the general area. Finding the precise location is also crucial to locating the arrow on a pass-through. Hunters should spend thirty minutes or more before determining the animal wasn't hit. It is a terrible waste for a hunter to walk away from a downed animal which is only a few yards away because he gave the hit site only a casual glance.

Any sign found at the site of the hit must be interpreted correctly and then acted upon in the best manner. If bowhunters can find their arrow, it can be extremely helpful. Unless it is raining or snowing heavily or the arrow passed through something else after striking the animal, a clean arrow with no blood, fat or hair indicates a clean miss. In this case, it is still a good idea for the bowhunter to make a quick search of the area to confirm a clean miss. A few minutes search in these cases sometimes uncovers a dead animal with no explanation for the clean arrow.

Any sign the hunter finds can indicate what type of wound the animal has. Hair color and length can reveal where the animal was hit. Back or neck hair is longer and darker on most animals; leg or stomach hair is lighter and shorter. Remembering the animal's specific coloration can help interpret any hair sign correctly. Hair with no blood may mean just a graze, but hair with a little blood may also mean just a graze. If there is also tallowy fat included, this often means a back shot because there is a lot of this along most animals' backs. Arrows which are covered with fat and little blood often mean a back or upper ham shot, but with fall bears this may indicate a hit anywhere on the body.

Heart-shot animals usually hunch their backs, then take off at a dead run, leaving a short trail of sprayed bright red blood. This is exactly what happened with this whitetail taken by Tony Russ (r.) with the help of Carl F. Brent.

Hunters must know how to interpret the quantities of blood they find. The primary rule to remember is: a little blood goes a long way. Blood has such an outstanding color that an occasional smear on yellow grass or regular drops along a trail are often interpreted incorrectly by anxious hunters as large quantities. Large quantities of blood from a solid hit on a game animal means pools of blood several inches across or walnut-size clumps of it. Continuous pools or blobs of blood like this which are easily seen twenty or thirty feet ahead on a trail often indicate a downed animal just a few yards ahead. Lesser amounts of blood, yet still enough for good tracking, indicates a fairly solid hit; but an animal with this type of wound may still go one-half mile before expiring, or it may survive. A blood trail of only occasional drops which is difficult to follow and requires frequent stops to locate usually means a poorly hit animal. It will seldom die within twenty-four hours and likely not at all without a finishing shot. Remembering these characteristics of blood trails can prevent hopeful hunters from misinterpreting the quantities of blood they find and then reacting inappropriately because of their mistakes.

The color of any blood found is a good indicator of the location of the hit. This should be used in conjunction with the animal's reaction to the hit to form conclusions about the location and severity of the wound. Bright red blood—sometimes almost pink—indicates a lung, heart or arterial hit. If bubbles are also present, this specifically points to a lung shot. With major arterial hits, blood is usually sprayed in a wide arc along the animal's escape trail or at least splattered to the side. All of this sign indicates a hard-hit animal which will probably be found within 100 yards of the hit location. In these cases, hunters can follow the trail immediately, but, as always, with caution.

Dark blood means a liver or muscle hit. A solid liver-hit animal is going to die and probably rather quickly. There are usually good quantities of blood at the hit site and/or on the first few yards of the trail. Sometimes there are also small bits of green, intestinal fluids or particles if the shot passed through the paunch area as well as the liver. Because the wound may not be as severe as the hunter thinks, a liver-hit animal should be given from 30 minutes to two hours to die before being pursued. As is the case whenever tracking a wounded animal, the hunter should be very alert because it may appear at any point along the blood trail.

A solid muscle hit may bleed good quantities of dark blood at first—the color indicates a venous hit, not arterial—and fool the hunter into believing the downed animal is near. However, venous muscle hits usually bleed much more at first and then close up and bleed only a little–if at all. Venous blood is sometimes splashed to the side of the blood trail, but more often is indicated by drops directly below the animal. Rapidly moving animals will spray blood to the sides of their trail. Drag marks or unusual track patterns accompanying these types of wounds usually mean a leg hit. This may mean the animal will be slower–depending on the difficulty of the terrain. When major muscle hits are indicated, the hunter has two choices. The first choice is to follow after 30 minutes and hope the animal has bled out or is slowed down enough so the hunter can get in a finishing shot. By pushing the animal, the hunter may be able to keep the wound open and bleeding, and recover an animal which would otherwise get away. The alternative is to give the animal two or more hours to bleed and weaken before trailing it. The choice depends on the sign found, time of day, weather, tracking conditions and the hunter's weapon. These types of wounds from arrows often heal; bullet wounds of this type sometimes heal.

Small amounts of dark blood indicate a minor muscle wound. There may be some sprayed blood at the point of impact which misleads the hunter into thinking it is a more serious wound. However, there will be almost no blood on the first part of the trail

Snow on the ground usually makes tracking wounded animals easier and recovery more certain, but falling snow can obliterate even the best blood trail. Chris McKinnon and a nice whitetail.

and this will virtually stop after only a few yards. These types of wounds will almost always heal. The hunter's choices are to let the animal go or try to catch up with it and get in a fatal shot. The animal will basically act healthy, but alerted, so this will affect how the hunter follows up on this type of hit.

Animals hit in the paunch will usually bleed a few drops of dark blood at the site of the hit and sometimes intestinal material will also be found. Arrows may have green fluid, food particles, a few drops of blood, possibly some fat or a distinctive intestinal smell. The blood trail will be sporadic and usually sparse. Paunch-hit animals should not be trailed for two to twenty-four hours, depending on conditions. If it is cool and late in the afternoon, hunters should wait overnight. If it is warm and early morning, hunters should wait the minimum time of two hours and then begin trailing the animal.

Paunch-hit animals will usually run for the first 100 yards, or until out of sight, and then walk another 100-400 yards and lie down. If they are not pushed by hunters the animal will typically die in this first bed within 500 yards and 12 hours of where they were hit—although paunch-hit animals may live as long as 36 hours in extreme cases. When paunch-hit ruminants (horned and antlered game animals) lie down, additional blood goes to their stomachs and causes them to bleed through their paunch wound more than if they were walking—when blood is diverted to their muscles. Because of this, they will die quicker when left alone to lie down.

Hunters who push paunch-hit animals will significantly decrease their chances of recovering the animal. The animal will bed down so it can watch its backtrail for following hunters. Animals which get up and continue on leave only an occasional drop of blood and may go for a mile or more with these types of wounds. These facts make it very difficult to track the animal successfully after it leaves its first bed.

Because animals with similar hits don't all bleed the same and sign can be misinterpreted, hunters should always follow an animal they have shot at for at least 50 yards. This can give the hunter additional evidence to confirm or deny his conclusions about the results of the shot. On the first 50 yards of the trail, the hunter may find the downed animal, he may find evidence indicating the dead animal should be found in the next 100 yards, or he may find more revealing evidence about the animal's wound. As much evidence as possible is necessary for hunters to correctly determine their next course of action.

Tracking and Reading Sign of Wounded Animals

A hunter who is trailing a wounded animal will increase the chances of recovery significantly if he can spot the animal before it sees him. The best way to accomplish this is by employing still-hunting techniques. A solitary hunter who is trailing a wounded animal should go very slow, keep noise to a minimum, and spend more time looking than moving. Spotting the wounded animal without being seen will help the hunter decide whether to shoot it again if it is within range, stalk closer for a shot, or back off and wait if the animal appears on the verge of dying.

When possible, it is almost always better to have two hunters to follow a wounded animal. These hunters should function like still-hunting partners. One partner looks for sign to follow the trail while the other hunter is always looking ahead for the animal. Depending on the situation, the watching partner can stay off to the side up to 100 yards or more if this gives him a better view of the terrain ahead while still keeping the tracking partner in view. This trailing method may help him spot a wounded animal which has curled back on his trail to look for a following hunter. There should be no talking between partners which is loud enough to alert the wounded animal.

There are several more guidelines to follow while tracking wounded animals. Hunters should not walk directly on the animal's

Bowhunters must follow wounded game more carefully than firearms hunters because they cannot shoot as far nor as quickly. Dave Widby approaching a downed deer with an arrow ready.

trail so they don't destroy important sign. Hunters may have to backtrack, so sign should be left intact as much as possible. Whenever obvious sign—usually blood—stops, a marker should be placed by the last piece of sign. Branches can be broken in obvious ways or small pieces of tissue paper can be stuck on brush as markers. Pieces of tissue paper placed at short intervals along a blood trail allow trackers to look back and easily identify the animal's pattern of movement. This helps predict the animal's direction of travel or final destination if the trail is lost. In very wet or windy weather, cloth flags can be tied to branches and then recovered and leapfrogged ahead in intervals along the trail. The distance between front and rear feet and any unusual characteristics of the tracks—like chipped hooves or extremely large tracks—should be noted from the onset of tracking to help stay on the wounded animal's trail.

If the trail is lost for more than a few minutes, hunters need to mark the last known sign before continuing. Then, hunters should look ahead for the most likely route the animal took. These can be checked out one by one while being careful to not step on and ruin small pieces of sign. It is best to walk off trails when doing this since these are the most likely places where sign will be found. Places like streambeds, muddy patches of ground, roads or any soft earth are good places to look for a continuation of the trail. If this doesn't work, concentric circles around the last piece of sign can be made to look for the next piece. If neither of these methods work, the hunter can predict where the animal is headed and go in that direction, trying to pick up the animal's trail again. If all else fails to turn up the trail or the animal, the hunter(s) should either find a good vantage point and make some noise or walk through the area while making noise—hoping to make the animal move into view. This is the last method to try and locate a lost animal, but it is better than just giving up and going home. Hunters should also be watchful for fox, crows, magpies, ravens, or other scavengers as a sign of a dead animal—both while tracking and if they return on subsequent days to where the wounded animal's trail was lost.

Some habits of wounded animals which hunters should remember when trailing them are: animals—particularly those like deer which live near dense cover—often circle back to the area they were wounded; wounded animals typically head for the thickest cover in the area—bears do this almost 100% of the time; and wounded animals often head for creeks, lakes, swamps, etc. to drink, lie down in or use to cover their trail (I once followed a wounded deer which walked over 100 yards through a tiny stream in winter before getting out on the same side in an effort to lose me). The overall pattern of a wounded animal's trail may reveal more about its wound to attentive hunters.

Approaching Downed Game

It is crucial for a hunter who finds a downed animal to make sure it is dead before celebrating or touching it. Don't rush in and have your "dead" animal get up and run off or turn on you. After sighting a downed animal the first thing to do is find a vantage point and watch it for a few minutes. This will sometimes reveal slight

Downed animals should always be approached from their back or rear and only after observing them for signs of life. The hunter should have his weapon ready in case a killing shot is needed.

movements which may mean the hunter will have to deliver a killing shot to the animal. This should be done from as close as feasible without risk of the animal getting up and running away. The hunter should keep the animal in view and be ready to shoot as he approaches it. Better yet is to have a partner get into a vantage position where he can shoot if necessary, while the hunter approaches the downed animal.

If necessary, a close-range killing shot should be fired into the brain, or neck in the case of animals whose skulls are to be salvaged. If the range is too far, killing shots can be fired into the standard kill zone in the chest cavity. Hunters approaching game should always plan for a necessary kill shot by positioning themselves and any partners so everyone has safe angles to fire. A typical setup is to have a watchful partner stand to the side as the hunter approaches the animal, with communication beforehand about not firing should the animal get between the hunters.

Always approach a downed animal from its back end, from uphill if possible so it will be slower if it comes for you, with your gun ready and a cartridge in the chamber and, if possible, a partner watching from a safe angle. Most big game animals outweigh hunters, they have dangerous hooves or claws, and (when wounded) they are fighting for their lives.

Animals with clear eyes and their heads upright may not be dead.
Hunters have lost apparently dead animals by approaching too
quickly and not being ready to shoot if necessary.

Dead animals typically have open mouths, glazed eyes, flopped-over ears and are loosely sprawled on the ground in awkward positions. If the legs are bunched up under the body and it is in an upright position, the animal may still be alive. An upright head or laid-back ears also indicate it is alive. Stop ten to twenty feet from the animal and look for the chest moving as it breathes. You should stop if there are any of these indications the animal is still alive. A killing shot can them be delivered. If you are unsure about the animal's state, throw rocks or sticks at the animal and be ready to shoot if there is movement. Extra shots into the animal are better than possibly losing it or being attacked if it does get up.

The recovery process begins the minute a hunter fires at an animal. Everything he does from that moment on will affect his chances of recovering the game animal. Hunters who plan ahead for this phase of the hunt are more likely to act in ways which best increase their chances of recovering animals they shoot. Celebrations by hunters should wait until the animal has been found and approached in a safe manner to verify the kill. Only then should the hunter's success be celebrated.

Chapter 32
CARE OF GAME MEAT

Game meat which has been properly cared for is high in protein, low in fat, tender and very tasty–for the most part. There are a few species of North American big game animals (caribou and goats) which, during the peak of their rut, have strong, offensive tastes and don't make good table fare during these brief, two or three-week periods. Otherwise, successful hunters should expect to take home from twenty to six hundred pounds of high-quality meat for their freezers. Even black bear and cougar are excellent eating if properly cared for in the field and the kitchen.

The nutritional composition of game meat is often preferred to that of farmed animals. Game meat has more protein, less fat and fewer calories than beef or pork. Table 32.1 shows how one-half cup (100 grams) of beef compares to the same amount of caribou meat.

Table 32.1	Nutrient	Lean Beef	Caribou
	Fat	28.0 grams	1.2 grams
	Calories	323. calories	120 calories
	Protein	16.5 grams	27.2 grams

Although caribou is one of the leaner game meats, comparisons of most game meats to farm-raised animals would still lead to the following conclusion. That is, substituting game meat for beef or pork will increase protein intake while reducing fat and calorie intake–a healthier diet by most standards (see Chapter Five on nutrition).

Plan Ahead

The quality of game meat a hunter can expect to take home depends on many factors, some occurring before the animal is shot. An overly excited game animal or one that has been running will have reduced sugars and increased levels of lactic acid in its muscles. This combination makes the meat tougher, stronger-flavored and harder to care for in the field. These affects are one more reason for hunters to strive for clean kills as much as possible. Rutting animals are usually still good table fare, but more care must be taken to avoid getting hair on the meat. Since animals in the rut—both males and females—have active scent glands and they cover themselves with their own urine, their hair has odors and flavors that are better left in the woods, and not brought home on game meat.

Once the animal is killed, the work of caring for the meat begins. The important factors to remember during the entire process are to keep the meat clean, cool and dry. Clean meat is free from hair with its various odors, as well as sand, mud, leaves, grass, etc. Care taken in the field to keep the meat as unsoiled as possible will also save time later when cleaning the meat at home.

The best way to protect game meat in the field is to use game bags. Cheesecloth is often used for this purpose because it allows air circulation to cool the meat while keeping it clean. However, for optimal utility, cheesecloth bags must be tightly woven to keep out dirt and insects, strong enough to hang the meat when required and still allow circulation. An alternative (which I recommend) is to make or buy muslin bags. Muslin is an inexpensive, whitish, tightly woven cotton material which comes in many thicknesses. Muslin game bags with good draw-cords sewn around their tops will protect meat from dirt and insects, can be made strong enough to hang any size chunk of meat (just choose heavier material for heavier chunks), are inexpensive and reusable. Generally, game meat should not be put in plastic bags or other airtight materials because these will hold in heat and moisture–both of which increase bacterial growth.

Game meat should be kept cool and dry to slow the growth of bacteria and to keep the PH level down. Bacteria are the tiny organisms (found everywhere in our world) which will cause meat to spoil. The minute a game animal is killed, the muscle tissue (the meat) starts to breakdown (tenderize) from enzymes within the meat and bacteria begin to grow on the surface. When game meat or beef is hung to age, this is a slow, controlled process of decay which is used to tenderize meat and improve its flavor. In the field hunters need to control bacteria by cooling the meat as quickly as possible and keeping it dry. Bacteria thrive on warm, moist environments with high PH levels, which is precisely what a warm animal carcass presents immediately after the kill. Unless it freezes solid, bacteria will ruin a game animal carcass for human consumption within 12-48 hours *if nothing is done to slow their growth.*

The quality of meat produced from a game animal carcass depends a lot on what the hunter does in the first thirty minutes after the animal dies. When a ruminant (any cud-chewing animal like deer, moose, sheep, etc.) dies, digestion gases are trapped in their stomachs

Hunters should clean animals as quickly as possible to avoid excess bloating. When possible, cuts should be made with the direction of the hair to minimize hair on the meat.

which causes swelling almost immediately. This doesn't affect the meat, unless the stomach is punctured and its contents get on the carcass. By opening the animal as quickly as possible before the stomach swells to maximum size, the hunter has less chance of puncturing it and the animal will start to cool sooner. The meat from animals which are not cleaned and cooled right away, but left overnight or transported back to a home or hunting lodge (for pictures, perhaps?) will have an increasingly stronger taste and smell—called gaminess.

Hunters in more southern areas of North America or those hunting in early seasons everywhere have to contend with much warmer temperatures than hunters in northern areas or later, colder seasons, so they have to make greater efforts to cool game animals soon after the kill. When temperatures never rise above 50° F, like many hunting seasons in Alaska or Canada, it is much easier to cool game meat than when temperatures are in the 80's or 90's, like it is in more southern—and warmer—regions. This simple fact of temperature difference is why northern or later-season game meat often has a better flavor and is less gamey than that from southern areas or early seasons. Quick cooling of meat is also the reason game taken on remote hunts is often better than that taken when mechanized transportation is available close to the kill site. Since remote hunters typically have to cut up the animal carcass into pieces for packing, they consequently cool their game meat much quicker; while urban hunters often move the entire carcass before skinning or even gutting– sometimes waiting several hours before even applying a knife. For the best flavor in any game meat, the carcass must be cooled as quickly as possible.

Although it is best to cool meat as quickly as possible, it should not be allowed to freeze for at least twelve hours after the animal dies, and preferably not until it is cut, wrapped and goes into the hunter's freezer. Game meat undergoes a chemical change from when the animal dies until rigormortis occurs, and this change tenderizes the meat. Game meat which freezes before rigormortis sets in (about twelve hours) will be much tougher because of this. Game animals which are killed at below-freezing temperatures should be covered with tarps and insulated if necessary to prevent freezing. The hides can also be left on to help prevent freezing. After rigormortis sets in it is okay to let the animal freeze if this is unavoidable, although the meat quality will be higher if it is only frozen once–when it is wrapped and in the hunter's freezer.

Two more important factors when trying to cool game meat are removing excess blood and the hide. Any animal killed with a solid heart/lung or liver shot should be bled sufficiently. Cutting an animal's throat will not help bleed it unless no shots were in this area and the throat is cut very quickly after it dies. A better way to help bleed an animal and remove excess heat is to very quickly open it and remove the vital organs from the chest cavity. Removal of the hide from a game animal is also very important to the cooling process. Most animals' hides have enough insulating value to keep them warm in below-freezing temperatures, so these thick coats of hair and skin will hold body heat in their carcasses for many hours, or even days. The hide should be skinned from an animal carcass right away to start the cooling process. The only exceptions to this are when the hide is left on the carcass or the quartered animal to protect it from moisture, dirt or freezing. However, this should only be done in cooler temperatures (below 50°), when these factors would do more damage than the lack of cooling and only for as long as absolutely necessary. Large animal carcasses and quarters hold an astonishing amount of heat; unskinned quarters may take 24 hours to cool completely and carcasses may require 48 hours. Any game meat which has its hide left on for any length of time will have a much stronger flavor because of the extended cooling time.

Game bags protect meat from dirt and insects as well as making it easier to hang and transport.

High PH levels in game meat also encourage rampant bacterial growth. One way to reduce the PH and slow this growth is by using citric acid directly on the meat or by soaking game bags in it. A mixture of one large bottle of lemon juice to one bottle of

Tabasco™ can be used or a commercially produced, dry product can be carried into the field and mixed with water when needed. This not only lowers PH to reduce bacterial growth, it also keeps flies off the meat. The citric acid on the surface of the meat or on the game bags (soak them in it, hang dry, then pack in Ziplocs™ to carry into the field) will burn the insects' feet and they won't stay on meat nor lay eggs. The acidic solution can just be washed off when the meat is butchered with no aftertastes.

Another way to keep egg-laying insects away from meat is to make a fly trap. A fly trap is made by laying a few branches on the ground, piling meat scraps on the branches, pouring powdered insect poison on top, covering the entire pile with black plastic which has a slit in the top. Make this pile eight to ten feet away from where game meat is stored to lure flies away from it and to the trap. (Drum, *Care of Game in the Field*)

Preparations to Clean an Animal

The first thing to do when arriving at a kill site is to locate the best spot to clean (and photograph) the animal. In the case of a large animal, this spot may have to be right where it dropped. If the animal can be moved, hunters should look for a clean, open area with good visibility. Avoiding sandy, muddy or wet areas will keep the meat cleaner. Moving away from trees or heavy brush will make moving around the animal during the cleaning process much easier. And open areas give the hunter better visibility to watch for bears or other hunters. It is also a good idea to hang up colorful (blaze orange?) clothing or packs to alert other hunters to the kill site. If the kill will have to be revisited to finish the cleaning job or to pick up more meat to pack out, it is a good idea to hang markers in the area to relocate the site and warn other hunters about the kill if in bear country. Flagging tape is a good item to carry for this purpose.

The next thing to do is lay out all the tools and materials needed to clean the animal and prepare it for transportation. Knives, saws, sharpening tools, surgical gloves, game bags and rope should all be laid out in a convenient, yet safe location where they will not be lost or stepped on. Surgical gloves are a lightweight and extremely useful item for hunters to carry. They will keep most of the blood and gore off hands, help protect hands from sharp bones and knives, and help prevent infection. Protective gloves should always be worn when cleaning bears to help prevent trichinosis infection. It is also convenient to prepare places to lay pieces of meat. Large rocks can be cleaned off, brush can be stacked and plastic or game bags can be laid out anywhere for this purpose. It is also a good idea for hunters

By getting all the necessary field-dressing items out and readily accessible, the process goes much smoother and bags are available to protect the meat as soon as necessary.

to have a quick snack and something to drink to prepare them for the hours of hard work to come.

The type of trophy desired and the method of cutting the meat have to be decided upon by this time. The skinning cuts to be made for shoulder mounts, life-size mounts or European mounts differ, so the hunter's choice will affect the skinning method used (see Chapter Thirty-Three for details on trophy care). The carcass can be either field-dressed, gutted and skinned, skinned and quartered, or boned-out—depending on the hunter's preference and the situation. An animal can be field-dressed if the whole body is small enough to move given available transportation and this will allow the meat to cool adequately. This depends on the temperature and how long it will take to transport the carcass to the location where the hide will be removed. It is better to gut and skin the animal immediately for the purpose of cooling the meat. However, once the skin has been removed the hunter must have a way to keep the carcass clean. Whole-body game bags can be used for this, but only in the case of smaller game animals.

With larger animals and in remote areas where the animal has to be packed some distance, the animals should be gutted, skinned and quartered to be packed out in pieces. In these situations, the pieces should be laid out to cool as they are separated from the carcass. If the animal is too large to pack out in one trip, hunters should pre-select hanging spots to cool meat and keep scavengers away. In brown/grizzly bear country, meat must be hung fifteen feet off the ground to keep it out of reach of the largest bears. Black bears and even some brown/grizzly bears can climb, so meat has to be suspended from ropes and not just set on limbs. Since bears go for the innards of an animal first, it is best to move all the meat and the trophy at least 200 yards from the kill site before hanging. By piling all other cleaning leftovers on the gut pile, any bears who come around should be in one known location. Moving all the meat and trophies and hanging them out of reach should protect them until they can be packed out. However, if bears do get to game meat, it becomes their property and hunters should leave them alone. Regulations generally do not allow hunters to kill bears to recover game meat or trophies.

When backpacking long distances, the meat can be boned to reduce weight and bulk. The meat can be laid out to cool and dry as it comes off the animal and then placed in game bags when it is time to start packing. The drawback to boning meat is that more surface area is exposed to dirt, moisture and insects. However, experienced backpacking hunters can reduce the weight of quartered game meat by 40% with proper boning and removal of all inedible tissue. And, on overnight or longer trips, the meat can be laid out to dry—out of any direct sunlight—and the weight reduced even further.

Any animal which has to be left overnight or for other unavoidable reasons must be at least field-dressed if the hunter expects to eat the meat. The meat from an animal carcass which is left overnight without being gutted is very strong-flavored, tough and difficult to swallow.

The final preparation to ready the animal for cutting are to prop it up on its back and/or tie it off to brush or trees. Smaller animals like deer and sheep which can be moved and situated before and during the cleaning process seldom need to be tied off. Moose and elk-sized animals are often too big for a lone hunter to turn over, so ropes can be looped around trees for leverage to move them, turn them over, and position them on their backs. Animals which can't be moved or turned over have to be cleaned as they lay and moved as they get lighter. Situations when large animals like moose die in water and have to be cut up and carried away from the water in pieces are necessary to teach some hunters they should avoid killing large animals in these or other difficult places.

Animal carcasses can be boned to remove excess weight when meat will have to be packed long distances. This caribou front quarter has been boned and laid out to cool on top of a game bag.

Cleaning the Animal

The first step in cleaning an antlered game animal is to remove the scent glands. These are found on the metatarsal bones (hocks) of the hind legs of both sexes. All the skin and hair should be cut from both legs and discarded, then the knife and the hunter's hands washed before proceeding. Any hair from these areas which touches meat will give it a strong, offensive smell and taste, so if this happens, hunters need to clean the affected area or strip the outer layer of meat to prevent further contamination.

One important guideline to observe whenever cutting the hide of an animal is to cut in the same direction as the hair grows and try to get the knife inside the skin and cut outward. By doing so, fewer hairs will be cut–producing a better mount and cleaner meat. With this in mind, the first cut to make when field-dressing an animal is to start at the sternum and go to the anus–not from the back to the front as is commonly taught.

As the hunter continues the cleaning process, he makes the appropriate cuts for the desired trophy. As the skin is removed from the animal, the carcass is turned as necessary to facilitate the process–while keeping the meat clean. Quarters and/or pieces of meat should be removed as they are exposed and then set aside to cool in pre-selected, clean areas. Hunters should watch for tumors or spots on internal organs which may indicate a diseased animal. In affected areas of the country, hunters should also watch for and avoid deer ticks. Any digestive material or excreta which touches the meat should be immediately removed or the affected meat surface stripped off. Either of these substances will taint the meat. Even a small amount of meat tainted in this way will ruin substantially more if placed into bags with otherwise unsoiled meat.

Digestive material must also be kept off any parts of the hide the hunter wants because this may cause the hair to slip (fall out). The inside of the hide should be cleaned of fat and muscle tissue as much as possible to reduce weight and moisture—particularly if it must be carried a long distance and won't get out of the field for several days.

Organ meats—heart, liver and kidneys—are all edible and taken home by many hunters. These organs are much tastier if they can be soaked in clean, cool water immediately upon removal from the carcass. This will leach out excess blood which improves flavor and prevents spoilage.

One method of cooling meat quickly when clean lakes or streams are close to the kill site is to immerse it for a short time. Meat should be immersed only long enough to bring the temperature down, but not completely cool it. There should be a little heat left in the meat to dry the surface after the meat is removed from the water. The meat should be laid on a piece of plastic or a tarp in the water to keep it clean. Immerse the meat in the water for 25 to 60 minutes, depending on the size of the pieces. Once the meat is taken out, most of the surface water can be removed by the hunter using his hand like a squeegee. The heat left in the meat will finish the drying process (Drum, *Care of Game in the Field*).

After a carcass has been completely cleaned and cut as desired, the next step is either to hang it or transport it to where it will be hung. If meat is to be hung in the field, remember to hang it in the shade, in a high spot safe from scavengers, and away from the gut pile. If clean blood can be smeared on the meat and left to set for about an hour, this will form a hard case which protects it from insects. Black pepper can help keep flies off the meat. It is important that meat is hung where the air is moving to dry the meat and cool it. If meat develops a hard outer case and is cool before game bags are put on, it will be better protected from dirt and insects and taste better in the long run. Liquid citric acid solution can also be sprayed

Game meat can be kept cool and out of reach of predators by hanging (high) in trees. Hunters must plan ahead for this by bringing ropes and pulleys if necessary.

directly on the meat to drive off insect pests (Drum, *Care of Game in the Field*). After this dries, game bags can be put over the meat.

Transportation

When transporting game meat (or trophy hides) the same principles apply as in every other phase of caring for meat–keep it clean, cool and dry. Game bags should be left on whenever possible to keep the meat clean. When game meat is transported during the day, it is important to keep it out of the sun or cover it with a light-colored tarp. However, there should be air circulation to prevent condensation and moisture buildup. White game bags are good for reflecting the sun's rays if the transport time will be short, but it would be better to have another light-colored tarp over the bags for longer trips. Hunters must plan ahead to protect their game meat.

Un-skinned game animals should not be transported over thirty minutes during the day, unless the temperature is below 50° F or they are covered with a light-colored tarp. Leaving an un-skinned carcass in the sun will prevent heat from escaping or heat it up further and will surely produce strong-tasting meat.

Whenever transporting meat in boats or canoes, hunters must be careful to keep the meat off the bottom where water can accumulate. Branches set in the craft before the meat will keep it dry and provide good air circulation. If water transport lasts overnight, the meat should be taken out and hung up in a covered location each night to provide circulation, protect it from scavengers, and keep it cool and dry.

Backpacking hunters must take special care of meat to get it home in the best condition. Meat which is jostled around inside a pack on a sweaty hunter's back for days can get warm and moist. To prevent direct sun on a pack with game meat inside, a light-colored cover should be draped over the pack during the day. White game bags or white plastic bags work well for this.

When backpacking meat, it is okay to put it inside a plastic bag while in the pack. Most packs are waterproof anyway, so no air would get to the meat without the plastic. However, putting the game bag full of meat inside a plastic bag before it goes into the pack will prevent blood from getting all over the pack, its contents, and the packer. This blood will just attract (undesirable) flies and bears. However, meat should not be left inside a plastic bag or a sealed pack overnight or it will spoil more quickly. The meat should be taken out at night, the blood drained and wrung from the game bag, and then the meat laid out to dry overnight. It will have to be protected from rain and scavengers of course.

For safety reasons, backpacking hunters should never carry un-skinned, exposed game heads on their packs. This is just asking for an accident to happen if another hunter sees this trophy head

When motorized transportation is close to a kill site, it is tempting to leave the carcass whole for convenience and to keep the meat clean. However, these advantages must be carefully weighed against the need to cool the meat quickly to assure optimal flavor.

bobbing along through the woods or just coming over a hill.

Aging, Preserving & Cooking

When game meat is hung to age, there must also be good air circulation and protection from egg-laying insects, just like in the field. Aging is a slow, controlled decaying process which helps tenderize meat by natural enzyme action within the muscle tissue. Most hunters do not have the necessary facilities to age their game meat at the perfect temperature of between 34° and 38° F. These low temperatures control bacterial growth without stopping the breakdown of muscle tissue by natural enzymes. At these temperatures game can be aged five to seven days without significant losses due to spoilage.

Most game meat is aged at temperatures between 40° to 60° F. At these temperatures there is considerable more bacterial growth and resulting spoilage. When temperatures are high (above 60° F) and hunters have no way to cool meat, or when meat comes out of the field in poor condition and aging will only cause more loss of meat, it may be best for hunters to butcher the meat immediately.

Some studies have concluded that game meat is best aged only five to seven days, even at optimal temperatures. After this time, the gains from tenderization are minimal, gaminess increases significantly and the meat dries out. The condition of the meat before it is hung, the temperature, potential losses to flies or spoilage, and the final consumer must all be considered to determine how long to hang game meat. It must be watched closely and butchered when potential losses will override any gains from the aging process.

Freezing game meat is the most common way to preserve it for future consumption. The first step to proper freezing is to remove as much visible fat as possible. Unlike beef or pork fat, game fat will only keep three to four months in a freezer before it becomes rancid. Game meat which is properly wrapped in two airtight layers can be kept two or three years in a freezer at -20° F—if the fat has been removed. Any fat left on will give the meat a distinctive, strong flavor, and further add to some people's belief that game meat is not good table fare. For this same reason, game fat should never be used to make burger; pork or beef suet should be used. Any fatty cuts like ribs should also be eaten quickly before their flavor deteriorates.

One of the attractive qualities of game meat is its low fat content. However, this also means it can become dried out with improper cooking. Cooks should allow for this by using moist heat methods like Swissing (steaks), roasting in covered pots with water, simmering, or boiling. Oven-roasting and barbecuing will tend to dry out game meat, but using tight covers, roasting bags, or sauces in these cases can help.

Using marinades are another good way to moisturize game meat. Dry teriyaki marinade is a universal favorite of hunters, both in camp and at home. The ginger in this marinade is the active enzyme which helps tenderize meat. A ginger-based tenderizing marinade can also be made by combining one-half cup soy sauce, one-half cup water, one tablespoon sugar and one teaspoon ginger. Meat should be marinated at least two hours, but up to forty-eight hours is better for tenderizing the meat as well as driving in the flavor. Other natural enzymes which can be used as a basis for sauces and marinades are papaya, pineapple, asparagus and sherry. These all help tenderize meat and add their own distinctive flavor.

Hunters who plan ahead can bring home the maximum amount of tasty game meat. Planning means having all the right tools and materials to properly care for the animal once it is down. Planning also means striving to shoot the animal at a time and place which will be conducive to proper meat care. Once the animal is down, the cleaning and cooling process must be accomplished as quickly as possible for the highest quality meat. First-rate care when handling the meat, during transportation from the field, and during the aging process is also vital to producing the best possible game meat. The

There are about 400 pounds of excellent meat on this paddle-horn bull for a hunter who takes proper care of it. Randy Russ (pictured) and the author enjoyed this moose meat immensely.

final test of a hunter's success at caring for his game meat comes when he sits down for a meal. High-quality table fare is the reward for all of his efforts.

Bringing home quality game meat from remote areas such as this on the Kenai Peninsula of Alaska requires the best of care. Dan Haskins with a nice goat.

Chapter 33
TROPHY CARE

A trophy taken home by a hunter is a reminder of the hunting experience for years to come. A trophy's primary purpose is not to show off to the world, it is a visual clue for a hunter which helps him relive the hunt over and over again from the comfort of his home. Mounted trophies are also a way to display wild animals for many people to see and appreciate–many of whom would never get to view these beautiful animals close up. A trophy can be horns, skulls, skins, or professionally mounted replicas of the animal. Regardless of the trophy size or shape, it is first and foremost a way to keep the hunter's memories vivid and enjoyable for years to come.

Basics of Trophy Care

To preserve the necessary parts of a trophy animal in the field so these can be turned into the most realistic reproduction of the animal requires skill and know-how. An animal mount should be a work of art–and it can be if the hunter takes proper care of the hide and horns in the field and then takes them to a reputable taxidermist. The first step for the hunter should be to visit his taxidermist. A hunter who has not chosen a taxidermist should pick an established shop in his area. Taxidermists can describe to the hunter all the details of how to take care of trophies of any kind in the field. Inexperienced hunters may even want to spend some time at the shop watching experienced skinners handle capes and hides. The most detailed description of skinning technique will not teach a beginner as much as an hour of watching an experienced skinner.

The first tasks to complete upon taking an animal which is going to be turned into a mounted trophy is to take a few simple measurements. These will help the taxidermist recreate the animal's size and proportions to represent the actual animal. The measurements to take for a shoulder mount are:

•Distance from inside corner of eye to outside corner of nostril
•Distance between inside corner of eyes
•Circumference of neck at base of skull

For life-size mounts, add:
•Length from top of nose to base of tail along curves of body
•Circumference of chest behind front legs
Although these measurements are not essential and most hunters do not take them, those who do will receive a more realistic representation of their trophy back from the taxidermist. At the least, hunters should take good photos from several angles. These should be given to the taxidermist when the trophy is dropped off so he can see any abnormalities of the trophy.

Common trophies from a big game animal are horns, antlers, European mounts (entire skull with horns attached), skulls, hides, rugs, shoulder mounts, half life-size and life-size mounts. On record-book size antlered animals, hunters must remember that the skull between the antlers cannot be broken for the animal to be officially scored and entered. Hunters must take care when cutting and transporting these possible book trophies. Skulls, horns or antlers do not have to be cleaned of fat or meat in the field, but, for aesthetic reasons during transport, they should be kept dry and protected from flies. Horns in velvet are fragile and need special care. They should be kept cool and can be injected with formalin or another preservative in the field to help preserve them. When velvet trophies are expected, hunters should check with a taxidermist before heading into the field for a kit to protect the velvet. Such a kit usually contains a syringe and a liquid preservative.

The proper cuts to make on a hide for mounting purposes vary. A good habit is to cut with—rather than against—the direction of the hair growth. This will cut fewer hairs and result in a better mount. For a shoulder mount, the hide is cut around the animal behind the shoulders, up the back of the neck to each horn and around each front leg at the elbow. One of the guidelines to remember on shoulder capes is to cut them larger when in doubt. Making the cut a few inches farther behind the shoulders will only add a few ounces to the total weight (a Dall sheep cape only weighs about five pounds total), will give the taxidermist much appreciated extra hide to work with, and result in a better mount. The biggest complaint of taxidermists is that capes are cut too small. Figure 33.1 shows the cutting pattern for a shoulder mount and the cutting line to remove horns or antlers. Cut as close as possible around the horns or antlers. A screwdriver works well to pry away the skin at the base of antlers. The skin around horn bases must be cut carefully to get all of the hair with the hide, since horns actually grow out of the skin and their edges are not always distinct to a careless skinner. A good

SKINNING FOR A SHOULDER MOUNT

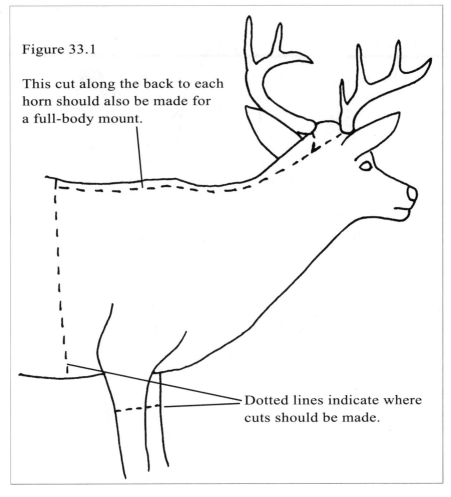

Figure 33.1

This cut along the back to each horn should also be made for a full-body mount.

Dotted lines indicate where cuts should be made.

general rule to follow is to make all cuts with the appearance of the final mount in mind. Taxidermists can sew up small nicks, especially on long-haired hides, but facial cuts or abrasions are hard to cover up and can mar the appearance of an otherwise beautiful mount.

A life-size mount or rug usually requires cuts from the underside of the animal, although some taxidermists want back cuts for certain mount positions. Hunters should always check with their taxidermists before going into the field. Figure 33.2 shows the cuts for most life-size mounts and rugs. The animal is cut up the center of the belly from anus to the base of the neck (to the chin for rugs), then along the underside of each leg to the foot or hoof. Horned or antlered animals are also cut along the back of their necks to each horn as in a shoulder mount.

SKINNING FOR A LIFE-SIZE SKIN OR MOUNT

Figure 33.2

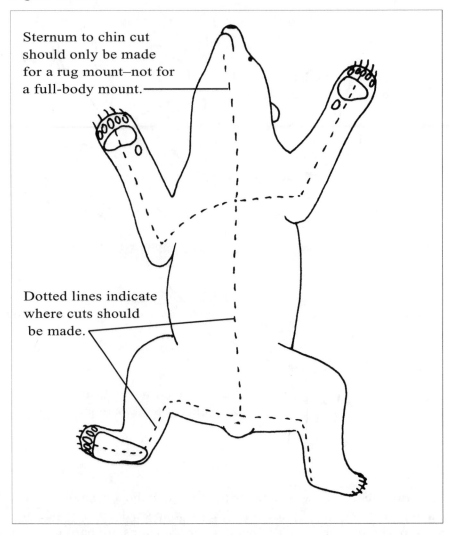

Sternum to chin cut should only be made for a rug mount–not for a full-body mount.

Dotted lines indicate where cuts should be made.

When removing the skin around the face it is important to cut against the skull and not the hide. This will prevent nicking the face and leave more nose, ear, eye and lip tissue on the skin. The more of these features left on the mount, the better for the taxidermist and the final appearance. Skinners should use one hand outside the hide when skinning around the facial features. By feeling for the knife blade inside the skin with this hand, the skinner can tell when the hide is likely to be nicked. Another trick is to cut the lips and nose free from the skull from the outside of the hide rather than from the inside. This allows the skinner to see rather than feel what the knife is doing. Special care should be taken around the forward corner of the eye because the skin is tucked into a depression there. The point of a knife should be used to cut into this cavity to get the skin out without nicking it.

The basic guidelines of trophy care are the same as caring for game meat in the field. Horns and hides should be kept clean, cool and dry. Hides which are warm and moist are breeding grounds for bacteria, which can eat away at the skin and cause hair slippage. Remember, the sooner the hide is removed, the quicker it and the meat will cool.

If temperatures are cool (below 50° F), bloody hides can be washed. This is particularly important for animals with any hollow white hair—like sheep, deer, caribou or pronghorn—because any blood which dries inside the hair will be impossible to clean entirely. If no water is nearby, the damp, bloody hide can be put in a plastic bag briefly to keep it moist until the hunter can reach a creek or lake. Then the hide should be soaked for ten to fifteen minutes to remove the blood (running water is better, if available). After removing the hide, all the excess water should be gently squeegeed out by hand. Then it can be hung up in the shade to drip-dry. At the least, bloody white hair can be gently dabbed with moss, paper towels, tissue or cloth to remove the excess blood.

Hides should be fleshed carefully to remove all fat and muscle tissue. The ears, lips, nose, eyes and feet have to be turned or split and then fleshed. Hides need to be split to the last joint on a hoofed animal and the last bone of the claws on carnivores. It is necessary to remove as much fat and muscle tissue from the hide to help dry it out. If the hunter can keep the hide at cool temperatures below 50° F it will probably not spoil without fleshing for a few days, but this is always risky. If facilities are available, freezing will preserve a hide for several months without fleshing.

After a hide is thoroughly fleshed, it should be dried to prevent bacterial growth. Thin hides like those from sheep or deer that are properly fleshed can be sufficiently dried in the field without salt, then salted by the taxidermist when the hunter returns. However, using salt is a safer method and it only takes a few pounds of salt for small capes. A large bear hide may take twenty-five pounds or more. Salt must be rubbed into all parts of the hide, including noses, ears, toes, etc., and care must be taken to get salt on all the edges–these tend to curl over and are frequently missed. Any part of a hide which is not dried can slip within a day or two, damaging it or ruining it completely. The hide should be laid out on a slanted surface to drain.

After 24 hours or more, the wet salt is removed and dry salt applied again. After another draining period, the hide can be loosely rolled with the flesh side inward and stored in a cool spot. If the hide stays in the field, it should be unrolled, drained, checked for wet spots and re-salted every few days. To ensure that hides do not spoil, they must be monitored closely to be sure they are cool, dry and bug-free until they get to the taxidermist.

When drying a hide with or without salt, it must not be exposed to sun or fire. A warm hide which is still moist will likely spoil quickly—within a few hours in some cases. Hides should be hung or loosely rolled in the shade in the coolest, driest locations available. Flies must also be kept away from the hide as they may lay eggs which can turn to destructive larvae within one hour.

Transportation

When transporting a hide, it must be treated with the same care as game meat. Both must be kept cool and dry. Backpackers should not tie hides on the outside of a pack or put them inside the top portion of the pack where they will get direct sunshine—unless a white cover is used. A hide inside a dark-colored pack or in a dark bag tied on top of a pack in the sun will quickly heat up and be destroyed—even in cool weather. Hides should also be taken out at night just like game meat and laid out or hung to cool and dry. Before being placed back in the pack, the hide should be rolled up with the flesh side in and carefully put in a protective game bag. Just as with game meat, hides can be placed in plastic bags while in the pack to keep the blood contained, but they must be taken out of any plastic at night.

Hides which are transported by car or plane must be dry and cool to withstand the trip. If the hides are shipped, it is best to let a reputable expeditor handle the hide. They will dry it sufficiently so it will last for months and arrive at your taxidermist in good condition. Antlers which are to be carried on planes or shipped should be crated if possible and the tips protected. Short sections of garden hose stuck over antler tips are a convenient, safe way to do this which satisfies airlines' requirements.

Home Care

After the mounted trophy has gone home with the hunter, its beauty can be preserved with just a small amount of care. Wall mounts should be securely fastened. There is no excuse for failing to protect a trophy into which a hunter has put considerable time, effort and money. Double nails should be securely driven into studs and tested before shoulder mounts are hung. Life-size wall mounts may require heavier fasteners like lag bolts or brackets to hang safely.

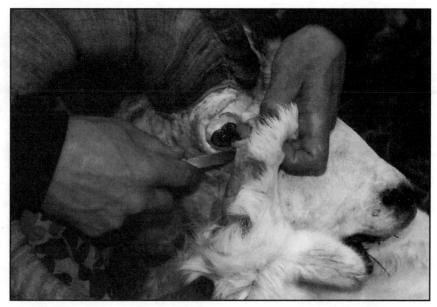

Hunters should use their fingers as guides when skinning around the eyes and lips of trophies to prevent damaging them. This hunter has his finger through the eye opening from the outside– which helps him cut as close to the skull as possible.

Trophy mounts should not be exposed to direct sun, excessive heat or smoke. All of these can permanently damage their appearance. White-colored mounts like sheep and goats are particularly susceptible to sun and smoke. Since trophies are a work of art meant to be looked at and not touched, they should be placed out of reach as much as possible. Human hands have oils and dirt which will quickly degrade the appearance of mounts. Anytime a hollow-haired animal is touched some of the brittle hair is broken–which damages them beyond repair. If mounts must be touched, the back of a clean hand can be gently stroked in the direction of the hair growth. Furred animal mounts like bears are more forgiving than hollow-haired mounts, but excessive touching will also degrade their appearance.

Trophy mounts should also be cleaned when necessary. As dust collects on mounts it dulls the appearance of the hair and horns. The horns and hair should first be gently vacuumed to remove dust. Then a clean, damp cloth can be used to wipe the horns and the hair. There are commercial products available which can be used to clean the hair and prevent it from getting brittle. Horns can be lightly waxed with any furniture wax to bring out their color and shine. Eyes can be cleaned with glass cleaner and Q-tips. Mounts which are very old or badly soiled can also be professionally cleaned. Just a little

Once trophies are in a hunter's home, they must be maintained to preserve their appearance. These are only a few of the trophies of one very successful bowhunter.

attention and care can keep mounts looking like new for twenty, thirty or more years, depending on the environment where they are kept.

Proper care in the field will greatly affect the final appearance of game trophies. Hunters must first learn how to remove hides and horns correctly for the type of mount they prefer. Hides must then be kept clean, cool, and dry for them to arrive in good condition at the taxidermist. After finished trophies arrive at the hunter's home, they should be protected and cared for to keep them looking their best. Well-maintained trophies will give hunters maximum enjoyment as they sit back and relive their hunting experiences and successes.

Chapter 34
Memories

Every hunter has at least one hunting trip which will always have a special place in his or her memory. These special memories are what we hunters daydream about during the time between hunting seasons. They are what keep us coming back each season to pursue our favorite game animal in the hopes of creating another outstanding memory.

Fred smiling as he hesistantly makes his bed.

Fred feeling a little more comfortable with our casket-like enclosures.

I often reminisce about a guided sheep hunt in Alaska in August of 1995. My client was Fred Gonzalez, the owner of Northern Outfitters–the cold-weather gear company. He had brought along his 21-year-old, non-hunting son Brett, to share the experience.

After flying into a high airstrip in the Chugach Mountains, the three of us went after three good rams we had spotted. We spent one long day climbing after the rams, only to have two other hunters spook them at the last minute by walking up the middle of the valley. We returned to the strip to wait for our pilot.

When Fred and I were moved to another hunting area on the third day, his son Brett decided to return home to Utah. For the next three days Fred and I dealt with fog and rain and did some extreme mountain climbing, but didn't have a chance at a ram. On the seventh day we moved again, this time to the Talkeetna Mountains. After being dropped off by the plane, Fred and I climbed for three hours up a steep, loose scree slope which was barely negotiable. At the top of the ridge we peeked over to see four rams, with at least one good one in the group.

We cannot shoot the same day airborne in Alaska, so Fred and I prepared to sleep right there on the ridge top. We moved slightly back down the far side of the ridge from the sheep to prevent our scent from drifting down to them with the evening thermals. Fred was very skeptical—to say the least—when I told him we were going to sleep at the top of the steep, scree slope we had just barely been able to climb. But, after pushing rocks away from the base of an overhanging boulder, flattening a strip of mountainside, and building an eighteen-inch-high retaining wall to prevent us from rolling downhill in our sleep—he was almost convinced we would be safe.

That night we went to sleep under a clear sky, with a gorgeous sunset, and then a full moon. By the time we awoke in the predawn and watched the beautiful sunrise from our sleeping bags while munching on our energy-bar breakfast, Fred was finally convinced we had chosen a good spot.

We crept to the top of the ridge, spotted the now-feeding rams and descended toward them. The rams were out of sight below the curve of the mountain as we made our slow descent. Suddenly they came into view below us, climbing up to their mid-morning beds. We both dropped to prone positions before any one of the four rams had spotted us. Fred and I enjoyed the next twenty minutes of watching the rams make their way up toward our position on the ridge, knowing the hunt was coming to a climax. When the biggest ram got within good rifle range and Fred and I were both set, Fred fired. At the shot, Fred's ram plunged downhill for a few seconds, fell over, and rolled to a stop.

We walked down to the ram and admired the magnificent animal. The striking beauty of their dark, curling horns paired with their radiant white coats always impresses me, no matter how many times I see them. We commemorated the moment with congratulations for the hunters and honor for the animal.

After the mandatory photograph session, we removed the cape, boned the meat, and loaded these and the horns in our packs. As it was only noon, we were able to take our time descending the additional 2,000 feet to the river and our pickup spot. Our pre-selected gravel bar landing strip was on the far side of the glacial river. At the river crossing, Fred was again hesitant because he had never crossed a turbulent, milky-colored river such as this. After some convincing and my successful crossing, Fred followed my route with some trepidation. However, his anxiety turned to the most remarkable smile—a combination of relief and achievement—when he reached the gravel bar airstrip. Shortly thereafter we were picked up by twin Super Cub aircraft and whisked away–back to civilization.

The memories I have from spending time with Fred are some of my finest. Fred was one of the best hunting companions I have ever had–friendly, helpful, competent and willing to try the outrageous things I proposed during the course of the hunt. We got to plan strategies, stalk several sheep and enjoy a variety of hunting situations. Fred got to sleep on top of a mountain, take a splendid Dall ram and cross a glacial river–all new experiences for him. I thoroughly enjoyed each of these accomplishments as if I was experiencing them for the first time myself.

Although this hunt was not the longest, the toughest, or the most exciting, and did not produce the biggest trophy, it will always be one of my life's best memories. This is why I hunt.

~

I hope this book of skills can help you achieve the hunting goals you have. I wish you well in all your hunting endeavors.

Tony Russ

Fred Gonzalez with a magnificent trophy–and memories for many years to come.

BIBLIOGRAPHY

Adams, Chuck; *Bowhunters Digest*; DBI Books; Northfield, Illinois, 1981.

Angier, Vena and Bradford; *At Home in the Woods*; Collier Books; New York, New York, 1951.

Askins, Bill – Editor; NRA Publications' *The Deer Hunter's Guide*; National Rifle Association; 1978.

Batin, Christopher; *Hunting in Alaska: A Comprehensive Guide*; Alaska Angler Publications; Fairbanks, Alaska, 1995.

Burt, William H., and Richard P. Grossenheider; *A Field Guide to the Mammals*, Third Edition; Houghton Mifflin Company; Boston, Massachusetts, 1976.

Clancey, Gary, and Larry R. Nelsen; *The Complete Hunter – White-Tailed Deer*; Cowles Creative Publishing, Inc.; Minnetonka, Minnesota, 1991.

Drum, Doug; *Care of Game in the Field*; Indian Valley Meats; Indian, Alaska.

Groves, David; "Everybody Hunts," *Mens Fitness*; April, 1996; pp. 64, 67-68.

Hillsmeyer, Tim; "Still-Hunt Your Way to Success," *Whitetail Bowhunter*; 1995; pp. 46, 48, 122, 123.

James, M. R.; *Bowhunting Big Game Records of North America*, Fourth Edition; Pope & Young Club; Chatfield, Minnesota, 1993.

Jansen, Charles; *Lightweight Backpacking*; Bantam Books; New York, New York, 1974.

Lippert, Joan; "Protein Power," *Men's Health*; December, 1994; pp. 77-78.

Marchand, Bob; *The Hunter's Tip Book*; B.S. Publications; British Columbia, 1996.

McRae, Bill; "Building a Better Rifle Scope," *American Hunter*; July, 1998.

McRae, Bill; "The Art & Science of Spotting Game," *American Hunter*, April, 1996; pp. 39-41, 61.

Mills, Kathy D.; *Live by the Law: Hunter Orange Regulations by State and Province*; Highland Industries, 1990.

Nordberg, Dr. Ken; *Whitetail Hunter's Almanac*, 3rd Edition; Shingle Creek Outdoor Productions; Minneapolis, Minnesota, 1990.

Ormond, Clyde; *Complete Book of Hunting*, Ninth Printing; Outdoor Life/Harper & Row; New York, 1966.

Ormond, Clyde; *Outdoorsman's Handbook*; Berkley Publishing Corporation; New York, New York, 1974.

Petersen, David; "Back to Basics," *Whitetail Bowhunter*, 1995; pp. 60-61.

Posewitz, Jim; *Beyond Fair Chase*; Falcon Press; Helena, Montana, 1994.

Reneau, Jack and Susan C. – Editors; *Records of North American Big Game*, Tenth Edition; Boone & Crockett Club; Missoula, Montana, 1993.

Russ, Tony; *Sheep Hunting in Alaska*; Northern Publishing; Wasilla, Alaska, 1994.

Schuh, Dwight; "No Sweat," *Bowhunter*, April/May 1996; pp.66-67.

Sell, Francis E.; *The Deer Hunter's Guide*; The Stackpole Company; Harrisburg, Pennsylvania, 1964.

Thomas, E. Donnall Jr., M.D.; "The Ears Have It," *Bowhunter*, April/May, 1996; pp.34-36.

Wadsworth, William H. – Editor; *International Bowhunter Education Manual*; National Bowhunter Education Foundation; 1986.

TONY RUSS
REGISTERED ALASKAN GUIDE

SPECIALIZING IN:
TROPHY DALL SHEEP HUNTS IN THE TALKEETNA
AND CHUGACH MOUNTAINS

As of 1998, Tony has taken five Pope & Young Record Book Dall sheep with bow & arrow–including the P&Y **WORLD RECORD DALL SHEEP.** Rifle hunters or bowhunters will hunt in open or draw areas. For more information write: Tony Russ, P.O. Box 871803, Wasilla, AK, 99687-1803 or tony@tubooks.com

Client Mike Traub with 1998 Dall sheep taken in the Chugach Mountains of Alaska with guide Tony Russ. This ram was awarded the Archery Gold Medal at FNAWS for 1998.

HORN & ANTLER CARVINGS
by TONY RUSS

Native Alaskan, guide, writer, and bowhunter.

Creations that depict the beauty and majesty of Alaska and her wildlife, captured in materials from the animals themselves.

(Contact Tony at address/phone number on facing page.)

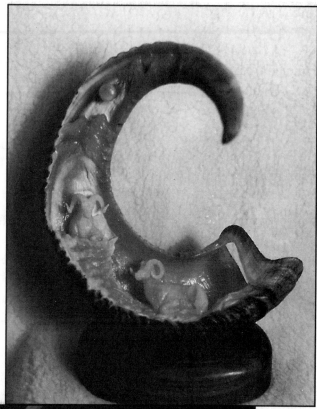

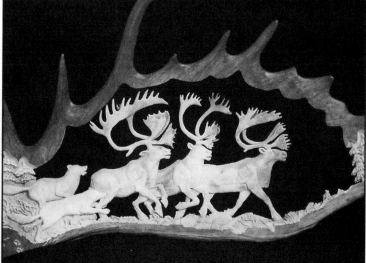

Moose, Caribou, and sheep horn carvings from your design or mine.

NORTHERN PUBLISHING – ORDER FORM

SHEEP HUNTING IN ALASKA: The Dall Sheep Hunter's Guide - second edition, by Tony Russ, 224 pages, 100 photos, softcover - $19.95, HARDCOVER - $29.95 ....$_____

THE MANUAL FOR SUCCESSFUL HUNTERS: Why 10% of the Hunters Take 90% of the Game, by Tony Russ, 400 pages, 174 photos, 40 Illustrations, softcover - $24.95, HARDCOVER - $32.95 ....$_____

THE QUEST FOR DALL SHEEP: A Historic Guide's Memories of Alaskan Hunting, by Jack Wilson, edited by Tony Russ, 224 pages, 90 photos, $19.95..$_____

BOWHUNTING ALASKA, A How-to Guide by Ron Swanson, updated in 1997 by Tony Russ, 62 pages, 33 photos, 10 maps, softcover - $10.00..$_____

ALASKA BOWHUNTING RECORDS: Bowhunting Records of Alaska's Big Game Animals, by Tony Russ, 128 pages, 23 photos, HARDCOVER - $25.00....................$_____

ALASKA WEAR: The Visitor's Guide to Clothing and Gear, by Tony Russ, 200 pages, 150 photos and graphics, softcover - $15.95 ....$_____

GREAT ALASKAN ADVENTURES, available in September, 2002, 256 pages, photos, softcover - $15.95 ....$_____

BEAR HUNTING IN ALASKA, available in December, 2002, 224 pages, photos, softcover - $19.95 ....$_____

BOOK TOTAL..$_____
SHIPPING – $4 per order ....$ 4.00
TOTAL ENCLOSED (check or money order made out to Northern Publishing).......$_____

Mail Order Form to: Northern Publishing, P.O. Box 871803, Wasilla, AK 99687-1803 or visit www.tubooks.com to order